Variorum Reprints:

JOHN WILLIS CLARK
The Care of Books. An Essay on the Development of Libraries and their
Fittings, from the earliest times to the end of the 18th century.
Cambridge 1902 definitive edition

OSKAR HALECKI
Un empereur de Byzance à Rome
Warsaw 1930 edition

In the Collected Studies Series:

JOHN W. O'MALLEY
Rome and the Renaissance: Studies in Culture and Religion

CECIL H. CLOUGH
The Duchy of Urbino in the Renaissance

RUDOLF HIRSCH
The Printed Word: its Impact and Diffusion (primarily 15th-16th centuries)

MARSHALL CLAGETT
Studies in Medieval Physics and Mathematics

DAVID HERLIHY
Cities and Society in Medieval Italy

DAVID HERLIHY
The Social History of Italy and Western Europe, 700-1500

JACQUES HEERS
Société et économie à Gênes (XIVe-XVe siècles)

KENNETH M. SETTON
Europe and the Levant in the Middle Ages and the Renaissance

JOSEPH GILL
Church Union: Rome and Byzantium (1204-1453)

BRIAN TIERNEY
Church Law and Constitutional Thought in the Middle Ages

WALTER ULLMANN
Jurisprudence in the Middle Ages

STEPHAN KUTTNER
The History of Ideas and Doctrines of Canon Law in the Middle Ages

LEONARD E. BOYLE
Pastoral Care, Clerical Education and Canon Law

Culture and Censorship
in Late Renaissance Italy and France

Professor Paul Grendler

Paul F. Grendler

Culture and Censorship
in Late Renaissance Italy and France

VARIORUM REPRINTS
London 1981

British Library CIP data

Grendler, Paul F.
  Culture and censorship in late Renaissance Italy and
  France. — (Collected studies series; CS138)
  1. Renaissance — France   2. France — Civilization —
  1328-1600   3. France — History — 16th century
  4. Renaissance — Italy   5. Italy — Civilization
  — 1328-1600   6. Italy — History — 16th century
  7. Censorship — France — 16th century
  8. Censorship — Italy — 16th century
  I. Title   II. Series
  944'.02   DS33.3

  ISBN 0-86078-084-8

Copyright © 1981   Variorum Reprints

Published in Great Britain by   Variorum Reprints
                                    20 Pembridge Mews London W11 3EQ

Printed in Great Britain by   Galliard (Printers) Ltd
                                    Great Yarmouth Norfolk

                                    VARIORUM REPRINT CS138

CONTENTS

This volume contains a total of 318 pages

PREFACE

The studies in this volume have two scholarly foci. The first eight, all written in the 1960s, analyze the cultural ferment of the late Renaissance, c. 1530 to c. 1600. Ideas and values inherited from the earlier Italian Renaissance of the fifteenth century spread to a broader, less learned public. But intellectuals also sharply criticized received cultural assumptions. The first study assesses the mass of popular history circulated by the vernacular printing press. The second and third analyze the iconoclasm in learning and religion typical of Italy in the middle third of the century. One correction should be noted: subsequent research has shown that Ortensio Lando was more Protestant than I supposed in III, pp. 34-35. Dreams of a utopian new world, intermingling hope for social equality and sardonic criticism of contemporary life, are the subjects of IV. While some intellectuals criticized inherited values, others reaffirmed traditional definitions of humanist and humanism, the themes of V and VI. In late Renaissance France, Pierre Charron used humanistic Neo-Stoicism to formulate a new political philosophy at a time of crisis. This is the topic of the seventh and eighth studies, which should be read together.

In the 1970s, I turned my attention to another reality of late Renaissance Italy, the censorship of the printing press imposed by the Index of Prohibited Books and enforced by the Inquisition. In the second half of the sixteenth century, Italian authors and printers operated against the background of an omnipresent but not always effective censorship. Study IX offers an overview of censorship in Venice, the home of the major Italian press. Subsequent studies develop aspects of the censorship. The tenth study examines the political biographies of the 117 powerful Venetian patricians who assisted the Holy Office between 1547 and 1605. It also reveals how concentrated and gerontocratic was political power in the Republic. Study XI, co-authored with Marcella Grendler, surveys the Counter Reformation hostility toward Erasmus and the results, as seen through a survey of the current

Erasmus holdings of major Florentine and Venetian libraries. The opportunity has been taken to correct two or three shelfmarks. Hebrew books also suffered, not from Index and Inquisition, but from Venetian governmental hostility. Yet, through smuggling and subterfuge, the Jewish community obtained the books that it needed; these are the topics of XII. Study XIII discusses the smuggling of other kinds of books during the interdict struggle of 1606 and 1607.

I wish to acknowledge and thank the following journals, publishers, and learned organizations for permission to reproduce these studies: The Renaissance Society of America (I, II, and V); The Canadian Catholic Historical Association (III); *The Journal of the History of Ideas* (IV); The Northern Illinois University Press (VI); *Romance Notes* (VII); *The Review of Politics* (VIII); The University of Chicago Press (IX); The Istituto per la Storia della Società e dello Stato Veneziano (X); University of Toronto Press (XI); The American Academy for Jewish Research (XII); The Harvard University Center for Italian Renaissance Studies and La Nuova Italia (XIII).

My thanks go to Kenneth Setton who first suggested this volume, to Eileen Turner who gracefully shepherded it into existence, and to my wife, Marcella, the co-author of XI. This volume is dedicated to George Mosse of the University of Wisconsin as a *Festschrift* offering. He first introduced me to the complex and strife-torn world of the late Renaissance, and to the study of secondary intellectuals as a splendid and engrossing way to understand the culture of an epoch.

PAUL F. GRENDLER

University of Toronto
January 1981

I

Francesco Sansovino and Italian Popular History
1560–1600*

OPULARIZATIONS attempt to present a body of information in an intelligible form to the non-specialist. Sometimes their goal is simply to enable the reader to pass the time in an interesting way. In this case, the popularizer has no other goal than entertainment. Other popularizations have the serious purpose of being of some utility to their audience. Today in North America, serious popularizations attempt to bring the work of experts to the attention of the general public. At times the author's purpose is not only to disseminate information but to stimulate public policy along certain lines. When such books are well-written and convey the enthusiasm or outrage of the author, they can have great influence.

Today popularizations in the fields of sociology and economics are probably more numerous and more influential than popularizations of history. In sixteenth-century Italy history was an important subject matter of popularization. History's purpose in the Renaissance was to give advice to men on how to live and to princes on how to rule. Historical precedent was of great importance; rulers consulted ancient and modern historical examples before making decisions. Even when they disregarded history, they and their representatives paid lip service to it. Ambassadors portrayed the policies of their princes in historical terms. History provided a frame of reference for sixteenth-century life.

Sixteenth-century popular histories filled several needs. They were written for those who could not or did not wish to read the original Latin and Greek. The busy statesman who lacked the time to read long original histories found useful information quickly in popularizations. Readers who lacked the critical insight to extract the lessons from history

* I wish to thank the Canada Council and the University of Toronto Humanities Research Fund for enabling me to travel to Venice, Florence, and elsewhere for research, and the Institute for Research in the Humanities for providing the time to write, with a Postdoctoral Fellowship in 1967–1968.

looked to popularizations which presented the lessons in clear and simplified form. Merchants and secretaries who wanted reference information on an event, person, or place looked to popularizations.

Because popularizations are related to their audience, they and their authors can be of use to the intellectual historian. An effective popularizer must know his audience and relate his material to it. Perhaps effective popularizers are as often experts on their audience as in the material that they are transmitting. Today, for example, few experts popularize their work; they leave that task to others to whom such work is temperamentally more congenial.

Popularizations give an idea of the intellectual nourishment and the interests of the general reading public. Popular histories can be compared with original histories in order to see which historical conceptions are retained or altered in popularization. Then, by examining the popular histories one can ascertain the interests of the readers; if certain subject matter appears often, it indicates an audience interest.

The forms of popular histories are also informative. The approach to history of the popularizer and the way in which he organizes his book may indicate habits of mind of both the popularizer and his audience. The popularizer is a junior partner in the creative process. Popularization is not simply passively receiving and transmitting material; the popularizer almost inevitably alters the material, either slightly or a great deal. Popularization is essentially a problem of organization; the popularizer must shape his material into some form that is intelligible to his readers. This may mean imposing a new framework, relating it to the needs and interests of the audience, or drawing practical conclusions when the original matter lacked them. Condensation and simplification are part of organization. With popularization there are often great or small substantive differences from the original. This point does not need to be labored; any lecturer attempting to convey technical material to a non-specialized audience discovers this. Through popularization certain themes may become more prominent, or a complex historical situation may become black and white. This gives some insight into the mentality of the popularizers and their audience.

An efflorescence of popular history occurred in the second half of sixteenth-century Italy. Two phenomena made it possible: the preference for the vernacular as the language for the dissemination of knowledge and the growth of the Venetian vernacular presses.

After 1525, when Pietro Bembo argued in his *Prose della Volgar Lingua* that the vernacular was preferable to Latin, the majority of authors except in theology, law, and possibly philosophy, followed him into the vernacular. Italian classics such as Castiglione's *Courtier* (published in 1528) and Ariosto's *Orlando Furioso* (1516) further stimulated the vernacular. The popularity of these and other literary works led to the adoption and defense of the vernacular as the chief medium of expression. Latin continued, especially in the schools, but the language of literature, history, and politics was usually the vernacular. The famous *Questione della lingua* was not Italian versus Latin but which form of Italian was preferable.

The Venetian printers responded to and encouraged the new enthusiasm for the vernacular. In the early sixteenth century, the Aldine press provided an indispensable service by printing Greek and Latin editions of the classics. The following generation of printers produced vernacular translations of these same classics, and many new vernacular works. Such Venetian printers as Gabriel Giolito de' Ferrari (d. 1578) played a key role in stimulating vernacular literature of all kinds. Soon after his arrival in Venice in 1536, he adopted italic type and lengthened letter forms in order to cut costs. Then with greater vision and resources than his rivals, he refused Latin works but actively supported vernacular authors. He printed numerous vernacular books including many popular histories.[1]

The central figure in this study is Francesco Sansovino (1521–1583), the most industrious, gifted, and informative Italian historical popularizer of the period. Born in Rome, he was the son of the sculptor Jacopo Tatti (Sansovino) by either a wife or an unfaithful concubine, and Jacopo always harbored doubts about Francesco's paternity. In the aftermath of the sack of 1527 father and son left Rome for Venice, where Jacopo's many works won him enduring fame. After youthful study of letters including Greek, Francesco obeyed his father and studied law in Padua from 1536 to 1540, in Florence in 1541, and in Bologna where he earned a degree in jurisprudence in 1542. Unhappy with law, Francesco quarreled with his father and began to write poetry and imaginative vernacular literature in the 1540's. In 1550 Jacopo, still desirous that his son should travel the road to wealth and position, arranged for an appointment at the papal court of Julius III, who had held Francesco at the baptismal font. But Francesco disliked courtly intrigue and after a brief

[1] On Giolito see Salvatore Bongi, *Annali di Gabriel Giolito de' Ferrari da Trino di Monferrato, stampatore in Venezia.* 2 vols. (Roma, 1890–1897).

period returned to Venice. In 1553 he married a Venetian girl of good but non-noble family and settled down to a tranquil life of study and writing.

In his career Sansovino wrote, translated, or edited about eighty books, nearly half of an historical nature. He worked on his own initiative and lived on the income of his books; with one exception he did not write commissioned histories. His income came from sales, from editing fees, and from the gifts of dedicatees. From 1560 to 1570 and again from 1578 to 1581 he operated his own press. Since the majority of his printings were his own compositions and translations, he probably realized a greater profit by controlling the entire operation. At the same time he continued to compose and edit for other vernacular presses as well, probably on a fee or commission basis. Then he dedicated his books to wealthy princes and prelates who sometimes rewarded him— and sometimes did not. He was not financially secure until 1570 when after a bitter legal struggle he won an annual stipend of sixty ducats from the Venetian government for unpaid fees owed to his father for some commissioned works.[2]

Sansovino was acquainted with nearly all the popular vernacular authors whose publishing careers centered in Venice—Pietro Aretino, Anton Francesco Doni, Ortensio Lando, Luca Contile, Andrea Calmo, Bernardo Tasso, Lodovico Dolce, and many others. Since he avoided the personal quarrels which flourished in this literary society, he was probably of a calm and peaceable temperament. He enjoyed some recognition with memberships in literary academies, and in 1573 was made a cavalier of the Order of Constantine. Ceaseless literary activity weakened his eyes in his last decade although he continued to write until his death in 1583.

[2] On Sansovino see Emmanuele A. Cicogna, *Delle iscrizioni veneziane* (Venezia, 1834), IV, 31–91 with a bibliography of his works; Giovanni Sforza, 'Francesco Sansovino e le sue opere storiche', *Memorie della R. Accademia delle Scienze di Torino*, serie II, 47 (1897), 27–66; and Guido Pusinich, 'Un poligrafo veneziano del cinquecento', *Pagine Istriane*, VIII (1910), 121–130, 145–151. The sponsored work was *L'historia di Casa Orsina Di Francesco Sansovino Nella quale oltre all'origine sua, si contengono molte nobili imprese fatte da loro in diverse Provincie fino a tempi nostri* . . . (In Venetia, Appresso Bernardino, & Filippo Stagnini, fratelli. MDLXV). Concerning Sansovino's annual income: on 31 March 1582 he reported a year's income of 119 ducats from the rental of four houses and over forty fields. This was in addition to whatever income he enjoyed from other sources—such as the proceeds from his books and the government stipend—which he was not required to report. He was well-off but far from wealthy, at the level of moderately successful merchants and professionals. Archivio di Stato, Venezia, Dieci Savi sopra le decime a Rialto. Condizioni di Decima, 1581, San Marco, **Busta 157, no. 340.**

This study will discuss some examples of Italian popular history in the last forty years of the sixteenth century.[3] It will begin with an examination of the practice and theory of original history which provided the model for the popularizers. It will then analyze the ideas on history of the popularizers. This will be followed by a look at some of the popular histories—scissors-and-paste compilations, epitomes, chronicles, popular lives of famous men, and, above all, works which tried to present in simple form the lessons to be derived from history—in order to see what interests were present and how the popularizers organized their materials to meet these interests. Finally, some evidence that the popular histories found their way into private libraries will be noted.

I

One must first survey the practice and theory of original history in the Italian Renaissance in order to understand the tradition within which the popularizers worked. History was one of the more practiced and discussed arts, and after the middle of the sixteenth century a rich literature existed. The development of Italian historiography was a fruitful interplay between classical texts and contemporary events which stimulated new historical questions. Founded on the ancients and humanist historiography, sixteenth-century Italian historiography expanded its horizon and sharpened its insight.

The basic framework was the theory and practice of humanist historiography.[4] A few texts from the ancients heavily influenced fifteenth-century historians and continued to sway historians in the following century. Cicero was most influential, especially in the *De Oratore* where he lauded history 'which bears witness to the passing of the ages, sheds light upon reality, gives life to recollection and guidance to human existence, and brings tidings of ancient days' (II, ix, 36). Other classical

[3] For English popular history at this time, see Louis B. Wright, *Middle-Class Culture in Elizabethan England* (Ithaca, 1958), pp. 297–338.

[4] For the following summary, see especially Giorgio Spini, 'I trattatisti dell' arte storica nella Controriforma italiana', *Contributi alla Storia del Concilio di Trento e della Controriforma*. Quaderni di 'Belfagor' I (Firenze, 1948), 109–114. On late fifteenth-century humanist historiography, see Felix Gilbert, *Machiavelli and Guicciardini. Politics and History in Sixteenth-Century Florence* (Princeton, 1965), 203–226. His analysis of Giovanni Pontano's dialogue on history, *Actius*, is particularly valuable. Also see Beatrice Reynolds, 'Shifting Currents in Historical Criticism', *Journal of the History of Ideas*, XIV (1953), 471–480; and the same author's 'Latin Historiography: A Survey 1400–1600', *Studies in the Renaissance*, II (1955), 5–66. All translations from and references to classical texts are from Loeb Classical Library editions.

texts which guided Renaissance historians were Aristotle, *Poetics*, IX, and Quintilian, *Institutiones oratoriae*, X, I, 31. Lucian's small treatise, *How to Write History*, grew in influence in the sixteenth century.

Guided by classical antiquity, humanist historiography sought to relate truth, to teach by way of moral example, and to please as literature. As Lucian explained, the historian's source was the truth; he should have independence of spirit in order to write the truth fearlessly. He should carefully investigate the facts of the matter and then put them into order. Cicero argued in *De Oratore* that with the light of the past before them, men could emulate the great men and deeds of the past and avoid their vices. The historian could, when he deemed it useful, interrupt his narrative in order to underline the moral lesson to be learned. Good writing was essential if history was to be pleasing and useful. Cicero laid down literary rules which included clear chronological order and a balanced evaluation of the consequences of an historical deed (*De Oratore*, II, XV, 62–64). The historian also had to learn to keep a proper balance between matters of importance and details. Humanist historians preferred a limpid style and sober language; if he did not naturally possess a good literary style, the historian should study classical models to acquire it.

Fifteenth-century historians honored Caesar, Sallust, and Livy as the greatest historians. Like their models, they narrated political and military events chronologically. Humanist historians concentrated on single or limited events, as the history of one war or a single city. Through the use of orations attributed to historical actors, the historian interpreted motivation. Since he was to be judge and educator, he should not have been personally involved in the events which he narrated; nor did he have to possess political and military experience in order to write.

In addition to the norms of humanist historiography, Italian historians of the second half of the sixteenth century had as models the two best-known histories of their day: Francesco Guicciardini's *Storia d'Italia* (written 1537–1540 and first published in 1561 but lacking the last four books) which narrated events from 1494 to 1534, and Paolo Giovio's *Historiarum sui temporis* (written over a thirty-year period and published in 1550–1552) which described the period 1494 to 1547. Both works stood head and shoulders above contemporary histories.

The virtues of Guicciardini's work are so well known that they do not need enumeration, nor does the high ranking accorded him need explanation. Scholars have been less kind to Giovio but despite its weaknesses, his history was comparable to Guiccardini's both in scope and execution.[5] In the sixteenth century it was printed and cited as often as the *Storia d'Italia*. Giovio was at his best as a military historian; his military information was reliable and is still useful, an important virtue for an historian writing of a period with numerous wars. His voluminous correspondence showed that he repeatedly sought information from the participants on the number of men involved in a battle, the details of armament, the development of the fighting, and so on. Military prowess and courage aroused his admiration even when he was hostile to the aims of the combatants. He praised the courage of the Florentine republicans and narrated well their struggle of 1530 although he endorsed their defeat and was unsympathetic to their form of government. In style the early books notably demonstrated sober language, clear structure, and good balance between general considerations and details. The later books sometimes seemed to be one battle after another; but in fairness to Giovio, the major feature of European political history at that time was the Habsburg-Valois struggle.

His major deficiency was his partiality for princely rule in general, and for Charles v and his Medici patrons (the Medici popes and Cosimo I) in particular. He disliked those who rebelled against princes because they disturbed the political order. He supported Charles v because he felt that the Emperor was the only guarantee of peace in Italy and defense against the Turks. But he discussed frankly the inadequacies of Leo x and Clement vii. Moreover, sixteenth-century editors and historians partially compensated for Giovio's biases. The editor of the 1560 vernacular edition annotated marginally Giovio's partiality toward Charles v (e.g., ii, 266), and Florentine historians took Giovio to task for his account of Florentine affairs.[6]

---

[5] The edition used and cited in the text is *La prima [seconda] parte dell'istorie del suo tempo di Mons. Paolo Giovio da Como, vescovo di Nocera, tradotta per M. Lodovico Domenichi . . . Con un supplimento sopra le medesime Istorie, fatto da Girolamo Ruscelli . . .* (In Venetia, Appresso Giovan Maria Bonelli. MDLX). A balanced evaluation of Giovio is Federico Chabod, 'Paolo Giovio', *Periodico della Società Storica Comense*, 38 (1954), 7–30, and reprinted in Chabod's *Opere*, vol. ii, *Scritti sul Rinascimento* (Torino, 1967), 241–267. Hostile to Giovio but useful are Michele Lupo Gentile, 'Studi sulla storiografia fiorentina alla corte di Cosimo I de' Medici', *Annali di R. Scuola Normale Superiore di Pisa*, xix (1906), 47–58; Felice Scolari, 'L'assedio di Firenze (1529–1530), Francesco Ferrucci e il nostro storico Paolo Giovio', *Periodico della Società Storica Comense*, 27 (1930), 11–65; and Benedetto Croce, 'La grandiosa aneddotica storica di Paolo Giovio', in *Poeti e scrittori del pieno e del tardo rinascimento* (Bari, 1958), ii, 27–55.

[6] See M. L. Gentile, as cited in n. 5.

Guicciardini and Giovio conceived their works within the canons of humanist historiography. Giovio in his introduction invoked the trinity of Caesar, Sallust, and Livy favored by the humanists. Both Guicciardini and Giovio followed the humanists by beginning individual books with brief general considerations, and then presenting an annalistic narration of political and military events. Giovio wrote in Latin while Guicciardini wrote in Italian, but both tried to achieve good humanist style. Both used orations to delineate motive and alternatives.

But the completed histories differed substantially from humanist historiographical canons. Both authors broke with the humanist exemplar of the history of a single political or geographical unit and moved toward universal history. Political events forced Italians to discard their historiographical insularity; as their destinies began to be determined outside of Italy, they followed European politics with closer attention. In the opening lines Guicciardini took as his theme the history of the disasters that had befallen Italy since the halcyon days of Lorenzo de' Medici, and brought in European affairs when necessary in order to clarify Italian events. Giovio's vision was broader. In the opening lines (I, 1) he noted that the whole world had been in a state of peace before 1494 but in the next fifty years Italy, then all of Europe, and finally faraway Asia, were ravaged by war. In so far as Giovio had a discernible theme, it was the gradual spread of war. He broadened his vision to the point that he came close to writing a history of Europe and the Near East; by the time his account reached the 1540's (Bks. 41 ff.) Italy was only one part of the whole. He followed the Emperor's efforts to maintain a unified *Respublica Christiana* by narrating Spanish and northern European affairs. He noted the discoveries of the New World (II, 392 ff.). In order to alert his readers to the growing Turkish menace, Giovio discussed the Turks at length. He also intuited the importance of non-political and non-military factors. When introducing a distant political unit, he presented a short geographical description and mentioned a few indigenous customs. For example, in an account of the wars between Poland and Moscow, he noted the agricultural production of the Volga River plains. Elsewhere he included a page on the nature, customs, and food of Arabs.[7]

Guicciardini and Giovio reflected the change in the ideal of the historian: he was no longer an inexperienced and detached observer but a

[7] On Giovio's inclusion of non-political and non-military factors, see Chabod, 'Giovio', 21–22.

man of political and military experience. Lucian, in *How to Write History*, 37, stressed that the historian should acquire political insight through participation in political affairs, and that the historian should serve as a soldier, or at least visit military camps and study military affairs. Guicciardini best fulfilled this condition, but it was Giovio who brought it to the attention of his readers as one of his qualifications as an historian. He emphasized in the preface to the *Historiarum sui temporis* that he had spent thirty-seven years in the courts of the mighty learning of affairs (I, sig. *iv^r), and he pointed out in his narrative where he had played an active, if minor, role (II, 264–265, 462, 693).

Guicciardini and Giovio went beyond humanist historians in their appreciation of documentary evidence from archives. Humanist historians did not boast of exploiting archives, nor did they claim that they were good historians because they used documents. With the notable exception of Flavio Biondo they probably used documentary evidence only sporadically; most often they followed what they felt were reliable narrative accounts, assigning highest credibility to witnesses. Guicciardini used documentary evidence extensively,[8] but again it was Giovio who emphasized its significance. He claimed to use archival materials, but his use of documentary archival evidence has not been investigated. In his life of Giangaleazzo Visconti (1351–1402), Giovio noted that Giangaleazzo had had a well-organized chancellery and advertised that he had seen these archival documents. He wrote that anyone who wished to write a 'just history' could not want more abundant or accurate material; from these records the historian could trace the causes of wars, the success of enterprises, and negotiations.[9] Similarly, in his list of sources used for his life of Francesco Sforza (1401–1466), he included *Archivij Romani* in the midst of other histories and eyewitness accounts of old soldiers.[10] Giovio's statements indicate that the use of documentary evidence was coming to be one of the prerequisites of the good historian.

One of the signs that Italy and Italian historiography were in a differ-

---

[8] On the humanist historians' use of documents, see Gilbert, *Machiavelli and Guicciardini*, 221–226, 334–335, and for Guicciardini's use of documents, 296–297.

[9] 'Ho veduto io ne gli armari de' suoi Archivi, maravigliosi libri in carta pecora, i quali contenevano d'anno in anno i nome de' capitani, condottieri, & soldati vecchi, & le paghe di ogniuno . . . [he noted the registers of letters] . . . talche chi volesse scrivere una istoria giusta, non potrebbe desiderare altronde nè più abondante nè più certa materia: percio che da questi libri facilissimamente si traggono le cagione delle guerre, i consigli, & i successi dell' imprese.' *Le Vite di dicenove huomini illustri, descritte da monsignor Paolo Giovio* . . . (In Venetia, Appresso Giovan Maria Bonelli, MDLXI), p. 48^v.

[10] *Ibid.*, p. 59^v.

ent era in the second half of the sixteenth century was the growth of the influence of Polybius.[11] Leonardo Bruni derived from Polybius the distinction between the literary genre of 'panegyric' and objective 'history' and made a partial Latin adaptation of Polybius in 1418–1419. Complete Latin editions were printed later in the fifteenth century, and Machiavelli studied Polybius; but the work of Polybius did not become important in historiography until after Lodovico Domenichi's Italian translation of 1545. When the problems of republican institutions versus the rule of princes, or the defense of the *libertà* of an independent city-state, dominated Italian affairs, historians looked to the historians of republican Rome. When the Spanish Empire dominated Italy, they sought out Polybius (c. 200–c. 118 B.C.) a Greek who witnessed the period in which Greece and much of the rest of the world fell to Rome. He wrote the history of the era 220 to 168 B.C. in order to explain to his fellow Greeks how disaster had befallen them and to teach them how to bear it. Similarly, Italians tried to understand how Italy had fallen under the influence of Spain, and how to cope with this new political balance.

Polybius reinforced historiographical tendencies stemming from Guicciardini and Giovio. In contrast to the normal practice of ancient historians, but like Guicciardini and Giovio, Polybius wrote universal history. He argued that since 220 B.C. the world had become an organic whole with the affairs of Italy, Libya, Greece, and Asia intertwined, and that they should be treated as a whole (Book I, 3–4). Like Giovio, Polybius stressed that an active role in politics and military affairs, rather than rhetorical training, was the appropriate preparation for the historian. And like other ancient historians, and practically all Renaissance historians, Polybius believed that history was the best possible preparation for the active, political life, especially in periods of disaster. Indeed, history was 'the only method of learning how to bear bravely the vicissitudes of fortune' (I, I. 2). Then too, Polybius' theory of anacyclosis in Book VI, i.e., the process of cyclical development of states through vari-

---

[11] On the growing popularity of Polybius in the late sixteenth and early seventeenth centuries, see Peter Burke, 'A Survey of the Popularity of Ancient Historians, 1450–1700', *History and Theory*, V (1966), 143–145. For Polybius' influence on historical theory in the second half of the sixteenth century, see Reynolds, 'Shifting Currents in Historical Criticism', 472–473, 487, 490–491. On Polybius, see F. W. Walbank, *A Historical Commentary on Polybius*, vol. I, *Commentary on Books I–VI* (Oxford, 1957), esp. pp. 1–37. For Bruni and Polybius, see Hans Baron, *The Crisis of the Early Italian Renaissance. Civic Humanism and Republican Liberty in an Age of Classicism and Tyranny*. Rev. ed. (Princeton, 1966), pp. 216–217, 410, 508 n. 14, 553 n. 16.

ous constitutional forms, had great influence especially on Machiavelli.[12]

Above all, Polybius was congenial to the second half of the sixteenth century because he tended to see history not as a branch of rhetoric but as an objective science which would yield political wisdom. First, he made a determined effort to wrest history from the hands of the ancient rhetoricians who, Polybius believed, were interested in praising friends and condemning enemies rather than telling the truth. The historian had to follow the facts objectively, sparing neither friend nor foe, and Polybius often interrupted his narrative to correct other historians. He also insisted upon an analysis of causes. 'For if we take from history the discussion of why, how, and wherefore each thing was done, and whether the result was what we should have reasonably expected, what is left is a clever essay but not a lesson, and while pleasing for the moment of no possible benefit for the future' (III, 31. 12–13). Historians should pay more attention to causes and results, and less to the narrative of events. The purpose of objective analysis was to yield practical political wisdom. Polybius habitually summarized the lesson to be derived from a war or political maneuver in a pithy political maxim. These maxims were distilled political wisdom devoid of moral considerations, much like the *Ricordi* of Guicciardini. He avowed that the political truth might be bitter but was always instructive. This was the approach to history which Polybius brought to the second half of the sixteenth century. Theorists of history such as Jean Bodin in his *Methodus ad facilem historiarum cognitionem* (1566) praised Polybius and wrestled with his dicta.[13]

Historians in the second half of the sixteenth century could also look to a growing number of treatises on the art of writing history. From Giovanni Pontano's *Actius* (published 1507) until mid-century there were no treatises on history, but then they appeared in abundance. Francesco Robortello (1548), Dionigi Atanagi (1559), Ventura Cieco (1563), Antonio Riccoboni (1568), Giannantonio Viperano (1569), Uberto Foglietta (1579), and Alessandro Sardi (1586) wrote treatises which explained and amplified Aristotle, Cicero, Quintilian, and Lucian.[14] More

[12] See Gennaro Sasso, *Studi su Machiavelli* (Napoli, 1967), pp. 161–280.

[13] For Bodin on Polybius, see Julian H. Franklin, *Jean Bodin and the Sixteenth Century Revolution in the Methodology of Law and History* (New York, 1963), pp. 139–146.

[14] Spini, 'I trattatisti dell'arte storica nella Controriforma italiana', *Contributi alla Storia del Concilio di Trento e della Controriforma*. Quaderni di 'Belfagor', I (Firenze, 1948), 109–114. See also the article, with selections from the texts of these treatises on history, by Ferdinando Vegas, 'La concezione della storia dall'Umanesimo alla Controriforma', in M. F. Sciacca ed., *Grande Antologia Filosofica*, vol. 10, *Il Pensiero della Rinascenza e della Riforma (Protestantesimo e Riforma Cattolica)* (Milano, 1964), pp. 1–177.

concerned with style than evidence, the treatises were jejune and academic until the end of the century. Perhaps the fact that, with the exception of Foglietta, the above were philosophers and rhetoricians rather than practicing historians, helps to account for the sterility of their work. The practice of history was better than the theory.

By the end of the century the theory caught up with the practice. The philosopher Francesco Patrizi in his *Della Historia* (1560) questioned Ciceronian canons and argued tentatively that the historian was not a rhetorician concerned with style but a scientist trying to judge the veracity of his sources. Patrizi discussed the degrees of objectivity and accuracy that an historian might find in different types of historical evidence.[15] Patrizi raised questions but presented few answers. After him, Bodin (*Methodus*), Antonio Possevino (1593), and Paolo Beni (1611) developed the idea that history was a science dealing with the past seen as an organic whole. For example, Beni argued that the historian ought not limit himself to political and military events but should also include judicial institutions, economics, and opinions. He went on to stress causes in history, and to insist that history must produce human utility.[16]

Historiography in the second half of the sixteenth century was also closely related to political speculation. The great political changes of the century stimulated much political thinking, expecially on problems related to the state, e.g., the best form of government or how to preserve the power of the state. Political writers depended upon both ancient and modern histories for the raw materials of their analyses. The close link between history and political speculation was shown by the number of men who wrote both history and political speculation, e.g., Machiavelli, Guicciardini, Paolo Paruta, and Scipione Ammirato.[17] History provided the lessons which might be applied to modern politics, and examples to prove or disprove political theory. By the end of the century the tendency to view history as a laboratory of politics appeared in some of the treatises on history. Jacopo Aconcio (who wrote c. 1562 but whose work was not published until the twentieth century), Giovan

[15] On Patrizi, see Franklin, *Jean Bodin*, 96–102; and Spini, 'I trattatisti dell'arte storica', 115–118.

[16] Spini, 'I trattatisti dell'arte storica', 118–123. See also the selections from Beni in Vegas, 'La concezione della storia', 157–158.

[17] See Rodolfo De Mattei, *Aspetti del pensiero politico Europeo del Cinquecento* (Roma, 1957), 6–13; and Carlo Curcio, *Dal Rinascimento alla Controriforma. Contributo alla storia del pensiero politico italiano da Guicciardini a Botero* (Roma, 1934), 24–57.

Michele Bruto (1589), Lorenzo Ducci (1604), and Traiano Boccalini in his *Ragguagli di Parnaso* (1612–1613) argued that by using an inductive method on the past one could construct a technique of politics useful to statesmen. In addition, the fascination with reason of state and the attempt to analyze it with reference to Tacitus also stimulated the view of history as a laboratory of politics.[18]

Sixteenth-century historiography was founded on the canons of the ancients and humanist historiography. But with Guicciardini and Giovio it broadened to include universal history and non-political and non-military factors. Polybius reinforced the example of Guicciardini and Giovio. Historiography became more scientific with the search for better documentation and concern to understand causes. The preparation of the ideal historian included personal experience in political and military affairs. As political speculation increased, history became a laboratory for political theory. This was the form of original history which the popularizers organized, simplified, and presented to their readers.

II

The popularizers occasionally pondered man and history. They wrote no formal treatises but they wrote many prefaces and dedicatory letters in which it was standard procedure to discuss briefly the purpose of a work and to reflect on man and history.

The popularizers accepted without question the Renaissance *vita civile* and the role of history in preparing men for it. In this they were the descendants of fifteenth-century humanists who taught that history was part of the *studia humanitatis*, which inculcated virtue and learning to prepare men to live the active life as head of the family, in business, and in service to the state. In the *studia humanitatis* history provided examples from the past to supplement moral philosophy. Sansovino in 1554 advocated the program of the *studia humanitatis* for the *vita civile* as the appropriate education for a young boy whatever his adult profession.[19] And he praised Venice for the usual reasons which comprised the 'myth of Venice', but especially because Venice nourished the *vita civile*.[20]

[18] Spini, 'I trattatisti dell'arte storica', 118–119, 124–128.

[19] *Francesco Sansovino. L'avvocato e il segretario*, a cura di Piero Calamandrei (Firenze, 1942), 101–102, 104, 109–111. The first edition was 1554.

[20] *Venetia città nobilissima et singolare, Descritta in XIIII Libri da M. Francesco Sansovino...* (In Venetia, Appresso Iacomo Sansovino. MDLXXXI), fs. 3ʳ–4ʳ. On the 'myth of Venice' see Franco Gaeta, 'Alcune considerazioni sul mito di Venezia', *Bibliothèque d'Humanisme*

Influenced by the events of his century and current discussions of man and history, Sansovino assigned limits to man's participation in shaping his world. He believed that man could shape his political destiny in day-to-day affairs but that politics was in the long run subject to an inevitable cycle. Sansovino viewed the growth and decline of states in terms of Polybius' anacyclosis. The initially good government of one man, monarchy, became a tyranny. Then the state was renewed by the efforts of a few good men who made it an aristocracy. This in turn decayed into oligarchy and was replaced by democracy which became mob rule which, in turn, was supplanted by one-man rule as the cycle continued. Sansovino noted that worthy men attempted unsuccessfully to establish principates or republics to endure a thousand years. The reasons for failure were twofold. By their nature all human institutions carried within themselves the seeds of corruption which were human excesses and disorders. Second, one could not provide for everything. The accidents which befell states were so many and so diverse that it was impossible to provide against, or to correct, all of them.[21]

Although governments were subject to inevitable corruption in the long run, men could control their immediate destinies through their daily political decisions, and history enabled men to make intelligent decisions. The study of history was useful because human actions were normally consistent in every period and for most men. Political precepts learned from history could not be 'determined and fixed rules', but they were useful to intelligent statesmen who understood the nature of reality.[22] Unexpected and incomprehensible misfortunes overtook men from time to time but the fault did not lie in the study of history and politics.[23]

_____

et Renaissance, XXIII (1961), 58–75; and Brian Pullan, 'Service to the Venetian State: Aspects of Myth and Reality in the Early Seventeenth Century', Studi Secenteschi, v (1964), 95–147.

[21] Propositioni overo considerationi in materia di cose di Stato, sotto titolo di Avvertimenti, Avvedimenti Civili, & Concetti Politici, Di M. Francesco Guicciardini. M. Gio Francesco Lottini. M. Francesco Sansovini. [sic] Di nuovo posti insieme, ampliati, & corretti, à commodo & benefitio de gli Studiosi. Nelle quali si contengono, leggi, regole, precetti, & sentenze molto utili à coloro che maneggiano, cosi i Principati & le Republiche, come ogni altra sorte di governo . . . (In Vinegia, Presso Altobello Salicato, 1583. Alla Libraria della Fortezza), sigs. *2ʳ–*3ʳ.

[22] Ibid., sig. *3ʳ.

[23] Concetti Politici di M. Francesco Sansovino. Raccolti da gli Scritti di diversi Auttori Greci, Latini, & Volgari, à benefitio & commodo di coloro che attendono à governi delle Republiche, & de Principati . . . (In Venetia, MDLXXVIII. Appresso Giovanni Antonio Bertano), sig. *4ʳ.

Sansovino filtered and simplified current speculation on the problem. He could have derived his notions of anacyclosis and human corruption from either Polybius or Machiavelli. His rejection of 'determined and fixed rules' because of the mutability of life echoed Guicciardini's approach. However, Sansovino's resolution of human intervention and historical inevitability begged questions. What was the relationship between the actions of statesmen and incomprehensible misfortune? To what extent were human actions consistent from period to period in history? However, neither the popularizers nor their readers were philosophers of history. Sansovino formulated a simple pragmatic resolution which assumed that men would continue to live the *vita civile* and which justified the study of history. Neither very pessimistic nor excessively optimistic, Sansovino's views reflected Italian political reality. He did not share the hope of Polybius and Machiavelli that a mixed constitution would check the cycle, but he believed that men normally could control their own affairs and learn from the experience of others. Sansovino's view corresponded to the Italian political situation. An independent city-state like Venice had broad if not unlimited freedom to make its own policy, but the possibility of a major power intervention which would destroy the Italian political order existed.

Like fifteenth-century humanists, Sansovino believed in the *vita civile* and history's contribution to it, but he changed the emphasis. Political activity was the most important part of the active life. In Sansovino's words, *cose di stato*, or the knowledge and practice of politics, were the most important concerns of this world. In his *Secretario* (1564), a work designed to teach men how to be secretaries to princes, Sansovino argued that the great dignity of the secretary stemmed from the fact that he was close to his prince with advice in matters of state, and 'affairs of state are the chief matters of this world'.[24] Similarly, in the capsule summaries of the careers of men which dotted his histories, Sansovino's highest praise, reserved for only a handful of princes and students of politics, was that someone possessed skill in *cose di stato*. Neither sycophancy nor devotion to Venice swayed Sansovino's evaluations. He praised Lorenzo de' Medici as a 'rare man in *cose di stato*' because he preserved peace in Italy. Charles V 'stood above all others in understanding

---

24 '. . . perche le materie di Stato sono le principali di questo Mondo', *Del secretario Di M. Francesco Sansovino libri quattro Ne quali con bell'ordine s'insegna altrui à scriver lettere . . .* (In Venetia, Appresso Francesco Rampazetto. 1564), f. 1ᵛ.

cose di stato'.[25] And, of course, he praised Machiavelli as being of 'profound and subtle intelligence in *cose di stato*'.[26]

Sansovino elevated but narrowed the contribution of history to the *vita civile*. He had little interest in the contributions which moral philosophy, literature, and the rest of the *studia humanitatis* could make to the *via civile*, nor was he interested in the importance of history for the non-political part of the *vita civile*. History provided concrete lessons in the negotiations and administrative actions of statesmen. In 1580 Sansovino wrote that history was 'most necessary' to men who headed governments because history demonstrated the 'direct way of civil administration'. In particular, Guicciardini's history was good because the author treated in excellent fashion causes, consultations, deliberations, and the execution of affairs of state. From it one could learn the true terms of how to manage important affairs in every kind of state.[27] Absent was the humanist belief that the purpose of history was to influence the whole range of man's life, his moral character as well as his political deeds. Neither was Sansovino interested in what history had to teach about men and states in general. History provided lessons of civil administration.

Sansovino simplified the role of history in such a way that his readers could easily understand the reasons for studying it. He enlarged one element of the Renaissance view of history's contribution to the *vita civile*: history had narrow, concrete, and practical goals. Practical politics became a major subject matter of popular history.

Another feature of popular history was its secular character. In these years of the impact of the Counter-Reformation, some Italian historians sought to place history at the service of religion. They attempted 'to con-

---

[25] Sansovino's *Sopplimento* has a separate title page dated 1574 within the *Cronica Universale* but the paging is continuous. *Della Cronica Universale del Mondo chiamata gia sopplimento delle croniche Parte Terza . . . da M. Francesco Sansovino. Nella qual si contengono tutte le cose avvenute dall'anno 1490. fino al presente 1574. cosi in Italia come fuori, & per tutte l'altre Provincie . . .* (In Venetia, MDLXXIIII), in *Sopplimento delle croniche universali del Mondo di F. Iacopo Filippo da Bergamo. Tradotto nuovamente da M. Francesco Sansovino* (In Venetia, MDLXXV), fs. 569ᵛ, 584ᵛ. This was not sycophancy; Sansovino also rebuked Charles V for permitting the sack of Rome and pointed out the grievous damage to Italy which his wars brought. *Ibid.*, fs. 589ᵛ, 584ᵛ.

[26] *Dante con l'espositioni di Christoforo Landino, et di Alessandro Vellutello . . . reformato . . . Per Francesco Sansovino Fiorentino.* (In Venetia, Appresso Giovambattista, Marchiò Sessa, & Fratelli. 1578), sig. A8ʳ.

[27] *Dell'Epitome dell'historia d'Italia di M. Francesco Guicciardini Libri XX . . .* (In Venetia, Per ordine di Iacomo Sansovino. MDLXXX), sigs. a2ʳ–a3ʳ.

struct an orthodox interpretation consistent with the interests of the church'.[28] For example, the *Annales ecclesiastici* (1588–1607) of Caesar Baronius were polemical in intent as well as being of great value as a repository of sources of ecclesiastical history. The popularizers maintained the secular nature of history. Like Guicciardini and Giovio, they treated religious history in the same way and within the same context as profane history. For example, they viewed the religious aspects of sixteenth-century wars within a political framework. While unsympathetic to Protestantism, the popularizers were not overly biased; and they did not omit the political and moral failures of popes and prelates.[29] The Venetian environment probably influenced the popularizers, especially Sansovino, as Venetian historians through Paolo Sarpi (1552–1623) were consciously secular and often unsympathetic to the religious aims of Rome.[30]

Not surprisingly the popularizers looked to the major histories of their century as the best examples of the historian's art. Guicciardini received highest praise. According to Sansovino, the world judged Guicciardini to be a better historian than Giovio, Machiavelli, or the ancients. The reasons were his veracity, his excellent understanding of the affairs of state, and his marvelous order and language.[31]

Through editorial labors, the popularizers played an important role in bringing the histories of Guicciardini and Giovio to the public. Preceded only by the Florentine edition of 1561, Giolito published a Venetian edition of the *Storia d'Italia* in 1562. Sansovino edited this edition and added a brief life of Guicciardini. This edition was reprinted several times, and Sansovino's life appeared in seven editions between 1562 and 1645. A second popularizer, Remigio Nannini (Fiorentino) edited for the Venetian press of Bevilacqua in 1563 the *Storia d'Italia*

[28] William J. Bouwsma, 'Three Types of Historiography in Post-Renaissance Italy', *History and Theory*, IV (1965), 307.

[29] For examples, see Sansovino, *Sopplimento*, 1575 ed., 605 r–v, 632r; and Girolamo Garimberto's *Le Vite d'alcuni papi et cardinali* discussed below in section IV.

[30] Bouwsma, 'Three Types of Historiography', 309–314. Now also see Bouwsma's *Venice and the Defense of Republican Liberty. Renaissance Values in the Age of the Counter Reformation* (Berkeley and Los Angeles, 1968).

[31] '[Guicciardini] scrisse la historia di Italia . . . nella quale per giuditio del mondo, se portato di modo, che è tenuto non pur veridico, ma anco il piu illustre che sia stato da gli antichi in qua, non pur per intelligenza di stato, quanto anco per gravità di dire & per ordine maraviglioso, onde havendo esse oscurata la gloria del Giovio & di Nicolò Machiavello tanto celebre innanzi a lui . . .' *Sopplimento*, 1575 ed., f. 689v. This judgment was repeated in his *Venetia*, 1581 ed., f. 253v.

adding marginal notes and a longer life of Guicciardini which appeared nine times by 1640. Still another popularizer, Tommaso Porcacchi, edited the new 1574 edition for the printer Angelieri of Venice, again with marginal notes, tables, and a panegyric of the *Storia*. Each new edition of the *Storia d'Italia* contained more information on the author, summaries, tables, commentaries, and so on, as the editors made the work more intelligible and useful to their readers.[32] For Giovio, Lodovico Domenichi provided a vernacular translation of the *Historiarum sui temporis* in 1551–1553. Reprinted in 1555, 1560, 1565, 1572, and 1581, with the same accretion of tables, marginalia, and evaluations, Domenichi's translation was reprinted more often than the Latin original, and gained many readers for Giovio. In addition to the editions and translations, the popularizers produced epitomes of Guicciardini and Giovio.[33]

Often the popularizers translated, rearranged, and rewrote the histories of others. But when the occasion to use documentary sources arose, Sansovino employed them objectively and intelligently. He never discussed formally the problem of evaluating sources, but he formulated his own pragmatic criteria. For his *Origine delle famiglie illustri* he claimed to have used archival sources, *relazioni*, and *registri* as well as histories and *annali* of various cities,[34] and he used this evidence to dispose of legends. For example, he rejected the legend that the Bentivoglio family of Bologna were descended from King Enzo of Sardinia (c. 1220–1272), a natural son of Emperor Frederick II. According to the legend, Enzo begot a son through a union with a Bolognese woman. Then upon imprisonment he repeatedly protested his affection for her with the words 'Ben ti voglio' until his death shortly later. Hence the name, and through the son, the origins of the Bentivoglio family. In evaluating the possibility of heirs to Enzo, Sansovino noted that there were several autograph chronicles written by Bolognese citizens of the period. Sansovino found them filled with daily detail. In comparing them, he found them to agree and concluded that they could be accepted as truthful. These chronicles described in detail the imprisonment, death, and burial of Enzo but made no mention of issue. Sansovino concluded that

[32] Vincenzo Luciani, *Francesco Guicciardini e la fortuna dell'opera sua*. Ed. ital. a cura di Paolo Guicciardini (Firenze, 1949), pp. 16–26.

[33] See below, section IV.

[34] '. . . alcuni memoriali, & fragmenti de gli annali del Frignano, posti nell'Archivio del Duca di Ferrara, che dicono a questo modo . . .' *Della origine, et de' fatti delle famiglie illustri d'Italia, di M. Francesco Sansovino Libro Primo* . . . (In Vinegia, Presso Altobello Salicato. MDLXXXII), f. 171ᵛ. This work was reprinted in 1609 and 1670 in Venice.

since these writers were true observers of little things, they could be followed on a major matter, and rejected the legend of the origins of the Bentivoglio.[35] The example showed intelligent rule-of-thumb discrimination.

Sansovino's objectivity on the origins of noble families was laudable. Family histories at this time generally found in ancient Rome and Greece flattering ancestors of dubious historicity. Sansovino accepted no origin that he could not support with evidence. When he wrote of the Medici of Florence, he noted the claim that the Medici had Greek roots and that Medici forefathers had ruled Greek cities. But Sansovino wrote that he could not find any evidence of this. He began his account of the Medici with a reference to a Giovanni de' Medici shortly before 1348 in Giovanni Villani's chronicle.[36] Sansovino's caution and objectivity can be compared with the sycophantic *Vita di Cosimo [Primo] de'Medici* (1586) of Aldo Manuzio il Giovane (1547–1597), which accepted and 'documented' at length the Greek origins of the Medici.[37] Similarly, when Sansovino wrote of contemporary history he also claimed to base his account on primary sources and reliable secondary accounts. At times he even inserted into the text quotations from primary sources.[38]

The popularizers had a clear idea of the nature of history and of its value to man. Although man's affairs were subject to occasional intervention by Fortune, they believed that man normally could control his own destiny. The most important part of the active life was politics, and history's task was to help men to make practical political decisions. The popularizers praised, edited, and translated the histories of Guicciardini and Giovio, and like them saw history as a secular science guided by considerations of evidence and objectivity.

[35] '. . . per le mani di diversi gentilhuomini & cittadini Bolognese diverse Croniche, delle quali con tutto che siano scritte molto alla grossa & da persone idiote, se ne cava però molta verità, & confrontate tutte insieme, si trovano poco differenti l'una dall'altra. Et per che riferiscono con molta sincerità quello che di giorno in giorno è avenuto, non si puo credere, che trovandosi scritto minutamente da cotali autori, tutte le conditioni della prigionia, della vita, della morte, & della sepoltura d'Enzo, non si trovasse ancora fatta memoria del figliuolo se lo havesse havuto, & della sua soccessione, con tante ricchezze, che si dice che gli lasciò, & che senza dubbio lo harebbono messo in consideratione: essendo essi scrittori osservatori di ogni picciola cosa, non che di questa, che era importante, se ciò fosse stato vero.' *Ibid.*, f. 172[r].

[36] *Ibid.*, f. 125[r].

[37] *Vita di Cosimo de' Medici, primo Gran Duca di Toscana, Descritta da Aldo Mannucci* (In Bologna, MDLXXXVI), pp. 10–13.

[38] For example, see *Sopplimento*, 1575 ed., fs. 642[v]–643[r].

I

III

The notion that history taught concrete lessons of politics stimulated some of the most interesting popularizations. The popularizers argued that history would be most useful if they extracted from it the pertinent political information. Then they would systematize the information and present it in some methodological order so that readers could quickly find what they desired.

The most ambitious project of this kind was the series of ten volumes of 'a chain of historical jewels' (*gioie historiche*) under the general editorship of Tommaso Porcacchi and published by Giolito in Venice between 1557 and 1570. The historical jewels were designed to accompany the *Collana Historica*, a series of volumes of vernacular translations of Greek historians—Dictys Cretensis and Dares Phrygius on the Trojan War, Herodotus, Thucydides, Xenophon, Polybius, and others—also edited by Porcacchi and published by Giolito. The historical jewels linked together the ancient histories, i.e., they systematized the political lessons to be derived from these histories.

Porcacchi explained in a general introduction to the series that the historical jewels were planned around war.[39] He argued that since the actions of states depended on war it was the most important factor in history. Because wars had to have causes, the first book in the series, written by Porcacchi, dealt with the causes of wars. A cause for war existing, the next step was to prepare for hostilities. The first necessity was a good captain for the army, so the second book in the series dealt with this subject. Next followed a book on the master of the military camp. Since one needed soldiers, one needed a book which discussed the true soldier, the next historical jewel. Then there was a book on making war, followed by one which discussed great ancient and modern military deeds, a book on how to make a military camp, a book on military strategy, and finally a book of orations to help the military leader or

[39] *Ditte Candiotto et Darete Frigio della Guerra Troiana, Tradotti per Thomaso Porcacchi da Castiglione Arretino: Il quale v'ha aggiunto l'ordine, che s'ha da tener nella concatenation dell'historie, & le Vite di tutti quelli historici antichi Greci, de' quali è formata la sua Collana. Et questo, secondo l'ordine da lui posto, è el primo Anello d'essa Collana historica . . . (In Vinetia Appresso Gabriel Giolito di Ferrarii. MDLXX), sigs. d iii ᵛ–d ivᵛ. This is the most complete description of the historical jewels. Porcacchi does not give a precise list of titles and authors, but one can reconstruct the series by checking Bongi, Annali di Giolito, passim, and the books.*

statesman to persuade and negotiate.[40] The authors were Tommaso Porcacchi,[41] Ascanio Centorio degli Hortensii,[42] Remigio Nannini,[43]

[40] The ten historical jewels were as follows: *Le Cagioni delle guerre antiche* (1564, with some copies of 1565 and 1566) by Porcacchi; *Il Primo Discorso di Messer Ascanio Centorio, sopra l'ufficio d'un Capitano Generale di essercito* (1557) by Ascanio Centorio degli Hortensii; *Il Terzo Discorso di M. Ascanio Centorio, nel quale si tratta della qualità, ufficio, et Autorità d'un Maestro di Campo Generale* (1558); *Il Soldato* (1570, with some copies of 1569) by Domenico Mora; *Il Quinto Discorso di Guerra ... appartenenti all'arte della militia* (1562) by Centorio; *Del Governo della Militia* (1570 in two parts) by Bernardino Rocca; *Paralleli o essempi simili* (1566) by Porcacchi; the eighth jewel was to be a book on how to make military camps which apparently never appeared; *Imprese, stratagemi, et errori militari* (1566) by Rocca; and the tenth jewel the *Orationi militari* (1577) by Remigio Nannini, and perhaps his *Orationi in materia civile, e criminali* (1560) as well.

The reason for uncertainty on the tenth jewel is that on one occasion Porcacchi listed the *Orationi militari* and on another occasion listed both volumes of Nannini's *Orationi* as the tenth jewel. See Porcacchi, *Ditte Candiotto et Darete Frigio*, 1570 ed., sig. d iv^v; and *Il primo volume delle cagioni delle guerre antiche di Thomaso Porcacchi, tratte de gl' historici antichi greci a beneficio di chi vol'adornarsi l'animo delle Gioie dell'Historie ...* (In Vinegia appresso Gabriel Giolito de' Ferrari. MDLXIIII), Prohemio, sig. ***iiii^v.

Title page announcements that a book was a particular jewel sometimes differed from Porcacchi's overall plan. In addition, it seems evident that the series was conceived after several of the books had appeared. The four volumes before 1564 made no mention of being part of the historical jewels. In 1564 the first notice of the plan appeared, and the five volumes of 1564 through 1570 referred to the historical jewels.

[41] Tommaso Porcacchi (c. 1530–1585) was born in Castiglione Aretino in Tuscany and moved to Venice in 1559, after some of the historical jewels had appeared. He spent the rest of his life near the Venetian presses, translating, editing, and writing several popularizations: *L'isole più famose del Mondo* (1572), a work of popular geography; *De funerali antichi di diversi popoli, e nazioni* (1574), a popular antiquarian work; and *La nobiltà della Città di Como* (1569), a popular history. See *Teatro d'huomini letterati Aperto dall'abbate Girolamo Ghilini ...* (In Venetia, Per li Guerigli. MDCXLVII), I, 217–218; and the *Enciclopedia Italiana*, XXVII, 934.

[42] Ascanio Centorio degli Hortensii (fl. 1553–1579) was born in Milan and was a Cavalier of San Giacomo della Spada. He wrote a number of works: *rime*, a book on the plague in Milan, and other historical works. He was the friend of Giovan Battista Castaldo, Marchese di Cassano and Conte di Piadena, who fought in the service of the Emperor; and it is thought that for the *Discorsi di Guerra* Centorio served as Castaldo's amanuensis. He wrote five *Discorsi di Guerra* (printed together by Giolito in 1566 and 1568) of which three were historical jewels. On Centorio, see Ghilini, *Teatro d' huomini letterati*, II, 31; and Filippo Argelati, *Bibliotheca scriptorum Mediolanensium* (Mediolani, 1745), II, 409–410; IV, 1976.

[43] Remigio Nannini or Remigio Fiorentino (1521–1581) was born and died in Florence, where he was a Dominican monk at Santa Maria Novella. But he lived most of his life in Venice, where he wrote poetry and historical works, translated, and edited. In addition to the *Orationi*, he edited Guicciardini's *Storia d'Italia*, and wrote *Considerationi Civili sopra l'Historie di Guicciardini, e d'altri Historici* (1582) which appeared in French and English translations. See Tommaso Bozza, *Scrittori Politici Italiani dal 1550 al 1650: Saggio di bibliografia* (Roma, 1949), pp. 57–58.

Domenico Mora,[44] and Bernardino Rocca.[45] They could at least partially fulfill the requirement of military experience: Mora was a professional soldier who fought all over Europe, Rocca had some military experience although the details are unknown, Centorio was a writer who
was thought to have been the amanuensis for a soldier; while Porcacchi
and Nannini were professional authors who had no known military experience.

Porcacchi argued that by approaching history with method and order
one could obtain full practical value from it. He noted, in conventional
terms, that men learned moral attitudes and practical advice from history, especially for governing states. The best way to gain this knowledge was to individuate materials dealing with war, peace, or any other
topic, under these headings so that the reader could in an instant locate
what he needed to know.[46]

Porcacchi and his collaborators attempted to reduce historical reality
to static, easy-to-learn commonplaces. In his *Paralleli o essempi*, Porcacchi repeated Sansovino's formulation concerning the relationship between repetition and change. Men usually repeated the deeds of the past;
the means and circumstances changed but the substance remained the
same. Thus one could construct historical 'commonplaces' from history.[47] The commonplaces of the book were illustrious military deeds
demonstrated by parallel ancient and modern examples. The *Imprese,
stratagemi, et errori militari* of Bernardino Rocca was organized in the
same way. At the beginning was a table of commonplaces of stratagems.
Then Rocca examined in detail some cases of ancient and modern military strategy in order to point out the correct moves and errors of the

---

[44] Domenico Mora (1536–post 1600) was a professional soldier from Bologna. He
fought against the Huguenots in France and acquired the title of gentleman in the Grisons,
where he commanded soldiers. He fought the Turks under the Venetian flag, and in 1579
went to Poland, where he was a military commander. He also fought in Transylvania
against the Muscovites before returning to Italy in the early seventeenth century. In addition to *Il Soldato*, he wrote *Il Cavaliere* (Vilna, 1589), and military works. See Bongi,
Annali di Giolito, II, 301–304.

[45] Bernardino Rocca, called il Gamberello (c. 1515–1587) came from Piacenza and
died in Venice. He had some military experience and became a priest in the last four
years of his life. He also wrote *Discorso dell'amor di Dio* for Giolito (1572), *Discorsi di
guerra* (1582), and did translations. See Bongi, *Annali di Giolito*, II, 228–229.

[46] *Le Cagioni delle guerre antiche*, 1564 ed., Prohemio, sig. ***iiiiᵛ. Also see *Ditte Candiotto et Darete Frigio*, 1570 ed., sigs. c iiʳ–d iiʳ.

[47] *Paralleli o essempi simili di Thomaso Porcacchi cavati da gl'Historici . . . È questa, secondo
l'ordine da lui posto, la seconda Gioia, congiunta all'Anella della sua Collana Historica . . .* (In
Vinegia Appresso Gabriel Giolito de' Ferrari, MDLXVI), Prohemio, p. 4.

leaders. He claimed that his readers would learn better how to avoid error by following his book with its organization than by reading the histories of Plutarch, Polybius, Livy, Caesar, and Appian.[48]

In the first of the series, *Le Cagioni delle guerre antiche*, Porcacchi discussed the cause and then the development, conduct, and result of wars taken from ancient Greek historians. He summarized or paraphrased excerpts from the histories and added his own marginal comments designed to elicit the knowledge to be gained. At times he merely noted the high points of the wars but more often he stated in a political maxim the lesson to be derived. Unfortunately, his maxims were usually superficial and sometimes even banal: 'Weak and neutral cities become powerful while the great cities war among themselves', 'Good advice and money produce victory in wars', 'Most often the causes of wars depend on the thirst for power.'[49]

Porcacchi and his collaborators recognized an audience interest in military history, and rearranged historical materials in an imaginative way to cater to it. Unfortunately, the qualitative results of the historical jewels were somewhat disappointing; because the authors, Porcacchi in particular, lacked the powers of analysis to fulfill their methodological insight.

The attempt to extract methodical political knowledge from history gave birth to a treatise of comparative government by Sansovino. In his *Del governo dei regni et delle republiche* (1561), he expressed the desire to formulate a *nuova Politica* by describing governments as they existed or had existed in the past. With the examples of many governments before him, the reader could discern for himself what was good and bad, and devise his own improved form.[50] Sansovino's comments implied criticism of theoretical treatises as he emphasized the actual practice and pro-

---

[48] *Imprese, stratagemi, et errori militari di M. Bernardin Rocca Piacentino, detto il Gamberello . . . È questa, secondo l'ordine da noi posto, la Quarta Gioia, congiunta all'Anella della nostra Collana Historica . . .* (In Vinegia Appresso Gabriel Giolito de' Ferrari, MDLXVI), sigs. C^r, c iii^r–^{v}.

[49] 'Le città deboli & neutrali, diventano possenti, mentre le grandi guerreggiano fra di loro.' 'Il consiglio e i denari acquistano vittoria ne le guerre.' 'Il piu quasi delle cagioni delle guerre dependono dall' ingordigia di signoreggiare.' *Le Cagioni delle guerre antiche*, 1564 ed., pp. 36, 34, 46.

[50] *Del governo de i regni et delle republiche cosi antiche come moderne libri xviii. Ne quali si contengono i Magistrati, gli Offici, & gli ordini proprij che s'osservano ne predetti Principati. Dove si ha cognitione di molte historie particolari, utili & necessarie al viver civile di Francesco Sansovino . . .* (In Venetia, Appresso Francesco Sansovino. MDLXI), sig. *3^r. It was reprinted in 1566, 1567, 1578, 1583, and 1607, always in Venice.

I

cedure of governments. The book contained short descriptions of the
constitutional structure of the governments of contemporary France,
Germany, England, Spain, Turkey, Venice, Rome, Lucca, and Genoa;
Sparta, Athens, and Republican Rome of antiquity; and concluded with
the government of Utopia. Subsequent editions added more governments.

The chapters were rapid surveys of the organs of government and the
functions of various offices in the states. Sansovino took his information
from standard histories, and when such a history was lacking, as in the
case of Lucca, he wrote his own account. But he added no comment or
analysis, and with the exception of the lengthy section on Venice, taken
from Gasparo Contarini's *De magistratibus et Republica Venetarum*, the descriptions lacked depth and detail. On the other hand, the work demonstrated that Sansovino thought it useful for his readers to learn from
non-Italian examples. He also showed an awareness of the importance
of understanding indigenous customs in order to comprehend the workings of the government. For example, with his analysis of the English
government, Sansovino devoted a page to English manners, habits,
dress, and modes of speech, although he failed to relate them to the
workings of the government.[51] The last section of the book, the government of Utopia, was a shortened version of Thomas More's *Utopia*
from the Italian translation of Ortensio Lando first printed in 1548. Sansovino explained that More had written his book because he had been
sickened by the corruption of the century. He justified its inclusion in a
book devoted to the descriptions of actual governments with the comment that men might learn from the *Utopia* the true way of living well
and happily.[52]

Bodin wrote that it was useful to the historian to compare the forms
of government of different states, and sixteenth-century Italians were
engrossed in the search for the perfect form of government.[53] *Del governo
dei regni et delle republiche* provided in a convenient format some raw
materials for the quest. Sansovino enabled the general reader to consider
historically the issues raised by learned commentators.

The popularizers gave to their readers more political wisdom by publishing political maxims extracted from histories. The practice of distill-

[51] *Ibid.*, f. 31ʳ.
[52] *Ibid.*, f. 184ʳ.
[53] *Methodus*, ch. VI, in Vegas, 'La concezione della storia', p. 176; and Curcio, *Dal Rinascimento alla Controriforma*, pp. 77–138.

ing years of political experience into pithy sentences existed as early as the fifteenth century. For example, the Florentine Gino di Neri Capponi just before his death in 1420 wrote for his son maxims of political conduct which had a Machiavellian ring in their stress on political to the exclusion of moral considerations.[54] For the second half of the sixteenth century, Machiavelli was an important source for maxims and Guicciardini's *Ricordi* were very influential. Sansovino credited Guicciardini with being the inventor of 'these propositions, rules, maxims, [and] axioms' of politics.[55] In 1578 Sansovino published his maxims as *Concetti Politici*. In 1583 he collected the *Ricordi* of Guicciardini, the *Avvedimenti Civili* of Giovanni Francesco Lottini, and his own *Concetti Politici*, and published them as *Propositioni overo considerationi in materia di cose di Stato*.

As usual Sansovino stressed that each of the groups of maxims was useful to men involved in political affairs. He also stressed that practical experience in affairs of state qualified the authors to propose maxims. The claim was more than justified with Guicciardini; for Lottini Sansovino claimed that he had made 'an exquisite practice in maters of state' expecially under the Grand Duke of Tuscany, Cosimo I de' Medici. This was true; Lottini (1512–1572) was an experienced ambassador and courtier who probably organized the assassination of Lorenzino de' Medici for Cosimo.[56] But Sansovino was on shaky ground when he came to his own practical experience. He could only mention his brief and inconsequential career at the court of Julius III.[57]

Nevertheless, the maxims of Sansovino contained some of the best political wisdom of the century. In the original edition of the *Concetti Politici*, but not in the subsequent *Propositioni . . . di cose di Stato*, Sansovino listed twenty ancient and sixteen fifteenth- and sixteenth-century authors as the sources for his 803 maxims. The list included the major ancient Greek and Roman historians, moderns such as Giovio, Guicciardini, Sabellicus, and Leonardo Bruni, plus a few non-historians like

[54] Renzo Sereno, 'The *Ricordi* of Gino di Neri Capponi', *American Political Science Review*, LII (1958), 1118–1122.

[55] 'Perche il Guicciardino fu il primo inventore di queste Propositioni, Regole, Massime, Assiomi, Oracoli, Precetti, Sentenze, Probabili, o per qualunque altro nome possino esser chiamati.' *Propositioni . . . di cose di Stato*, 1583 ed., f. 100ᵛ. The *Concetti Politici* were printed separately in 1578 and 1603 in Venice, and an English translation under the title of *The quintesence of wit* appeared in London, 1590. The complete *Propositioni . . . di cose di Stato* were printed in 1583, 1588, 1598, and 1608, always in Venice.

[56] *Ibid.*, f. 12ᵛ. On Lottini, see Bozza, *Scrittori Politici Italiani*, pp. 46–48.

[57] *Propositioni . . . di cose di Stato*, 1583 ed., f. 100ʳᵛ.

Cicero and Giovanni Della Casa. Sansovino did not include Machiavelli although an anonymous *History of Florence* was listed.[58] The truth was that Sansovino took about one-fourth of his maxims from all the major works of Machiavelli, and slightly less than forty percent from the works of Machiavelli and Guicciardini combined.[59] Moreover, readers had little difficulty in identifying the authorship of the great Florentines. John Donne owned a copy of the 1588 edition of the *Propositioni . . . di cose di Stato* and correctly annotated Machiavelli and Guicciardini as the authors of many maxims.[60] Although Machiavelli was banned and references to him were being dropped from books,[61] the popularizers helped to bring his political insights to their readers.

One could object that distilling history into maxims distorted history and that the result paled in comparison to the richness of the original works. But Italians in the second half of the sixteenth century viewed historiography as a mine of political maxims. Esteemed histories like the *Storia d'Italia* of Guicciardini were published with apparatus which helped the reader to find maxims in the work. Remigio Nannini performed this function in an edition of the *Storia d'Italia* published by Giolito in 1568. One of the tables at the front of the book listed fourteen sentences, i.e., maxims, which Nannini felt were important and useful. One reader of this edition was not content with the editor's selections and underlined in the text many other maxims as well.[62] The popularizers simply responded to this reader preference.

58 *Concetti Politici*, 1578 ed., sig. **4[v].

59 See Vincent Luciani, 'Sansovino's *Concetti Politici* and their Debt to Machiavelli', *PMLA* LXVII (1952), 823–844; and 'Sansovino's *Concetti Politici* and their Debt to Guicciardini', *PMLA*, LXV (1950), 1181–1195.

60 *Propositioni, overo considerationi in materia di cose di stato* . . . (In Vinegia, Presso Altobello Salicato, 1588. Alla Libraria della Fortezza.) Donne's copy is at Harvard University, Houghton Library Nor 5200.7*. Donne identified some of Sansovino's *concetti* as those of Machiavelli and Guicciardini, and annotated many of Guicciardini's *Ricordi*.

61 Actually Sansovino continued to praise and identify Machiavelli longer than other —more cautious—popularizers. In the early 1560's Machiavelli's name began to disappear as an historical source. For example, in the tenth historical jewel, the *Orationi militari*. *Raccolte per M. Remigio Fiorentino, da tutti gli historici greci e latini, antichi e moderni* . . . (In Vinegia Appresso Gabriel Giolito de' Ferrari, MDLX), sig. **x[v], Machiavelli's *History of Florence* was listed as a source. But in the edition of 1561, only an anonymous *History of Florence* was listed.

62 *La Historia d'Italia di M. Francesco Guicciardini Gentil'huomo Fiorentino, Dove si descrivono tutte le cose seguite dal MCCCCLXXXXIIII per fino al MDXXXII. Riscontrate dal R. P. M. Remigio Fiorentino con tutto gli Istorici, c'hanno trattato del medesimo, e posti in margine i luoghi degni d'esser notati. Con tre tavole, una delle cose più notabili, l'altra delle sententie sparse per l'opera. E la terza de gli Autori co' quali sono state riscontrate. Con la vita del autore*

Through the application of 'method and order' the popularizers mined history for political lessons. These works showed an audience interest in concrete and practical political information. The popularizers responded by extracting this information from history and arranging it in easy-to-learn forms. They did violence to original historiography, to be sure, but their organization showed some creativity. In their attempt to present political lessons, the popularizers grasped the rudiments of a political science.

IV

Another large group of popular histories provided utilitarian information oriented toward the present. These books presented practical information for merchants, professional men, travellers, and other readers. They included historical guides to cities, chronologies, epitomes, family histories, and histories which gave information on the Turkish menace. On the humblest level there were anecdotal histories and popular biographies whose sole purpose was diversion.

In these works the popularizers demonstrated a preference for the history of their own century. Sansovino's narratives and compendiums, for example, became more full as they approached the present. Usually there were three or four separate levels of comprehensiveness. In the first stage, which normally began with a conventional starting point as Creation or the fall of Rome, the story was brief and sketchy until the mid-fourteenth century. An expanded second stage ensued until about 1500. A third stage after 1500 occupied still more space as Sansovino dealt with Italian events in more detail, added other European and Turkish events, and usually took a cursory glance at the New World. Sometimes a fourth expansion was noticeable as the narrative reached c. 1540 to c. 1560, the years in which the popularizers reached maturity.

The popularizers weighted their histories toward the present because they thought that men were more interested in their own times than in the past. Sansovino justified the greater attention that he gave the post-1500 period by noting that men were more interested in events that they

descritta dal medesimo, e co' sommarii a ciascun libro. (In Vinegia, Appresso Gabriel Giolito de' Ferrari, MDLXVIII). Nannini's *tavola* of sentences is on sig. ***iii^{rv}. For the example with the underscored maxims, see the copy Rinasc. G279° in the Biblioteca Nazionale Centrale in Florence, pp. 19, 45, 84, 167, 193, 253, 268, 273, 336, 354, 409, 424, 431, 541, 611, 666, 692, 778, 783. The title page carries the undated signature, 'Bartolomeo Francesionj'.

had witnessed or heard spoken of than in the past. Moreover, while allowing that the sixteenth century had been disturbed, he revealed no loss of self-confidence about his times. He admitted that many notable misfortunes, perhaps more than had happened in previous centuries, had occurred since 1500. But the present century had also witnessed a great efflorescence of military deeds, learning, and the arts, all of which gave perpetuity, glory, and splendor to an age.[63]

The presuppositions of sixteenth-century historiography also influenced these divisions. Italians believed that the Renaissance, or the modern age, had begun in the fourteenth century.[64] Vasari credited the rebirth of the arts to the age of Giotto; and when Porcacchi paralleled illustrious ancients and moderns, fifteenth- and sixteenth-century men were the moderns. Many sixteenth-century Italians were equally convinced that another dividing point had occurred with the invasions of Italy. Both Giovio and Guicciardini began their histories at 1494, and contrasted the peaceful days before with the new age of overturned states and the vast change in every field that followed. The availability of sources also helped to determine the allotment of space. Like original historians, the popularizers were conscious of the paucity of reliable sources for earlier periods. Sansovino often apologized for the brevity of his accounts of earlier periods by citing the lack of reliable sources. Once the narrative reached the sixteenth century, such good, comprehensive accounts as the histories of Guicciardini and Giovio were available. After 1550 it was a matter of relating current events, and a good popularizer like Sansovino kept himself well informed on these.

The union of the utilitarian and the present gave birth to historical guides to cities, perhaps Sansovino's best works. Other guide books to

63 'Nel primo adunque troverete con ordini, i soccessi dal principio della creatione fino all'anno 1579. è ben vero che giunto al 1500 sono stato da indi in quà più largo & più pieno, si perche in questi 78 anni passati, sono seguiti molti accidenti notabili forse quanti altri che avenissero mai ne secoli andati, & si perche diversi che gli hanno veduti vivono ancora, à quali peraventura saranno piu grate le cose vedute, ò sentite da loro, che le passate: & spetialmente questa età che ha fiorito cose largamente nella militia, nelle discipline, & nell'arti nobili che danno altrui perpetuità, gloria & splendore,' *Cronologia del mondo di M. Francesco Sansovino divisa in tre libri. Nel primo de' quali s'abbraccia, tutto quello ch'è avvenuto cosi in tempo di pace come di guerra fino all'anno presente. Nel secondo, si contiene un Catalogo de Regni & delle Signorie, che sono state & che sono, con le discendenze & con le cose fatte da loro di tempo in tempo. Nel terzo, si tratta l'origine de cinquanta case illustri d'Italia, co' soccessi de gli huomini eccellenti di quelle, & con le dipendenze & parentele fra loro* . . . (In Venetia. Nella Stamperia della Luna. MDLXXX), sig. *3ᵛ.

64 Wallace K. Ferguson, *The Renaissance in Historical Thought* (Cambridge, Mass., 1948), pp. 1–28, 60–66.

geography, architecture, and art of Italian cities, such as Leandro Alberti's *Descrittione di tutta l'Italia* (1550) were written in the sixteenth century. Sansovino's books on Venice surpassed the other guides by the wealth and broadness of their historical and contemporary information. His *Venetia Città Libera* (1581) was a detailed guide to the public and private institutions, buildings, and art of Venice. It also contained an account of the habits and customs of Venetians, the public pageantry of the city, brief lives of famous Venetians of public affairs and letters, and a short history of the city. Sansovino's use of historical material and his judgments were intelligent. Suffused with the author's love of the city, the book was accurate enough, and the topography of Venice has changed so little, that a twentieth-century tourist could still use it.[65]

Preceding the *Venetia* was Sansovino's *Delle cose notabili che sono in Venetia* (1561), an historical chronicle of the city with information on contemporary life. In addition to the history of Venice, one could find in it population statistics, its daily consumption of flour, a brief analysis of the functions of the chief courts, brief resumés of all the doges, and the location of the prostitutes (who were all foreigners according to Sansovino) with the information that they were fined twenty *soldi* if a patron became diseased.[66] The *Venetia* and the *Cose notabili in Venetia* were enlarged and often reprinted, testifying that readers found the books useful. Sansovino's historical guides were storehouses of the practical information that merchants and statesmen, as well as casual tourists, would appreciate.

In 1575 Sansovino accomplished for the rest of Italy what he had done for Venice by publishing a volume of short historical descriptions of Italian cities. In the *Ritratto delle più nobili et famose città d'Italia* he indicated his desire to be useful and his focus on the present. He stated that he was giving a portrait of 'those cities that live at present in Italy', and that anyone who wished to know something about his native city or any other city would find it here. He presented word-pictures from a

---

[65] The *Venetia* was enlarged and reprinted by Giovanni Stringa in 1604, and by Giustiniano Martinioni in 1663, with both editions published in Venice.

[66] *Delle Cose Notabili che sono in Venetia, quale con ogni verità fidelmente si descrive. Usanze antiche. Habiti & vestiti. Huomini virtuosi. Pittori & pitture. Scultori & loro opere. Fabriche & palazzi. Principi & vita loro. Tutti li corpi Santi. Numero delle parochie. Numero de Magistrati. Con le origine di esse Città, & un Sumario di tutte le guerre occorse dal 1496 fin'al tempo presente.* (In Venetia per Domenico de Franceschi. 1570), f. 6[rv]. The book appeared in editions of 1561, 1562, 1564, 1565, 1566, 1567, 1570, 1582, 1583, 1587, 1592, 1596, 1606, 1649, 1662, and 1671.

single page to forty pages of all major and many minor cities. All followed a pattern; the portrait of Florence began with what Sansovino judged to be her chief glory, the many brilliant Florentines in every field of activity. Then he listed his sources including works of Leonardo Bruni, Cristoforo Landino, Flavio Biondo, Machiavelli, and others. Next he briefly toured the city, describing important buildings, hospitals for the poor, major libraries, and works of art. After synopsizing Florentine history, he noted famous Florentines and concluded by listing the noble families of the city.[67]

An essential historical tool then as now was a chronology. Bodin wrote that a universal chronology was useful to the historian who needed exact dates to avoid mistakes and arguments.[68] Popularizers met this need with such works as Sansovino's three part *Cronologia* (1580). He apologized for the work's lack of eloquence and explained that his purpose was to provide a 'brief and succinct compendium' so that those whose time was limited because of their important affairs could 'comprehend in a moment' what many authors had written over centuries.[69] The first part of the book listed events and dates, with a little explanatory information, from Creation to 1578. In the second part Sansovino added more specialized information. This was a catalogue with brief historical information of reigns and rulers of Byzantium, ancient Greece and Rome, and the Near East, as well as western Europe. Sansovino assumed that his readers' interests and needs were much broader than Italy. In the third part he described briefly the origins of fifty illustrious Italian families.

Two years later he published his *Origine et fatti delle famiglie illustri d'Italia* (1582), an expanded version of the third part of the *Cronologia*. Sansovino did not write a narrative but collected historical information on eighty-one Italian families including the Medici, Sforza, Orsini, Co-

---

67 The *Ritratto delle città d'Italia* had a separate title page within the *Sopplimento delle croniche universali: Ritratto delle più nobili et famose Città di Italia di M. Francesco Sansovino, nel quale si descrivono particolarmente gli edifici sacri et profani cosi pubblici come privati, le famiglie illustri, gli huomini letterati, i personaggi di conto cosi morti come vivi et i dominii loro, con le reliquie de santi, le fertilità de territori, la qualità de paesi et il numero degli habitanti.* (In Venetia, MDLXXV), quote on f. 3r, portrait of Florence fs. 25v–31r. It was not reprinted.
68 *Methodus,* ch. viii, in Vegas, 'La concezione della storia', 176.
69 '. . . non per via di historia distesa & scritta con eloquenza, ma per modo di breve & soccinto compendio, accioche si possa da gli huomini grandi, & altri, à quali tempo è scarso per i negotij loro importanti, comprendere in un momento quello ch'è stato largamente trattato in tanti secoli da tanti Scrittori.' *Cronologia,* 1580 ed., sig. *2r. It was reprinted in 1582, Venice, omitting part three.

lonna, Este, etc. He discussed their origins, major figures, blood rela-
tionships, clientele, wars, and notable deeds down to the present. Within
families the arrangement was genealogical and chronological, and the
content mostly political and military history. Italian society was becoming more conscious of its aristocracy in the second half of the sixteenth
century, and Sansovino's book catered to that interest.[70] However, he
was not sycophantic; nor did he invent flattering origins for the nobles,
but confined himself to reporting from his sources.

Like Giovio, Sansovino aided the Italian understanding of the Turkish menace. He wrote two histories of the Turks, *Dell'historia universale
dell'origine et imperio de' Turchi* (1560) and *Gl'annali overo le vite de' Principi et Signori della casa Othomana* (1570). In the first work, Sansovino
collected and organized a large body of information from histories,
travellers' accounts, and so on. He did not limit himself to political and
military history but presented information on the religious laws and
practices, civil laws, customs, dress, eating and drinking habits of the
Turks, how they treated Christians in their realms, and much more. The
second work was a history of the Turks approached through their rulers.
Sansovino awakened Italians to the Turkish peril in a fair, informative
way. He admonished his readers that there was much that was admirable in the Turks. He praised their military valor and pointed out that
their ability to rule firmly and justly fostered peace in their realms.[71] He
was no friend of the Turks; in a pamphlet of 1570 he urged European
princes to make war on them, predicting success if they would chart a
bold course.[72] But he saw clearly that the historian's task was to inform
the public on the enemy's strengths.

On a humbler level were popular histories whose purpose was to save

[70] See Angelo Ventura, *Nobilità e popolo nella società veneta del '400 e '500* (Bari, 1964),
pp. 275–374.

[71] *Dell'historia universale dell'origine et imperio de Turchi parte prima. Nella si contengono
gli offici, le leggi, et i costumi di quella natione, cosi in tempo di pace, come di guerra. Con una
tavola copiosissima di tutte le cose piu notabili dell'opera. Raccolta da Francesco Sansovino* (In
Venetia Appresso Francesco Sansovino et compagni. MDLX). It was reprinted in 1564,
1568, 1573, 1582, 1600, and 1654, always in Venice. *Gl'annali overo le vite de' Principi et
Signori della casa Othomana Di M. Francesco Sansovino. Ne quali si leggono di tempo in tempo
tutte le guerre particolarmente fatte dalla nation de' Turchi, in diverse provincie del mondo contra
i Christiani . . .* (In Venetia MDLXXI. In fine: Appresso Iacopo Sansovino. MDLXX), sig.
a2ʳ–a3ʳ. It was reprinted in 1573, Venice.

[72] *Lettera overo discorso sopra le predittioni fatte in diversi tempi da diverse persone; Le quali
pronosticano la nostra futura felicità per la guerra del Turco, l'anno MDLXX. Con un Pienissimo
albero della casa Othomana tratto dalle scritture Greche, et Turchesche. Per Francesco Sansovino*
(in fine: Stampata in Venetia. Et ristampata in Modena.)

the reader's time. In 1580 Sansovino published an epitome of Guicciardini's *Storia d'Italia*, and in 1562 Vincenzo Cartari published an epitome
of Giovio's *Historiarum sui temporis*.[73] Using Guicciardini's words Sansovino retained intact the first few pages and format of twenty books of
the complete edition but reduced it to one-sixth of the original. Cartari
effected a similar condensation of Giovio's work. Sansovino's justification was that because of their multitudinous concerns, the great had
very little time to read and might miss Guicciardini's magnificent history.
Hence, he had selected a few precious jewels from the infinite treasure
of Guicciardini's book in order that the great could learn useful lessons
from it.[74] One wonders if Guicciardini, a busy statesman as well as historian, would have approved Sansovino's epitome.

Another time-saving book was Lodovico Dolce's posthumous *Giornale delle historie del mondo* (1572), a kind of historical diary. The editor
explained that the purpose of the book was to 'relieve the memory of
excessive weight.' Dolce had organized the illustrious deeds of the past
in day by day order so that one could easily find memorable facts to
include in a speech or letter on the appropriate date.[75] The book was
admirably organized to fulfill its purpose. Under each day of the year,
the author listed all the important historical events that had occurred on
that day: births, deaths, wars, battles, peace treaties, and so on. The
reader who had an event in mind but lacked the date could check an
eighty-six-page index to locate the page which would give him the day,
month, and year of the event. The earliest event noted was the founding

[73] *Compendio dell'Historie di Monsignor Paolo Giovio da Como Vescovo di Nocera, Fatto
per M. Vincentio Cartari da Reggio* . . . (In Vinegia Appresso Gabriel Giolito de' Ferrari.
MDLXII). Very little is known of Cartari. He was born in Reggio and visited France at
least once. Between 1551 and 1562 he published four books: *Le Immagini degli Dei antichi*
(which had eighteen editions between 1556 and 1674), *Il Compendio di Giovio*, a translation of Ovid's *Fasti*, and *Il Flavio intorno a' Fasti*. Girolamo Tiraboschi, *Biblioteca Modenese
o notizie della vita e delle opere degli scrittori natii degli Stati del Serenissimo Signor Duca di
Modena* (Modena, 1781–1786), I, 411–413; VI, 56.

[74] *Dell'Epitome dell'historia d'Italia di M. Francesco Guicciardini*, sig. a3r.

[75] *Giornale delle historie del mondo, Delle cose degne di memoria di giorno in giorno occorse
dal principio del Mondo sino a' suoi tempi, di M. Lodovico Dolce. Riveduto, corretto, & ampliato
da Guglielmo Rinaldi* . . . (In Venetia, Al Segno della Salamandra. 1572), sigs. iir–iiiv. It
was reprinted at Forlì in 1576. Dolce (1508–1568) was born, lived, and died in Venice
where he supported himself by writing, editing, translating, and teaching. In addition to
the *Giornale delle historie del mondo*, he wrote a *Vita di Carlo Quinto, Dialogo della Pittura,
Osservazioni nella volgar lingua, Vita di Ferdinando Primo*, and many dramatic works. For
his life and bibliography, see Emmanuele A. Cicogna, 'Memoria intorno la vita e gli
scritti di Messer Lodovico Dolce letterato veneziano del secolo xvi', *Memorie dell'I. R.
Istituto Veneto di scienze lettere e arti*, X (1862), 93–200.

of Rome and the latest in 1568, the year of Dolce's death. The births and deaths of both Italian and foreign rulers were listed as well as major Italian authors, and some lesser-known Venetian figures. Both ancients and moderns were amply represented while the period between c. 400 and c. 1350 received less attention. Dolce claimed as his sources a lengthy list of historians and chronicles including all the standard ancient and modern historians. The book fulfilled its purpose and doubtlessly proved of value to anyone in need of a date or historical allusion.

Finally there were popular histories whose sole purpose was diversion. Popular lives of the great comprised a large number of books of this sort. Perhaps the favorite subject of popular biography was Charles V. Lodovico Dolce's *Vita di Carlo Quinto* (1561) was a good example.[76] The book was a smoothly written portrait which viewed Charles as a Christian champion and slid over matters such as the sack of Rome. The author made no claim to originality, listing well-known historians like Giovio and Galeazzo Capella on Milan as his sources.

Sansovino added to this genre an unpretentious memoir, *Il Simolacro di Carlo Quinto* (1567). It included a brief summary of the origins, personal habits, important deeds in the Emperor's life (mostly wars), attributed sayings, and orations delivered at his death. The most interesting comment in the book was Sansovino's discussion of Charles' favorite reading. According to Sansovino, although the Emperor profited little from letters, four books (in translation) delighted him. They were Castiglione's *Courtier*, which he read for instruction in the *vita civile*, the *Prince* and *Discourses* of Machiavelli for *cose di stato*, and the history of Polybius to learn of military affairs.[77] Sansovino's comment illuminates current Italian judgment concerning the reading material useful to princes.

Even the popular history for diversion exhibited the tendency of the popularizers to categorize. Lodovico Domenichi published his *Historia*

---

[76] *Vita dell'invittiss. e gloriosiss. imperador Carlo Quinto, descritta da M. Lodovico Dolce* . . . (In Vinegia Appresso Gabriel Giolito de' Ferrari, MDLXI). It was reprinted twice in 1561 and in 1567, always in Venice.

[77] 'Studi. Parve che nelle lettere facesse poco profitto: non dimeno apprese la lingua Spagnuola, la Tedesca & la Francese. La latina intendeva cosi grossamente. Però si dilettava di leggere tre libri solamente liquali esso haveva fatto tradurre in lingua sua propria. L'uno per l'institutione della vita civile, & questo fu il Cortigiano del Conte Baldasar da Castiglione, l'altre per le cose di stato, & questo fu il Principe co Discorsi del Machiavello, & il terzo per gli ordini della militia, & questo fu la Historia con tutte le altre cose di Polibio.' *Il simolacro di Carlo Quinto Imperadore Di M. Francesco Sansovino* . . . (In Venetia, Appresso Francesco Franceschini, MDLXVII), f. 21ʳ.

Varia (1558), a collection of sketches of historical persons and deeds varying in length from a few lines to thirty pages, and often culminating in a well-turned phrase. These historical anecdotes were apparently chosen for their reader interest and were haphazardly grouped according to the names of the historical figures mentioned. The next, enlarged edition of 1564 added to each of the stories a heading which stated the category to which the story belonged. These categories were usually moral commonplaces: 'fortitude in sorrow', 'incontinence toward one's subjects', 'adulterers punished', and so on. Two ample tables of contents, organized according to the names of the historical personages and according to the moral commonplaces, enabled the reader to locate quickly the kind of anecdote which interested him.[78] Domenichi gave no reason for the new organization; probably either he or Giolito, his publisher, thought that readers would prefer this organization and would buy more copies.

Another anecdotal history organized by moral commonplaces was the *Vite d'alcuni papi et cardinali* (1567) of Girolamo Garimberto. His book was a popular version of the genre of short lives of illustrious men as the *Illustrium virorum vitae* of Giovio. Like the revised edition of Domenichi's *Historia Varia*, Garimberto's lives of fifteenth- and sixteenth-century prelates were grouped under moral commonplaces. Each sketch began with general comments on the given virtue or vice and then related a life or ancedote as illustration. Garimberto, who was a Roman courtier, avoided a dull moralizing book because he related some colorful tales probably based on court gossip. The lives illustrating vices were most interesting as Garimberto did not spare his clerical subjects.[79]

---

[78] *Historia di Messer Lodovico Domenichi di detti e fatti degni di memoria di diversi principi, e huomini privati antichi, et moderni* . . . (In Vinegia Appresso Gabriel Giolito de' Ferrari, MDLVIII). *Historia Varia di M. Lodovico Domenichi . . . Con due tavole, la prima de' nomi delle persone e delle cose notabili, & l'altra della proprietà delle cose* . . . (In Vinegia Appresso Gabriel Giolito de' Ferrari. MDLXIIII). Domenichi was born in Piacenza, studied at Pavia, lived in Venice from 1543 to 1546, and then moved to Florence where Cosimo I supported him. Domenichi was the author of *Nobilità delle Donne, Dialoghi*, and *La Donna di Corte*. He also edited a widely reprinted collection of *Facezie*, and translated several works of Giovio as well as many other works. For his life and bibliography see Cristoforo Poggiali, *Memorie per la Storia Letteraria di Piacenza* (Piacenza, 1789), I, 221–290.

[79] *La prima parte, delle vite, overo fatti memorabili d'alcuni papi, et di tutti i cardinali passati. Di Hieronimo Garimberto Vescovo di Gallese* . . . (In Vinegia, Appresso Gabriel Giolito de' Ferrari, MDLXVII). For colorful examples, see pp. 484–485, 498–501, 504–506. Garimberto (1506–1575) was born in Parma of a noble family and had a long career as a courtier in Rome where he died. He was named bishop of Gallese, a suppressed Tuscan diocese, in 1562. He was the author of *De Reggimenti pubblici delle Città, Della Fortuna, Problemi*

The moral commonplaces added nothing to an already interesting book, but either the author or the printer (Giolito) felt that they were necessary.

The common purpose of these historical guides, chronologies, epitomes, family histories, books on the Turks, anecdotal histories, and short biographies was to be of use to their readers. The uses ranged from providing reference information to helping the reader pass the time with historical tales of human interest. These books usually had a contemporary focus and demonstrated broad interests. They ventured beyond Italy to embrace universal history, and added other types of information to politics and military affairs. As with the popular histories which taught lessons of politics, these books showed a tendency to break down the content of history into categories. They were humble books, but many were well done and showed an intelligent author trying to meet needs and interests.

v

Sansovino judged that his works were of some use to men. Commentators agreed, and printers and booksellers made the popular histories widely available to readers who purchased them for their own libraries.

Sansovino evaluated his career modestly. In 1566 he wrote that he was born to write but lamented that he did not write well. He was referring to his lack of imaginative talent. But, he went on, because activity was more noble than idleness, it was better to write badly than not at all. Hence he was always adding and recording information, correcting errors, and leaving the material in better condition than when he found it.[80] This was an accurate self-evaluation. His editorial labors brought to his readers much historical information of which they might otherwise not have been aware, and in such a way that they could understand and use the information.

Observers praised Sansovino's corpus because it was useful to men. The editor of a 1587 edition of *Delle cose notabili in Venetia* praised Sansovino as an indefatigable worker whose books were of use to every degree and condition of mankind. The editor did not, however, credit

---

naturali e morali, *Concetti* (which had eight editions), and *Il Capitano-Generale* as well as the *Vite*. See Ireneo Affò and Angelo Pezzana, *Memorie degli scrittori e letterati parmigiani* (Parma, 1793, 1827), IV, 135–144; VI, part 2, 542–546, 970.

[80] Cicogna, *Delle iscrizioni veneziane*, IV, 90–91.

Sansovino with the authorship of the book but claimed it as his own.[81] Alessandro Zilioli (d. 1650), a Venetian literary scholar, praised Sansovino for producing books for the common good.[82] Similarly, in 1647 another historian of Italian literature praised Sansovino's *Del governo dei regni et delle republiche* because one could find in it information on the governments of foreign lands.[83] Other commentators praised Sansovino as an historian. Gabriel Naudé (1600–1653), French political writer and librarian to Cardinal Mazarin, praised Sansovino in 1633 for his *Origine delle famiglie illustri* and *Propositioni . . . di cose di Stato*.[84] The editor of the 1663 edition of the *Venetia* praised Sansovino for his invention, order, and erudition.[85]

The popular histories were widely available through Venetian booksellers. In 1584 a bookseller had eight copies of five titles of Sansovino for sale: his *Cronologia, Origine delle famiglie illustri, Ritratto delle città d'Italia, Historia universale de' Turchi,* and the *Epitome dell'historia di Guicciardini.*[86] A collector in 1604 had available nine titles of Sansovino: *Del governo dei regni et della republiche, Sopplimento, Venetia, Historia universale de' Turchi, Cronologia, Simolacro di Carlo Quinto, Epitome dell'historia di Guicciardini,* and *Concetti Politici.*[87] He also had three of the historical jewels: Rocca's *Imprese, stratagemi, et errori militari, Discorsi di guerra* of Centorio, and Mora's *Soldato;*[88] as well as Garimberto's *Vite d'alcuni papi et cardinali,* and Dolce's *Vita di Carlo Quinto* in his library.[89]

[81] *Delle cose notabili Della Città di Venetia . . . Fatta da Girolamo Bardi Fiorentino* (In Venetia, Appresso Felice Valgrisio. 1587), p. 199. This praise of Sansovino was repeated in the Bardi, Venice, 1606 ed., p. 132; in the Venice, 1662 ed., credited to Nicolò Doglioni, pp. 308–309; and in the Venice, 1671 ed., also credited to Doglioni, pp. 308–309.

[82] Biblioteca Marciana Venezia, MSS. Italiani, Classe X, No. I (6394), 'Istoria Delle Vite de' Poeti Italiani di Alessandro Zilioli Veneziano', p. 146.

[83] Ghilini, *Teatro d'huomini letterati,* I, 64.

[84] Gabriel Naudé, *La Bibliographie Politique* (Paris, 1642), 159–160. It was first published in 1633.

[85] *Venetia città nobilissima, et singolare, Descritta in XIIII Libri Da M. Francesco Sansovino . . . Con aggiunta Di tutte le Cose Notabili della stessa Città, fatte, & occorse dall'Anno 1580, sino al presente 1663. Da D. Giustiniano Martinioni . . .* (In Venetia, Appresso Steffano Curti. MDCLXIII), sig. *6v.

[86] Archivio di Stato, Venezia, Giudici di Petizion, Inventari, Busta 338, no. 44, fs. 6v, 10v, 22rv, 30r. (Hereafter abbreviated as ASV, GP Inv.) The bookseller was Auzollo Bonfadini. In addition he had three copies of *Avvedimenti Civili* which might have been Sansovino's *Propositioni . . . di cose di Stato.* ASV, GP Inv., Bu. 338, no. 44, fs. 5v, 29v.

[87] Biblioteca Marciana Venezia, MSS. Italiani, Classe X, No. lxi (6601), 'Inventario della Libreria di Giovanni Vincenzo Pinelli ereditata da Francesco Pinelli', fs. 47r, 81r, 83r, 86rv, 128v.

[88] *Ibid.,* fs. 45r, 76r, 84v.

[89] *Ibid.,* fs. 46v, 47r.

Sansovino's *Venetia* achieved instant commercial success. The editor of the second edition explained that the first edition (1581) had immediately sold out, and the author was preparing a new edition when he died in 1583. Twenty years later Sansovino's *privilegio* (copyright) had expired and this new edition appeared (1604).[90]

Limited evidence indicates that the popularizations found their way into contemporary private libraries of Venetians of varying social status and profession.[91] The inventory of a non-patrician Venetian at his death in 1584 included a copy of Sansovino's *Venetia* in a library of c. 130 titles.[92] The death inventory in 1600 of the widow of a Venetian patrician included the *Concetti Politici* of Sansovino within a collection of c. 180 titles.[93] At his death in 1624, a Venetian physician of modest means owned the *Sopplimento* of Sansovino, and possibly his *Historia universale de' Turchi* in a library of c. 320 titles.[94] At his death in 1631, Marco Dandolo, a wealthy Venetian patrician and statesman, had three titles of Sansovino, the *Ritratto delle città d'Italia*, *Gl'annali della casa Othomana*, and the *Cose notabili in Venetia*, within a library of 118 titles.[95]

---

[90] *Venetia città nobilissima et singolare; Descritta gia in XIIII libri Da M. Francesco Sansovino. Et hora con molta diligenza corretta, emendata, e piu d'un terzo di cose nuove ampliata dal M. R. D. Giovanni Stringa* . . . (In Venetia, Presso Altobello Salicato. MDCIII), sig. *3ᵛ.

[91] The following occurrences of popular histories are found in inventories of the possessions of deceased Venetians. The inventories were made by the court of the Giudici di Petizion when the owners died intestate or because there was a disputed inheritance. The records do not give the birth date or age of the owners; but if one estimates the age at death as from fifty to seventy years, then the titles in the library probably were acquired in the adulthood of the possessors, which would be thirty to fifty years before death. Most of the inventories listed only abbreviated titles, often omitting the author, and almost never including the place and date of publication. When the author's name and other information were omitted, it is easier to identify Sansovino's works than those of any other popularizer because he gave his books distinctive titles not repeated by others. This was not the case with other popularizers. For example, there were several entries of *Vita di Carlo Quinto* which could have been the book of Dolce, of Alfonso Ulloa, or of another author. Similarly *Discorsi di guerra* may or may not have been an historical jewel of Centorio, and *Orationi volgari* or *Orationi diversi* are difficult to pin down as Nannini's *Orationi*. Undoubtedly there were in these private libraries other copies of popular histories but only the clearly identifiable titles are noted.

[92] ASV, GP Inv., Bu. 338, no. 61, f. 2ᵛ. The profession of the owner, Ippolito Ganason, was not given.

[93] ASV, GP Inv., Bu. 342, no. 8, f. 6ʳ. This was the inventory of Maria Davila, widow of Benetto Memmo and sister to Bishop Ferdinando Davila.

[94] ASV, GP Inv., Bu. 349, no. 25, fs. 7ʳ, 9ᵛ. The owner, Alberto Quattrochi, had a house of eight rooms modestly furnished.

[95] ASV, GP Inv., Bu. 352, no. 99, items 60, 419, 426. This inventory is organized by items with printed books itemized with account books, contracts, *relazioni*, etc.

A Venetian with scholarly interests who died in 1640 had copies of the *Historia universale de' Turchi* (1600 ed.), the *Cronologia* (1580), *Ritratto delle città d'Italia* (1575), and *Venetia* (1604) of Sansovino.[96] He also owned two historical jewels, Porcacchi's *Le Cagioni delle guerre antiche* (1565) and Mora's *Il Soldato* (1569), as well as Dolce's *Giornale delle historie del mondo* (1570).[97]

By the mid-seventeenth century the popular histories appeared less frequently in the library inventories. The owners, who flourished in the first half of the seventeenth century, were more interested in the events of their own century, as for example, the Thirty Years War. Nevertheless, the continuing Venetian-Turkish conflict and interest in Venice meant that some of the popular histories continued to appear. Sansovino's *Venetia*, *Cose notabili in Venetia*, and *Gl'annali della casa Othomana* were in the library of a Venetian patrician in 1657.[98] Two non-patrician Venetians in 1658 owned copies of Sansovino's *Cose notabili in Venetia*,[99] and *Historia universale de' Turchi*.[100]

History was an important interest of the owners of these libraries. The inventories show that classical histories were usually present and that the histories of Guicciardini and Giovio almost always appeared, more often than any single title of popular history. The popular histories represented one part of the interest in history. Their appearance in these private libraries demonstrates that they were purchased and presumably read.

One can draw conclusions on the historical interests of readers from the remarks of the authors, and from the content and organization of the popular histories. The Italian reader accepted the Renaissance belief that history was useful to the active life because it taught political lessons. Beyond that, he was not very interested in theoretical considerations but wanted concrete useful information from the histories. Moreover, he preferred to have history reorganized in such a way that he could quickly locate the information that he sought. His historical interests were cath-

[96] ASV, GP Inv., Bu. 356, no. 67, fs. 8ʳ, 18ᵛ, 40ᵛ, 41ᵛ. Marco Antonio Felette, whose profession was not given, was the owner of this magnificent library of c. 3500 titles. About ninety per cent of the books were printed between 1550 and 1620, and the library was especially strong in the natural sciences, mathematics, and astronomy. The inventory is unusual in that it lists title, author, place, date, and occasionally printer.

[97] ASV, GP Inv., Bu. 356, no. 67, fs. 8ᵛ, 40ʳ, 63ᵛ. This inventory notes a 1570 (not 1572) edition of Dolce's *Giornale delle historie del mondo*. To date I have not located any copies of this edition.

[98] ASV, GP Inv., Bu. 366, no. 90 (Gasparo Chechel), fs. 19ᵛ, 30ʳ, 23ʳ.

[99] ASV, GP Inv., Bu. 367, no. 23 (Giacomo Farolfo), f. 3ʳ.

[100] ASV, GP Inv., Bu. 367, no. 32 (Anzolo Balbi), f. 4ʳ.

olic; he wanted to know about his own city, the rest of Europe, and the non-European world, especially the Turks. While ancient history was always popular, the reader was most interested in the present and the near past. On the other hand, he showed little interest in religious history. He enjoyed reading about famous men and hearing good historical anecdotes. Guicciardini, Giovio, and Machiavelli among the moderns, and Polybius of the ancients, were significant influences on his historical and political consciousness.

The most noticeable feature of the content of the popular histories was a great interest in politics. The popular histories showed a recovery of interest in the political world after a period of pessimism and withdrawal from affairs in the previous thirty years. Writing at the depth of Italian discouragement, from the sack of Rome in 1527 until peace in 1559, such popular vernacular writers as Anton Francesco Doni (1513–1574), Nicolò Franco (1515–1570), and Ortensio Lando (c. 1512–1554) bitterly criticized Italian political leaders and argued that men should withdraw from the *vita civile*.[101] With peace, the popular histories showed a revival of interest in politics.

But an air of unreality clouds the picture of a merchant poring over books which discussed the strategies of Charles V warring with Turk or Protestant while the fate of Europe hung in the balance. An atmosphere of make believe suffuses the image of courtiers affirming or disputing the means to effect a *coup d'état* proposed in the *Propositioni . . . di cose di Stato*. There was more political speculation but less political activity; or at least the sphere of political activity was more circumscribed. After 1559, with the major exception of Venice, Italian states were either in the Spanish orbit or were under the rule of Italian princes who practiced absolutism as far as possible. Italians had little opportunity to practice the maxims of *Realpolitik* learned from the popular histories. The major political activity of Europe went on elsewhere, a fact clearly recognized by the popularizers whose books discussed non-Italian affairs in detail. In the later years of the century, and in the seventeenth century as well, Italians went north, took an active role in the wars and diplomacy of northern Europe, and described them for an Italian audience.[102] Much of the interest in politics was necessarily armchair involvement.

[101] See Paul F. Grendler, *Critics of the Italian World 1530–1560. Anton Francesco Doni, Nicolò Franco, and Ortensio Lando* (Madison, Milwaukee, and London, 1969).

[102] For example, Enrico Caterino Davila (1576–1631) fought with Henry IV from 1589 to 1597 and then wrote his *Istoria delle guerre civili di Francia* (published 1630) which

The forms of the popular histories also suggest speculation on the habits of mind of the authors and their audience. In general, the popularizers followed the practice of the best original histories of their day. The popular histories fitted within the canons of historiography, the popularizers ordinarily practiced objectivity, and they understood the correct use of sources. But the popular histories differed from the original histories in two ways. First, the popularizers couched the lessons to be derived from history in concrete utilitarian terms. Second, the popularizers broke down the historical narrative and re-arranged history into analytical categories.

The emphasis on the concrete and the useful was evident in other fields of intellectual activity in Italy at this time. A growing number, but probably still a minority, of Italians placed a high value on experience and reality in opposition to the bookish and the abstract. In the late sixteenth century, educational critics proposed an education based on *cose* (things), i.e., reality and experience to prepare men for the world, in place of education based on *parole* (words), i.e., literary pedantry which filled the mind with abstract and disconnected words.[103] As early as the 1540's and 1550's, critics of society like Doni, Franco, and Lando proposed that the *studia humanitatis* was irrelevant and pedantic, and tentatively argued that men should look to experience and nature.[104] In 1572, Girolamo Muzio (1496–1576), courtier and author, wished a young prince to be taught things rather than words. Muzio meant that the boy should learn heroic example and moral principle related to the real world rather than literary detail. To bring about this kind of learning, Muzio insisted that the boy's tutor should be an honest man experienced in matters of the world, and he emphatically rejected a professor of humanistic studies because the latter lacked this experience.[105] In France, Montaigne in the *Apologie de Raimond Sebond* unfavorably contrasted the knowledge of the 'letter-struck' scholar with the practical knowledge of a peasant or shoemaker.[106]

---

narrated French events from Francis II through Henry IV (1559–1610). Guido Bentivoglio (1579–1644) had a similar career. See Giorgio Spini, 'La istorica del Barocco Italiano', *Belfagor*, 1 (1946), 326–327, for others.

[103] Eugenio Garin, *L'educazione in Europa (1400–1600). Problemi e programmi* (Bari, 1957), pp. 188–194, 225–228.

[104] Grendler, *Critics of the Italian World*, pp. 136–161.

[105] *Avvertimenti Morali Del Mutio Iustinopolitano. I quali sono Il Prencipe giovinetto . . .* (In Venetia, appresso Gio. Andrea Valvassori, detto Guadagnino. MDLXXII), pp. 18, 3–5.

[106] *The Essays of Montaigne*, trans. E. J. Trechmann, introd. J. M. Robertson (London, 1927), 1, 481–483, and passim.

This approach to education in the second half of the sixteenth century pointed toward the experimental and scientific temper of the seventeenth century. Then Tommaso Campanella in Italy and Francis Bacon in England argued against a learning of letters in favor of education based on experience, reality, and the book of nature.[107] The historical popularizers perceived this tendency; they tried to teach men something useful from history. To do this they stressed the concrete and practical in the historical experience.

The analytical organization of the popularizations showed a tendency at best to analyze—and at worst to pigeonhole—historical experience. This was related to a major tendency in Italian intellectual endeavor at this time. A concern for order, method, norms, and rules dominated Italian thought. The theoretical treatises on history tried to enunciate principles for writing history and using historical evidence. Italian literature was involved in formulating canons of literary criticism. Heavily influenced by Aristotle's *Poetics*, literary theorists applied categories and classifications to poetry and prose.[108] Pietro Aretino, opposing this tendency, wrote in 1537 that poetry was 'a whim of nature',[109] but the majority of authors in the second half of the century saw it as a literary science. Recently a scholar has noted a tendency among Florentines in the last quarter of the sixteenth century to view man in terms of abstract categories rather than in his complex human reality.[110]

The popular histories demonstrated the same tendency to categorize, organize, and arrange reality. The historical works of Sansovino contained all the elements of good sixteenth-century historiography but broken down into component parts. He devoted one book to chronology, another to the origins of families, another to a comparison of forms of government, and still other books to descriptions of cities. Never did he integrate the elements to produce complete history. Similarly, the popularizers excerpted nuggets of political wisdom from the historical context, organized them under commonplaces, and presented the results as universal keys to unlock the doors of politics. One suspects that a

[107] Garin, *L'educazione in Europa (1400–1600)*, pp. 219–252.

[108] See Giuseppe Toffanin, *La fine dell'Umanesimo* (Milano-Torino-Roma, 1920); and Bernard Weinberg, *A History of literary criticism in the Italian Renaissance*. 2 vols. (Chicago, 1961).

[109] Pietro Aretino, *Il primo libro delle lettere*. A cura di Fausto Nicolini (Bari, 1913), p. 187.

[110] Eric Cochrane, 'The End of the Renaissance in Florence', *Bibliothèque d'Humanisme et Renaissance*, XXVII (1965), 16–17.

statesman who attempted to rule by constant reference to the historical jewels or maxims would learn some useful information but that the everchanging reality would defeat his efforts. Nevertheless, the popular histories satisfied a keen historical interest in Italy.

University of Toronto

The Rejection of Learning in Mid-*Cinquecento* Italy

N THE years 1535 to 1555 a group of Italian authors rejected much of Italian Renaissance learning.[1] Humanists in the *Quattrocento* had wished to educate man for the active life. During the sixteenth century humanist education became a broad pattern of learning stressing grammar, rhetoric, logic, mathematics, history, and literature, based on both the Latin classics and vernacular models like Petrarch. Its purpose was the training of the young patrician to serve his family, city, or prince in the affairs of the world. But a group of critics mocked liberal studies, spurned the classical heritage, rejected authorities like Cicero and Pietro Bembo, ridiculed humanists, thought that history was widely misused, denied the utility of knowledge, and argued that man should withdraw into solitude. Nicolò Franco of Benevento (1515–1570), Lodovico Domenichi of Piacenza (1515–1564), Ortensio Lando of Milan (c. 1512–c. 1553), Giulio Landi of Piacenza (1500–1579), and Anton Francesco Doni of Florence (1513–1574) reached maturity in the fourth decade of the sixteenth century and expressed these critical themes in their many books published from 1533 to the early years of the 1550s.

Scholars know these authors primarily as *poligrafi*, low-born adventurers of the pen who followed in the footsteps of Aretino, producing amusing dialogues, not meant to be taken seriously, for a broad segment of the Italian reading public. Croce considered Lando and Doni as nihilists, lacking moral purpose.[2] For De Sanctis Franco and Doni were typical of the mediocrities whose contemporary popularity symbolized the corruption of the *Cinquecento*.[3] Twentieth-century scholarship has

---

[1] I wish to thank the Newberry Library for a grant-in-aid in the summer of 1964 which facilitated this research, and Dr. Hans Baron of the Newberry for his constructive criticism.

[2] Benedetto Croce, *Poeti e scrittori del pieno e del tardo Rinascimento* (Bari, 1945), I, 260–273; II, 126.

[3] Francesco De Sanctis, *History of Italian Literature*, tr. Joan Redfern (New York, 1931), I, 432–433.

devoted more time to their lively popular idiom than to the content of their writing.

However, the *poligrafi* had the serious purpose of criticizing sixteenth-century learning. In Doni's words, he wrote in order to 'chaff the world'.[4] Their attack on learning was an expression of their disillusionment with Italy in the *Cinquecento*. Moreover, the criticism was not limited to the low-born *poligrafi* as Count Giulio Landi, nobleman of Piacenza, joined them in mocking learning. These authors challenged sixteenth-century learning, adding an intellectual ferment to the declining political and economic fortunes, unsettled religious situation, and change to mannerism in art that marked the Italian *Cinquecento*.

The core of sixteenth-century learning was the *studia humanitatis*, defined by Kristeller as grammar, rhetoric, history, poetry, and moral philosophy based upon the reading and interpretation of its standard ancient writers in Latin and, to a lesser extent, in Greek.[5] Learning in the *Cinquecento* also included literature, defined as knowledge of the rules for writing poetry and prose, logic, philosophy, mathematics, geometry, arithmetic and, to some extent, law and medicine, based on the study of modern vernacular authors as well as the ancient Latin and Greek authorities. Its purpose was to train the young person to live virtuously at home, in the marketplace, or in service to city or prince.

In the fifteenth century Italians, especially Florentines, had developed a system of education which would train members of the urban patriciate to take their places as leaders in their family and in their city. Termed 'civic humanism' by Hans Baron and education for the *vita civile* by Eugenio Garin, the education favored by Leonardo Bruni, Matteo Palmieri, L. B. Alberti, and others sought to form critical judgment and moral obligation in the young student.[6] The recommended means were study and reading in the Latin classics and a reliance upon the past experience of man in history. Alberti urged man not to live alone but in the midst of other men. He warned that solitude and idleness quickly made one 'pertinacious, depraved, and bizarre'. If one wished to avoid the reputation of a rustic, one should be educated in letters, above all,

[4] '... egli c'è chi scrive per dar la baia al mondo, come il Doni' (A. F. Doni, *I Marmi*, a cura di Ezio Chiòrboli, Bari, 1928, 1, 131).

[5] Paul O. Kristeller, *Renaissance Thought: the Classic, Scholastic, and Humanistic Strains* (New York, 1961), pp. 10, 120–123.

[6] Hans Baron, *The Crisis of the Early Italian Renaissance: Civic Humanism and Republican Liberty in an Age of Classicism and Tyranny* (Princeton, N.J., 1955), and numerous articles; and Eugenio Garin, *L'umanesimo italiano: filosofia e vita civile nel rinascimento* (Bari, 1952).

but also in arithmetic, geometry, grammar, philosophy, oratory, and poetry. Alberti recommended such authors as Cicero, Livy, Sallust, Homer, Vergil, Demosthenes, and Xenophon. This scheme of education would make a child 'lecterato, costumato, savio e civile'. Joined with physical exercise and military training, the study of these subjects and authors would enable one to live the *vita civile*.[7]

In the sixteenth century vernacular literature grew in importance, and the urban patriciate.became a courtly society. With the exception of treatises inspired by Venice like Paolo Paruta's *Della perfettione della vita politica* (1572–1579), most sixteenth-century champions of education for the *vita civile* deëmphasized patriotism to a city and were less concerned with history than their *Quattrocento* predecessors.[8] The purpose of learning often became service to a prince at court rather than to one's native city in local government. Nevertheless, the basic program of studies whose purpose was to prepare the young man for life in society remained the same, as did the aversion to a rustic or solitary life. The ideal courtier of Castiglione should be well educated in letters, poetry, oratory, and history.[9] Giovanni della Casa affirmed in his *Galateo* (published in 1558) that any one who wished to live in fellowship with other men in populous cities, rather than 'in solitary and deserted places' like hermits, needed learning and skill in manners.[10] In *La civil conversatione* (1574) Stefano Guazzo argued that no sensible man would live in solitude, and provided a book which discussed relations between men. For Guazzo 'civil conversation' signified an honest and commendable kind of living in the world as citizen, neighbor, and spouse.[11] Romei, Nobili, Girolamo Garimberto, and Giraldi Cinthio discussed the education of man to fit him for an honored place within civil society.[12]

An example of the program of sixteenth-century learning at its best is Alessandro Piccolomini's *Della institutione dell'uomo nato nobile e in città libera* (1542) which went into fourteen Italian editions, three French,

[7] L. B. Alberti, *La Famiglia*, in *L'educazione umanistica in Italia*, ed. E. Garin (Bari, 1949), pp. 133, 137, 160–162, 145, 164.
[8] Hans Baron, 'Secularization of Wisdom and Political Humanism in the Renaissance', *Jour. of the History of Ideas* XXI (1960), 143–145.
[9] *The Book of the Courtier*, tr. Charles S. Singleton (Garden City, N. Y., 1959), p. 70.
[10] *A Renaissance Courtesy-Book, Galateo of Manners and Behaviours by Giovanni della Casa*, introd. J. E. Spingarn (Boston, 1914), p. 15.
[11] John L. Lievsay, *Stefano Guazzo and the English Renaissance 1575–1675* (Chapel Hill, N. C., 1960), pp. 19–44.
[12] Garin, *L'umanesimo italiano*, pp. 224 ff., 163.

and one Spanish between 1542 and 1594.[13] Piccolomini, Sienese noble-man, archbishop, philosopher, and a member of the influential *Accademia degli Intronati* of Siena, epitomized the *Cinquecento* learning to which Franco et al. objected.

In the *Prohemio* Piccolomini announced the purpose of the work. Since God has given man free will, and the privilege of living and governing himself as he wills, Piccolomini will offer a guide to 'finding the happiness that is appropriate to man as man'.[14] To accomplish this purpose, he will not speculate on the causes of things but will discuss the manner of educating children through knowledge and 'moral disciplines' to virtue and good habits (ff. 2ᵛ–3ᵛ). Like the *Quattrocento* Florentine humanists, he finds the center of life for the nobleman to be the active life in the city. His book would educate children in their actions and duties to God, parents, spouse, children, friends, servants, 'and in what manner they must live among citizens, in the forum, in the senate, and in whatever high place they should converse; and according to such duties, they came to act so that they could make their city similar to a celestial republic.'[15] Piccolomini even suggests that the young nobleman should not build a villa so far outside the city that he could not go and return in one day (ff. 237ᵛ–238).

The *humane lettere* were of central importance to Piccolomini's educational program. Early in the book (II, ch. 8, on 'la grammatica e humane lettere') he affirms that the boy should begin his study of Latin and Greek letters before any other discipline for the purpose of acquiring style, the comprehension of history, and the understanding of allegorical fables. The recommended authors are quite similar to Alberti's list; for Greek history, Plutarch, Polybius, Xenophon, and Thucydides, and for Roman history, Plutarch again, Livy, Caesar, Sallust, and Suetonius. He recommends for poetry Homer, Horace, Pindar, Menander, Hesiod, Euripides, Sophocles, Vergil, and Terence. For Latin prose style Cicero is the most important model.

Of equal importance to Latin literature is Tuscan. As a guide for writ-

---

13 *De la institutione di tutta la vita de l'huomo nato nobile e in città libera* . . . (Venetiis apud Hieronymum Scotum, 1542). Piccolomini revised the work in 1560, adding new material and changing the title to *Institutione morale*. For bibliography see Florindo Ceretta, *Alessandro Piccolomini: letterato e filosofo senese del Cinquecento* (Siena, 1960), pp. 184–186.

14 '. . . di trovar la felicità che si conviene al' huomo come huomo . . .' (f. 2).

15 '. . . e in che maniera si debbi vivere tra i cittadini, nel foro, nel senato, o in qual si sia altro luogo, dove uopo faccia di conversare: e secondo tali officij operando; venivano a far si che la città loro ad una celeste republica assomigliavano' (f. 3ᵛ).

ing vernacular verse Piccolomini approves the rules of 'the most learned Bembo', and *La Poetica* of Bernardo Daniello. As models he offers Petrarch, Bembo again, Molza, Giovanni della Casa, and Benedetto Varchi. He also recommends Boccaccio as a prose example, the dialogues of Sperone Speroni for their conceits, and the 'most ingenious' Claudio Tolomei. In short, Piccolomini's list of recommended authors is practically a roll-call of approved authors in the sixteenth century (II, ch. 8).

After the boy has established the foundation of humane letters, he studies other disciplines. Piccolomini recommends the same curriculum as Alberti—rhetoric or oratory, dialectic and logic with Aristotle the approved guide (III, chs. 7–8), mathematics, geometry, and arithmetic (III, chs. 14–15), and natural and moral philosophy based on Aristotle and Plato (III, ch. 4). Thus Piccolomini enunciates the *Cinquecento* version of education for the *vita civile*.

Against this program of learning Nicolò Franco launched a satirical and raucously humorous attack. Franco's importance lay in the iconoclastic spirit which he brought to his attack. His criticism was based on his view of Italy in the sixteenth century. In Franco's eyes, conditions had deteriorated to such a point that learning was of no use to men. Further, the state of learning, sharing in decline, had fallen so low that it was trivial, irrelevant, and useless.

Born of a modest family, Franco left Benevento in his teens to search unsuccessfully for patrons until 1536, when Aretino discovered him in misery in Venice. Aretino took him as secretary to assist in the preparation of his letters for publication, and further honored his young protégé by addressing to him the letter in which the scourge of princes elaborated his theory of writing in accord with nature's whims rather than by pedantic rules.[16] But the ambitious Franco began to plagiarize Aretino. Driven out of Venice, he lived in Casale, Mantua, Cosenza, and Rome, writing constantly, until he was tried by the Inquisition for his pasquinades against Paul IV. He was hanged in 1570.[17]

Franco launched his attack in his two major works, the *Pistole vulgari* and the *Dialogi piacevoli*, both published in 1539. The *Pistole vulgari* contained a lengthy letter from *Lucerna* (the lantern) which announced

---

[16] Letter of 25 June 1537 in Pietro Aretino, *Il Primo libro delle lettere*, a cura di Fausto Nicolini (Bari, 1913), pp. 185–188.

[17] On Franco see Carlo Simiani, *Nicolò Franco: la vita e le opere* (Torino-Roma, 1894), and *Nicolò Franco: saggi* (Palermo, 1890). On Franco and the Inquisition see Angelo Mercati, *I Costituti di Niccolò Franco (1568–1570) dinanzi l'inquisizione di Roma esistenti nell'archivio segreto Vaticano* (Città del Vaticano, 1955).

Franco's iconoclastic aims. *Lucerna* wanders about at night in order to
see if what men write corresponds to reality. *Lucerna* comments that
many men write sonnets and *canzoni* in praise of the beauty and goodness of women, but discovers from peering into bedrooms that their
beauty is artifice and their supposed honesty, chastity, and virtue is in
reality lasciviousness, pride, perversity, and instability.[18]

Franco used the device of the peering *Lucerna* to uncover foolishness
beneath the pretensions of learning. In her wandering through the night
Lucerna comes to bookstores and laughs at high-sounding titles like *En-
chiridio*—possibly a mocking reference to Erasmus' *Enchiridion militis
Christiani*. Warming to her subject, she coarsely ridicules dialogues,
comedies, tragedies, books of epigrams, Petrarchan commentaries, *Or-
landi*, and *Rinaldi* (Ariosto).[19] Turning to the representatives of various
branches of learning, *Lucerna* mocks pedants, i.e., literary scholars and
teachers who could never write anything from their own imagination,
but instead compose lists of vocabularies, rules for writing verses, and
books of sentences. Mixed in with pedants are the grammarians who
waste their time investigating the lives and works of the classical authors. Of what importance was the question of the true fatherland of
Homer; what did it matter if Pliny came from Verona or Brescia, or
whether Ovid composed six or twelve books of *Fasti*? The foolish
grammarians quarrel day and night over the location of Vergil's tomb
and the names of Priam's fifty children. *Lucerna* ridicules their efforts to
understand dactylic meter, spondees, heroic verse, and the parts of
speech. The esteemed handbook of the liberal arts of Martianus Capella
is, in *Lucerna's* words, 'the goat of Martianus' to be compared with the
'ass of Apuleius'. In conclusion, Franco approves of the practice of the
Emperor Tiberius who taunted 'the bizarre wits' of this 'rabble'.[20]

Other branches of learning bewilder men or try to prove as true what
men know to be false. Contemporary philosophers are in a state of great
confusion because of their own writing, involved as it is with principles,

[18] *Le pistole vulgari di M. Nicolò Franco* (In Venetia ne le stampe d'Antonio Gardane a
li XX d'Aprile ne l'anno del Signore MDXXXIX), ff. LXXXIIᵛ–LXXXIII. The *Pistole
vulgari* were reprinted in 1542, and in expurgated editions of 1604 and 1615 which eliminated most of the letter of *Lucerna*.

[19] The criticism of Petrarchan imitators by Franco, Lando, and Doni has been noted
by Lea Nissim, *Gli 'scapigliati' della letteratura italiana del Cinquecento* (Prato, 1921).

[20] '. . . che non l'harebbe pensate Tiberio Imperadore, quando si pigliava spasso di
scalzare i cervellacci di questa gentaglia con dubbi fantastichi . . .' (*Pistole vulgari*, ff.
LXXXIIIIᵛ–LXXXVᵛ, esp. f. LXXXVᵛ). See Suetonius, *The Twelve Caesars*, tr. Robert Graves
(Baltimore, 1957), pp. 137, 139, 144.

ends, prime matters, and distinctions (Aristotle), atoms (Democritus), and ideas (Plato).[21] Arithmeticians foolishly attempt to measure everything from the height of the air to the house of God the Father with their lines and angles. Logicians try to prove that *si* denies and that *non* affirms; syllogisms prove what every one knows is false and never resolve anything. Legists are the 'scum of nature's generations', thieves who sell evil words for good money.[22]

Franco rejected the vernacular authorities of the sixteenth century as well. He attacks Bembo for establishing rules of writing as if he were a *duce* threatening 'the prison of infamy' for those who disregard his decrees.[23] When Bembo died (18 January 1547), Franco composed abusive sonnets condemning him as one who had led others into pedantry.[24] Among those who followed Bembo into pedantry were Molza, Speroni, Bernardo Tasso, Luigi Alamanni, Benedetto Varchi, and Luigi Tansillo. Piccolomini held several of these authors as models of style; Franco thought they had become lost in the 'shadows and clouds' of their own forms and were worthless.[25]

In the *Dialogi piacevoli* Franco repeated much of his criticism, mocking the classical heritage, poetry, and philosophy.[26] In a kind of *coup de grâce* he laughed at the basic assumption of educational treatises that learning was of value in the contemporary world. In the eighth dialogue one of the characters reads an advertisement that offers to teach men all manner of learning and virtue in a few days. First, Latin letters can be poured into the fortunate recipient, and on the second day, Greek. Hebrew can be learned in two more days, Chaldean in three, grammar in four, and logic in five, followed by philosophy, poetry, arithmetic, astrology, medicine, and 'all the rest' by the time that ten

---

[21] 'Veggo prima i PHILOSOPHI, e con essi la gran confusione de i lor scritti, i cui ciarlamenti, tutti sono impecciati di Principii, e di fini; di corporeo e d'incorporeo: di generabile, e di sensibile, e d'incorruttibile: di mortale, e d'immortale: di finito, e d'infinito: di materie prime, d'atomi, e d'Idee' (*Pistole vulgari*, f. LXXXV).

[22] *Pistole vulgari*, f. LXXXV.

[23] *Pistole vulgari*, f. LXXXVI^v.

[24] *Rime di Nicolò Franco contro Pietro Aretino* (Lanciano, 1916), pp. 97–100, sonnets 193–199. They were first published in *Delle rime di M. Nicolò Franco contro Pietro Aretino, et de la Priapea del medesimo, terza editione* . . . (no pl., 1548).

[25] *Pistole vulgari*, f. LXXXVI^v.

[26] The *Dialogi piacevoli* were printed in 1539, 1541, 1545, 1554, and 1559, all by Giolito in Venice; in expurgated versions of 1590, 1593, 1598, 1599, 1606, and 1609, all in Venice; a French edition of 1579; and incomplete Spanish editions of 1616 and 1617. Citations are from *Dialogi piacevoli di M. Nicolò Franco* (In Venetia per Gabriel Giolito de Ferrarii. M.D.XLI), ff. XCIX–CV^v, CXIII^v–CXXVIII^v.

days have elapsed. For only ten *scudi* a man can learn 'the true method of understanding every mystery'.[27] But the other character rejects the offer for the reasons that summarize Franco's opposition to learning: he is sated with the triviality of the *scienze*; letters have fallen so low that only a rogue tries to be learned. Moreover, the world has gone to ruin. Ignorant workers and tradesmen triumph in the world, so that one would be well-advised to learn a trade rather than acquire learning.[28] The dialogue continues to a comic end. One of the characters tries to sell books on various subjects, but finds that no one wishes to buy them. Even at the lowest price (one *scudo*) no one will buy anything on philosophy, law, astrology, and medicine. Poetry is not worth the price of a salad. They conclude that all learning is useless.[29]

Having criticized the state of learning, Franco offered the alternative of peace and solitude in the rustic life. *Lucerna* praises the life of shepherds and farmers who are content with a few slices of bread over a little fire. In contrast to Alberti, who condemned solitude as conducive to vice, Franco lauds solitude because it strips men of vain appetites.[30]

Franco was a rancorous ne'er-do-well who peppered princes and prelates with his shafts. Nevertheless, his attack on learning was as sincere as it was humorous; it was consistent through his writings and corresponded to his other attitudes. Closely linked to his rejection of learning is his social criticism, and his lamentations for the political misfortunes that Charles V and the Spanish had visited upon Italy.[31] Italy

[27] 'INVENTIONE BELLA, NUOVA, UTILE, ET ADMIRABILE AL PARAGONE, RITROVATA DA SANNIO, NE LA QUALE, CON L'AIUTO DI QUEL DIO CHE NASCENDO GLI DIEDE TANTA VERTÙ, PUOTE INFONDERE IN OGNI INTELLETTO OGNI DOTTRINA. PRIMIERAMENTE LETTERE LATINE, E GRECHE IN UN GIORNO AL PIU. HEBREE IN DUE. CALDEE IN TRE. GRAMMATICA IN QUATTRO. LOGICA IN CINQUE. FILOSOFIA IN SEI. POESIA IN SETTE. ARITMETICA IN OTTO. STROLOGIA IN NOVE. MEDICINA, E TUTTO IL RESTO IN DIECE. PROMETTE DOPO QUESTO, IL VERO MODO D'APPRENDERE OGNI MISTERO, E LA STRADA D'ASCENDERE AD OGNI GRADO, E TUTTO S'INSEGNA PER DIECE SCUDI' (*Dialogi piacevoli*, f. CVII^v).

[28] 'Io ti dico il vero, o Sannio, della pidocchiera delle scienze son tanto satio; che vorrei vomitarle, quando potessi. Le lettere oggi (merce del cielo) son ite tanto al basso che tristo chi pensa averne. Quanto l'uomo è più dotto è più carico di dottrine, più dolente e misero va piangendo. Oggi i meccanici e gli artigiani, per quanto veggo, trionphano di questo mondo. E percio avrei a caro di apprendere qualche buon'arte' (*Dialogi piacevoli*, f. CVIII).

[29] 'Ma andiarcene senz'altro dire, poi che siamo chiariti a fatto che hoggi l'avaritia del mondo e tale che più s'apprezza un quatrino; che l'imparare mille scienze' (*Dialogi piacevoli*, ff. CXI^v–CXII).

[30] *Pistole vulgari*, f. LXXXVII.

[31] For some examples of Franco's social criticism, see *Dialoghi piacevolissimi di Nicolò Franco*, introd. Gaetano Sborselli (Lanciano, 1924), I, 27, 96–102; II, 25, 45–46, 52–58.

had fallen upon evil days; the degeneration of learning was but one aspect of the general *malaise*.

Lodovico Domenichi joined Franco to ridicule humanists. Born in Piacenza and a close friend of Doni from 1543 to 1548, he wrote plays, dialogues, *facezie*, and translated several works.[32] In his *La nobiltà delle donne* (1549) Domenichi advised neither *astrologi* nor *humanisti* to marry.[33] In elaborating his reasons for counseling humanists not to take wives, Domenichi criticized the 'popolo de grammatici', who with 'terrible cries' preached Homer and Vergil in their schools.[34] Next he criticized the 'huomini dagli studi & lettere' who in school criticized the deeds of Venus and Mars, but later in bed 'verified in act' the fables of the gods.[35] These men of studies and letters are 'half men' ('mezzi huomini') who generate monster children.[36] Philosophers make poor spouses because they spend their nights imagining Utopias or contemplating Ideas. As a result they also generate monsters.[37] In addition to these remarks, linking humanists with astrologers indicates that Domenichi had a very low opinion of humanists because the *poligrafi* (Franco, Lando, Doni, et al.) constantly ridiculed astrologers and astrology. Lodovico Domenichi had no more use for humanists than Franco.[38]

For examples of his anti-Spanish sentiment see *Rime di Nicolò Franco contro Pietro Aretino*, pp. 31–33, 52–57; and *Delle Rime di M. Nicolò Franco contro Pietro Aretino, et de la Priapea . . .*, 1548 (reprinted London, 1887), pp. lxxi, lxxvii, lxxxi.

[32] On Domenichi's life, see A. Salza, 'Intorno a Lodovico Domenichi', in *Rass. Bibl. della Lett. Ital.* VII (1899), 204–209.

[33] 'Io veramente non consiglierei mai ne gli Astrologi, ne gli Humanisti, che prendessero moglie' (*La nobiltà delle donne di M. Lodovico Domenichi*. In Vinetia Appresso Gabriel Giolito di Ferrarii. MDXLIX, f. 89ᵛ). It was reprinted in 1551 and 1554 by Giolito. I have examined the 1551 edition and found the passages relating to the *humanisti* to be identical with the 1549 edition.

[34] 'Al popolo de grammatici suol le piu volte avenire, che mentre eglino con terribili grida predica Homero o Virgilio alla sua scuola' (f. 89ᵛ).

[35] 'Bel frutto traggono dunque gli huomini dagli studi & dalle lettere: poi che dichiarando essi nelle scuole i furti di Venere & di Marte, altri nel letto suo verifica in atto queste favole tali' (f. 90).

[36] 'Aggiungesi che questi mezzi huomini ingenerano le piu volte figliuoli stropiati & poco meno che mostri' (f. 90).

[37] 'Stanno i philosophi tutta la notte a vegghiare, mangiano poco, mentre ch'abbracciano la moglie, mentre si reputano prodi & valorosi guerrieri nelle battaglie amorose, stanno allhora contemplando le idee, & le sostanze separate; imaginansi la Utopia o una republica di Platone; cercano il cielo cristallino; disputano co i frati se la semplice fornicatione è peccato; & cosi avviene che dopo i nove mesi ne nasce poi qualche mostro, o cosa contrafatta' (f. 90).

[38] This use of *gli Humanisti*, not noted by Kristeller, *Renaissance Thought*, pp. 159–160, nn. 58–61, or Augusto Campana, 'The Origin of the Word Humanist', *Jour. of the War-*

Ortensio Lando treated the important issues and esteemed authorities of learning with a studied nihilism which mocked the whole structure. He defended first one side and then the other of sixteenth-century debates, leaving the impression with his readers that neither opinion was worth commitment. He criticized through ironic paradoxes; for example, he argued that it was better to be blind than to see—hence one would not see the evil conditions in Italy. If Franco was humorous, Lando was bitter and he named his targets more often.

Born in Milan, Lando studied at the University of Bologna and acquired a degree, although the place and date are not known. He began a wandering life in 1534, and in the next dozen years visited Milan, Lucca, Rome, Naples, Lyon, Basle, Piacenza, Venice, Trent, and most of the south of Italy. By his own admission Lando was contentious, unhappy, and a poor courtier. He gravitated to Venice in August 1546 and remained in or near the city as Giolito and other Venetian printers published his books, until his death at an unknown date in the 1550s.[39]

Lando's first published work, in which he parodied the debate over Ciceronianism, illustrated well his ambivalent attitude toward contemporary learning. In part one, *Cicero relegatus* (Lyon, 1533), a council of eminent Italians meet to judge Cicero. After lengthy discussion, with many references to his works, they decide that Cicero was inconsistent, boring, unlearned, and seditious, and sentence him to perpetual exile in the mythical land of Scizia. But in the second part, *Cicero revocatus* (Venice, 1534), the Roman's absence is so lamented that a second assembly decides to recall him to Italy in triumph.[40] Lando's mockery of the Cic-

---

burg and Courtauld Inst. IX (1946), 60–73, indicates that Domenichi either included philosophers within the term 'humanists', or saw philosophers as very similar to humanists. In the above passages, Domenichi differentiated between humanists and astrologers. After disposing of the astrologers with a satirical poem attributed to Thomas More, Domenichi criticized as unfit to be husbands the *popolo de grammatici, gli huomini dagli studi & dalle lettere* and *i philosophi*. Both the *huomini dagli studi & dalle lettere* and *i philosophi* generate monsters. Domenichi connected the *grammatici* and *huomini dagli studi & dalle lettere* with schools but not the *philosophi* although the latter 'dispute with the friars', and the most likely place for philosophic disputes would be an academic locale. If Domenichi did not clearly include philosophers within the term *humanisti*, the passages indicate that he saw them in close proximity and equally unfit to be husbands and fathers.

[39] Most of the information about Lando's life comes from his own scattered comments in his works. These have been summarized by Ireneo Sanesi, *Il cinquecentista Ortensio Lando* (Pistoia, 1893), pp. 5–25, and Giovanni Sforza, 'Ortensio Lando e gli usi ed i costumi d'Italia nella prima metà del Cinquecento', *Memorie della R. Accademia delle Scienze di Torino*, serie II, LXIV, no. 4 (1914), 1–68.

[40] *Cicero relegatus et Cicero revocatus Dialogi festivissimi* (Impressum Venetiis per Mel-

eronian and anti-Ciceronian polemics was so successful that contemporaries entertained contradictory evaluations of his real opinions.[41] However, Lando's fundamental attitude toward Cicero was probably quite hostile. In the *Paradossi* (Lyon, 1543) he rejected Cicero as an authority because he was ignorant of philosophy, mistaken in his historical facts, and taught a worthless oratory and rhetoric.[42] Lando's attitude contrasted with that of Alberti and Piccolomini, who praised Cicero as a model for style and content, or of Bembo, who propagated a vernacular Ciceronianism.

In his *Sferza di scrittori* (Venice, 1550) Lando extended his criticism to a general attack on learning. The book is an account of a dream in which the author accumulated so many books that they filled his house. They should have made him learned, but instead they 'confounded the wit and weakened the memory'. All these books contained a thousand defects because of the instability of learning and the imperfections of their authors. Among the authors whom Lando rejected were many admired by sixteenth-century educators: Herodotus, Xenophon, Livy, Cicero, Sallust, Plato, and among the moderns, Dante, Petrarch, Boccaccio, Valla, and Ariosto. Then, true to his style, Lando reversed himself in the second part of the work. He announced that he had been writing 'in jest rather than seriously' ('da scherzo e non da senno'), and exhorted his readers to study ancient and modern letters.[43] The result of

---

chiorem Sessam: Anno domini MDXXXIIII). The first part, *Cicero relegatus*, was printed in Milan, 1533. Both parts were printed together in Venice, 1534; Lyon, 1534; and Venice, 1718.

[41] Erasmus knew the *Cicero relegatus et Cicero revocatus* and commented that the book attacked Cicero harshly and defended him indifferently. 'In eo Cicero odiosissime laceratur, frigide defenditur' (*Opus epistolarum Des. Erasmi Roterodami*, ed. P. S. Allen, Oxford, 1947, XI, 134, ep. 3019, 21 May 1535). On the other hand, a letter of 29 October 1535 written by John Angelus Odonus to Gilbert Cousin, secretary to Erasmus, described Lando as an avid Ciceronian, claiming that he based his evaluation upon intimate acquaintance with Lando in Bologna and Lyon. See Izora Scott, *Controversies over the Imitation of Cicero as a Model for Style and some Phases of their Influence on the Schools of the Renaissance* (New York, 1910), pp. 85–88.

[42] *Paradossi, cioe, Sententie fuori del comun parere: novellamente venute in luce, opera non men dotta che piacevole: & in due parti separata* (In Venetia, MDXLV), ff. 80ᵛ–85ᵛ. The *Paradossi* were first printed in Lyon, 1543, then reprinted at Venice in 1543, 1544, 1545, and 1563; at Lyon, 1550; and in expurgated versions at Bergamo, 1594, Piacenza, 1597, and Vicenza, 1602. Charles Estienne made a French translation which appeared ten times between 1553 and 1638. Citations that follow are from the Venice, 1545 edition.

[43] *La sferza di scrittori antichi et moderni di M. Anonimo di Utopia alla quale, è dal medesimo aggiunta una essortatione allo studio delle lettere* (In Vinegia, MDL), ff. 3ᵛ–26ᵛ, 28ᵛ–36.

Lando's book was to mock the serious claims that these authors could teach either style or virtue.

Quattrocento humanists had stressed the utility of learning, claiming that it aided men in their affairs in the marketplace and in council chambers. This Lando denied. He held up for his readers' admiration Francesco Sforza, who had been learned in experience rather than in books on warfare. He approved the practice of the Luccan city government which forbade men of learning to sit in the magistracy because they always fomented disturbances. Lando could see no value in Renaissance educational treatises based on Aristotle's *Ethics* and *Politics*. How could the confused Aristotle advise the moderns about ruling family, household, and servants, Lando asked rhetorically.[44] He recognized that he was flouting the established educational and literary authorities of Italy. In paradox twenty-seven of the *Paradossi*, an attack on Boccaccio's works as worthless, Lando commented that he expected to provoke a tumult in the many academies of Italy. He expected the *Infiammati* of Padua led by the 'authoritative Speroni' to sharpen their pens against him, and the *Intronati* of Siena to war against him as if he had sinned against the divine, but Lando did not care.[45] As for Cardinal Bembo, Lando sneered at him as an irreligious 'wiseacre' (*baccalare*) who declined to pray in Lent.[46]

Like Franco, Lando rejected the active life of the noble in the city. In paradox fifteen of the *Paradossi* Lando argued that it is better to be born in small villages than in populous cities which are the locale of homicide, larceny, treason, and sedition. In paradox sixteen he argued that it is better to live in humble houses than in great palaces. The basis of his argument was the attitude that, when times were so bad, man should avoid risk to prevent losses and disaster. Some one of great wealth or of a great house was more often the prey of ambition and crime than the humble peasant.[47] But Lando did not praise pastoral life as an alternative. In a dialogue between a cavalier and a hermit in his *Vari componimenti* (1552), Lando criticized nearly every human profession or position, high and low, as dishonest or conducive to vice. He rejected *signori* (princes and nobles), councilors and rulers of cities, members of the legal profession, doctors, ambassadors, soldiers, merchants, the clergy, shipbuilders, and sailors, down to the lowly fishermen and

[44] *Paradossi*, ff. 12–17.
[45] *Paradossi*, ff. 70v–71.
[46] *Paradossi*, ff. 79–79v.
[47] *Paradossi*, ff. 43–46.

peasants. In conclusion Lando advised men to fleé not only cities and palaces, but also peasant villages and country villas. Only in complete solitude can man obtain peace.[48] Lando did not advocate religious contemplation in isolation; his point was that man could not achieve happiness in any way of life.

Thus Lando expanded the rejection of learning of Franco and Domenichi. Lando had little use for Cicero as a model, rejected many classical and modern authors esteemed by the *Cinquecento*, denied the utility of learning, and rejected the active life in the city. Lando's attack was sharper and better focused than that of Franco, probably because he had a better command of sixteenth-century learning and had traveled more widely than Franco. He was well acquainted with the educational structure that he tried to tear down. The fundamental reason for Lando's *malaise* was the same as for Franco's—his disillusionment with the sixteenth-century world.

Not all of the critics were low-born literary adventurers. Count Giulio Landi of the noble Landi family of Piacenza earned a degree in jurisprudence and served in high government posts and diplomatic missions, but joined the *poligrafi* in rejecting learning. He may have imbibed his ideas from them at Piacenza, for he was a member of the *Accademia Ortolana* between 1543 and 1545 when Doni and Domenichi were members of the group and Lando visited the city.[49] In 1551 Giulio Landi published his *Lode dell'ignoranza*. Parodying Aristotle, he announced that he was basing his tract on Aristotle's dictum that privation is the source of nature's production of new things. In the same way, ignorance is the privation of knowledge and thus praiseworthy as an acute stimulus to knowledge. However, he devoted the major part of his tract to a description of the pitfalls and inadequacies of current learning. Logic makes men insolent and tanglers of the truth, algebra is the tool of lying merchants, geometry makes men abstract. He noted approvingly that the Romans had banished poets and orators from the city. Landi criticized theologians for attempting to know the highest mysteries of God.

[48] 'Ragionamento fatto tra un Cavalliero errante, et un' huomo soletario, nel'quale si tratta delle fallacie, & malvagità mondane: mostrando non potersi in verun stato ritrovar alcuna bontà: con una lode nel fine della vita Soletaria', in *Vari componimenti di M. Hort. Lando nuovamente venuti in luce. Dialogo intitolato Ulisse. Ragionamento occorso tra un Cavalliere, & un' huomo soletario. Alcune novelle. Alcune favole. Alcune scroppoli, che sogliono occorrere nella cottidiana nostra lingua* (In Venetia appresso Gabriel Giolito de Ferrari, et fratelli. MDLV), pp. 89–128.

[49] For biographical information on Giulio Landi, see Cristoforo Poggiali, *Memorie per la storia letteraria di Piacenza* (Piacenza, MDCCXXXIX), II, 195–207.

Adopting momentarily the pejorative meaning of ignorance, Landi, a count and nobleman, described kings, princes, dukes, and counts as *stupidissimi*. Then, returning to his original meaning of ignorance, he concluded in terms similar to Agrippa's *De incertitudine et vanitate scientiarum*. Man is better and happier in ignorance and God can be known only through ignorance. Even the apostles Peter and John were simple, ignorant men. Ignorance rather than knowledge leads to modesty and virtue.[50] Landi's tract was not original; all of the themes and several of the examples had been stated earlier by Agrippa, Doni, Franco, or Lando. However, his tract indicates that the rejection of learning was not limited to lowborn literary adventurers scrambling to keep body and soul together by writing, but had penetrated to at least one member of the wealthy nobility as well.

Anton Francesco Doni went beyond Franco, Domenichi, Lando, and Landi in his rejection of *Cinquecento* learning. The others believed that learning had declined and attacked individual humanists, but Doni argued that the *studi liberali* were fundamentally inadequate to teach men virtue. The son of a Florentine scissors-maker, Doni became a Servite priest in the monastery of the Annunziata in Florence, but left the monastery in 1540 to follow a wandering life, living by his pen. From 1543 to 1545 he lived in Piacenza, then operated his own printing press in Florence until early 1548, when he moved to Venice. There he published his major works between 1548 and 1555 before his celebrated quarrel with Aretino caused him to leave. His major period of authorship was ended although he continued to live near Venice and to write occasionally until his death in 1574.[51]

Although Doni never returned to Florence after 1548, he often evoked the city and its people in his writing. His *I Marmi* (1552–1553), or conversations overheard in the evening on the marble steps of the Florentine cathedral, contains a dialogue in which he rejects the *studi liberali*. A poultry vendor, a broker, and an unidentified third person begin to discuss how to avoid vice and to foster virtue, defined in traditional terms as the love of *patria*, wife, and children. But the *studi liberali* can-

[50] *La vita di Cleopatra reina d'Egitto. dell'illustre Conte Giulio Landi con una oratione nel fine recitata nell'Academia dell'Ignoranti: in lode dell'Ignoranza* (In Vinegia [Giolito] MDLI), pp. 53–62. The *lode dell'Ignoranza* was reprinted in 1575 and 1601.

[51] For Doni's life see *I Marmi di Antonfrancesco Doni ripubblicati per cura di Pietro Fanfani, con la vita dell'autore scritta da Salvatore Bongi* (Firenze, 1863). For the bibliography of Doni's works see Cecilia Ricottini Marsili-Libelli, *Anton Francesco Doni, scrittore e stampatore: bibliografia delle opere e della critica e annali tipografici* (Firenze, 1960).

not teach virtue. 'Without the liberal studies one can come to wisdom, because, although it is necessary to learn virtue, nevertheless one does not learn it through the liberal studies.'[52] Grammar can teach style and poetry is important; history is 'noble', but knowledge of the lives and activities of the ancients has only a negative value, a warning to men to avoid their faults.[53] With arithmetic and geometry one can count one's possessions, but it is of no avail if one does not divide them for charity. Neither is virtue the result of the study of Stoic or Aristotelian philosophy. Books cannot teach men virtue because men have to learn from their own experience. In Doni's humble example, one can read 'fire burns', but if one does not touch the fire, one will never know the sensation of burning. Further, after one has learned through experience, one cannot teach another unless he also touches the flame.[54] In the same way, one cannot learn virtue from another or from books. Virtue is an innate knowledge of good and evil which man possesses through being a man.[55] He cannot possibly learn virtue through the liberal studies. Doni's attitude is in direct contrast to that of the *Quattrocento* humanists and the many educational treatises of the fifteenth century.[56]

Doni's attitude toward history is also in direct contrast to that of his Florentine predecessors. Although history can be a mirror before men's eyes, the 'teacher of life' (*maestra della vita*), and a means of acquiring immortality,[57] it is in practice a pack of lies written to cover up crimes

52 'Si può ancóra dir questo, che senza gli studi liberali si può pervenire alla sapienza, imperoché, benché sia necessario imparare la virtú, non di meno non s'impara per gli studi liberali' (*I Marmi*, 1928 ed., II, 67). After the first edition in 1552–1553, *I Marmi* was reprinted only once, in an expurgated edition of 1609, before the nineteenth century.

53 'Che mi fa egli che Eccuba fusse da manco che Elena o se Achille aveva tanti anni quanti Patroclo? . . . guardo in quello che fallasse Ulisse e considero bene in qual cosa egli errò, solamente per guardarmi di non errare' (*I Marmi*, II, 61).

54 ' "Il fuoco cuoce", trovo scritto: s'io non lo tócco, mai vi saprò dire che cosa sia fuoco; ma quando mi sentirò quell'incendio, allora non lo saprò insegnare ancóra, perché colui non saprá mai, a chi l'insegnerò, che cosa è fuoco, se non è tócco alquanto da esso' (*I Marmi*, II, 61).

55 'La umanità ti vieta che tu sia superbo alli tuoi compagni; viètati che tu sia avaro di parole, di cose, di affetti; ella è comune e facile a tutti, nessun male stima essere alieno, e il suo bene però grandemente ama, perchè sa che deve esser bene per qualche uno altro. I liberali studi t'amaestrano in questi costumi? Non più ti amaestrano in questo che nella semplicitá, nella modestia, nella temperanza la quale cosi perdona all'altrui sangue come al suo e sa che l'uomo non debbe usar l'uomo piú che non si conviene' (*I Marmi*, II, 66–67).

56 See William H. Woodward, *Vittorino da Feltre and other Humanist Educators* (Cambridge, 1921).

57 *I Mondi del Doni libro primo* (Jn Vinegia Per Francesco Marcolini, . . . MDLII), f. 84.

and to please readers.[58] Doni criticizes Herodotus, Diodorus Siculus, and Roman historians in general for including patriotic lies in their histories. He cites as an example the story of Mucius Scaevola, who was held to be 'a great father of his country' (*un gran pater patrie*) for saving Rome by impressing the Etruscan chieftain Porsenna with his courage in burning his hand in the fire. Doni's comment is that Mucius Scaevola's deed had nothing to do with Porsenna's actions or Rome's salvation.[59] Sixteenth-century historians are no better in Doni's opinion, but he does not list names and examples.[60] As for acquiring immortality through history, Doni mocks the Renaissance quest for fame and the recognition of posterity. He compares man's desire for fame in perpetuity to the desire of a flower which wanted to live as long as the sixty or seventy years allotted to man. The earth laughs at man's words, deeds, and statues designed to immortalize him.[61]

Other aspects of Doni's criticism of learning followed the lines of Franco, Lando, Domenichi, and Landi, but Doni, who was a more imaginative writer than his fellow discontents, cloaked his criticism in colorful images. In one of his most popular books, the *Inferni* (1553), a Dantesque journey through seven circles of hell, each filled with a different group of sinners, Doni dealt appropriate tortures to men of learning. In the first *inferno* doomed scholars (Doni did not indicate which scholarly discipline they followed) run around and around in a huge wheel with as many serpents pursuing them as they had written books. In Doni's words, the scholarly authors are bitten by the serpents as their books had bitten others on earth. Grammarians are condemned to carrying their moaning heads in their hands as they trudge around and around in the ghastly wheel.[62] In the fifth *inferno* legists are condemned to eating their own dull writings, and medical men who pretend knowl-

---

Doni's *I Mondi*, one of his most popular works, appeared in Italy eight times between 1552 and 1606, and in four French translations by 1583.

[58] *Lettere del Doni Libro Secondo* (In Fiorenza MDXLVII), ff. 44ᵛ–45.

[59] *I Mondi*, ff. 83–83ᵛ. M. Cary, *A History of Rome down to the Reign of Constantine* (2d ed., London, 1957), p. 64, agrees with Doni on the irrelevance of the action of Mucius Scaevola.

[60] *I Mondi*, f. 45ᵛ.

[61] *I Mondi*, ff. 74, 86–88.

[62] Doni was particularly hostile to grammarians. See also *La zucca del Doni Fiorentino* . . . (In Venetia, Appresso Fran. Rampazetto . . . MDLXV), ff. 124–125; and *Tre libri di lettere del Doni* . . . (Jn Vinegia per Francesco Marcolini MDLII), ff. 13–16.

edge by examining chamber pots are forced to eat the contents of the pots.[63]

Doni also objected to the abuse of learning. His objection was that men used learning to defraud others, or as an avenue to advancement. Doni railed against *dottori* who took the money of *signori* for educating their sons but returned the sons with a new complement of vices. Some learned *dottori* became bureaucrats and executioners rather than use their knowledge to teach the poor. Peasants and butchers sent their sons to universities in order to acquire degrees which would open the road to evil wealth and power. Unfortunately education did not improve the character of the rough peasants who then 'butchered' learning.[64]

Finally, Doni urged men to withdraw from the learned and committed life of activity into ignorant self-concern. Men ought to stop striving to change and improve the world and attend only to their own affairs. In *La Zucca* (1551) Doni lauded the life of 'good ignorance' (*ignoranza da bene*), a non-intellectual approach to life which meant living without thought or care and attending only to one's own affairs.[65] Explaining in more detail, Doni affirmed that learning is not necessary. Reverence for Cicero and an intense study of Priscian's grammar are superfluous. The learned rack their brains over whether the soul is mortal or immortal, they cry that the streets of the city were wrongly laid out, and that the architecture of the cathedral ought to be corrected. They are never satisfied to leave things as they are, and even assume that all the unlettered live dissolute lives. But the man of *ignoranza da bene* lives by a different, preferable credo. He is not interested in the knowledge of others. He has no concern for the way of life of others because he attends to his own affairs.[66] The best way of life is that of the simple, ignorant man who does not seek to interfere with others or to change the world.

---

63 *Inferni del Doni Academico Pellegrino. Libro secondo de mondi* (In Vinegia per Francesco Marcolini nel MDLIII), pp. 27–41, 156. The illustrations in the original edition vividly portray the torments. After 1553 the *Inferni* were always reprinted with the *I Mondi*.

64 *Inferni*, pp. 144–145, 160, 152–153.

65 'Ultimamente Ignoranza da bene, è quando l'huomo se ne va alla carlona, & non si da impaccio de fatti d'altri, come dire' (*La zucca*, 1565 ed., f. 66). *La zucca* appeared eight times in Italy between 1551 and 1615, and in one Spanish translation.

66 'E sarà uno ignorantaccio che sparlerà in questa forma, Il tale non ha lettere; (e mentirà per la gola), il quale fa la tal vita dissoluta, (e non serà vero) & quell'altro capiterà male. Colui che ha abbracciato l'ignoranza da bene, subito se ne va in la dicendo; io non vo sapere se egli sà, o se non sà, che vita sia la sua capiti dove e vuole la non m'importa nulla; assai ho io da fare ad attendere a casi mia' (*La zucca*, f. 66).

Doni preferred him to the striving busybodies who sought to improve the world.[67]

With Doni's espousal of ignorant withdrawal in 1551, these sixteenth-century authors turned their backs on Renaissance education for the active life. Franco, Domenichi, Lando, Landi, and Doni criticized sixteenth-century learning as worthless, and Franco, Lando, and Doni suggested that man would be safer and less vicious, if not happier, by withdrawing from the active life in the city. They voiced a mood of disillusionment in sharp contrast to the optimism and commitment to participation in affairs that marked the *Quattrocento* Florentine humanists as well as Alessandro Piccolomini in the sixteenth century.

To what extent did the rejection of learning of Franco et al. represent widespread discontent in sixteenth-century Italy? The large number of editions of their works indicates that their books were in demand. Taking only the more important works cited in this study (Franco's *Pistole vulgari* and *Dialogi piacevoli*, Domenichi's *La Nobiltà delle donne*, Lando's *Paradossi*, and *Cicero relegatus* and *Cicero revocatus* considered as one, Landi's *Lode dell'ignoranza*, Doni's *I Marmi*, *La Zucca*, and *I Mondi* and *Inferni*, also considered as one), there were twenty-four editions of these nine works before the publication of the Tridentine *Index* of 1564. Despite difficulties with the *Index* twenty-seven more editions of these works appeared from 1564 to 1615. In addition there were fifteen French and three Spanish editions of the above works. There were also three plagiarizations of Lando's works and Cesare Rao's (c. 1532–c. 1587) *L'Argute et facete lettere*, an extensive plagiarization of Doni, which appeared in fifteen Italian and two French editions between 1562 and 1622.[68] Clearly there was a large demand for the writings of the *poligrafi*, which would indicate that their writings struck a responsive chord in their readers.

These critical authors provoked some hostile reaction in the sixteenth century. Tomaso Garzoni (1549–1589) vented his hostility against 'Hortensio Lando who writes in his *Paradossi* with oversubtle reasons against wealth, liberty, and other things'; the 'extremely satirical' writings of Nicolò Franco; and the 'inventor of the *Sfera* [sic] *de' scrittori*', i.e.,

---

[67] *La zucca*, f. 67[v].

[68] *L'argute, et facete lettere di M. Rao di Alessano Città della Leucadia* . . . (In Vinetia, Appresso Giovanni Alberti, MDCXXII). On Rao, see Nicola Vacca, 'Cesare Rao da Alessano detto "Valocerca",' *Archivio Storico Pugliese* I, fasc. I (1948), 1–28. However, Vacca does not note the plagiarization.

Lando again.[69] In his *Teatro de' vari, e diversi cervelli* (1585) Garzoni included a discourse concerning 'malignant, perverse, divisive, perjured, perfidious, cursed, and invidious wits'. These 'invidious wits' who had 'passed the limits of justice and honesty in our age' were Aretino, Franco, Lando, and the 'new Momuses', i.e., Doni, because Momus (*Momo*) was his major mouthpiece in *I Mondi* and *Inferni*.[70] Bernardo Macchietta in his introduction to the 1597 expurgated edition of Doni's *I Mondi* and *Inferni* commented that Doni had uncovered the evils of diverse states and persons with his inventions and fables.[71] Gabriel Chappuys of Lyon (1546–1611), in his introduction to the French translation of *I Mondi* and *Inferni* of 1578, wrote that Doni used inventions and pleasant fantasies to hide the bitterness of his message, although Chappuys did not indicate what was Doni's bitter message.[72]

The *poligrafi* may have voiced the opinion of a broad cross-section of Italy. All but Landi came from low social origins, but traveled through much of Italy, visited the courts of prelates and princes, participated in literary academies of the townsmen, and wrote stories about artisans. Moreover, they were intimately associated with the vernacular presses, especially in Venice, as authors, printers, editors, and translators, and the shops of such printers as Giolito were natural places to learn new ideas and to exchange thoughts. Finally, they depended upon the sale of their books for their livelihood. As popular authors they had to write material that reflected the taste and opinions of their readers. In short, the *poligrafi*

69 'Ma i vitii loro communi sono questi . . . è Hortensio Lando, che fece quei Paradossi con troppo sottil ragioni contra la ricchezza, la libertà, & altre cose naturalmente al contrario desiate: alle volte troppo satirico, come Nicolò Franco insieme col suo maestro, & l'inventore della sfera de' scrittori' (*La piazza universale di tutte le professioni del mondo, nuovamente ristampata, & posta in luce da T. G. da Bagnacavallo.* In Venetia, Appresso Gio. Battista Somasco, 1587), p. 288.

70 Discorso XLVI, 'De' cervellazzi maligni, e perversi; divisi in perfidi, spergiori, maldicenti, & invidi.' 'E questa petulante maledicenza ha passato si i termini del giusto, e dell' honesto all'età nostra, che si sono visti novi Theoni da' denti rabbiosi, novi Zoili, e novi Momi, nell'Aretino, nel Franco, nel Lando, & in molti altri . . .' (*Il teatro de' vari, e diversi cervelli mondani nuovamente formato, & posto in luce da Tomaso Garzoni da Bagnacavallo* . . . In Venetia, Appresso Fabio, & Agostin Zoppini, fratelli, 1585), f. 94ᵛ.

71 '. . . sotto inventioni, favole, fittioni, e trovate scuopre i mali di diversi stati, e persone' (Bernardo Macchietta, 'Burattata sopra li Mondi del Doni', *Mondi celesti, terrestri, & infernali, de gli Academici Pellegrini composti da M. Anton Francesco Doni* . . . Jn Vicenza, Appresso gli Heredi di Perin Libraro, . . . 1597), f. 1.

72 *Les Mondes, celestes, terrestres et infernaux . . . Tirez des œuvres de Doni Florentin, par Gabriel Chappuis Tourangeau. Depuis, reueuz, corrigez & augmentez du Monde des Cornuz, par F. C. T.* A Lyon, pour Barthelemy Honorati, 1580, ff. 1–4.

were the nearest thing to journalists or columnists that the sixteenth century possessed.

The *poligrafi* mirrored a widespread discouragement and disillusionment in Italy during the years 1535 to 1555. It was a period of political resignation and self-concern, as the ruling classes were content to live under foreign domination so long as they were free of war.[73] It was a period of reaction against princes, politics, and old ideas. The rejection of learning was part of Italian discouragement in the *Cinquecento*.

University of Toronto

[73] Alessandro Visconti, *L'Italia nell'epoca della Controriforma dal 1516 al 1713* (Verona, 1958), pp. 51-55, 16.

Religious Restlessness in
Sixteenth-century Italy *

In this paper I would like to explore the religious turmoil of sixteenth-century Italy on a social level below that of popes, princes, and cardinals — the level of the concerned middle-class merchant, the courtier, and the literate artisan. The characters who will enable me to delve into the religious consciousness of middle and lower class Italy are the adventurers of the pen, the low-born followers of Pietro Aretino who wrote popular books, the paperbacks of the day. They wrote in order to earn money to keep body and soul together. In some cases their writing was little above twentieth-century newstand trash, but other parts of the corpus was of a higher order. In any case these men and their writings provide the avenue through which I will examine some aspects of religious restlessness in *Cinquecento* Italy.

In 1527 Pietro Aretino settled in Venice and supported himself by his wonderfully prolific pen. Plays, letters, tales, pornography, devotional treatises, and even a translation of the Psalms poured from his pen to the Venetian vernacular presses. Attracted by the example of Aretino, other penurious *poligrafi* came to Venice with the same desire to write freely away from the suffocating courts.

These authors both reflected Italian opinion and helped to mold it. In their restless lives they visited most Italian courts and cities and were alert to new ideas in the air. Indeed, their livelihood depended upon giving the reading public what it wanted to read. At the same time, since financial rewards were still quite limited, they had to write continuously — three to four books a year — to support themselves. This meant that they often filled their pages with ideas, gossip, and stories that were making the rounds of the city or court. For this reason, their books are a useful index to a primitive kind of public opinion in Italy. Although the number of their readers was limited by literacy, they included nobility, courtiers, merchants, professional men, perhaps literate artisans, and the academies were *letterato*, merchant, and noble met together. Their books were small in size, about four by six inches on the average, inexpensively printed,

* This is a slightly revised version of a paper read at the Canadian Catholic Historical Association meeting, June 10, 1966, at Sherbrooke, Que. I wish to thank Dr. James McConica for reading the paper when I was unable to attend. The documentation has been abbreviated.

and sometimes profusely illustrated. They fitted easily into pockets or saddle bags, and were avidly read in the long hours spent idling in courts, shops, or on sea and land journeys. These "pocket books" of the Cinquecento contained tales, poetry, plays, moral fables, travel literature, satires, letters and burlesques. From Aretino's arrival in Venice in 1527 until about 1560, the adventurers of the pen enjoyed their greatest fame and popularity.

Having introduced the adventurers of the pen, I would like to make some general remarks about the religious situation of *Cinquecento* Italy. In the early years of the sixteenth century, Italians in secular unconcern ignored religious revival, while northern Europe sought to understand the central paradox of grace and sin. Only after the penetration of the new ideas from the north and the hideous shock of the sack of Rome did latent Italian religious unrest find a focus. Then the anti-clericals saw the sack of Rome as a warning from God to correct abuses, while religious visionaries looked to Luther, although they did not always realize that his ideas were different from their native faith. [1] Throughout the 1530's and 1540's Italian churchmen and laymen wrote Scriptural commentaries, while vernacular translations of the Bible were printed by Venetian Dominicans in 1536 and 1538. Preachers devoted their Lenten exhortations toward inspiring an inner renewal along the lines of faith and Scripture. The interest in Scripture and faith was allied with the mounting desire to correct ecclesiastical abuses. When the Papacy seemed unresponsive, laymen and clergy sought new means. In November 1545, for example, an anonymous writer addressed an appeal to the new *doge* of Venice, begging him to use his power to effect reform in the Church. [2] New religious orders stressing worldly engagement rather than monastic isolation sought to meet the spiritual needs of the people through charitable activity in cities and towns. After their earlier lethargy, Italians took up religious concerns in the reign of Paul III (1534-1549), amid the desire for reform and reunion in the expectancy of the coming general council.

The study of the religious history of *Cinquecento* Italy leaves much undone. On one hand the Papacy, Council of Trent, and those movements called Catholic Reformation and Counter-Reformation have been studied extensively. Italians who opted decisively for the Protestant Reformation have had their lives minutely examined. It is an old cliché that there is a biographer for each sixteenth-century Italian Protestant — all six of them. A more recent tendency in scholarship is to find Italian Protestants under every rock of the Apennines, behind every workbench in Tuscany, and to speak of a vigorous plant cut down in full flower by the Counter-Reformation. But many of these Italian "Protestants" protested vigorously that they were "loyal sons

---

[1] Delio Cantimori, *Eretici Italiani del Cinquecento: Ricerche Storiche* (Firenze, 1939), 3-25.
[2] Aldo Stella, "Utopie e velleità insurrezionali dei filo-protestanti italiani (1545-1547), "*Bibliothèque d'Humanisme et Renaissance*, XXVII (1965), 133-182.

of the Roman Church" and considered Luther some kind of mad dog. They had no intention of breaking away from the Papacy. They did not flee to Protestant Switzerland.

Much of the religious activity of Italy in the first half of the *Cinquecento* does not fit neatly into older categories often derived from the study of Northern European religious history. The most useful term for the religious concern of Italians in the first half of the century is "Evangelism," an admittedly imprecise term for a phenomenon that was more an attitude than a movement. Evangelism included a desire to reform abuses, emphasis on Scripture, and the primacy of justification through faith without the omission of good works. Erasmus' concern for individual moral reform, the understanding of Scripture rather than commentaries, and the hope for union between all Christians influenced it. Delio Cantimori notes that in the period of Evangelism one cannot always distinguish between Catholic Reform, philo-Protestantism, or sympathy for Protestant ideas. Such diverse persons as the aristocratic ladies Vittoria Colonna and Giulia Gonzaga, the Spaniard Juan Valdés, cardinals Gasparo Contarini, Pietro Bembo, Reginald Pole, Giovanni Morone, Jacopo Sadoleto, and Girolamo Seripando could be termed Evangelicals at least part of the time. Some who fled Italy for Protestant Europe, as Bernardino Ochino, Pier Martire Vermigli, and Piero Paolo Vergerio, and others like Pietro Carnesecchi and Aonio Paleario, who remained and were executed in the 1560's as heretics, could be termed Italian Evangelicals. [3]

Only later were some men, books, and passages from the period of Evangelism judged heretical or close to heresy, and even after the decrees of Trent, distinctions were often difficult to make. To cite an example, the small but extremely influential *Beneficio di Cristo* was published anonymously in Venice in 1543. An *Index* of 1549 condemned it, although various cardinals praised the work. Despite the fact that entire heretical passages were copied or paraphrased from Luther, Calvin, and Melanchthon, modern scholars have found it difficult to detect open heresy in the work. [4] Drawing the line between Catholic and heretic involved definition and investigation. Only after the Council of Trent and general acceptance of its decrees could this be done with consistency.

---

[3] On Italian Evangelism, see Delio Cantimori, *Prospettive di storia ereticale italiana del Cinquecento* (Bari, 1960), 28, 32-34; Hubert Jedin, *Papal Legate at the Council of Trent: Cardinal Seripando*, trans. F. C. Eckhoff (St. Louis and London, 1947), 104-107; Jedin, *A History of the Council of Trent*, trans. Dom Ernest Graf O.S.B. (London, 1957), I, 363-367; and Eva-Maria Jung, "On the Nature of Evangelism in 16th-Century Italy," *Journal of the History of Ideas*, XIV (1953), 511-527, who limits it to aristocratic circles. Jedin makes a distinction between the "Erasmian programme of reunion" and "Evangelism" but states that "both were due to a tendency to seek an understanding with the Protestants on the basis of what both parties retained of the substance of Christianity." *History of the Council of Trent*, I, 370.

[4] See Ruth Prelowski's introduction and edition of the *Beneficio di Cristo* in John Tedeschi, ed., *Italian Reformation Studies in Honor of Laelius Socinus*, Università di Siena, Facoltà di Giurisprudenza, Collana di Studi "Pietro Rossi," Nuova Serie, vol. IV (Firenze, 1965), 21-102.

Evangelism flourished without difficulty until about 1542 when a series of reversals revealed that a chasm existed between Catholic and Protestant. Ochino, the brilliant preacher and general of the Capuchin order, fled Italy for Calvinist Switzerland. The shock to Italian public opinion was enormous. Contarini died, broken by the failure of the Ratisbon colloquy to come to an agreement with the Northern Protestants. The establishment of the Roman Inquisition, the constitution of the Jesuits, and the more militant stance of the German Lutheran princes all pointed to the coming strife. A second, crisis phase of Italian Evangelism occurred from 1542 to about 1560. [5] By the 1560's the cleric, gentleman, or commoner had to decide whether his religious conscience was fundamentally Catholic, or whether he should make the long journey over the Valtellina pass into Protestant Europe.

With these brief remarks about the religious situation of *Cinquecento* Italy, I would like to examine in the main body of the paper some of the religious views of the adventurers of the pen, and through them, those of middle and lower-class Italy.

The starting point for much of the religious concern of the adventurers of the pen was the desire for a simple religion of belief and good customs lacking a rational theology or elaborate ceremony. Aretino expressed this desire in both his devotional and secular writings. He saw religion as a matter of infused belief in the chief tenets of Catholicism, such as the Virgin birth. When he went to church, Aretino expected to hear a straightforward sermon on virtue and vice, not a "strident dispute." Such brazen arguments were "a reproach to the silence of Christ, who simply gave men a sign, in order not to take away the premium which He places on faith." These disputes had "nothing whatever to do with the gospels or with our sins." [6] Religion should be a personal benefit to man as well as a bond to a remote time of a better life. The characters in his stories looked back to a life of simple virtue and purity in the past. The simple devotion that he discribed in his saints' life typified his religious ideas. Although he practiced most of the sensual vices, Aretino propounded a religious ideal of simple faith and feeling. [7]

Another free-lance author who was much more deeply involved in Italian religious concerns, Ortensio Lando, was born about 1512 in Milan. [8] Although he once claimed that his mother was a noblewoman, it is unlikely that he enjoyed the advantages of noble birth.

[5] Cantimori, *Prospettive di storia ereticale italiana*, 28.

[6] *Primo libro delle lettere di Pietro Aretino*, a cura di Fausto Nicolini (Bari, 1913), I, 268; letter to Antonio Brucioli, 7 November 1537, Venice.

[7] See Giorgio Petrocchi, *Pietro Aretino tra Rinascimento e Controriforma* (Milan, 1948), 72-81.

[8] For Lando's life, see Ireneo Sanesi, *Il Cinquecentista Ortensio Lando* (Pistoia, 1893); Giovanni Sforza, "Ortensio Lando e gli usi i costumi d'Italia nella prima metà del Cinquecento," *Memorie della R. Accademia delle Scienze di Torino*, Serie II, LXIV, no. 4 (1914), 1-68; and Conor Fahy, "Per la vita di Ortensio Lando," *Giornale storico della letteratura italiana*, 142 (1965), 243-258.

He became an Augustinian monk as a youth, but left the monastery about 1530 because he found theology "too vague." He also studied medicine briefly at Bologna, but soon found his true vocation with the vernacular presses as copyist, editor, and finally, as a free-lance author writing for money. From 1533 through 1553, Lando published fifteen original works (usually anonymously), did two translations, and edited six other works. By 1650 his works had appeared in about 100 editions, including French and English translations.

Lando wandered constantly, rarely spending more than a few months in one place. He was to be found all over Italy from Sicily to Trent, in Lyons, at the court of Francis I of France, in Basel and eastern Switzerland, and in Germany. After 1545 he lived in or near Venice and its presses until his death c. 1554 or 1555. From time to time he was patronized by Italian princes or merchants, but never for long. By his own admission Lando found courtly sycophancy difficult, and more than once he lost the friendship of a prince with an ill-chosen word.

In his wanderings, Lando had ample opportunity for contacts with Protestants. He knew and approved the Protestants of the Tuscan city of Lucca and their concern for Scripture. He exhibited a good knowledge of Swiss Protestant leaders, especially those of Basel. In 1535 he may have been used as a messenger to carry letters back and forth from Martin Bucer to Lando's employer, a printer in Lyons. But despite occasional praise of Protestants for using Scripture rather than Scholastic commentaries, he did not become a Protestant and had little love for them.

Rather, Lando credited Erasmus as a formative influence on his religious thought. Writing in a dialogue published in Basel, 1540, he ecstatically described the impact of Erasmus and his message. Erasmus had struggled to bring people and nations to Christ through Scripture; he had brought men into light from the dark cloud which overshadowed them. Men were astonished and provoked, but they turned aside from prolix tomes (i.e., Scholastic commentaries) to examine the forgotten books of Scripture. Joyful letters spread the message of Erasmus to Italy, and many men opened the Gospel and moved forward to the glory of Christ. And Lando (speaking auto-biographically through one of the characters of the dialogue) explained that he himself had been persuaded to believe by Erasmus' message.

This dialogue also revealed Lando's lack of enthusiasm for the Protestant Reformation, and his dislike for the intense theological activity of Germany. Once emitting light, Germany was now a sordid and dark area of bawling theologians who ignored Erasmus. One man had thrown all into misery, and that man was Luther. At the same time, Lando faced the problem of whether Erasmus had been the fountain from which Luther issued. Thoroughly airing the problem, he concluded that Erasmus had not been a heretic. Lando did concede that Erasmus had had a sharp pen, and pointed out how it had provoked the illtempered Luther and Bucer. On the other hand, Erasmus often had overcome heretical men with his books. [9] In short, Lando admired Erasmus for teaching men to follow Scripture, but disliked Luther, Bucer, and German theologians. He absolved Erasmus from any taint of heresy, while admitting that his critical pen may have played a role in bringing on the Reformation. In the rest of the dialogue Lando amused his readers by chiding the Basel Reformers for their estrangement from Erasmus in the last seven years of his life. The Basel Reformed Church did not appreciate Lando's raillery and furiously denounced his book in the following year, 1541. [10]

The starting point of Lando's Evangelism was anti-clericalism. He flayed *Cinquecento* prelates for the abuses for which they were notorious: nepotism, non-residence, neglect of their dioceses, avarice, and politicking. On the other hand, he was willing to grant credit where credit was due. Lando praised the reforming bishop of Verona, the saintly Gian Matteo Giberti, whose reforms were codified in the Council of Trent. [11]

As might be expected, Lando sharply condemned the monastic life that he had left behind. His fundamental objection was that monastic orders had degenerated since their inception. In the early Church, monks had lived simple, holy lives in the wilderness but, as the world had declined, so little by little, had the lives of the monks. They had moved to the cities where they dressed well, made female friends, and mixed in worldly affairs. He urged monks to return to their holier ways as in the primitive Church. [12] Unlike Protestants, he did not advocate the abolition of monasticism.

Another element in Lando's Evangelism was a dislike of theology because it represented the attempt to apply reason to religion. Science *(scienza)* was an invention of the devil; Christ told men to forget the wisdom of this world and to know Him by ignorance. Scripture taught the word of God which was incomprehensible to reason. Theologians used all the trapping of reason — and ended by accusing one

---

[9] *In Des. Erasmi Rotherodami Funus, Dialogus lepidissimus, nunc primum in lucem editus.* Basileae, MDXL, foll. 12v, 14r-15v, 1v, 2v, 4r-6r, 14v, 16v, 17r-17v, 6v-10v.

[10] "Philopseudes, sive pro Desiderio Erasmo Roterodamo V.C. contra Dialogum famosum Anonymi cujusdam Declamatio, Joanne Herold Acropolita Auctore: In Gymnasio Basiliensi..." (5 August 1541), in *Desiderii Erasmi Roterodami Opera Omnia*... Lugduni Batavorum, MDCCVI, VIII, cols. 591-652. See cols. 600, 603, 615, 617, 621, 629-630.

[11] *Paradosi cioe, sententie fuori del comun Parere:* Novellamente venute in luce. Opera non men dotta Che piacevole: & in due parti separata. In Venetia. MDXLV, 24.

[12] *Commentario de le piu notabili, & mostruose cose d'Italia,* & altri luoghi, di lingua Aramea in Italia tradotto, nel quale s'impara, & prendesi estremo piacere... da Messer Anonymo di Utopia composto. In Venetia, Al Segno del Pozzo. MDL, 33-34v; *Ragionamenti familiari di diversi Autori*... In Vinegia al segno del Pozzo. MDL, 18-23v; *Erasmus funus,* foll. 19r-20v.

another of heresy. God came to simple, ignorant men who lived a good life in lowly places. [13]

In 1550 Lando linked justification by faith to belief in Scripture as an antidote for the ills of the Church. At the conclusion of a violent anti-clerical tract, he tendered advice to bishops. Above all, they should implant the Bible in the hearts of the faithful. In order to accomplish this, they had first to teach the force and true use of faith. Faith was a pure gift from God given to men to mortify the flesh, and for man's justification in Jesus Christ. Faith made good works spring up *(fa pullular le buone opere)*. By faith one came to works, and through works man was affirmed in faith. Teach the people, Lando admonished bishops, that works were signs of faith, faith a sign of grace, grace a sign of justification, salvation, and divine good will. [14] Lando's imprecise and untheological combination of justification by faith without omitting good works approximated the position of Italian Evangelism of Gaspare Contarini and Reginald Pole. [15]

Lando brought to fruition his belief in Scripture and faith in his *Dialogo della Sacra Scrittura* of April 1552 and repeated it in condensed form in another work published later in the year. Writing under his own name, Lando in the *Sacra Scrittura*, instructed Lucrezia Gonzaga of Gazzuolo, a minor Gonzaga princess and his current patroness, on the consolation and usefulness of Scripture by discussing its message book by book.

In his works of 1552 Lando strengthened his position of 1550 on justification by faith rather than works. Citing St. Paul's epistles to the Romans and the Galatians, he stated that men were born subject to sin, and only by the grace of Christ, and not through works or man's merits, were the believers justified. The epistle of St. James showed that true religion consisted not in words, nor in "easy boasts of faith," but only in piety, the soil of good works. [16]

Those who could hear the word of God were the elect. From the beginning of the world they had been "elected and predestined." Created to know and to serve God with perfect hearts, they were taught by God Himself because they had been given the power to hear the

---

13 *Paradossi*, 12v, 14-14v; *La sferza de scrittori antichi et moderni di M. Anonimo di utopia...* In Vinegia, MDL, 19-19v; *Quattro libri de dubbi con le solutioni a ciascun dubbio accomodate...* Vinegia, Appresso Gabriel Giolito de Ferrari, et Fratelli. MDLII, 309.
14 *Ragionamenti familiari*, 47v.
15 Jung, "On the Nature of Evangelism in 16th-Century Italy," 517, 521.
16 "Quivi [in Paul to the Romans] sopra ogni altra cosa egli disputa del peccato, & convince esser tutti gli uomini nati al peccato soggetti. Poscia egli disputa della giustitia; et dimostra che solo per la gratia di Christo, & non per l'opre, o per li meriti sono giustificati i credenti: non indugia molto, ch'egli esplica l'effetto della Gratia, & della fede, insegnando, che i Giustificati vivono una vita piena di penitenza guardandosi dalle mondane malvagità." *Dialogo di M. Hortensio Lando, nel quale si ragiona della consolatione, et utilita, che si gusta leggendo la Sacra Scrittura...* In Vinegia, MDL, al Scono del Pozzo. 51 (quote), 23, 53v.

Gospel. In answer to the objection that God wanted all men to be saved, Lando answered, citing St. Augustine, that God meant some men of all states and conditions, but not all men would be saved. Lando assured Lucrezia that her ability to listen avidly to him speaking on the glory of God was a sign that she was of the number of the predestined. [17]

Lando spoke of the Church in two senses: (1) a completely spiritual, invisible congregation of the good, and (2) a visible external union with a ministry and outward signs, a structure like the existing Catholic Church. Posing the question of what was the true Church, he answered that it was the "congregation of the good." It could not err, was without stain, and "completely spiritual" *(tutta spirituale)*. The Church was Christian, holy, annointed, with Christ as bishop, Pope, and mediator, at its head. [18] But the Church was also an external body with clear signs. In response to a question on the signs of the true Church of Christ, Lando answered: the preaching of the Word of God, confession of faith, baptism of water, correction of the errant, the Lord's Supper, and excommunication of the obstinate. Lando approved of infant baptism, and thought that the Church should include the "infirm" in faith. The Church had a ministry with priests *(sacerdoti)* who were to study, teach, and preach the word of God, dispense the sacraments, and minister to the poor. Lando affirmed that all the faithful were priests of an internal priesthood, but added that they were not the ministers of the sacraments. [19] Christ was the head of the spiritual Church, but Lando implied a hierarchy for the visible Church when he advised that correction of the vices of the heads of the Church was sometimes necessary. Excommunication was justified from St. Paul; those who were persuaded by another belief, or a salvation outside of Christ's, were to be excommunicated. [20]

Lando strayed from orthodoxy in his discussion of sacraments. Sacraments were "signs and testimonies" *(segnacoli e testimoni)* of divine benevolence and man's redemption. Their purpose was to restore and aid man's infirmity. [21] In his discussion of sacraments, Lando recurrently used the verb "signify." He posed the question, "What does the Lord's Supper signify? It signifies that all those who eat and drink together take part in the body and blood of Christ; in such a way they are united together with Christ through faith and charity

---

[17] "Hor poi che si avidamente m'udite favellare della gloria d'Iddio; ben è segno, che siete del numero de predestinati..." *Sacra Scrittura*, 9v (quote); *Dubbi*, 236, 273, 248, 259.

[18] Lando used the same words to describe the Church: "la congregatione de tutti i buoni" in *Dubbi*, 292; and "la congregatione dei buoni" in *Sacra Scrittura*, 7v; "tutta spirituale" was used in *Sacra Scrittura*, 7v, and *Dubbi*, 292. Also see *Sacra Scrittura*, 65v, and *Dubbi*, 241, 292.

[19] "Tutti i fideli sono sacerdoti? Cosi è... ma non propriamente ministri di sacramenti." *Dubbi*, 293; "Che tutti i fedeli sono sacerdoti del sacerdotio interno: & non dell'esterno." *Sacra Scrittura*, 7v.

[20] *Dubbi*, 276; *Sacra Scrittura*, 22, 15v, 41v, 66.

[21] "furono ordinati gli sacramenti, segnacoli, & testimoni della divina benivoglienza, & della nostra redentione..." *Sacra Scrittura*, 66; also *Dubbi*, 298.

like a body to the head in the same spirit." He went on to explain that whoever was not united to Christ in faith and to his neighbor in love, and yet participated in the Eucharist, was a hypocrite and simulator "showing himself to be what he was not." [22]

Lando stengthened this interpretation in his explanation of the "true use" of the Lord's Supper. It proved to the communicant himself that he had true faith and contribution for his sins, had charity toward his neighbor, and was not contaminated by vice. [23] In a strict sense, Lando implied that the sacraments were not necessary for salvation. But he added a strong plea for participation in the sacraments on the grounds that no one was perfect in faith. [24]

In his discussion of the Eucharist, Lando strayed furthest from Catholic orthodoxy. His discussion of the Lord's Supper was very close to Zwingli, who argued that the sacraments were signs and seals, not originating or conferring grace, but presupposing the grace of the elect. But at the same time, Zwingli acknowledged that the sacraments were necessary to strengthen man's faith. [25] Lando's words were close to the Zwinglians, but he did not deny that sacraments were channels of sanctifying grace, nor did he deny Transubstantiation; Lando made no mention of these.

Passing to other sacraments, Lando spoke of two kinds of confession, private and public. In response to Lucrezia's question, he defined private confession by the example of David who had confessed his injustice directly to God, who then loosed him from the impiety of his sins. Thus, Lando concluded, if we will confess our sins, God will faithfully remit them. Then he asked Lucrezia if she wanted to hear of public confession. She demurred and they went on to another topic. [26]

Ceremonies and religious practices were of little importance to Lando, but he did not eliminate them. He posed the question : if God wished to be adored only in spirit and truth, why did the Old Testament mention ceremonies? He answered : the Fathers of the Old Testament, who say that the Jewish people were childlike, instituted ceremonies to manifest God's glory and to provoke the Jews to remember the benefits received from God. Hence ceremonies remained in order to rouse the love of God and virtue in the hearts of men. Again Lando asked, why

---

22 "Che cosa significa la cena? Significa, che tutti coloro, che mangiono, & beveno [sic] insieme, hanno parte nel corpo & sangue di Christo, di maniera, che sono insieme uniti a Christo per fede, & charità come un corpo al capo in un medesimo spirito, & sono insieme uniti l'uno all'altro per carità, come un membro all'altro membro in un medesimo corpo. Talmente, che chiunque non è unito a Christo per fede, & carita, & al compagno per carità non puo degnamente convenire alla partecipatione della cena, anzi è hippocrita & simulatore mostrando essere quello ch'egli non è." *Dubbi*, 277.
23 *Paradossi*, 79v.
24 *Dubbi*, 301, 298.
25 Philip Schaff, *Creeds of Christendom* (NY and London, 1905), I, 372-375; III, 223.
26 *Dubbi*, 298-299, 252; *Sacra Scrittura*, 14v-15.

were so many devotional cults *(culti)* instituted in the Church, and answered that human reason always sought to justify itself through its own works. He did not attack any specific Catholic practices or ceremonies, but minimized the importance of fasts and abstinence from meat. [27]

But Lando spent little time discussing sacraments and ceremonies. The primary purpose of the *Sacra Scrittura* dialogue was to guide the reader to a better life through the reading of Scripture. The major part of the book was an explanation of the spiritual message of the Bible couched in terms of moral exhortation derived from biblical examples. Lando argued that the Bible was superior to all other models of conduct and learning. Scripture was better than Cicero, Seneca, Plutarch, and the early Renaissance educator, Pier Paolo Vergerio (d. 1414), for teaching virtue, including "civil faith" *(civil fede)*. The Bible was superior to any of the perfect types that inspired men : Cicero, the perfect orator; Thomas More's perfect reign of Utopia; Castiglione's perfect courtier; and Erasmus' perfect Christian knight of the *Enchiridion militis Christiani*. [28] Anti-clericalism was omitted from the *Sacra Scrittura* and the other work of 1552, as Lando proposed a positive religious program.

With the definition by the first session of the Council of Trent (1545-1547) Lando's position was heretical — more by omission than by assertion — on the sacraments, Eucharist, justification by faith, and predestination. But the Council was not completed, and the decrees were far from official promulgation, implementation, or widespread acceptance. Although some of the ideas of Lando's religious thought in 1552 were more heretical than orthodox, Lando, who was uninterested in theology, did not develop a complete heretical position. It is doubtful that he considered himself outside the Church. The circumstances of the publication of his religious ideas in 1552 argue that he did not consider himself a heretic. If Lando had thought of his *Sacra Scrittura* as heretical, or if he had foreseen difficulties with the Inquisition, he would not have published it under his own name. Two years later, when Lando ran into difficulty with the Inquisition because of the book, he protested that he was "a loyal son of the Roman Church." [29]

A great deal of Lando's religious thought would have been acceptable to Catholic, Lutheran, Calvinist, and Zwinglian. The only group whose doctrines he rejected by name were the Anabaptists. [30] Lando did not attack Catholic practices and beliefs, as purgatory, veneration of saints, the Virgin birth, the mass, tradition as a supplement to Scripture, indulgences, sacramentals, or holy orders. In most instances he made no mention of them. Lando did not work out the implications of his

---

27 *Dubbi*, 244, 315, 288, 259-260.
28 *Sacra Scrittura*, 26, 28, 31v-32.
29 Fahy, "Per la vita di Ortensio Lando," 255.
30 *Sacra Scrittura*, 16-17v.

religious ideas but, instead, propounded a simple, positive program based on Scripture and faith characteristic of Italian Evangelism.

Another vernacular author who exhibited a similar kind of religious belief was Anton Francesco Doni of Florence. Born in 1513, within a year of Lando, Doni was the son of an artisan, a scissors-maker. Like Lando, he became a monk, and priest of the Servants of Mary. Then at the age of 27 he left the order to embark upon the same rootless life of the literary adventurer. Like Lando, he settled in Venice from c. 1544 through 1556, and wrote prolifically for the popular presses. Then he resumed his fruitless travels, finally retiring to semi-isolation in rural Veneto until his death in 1574. [31]

By birth Doni was related to artisan circles and in his life maintained connections with the artisan classes, working as a printer himself. In a letter of November 1546, subsequently published in one of his books, he demonstrated that Italian Evangelism reached the level of Florentine artisans.

The letter recounted the confession of faith of a dying man, an anonymous unlearned weaver of Florence. Doni indicated that he was present at the man's death, and that he was happy to pass on the news, to communicate it to the other brothers *(fratelli)*. [32] The gist of the confession of the ignorant weaver was similar to Lando's thought. It affirmed faith in God as the foundation of salvation for the elect. Faith was a gift of God through which man had "certain experience" of the promise of God. Man was saved by God's grace through faith, not through his own efforts. [33]

The weaver implied a distinction between visible and invisible church. He confessed a church which was the gathering of all the elect "through divine predestination" and whose head was Christ. [34] Then he described a simplified external church with bishops and priests

---

31 On Doni's life, see my unpubl. diss. (Wisconsin, 1964), "Anton Francesco Doni : Cinquecento Critic," 91-143; and *I Marmi di Anton-francesco Doni* ripubblicati per cura di Pietro Fanfani con la vita dell'autore scritta da Salvatore Bongi. 2 vols. (Firenze, 1863). For a complete bibliography of Doni's works, see Cecilia Ricottini Marsili-Libelli, *Anton Francesco Doni scrittore e stampatore*, Biblioteca Bibliografica Italica, Vol. 21 (Firenze, 1960).

32 "A M. Basilio Guerrieri. Non sono quindici giorni passati, che venne a morte un fedel christiano . . . . Et questa fu la confessione & ragione che fece & rese di sua fede in propria persona di tal tenore . . . . la quale ellegrezza ho voluto participare con esso voi, come frutto della nostra novella amicitia : & voi sarete contento comunicarla a gli altri fratelli. State sano. Alli xxviij di Novembre. MDXLVI. Di Fiorenza." *Lettere del Doni Libro Secondo.* In Fiorenza MDXLVII, 50v, 52.

33 "Io confesso che la fede è dono d'Iddio, per lo quale sentiamo per prova, & habbiamo vera & certa esperienza della bonta & della promessa d'Iddio. Et certo noi siamo salvati per gratia per la fede, & non per nostro operare percioche questo è dono d'Iddio non dato per opere; accioche nessuno habbia di potersi laudate." *Lettere*, 51.

34 "Io confesso una sola chiesa, laquale è la ragunanza di tutti gli eletti per predestination divina; i quali sono stati dal principio del mondo & saranno insino alla fine; della qual chiesa è capo GIESU CHRISTO." *Lettere*, 51.

who had to be irreproachable in conduct and doctrine. On the sacraments, he affirmed a Zwinglian definition of the Lord's Supper. It was "a holy memory and thanksgiving of the death and passion of Jesus Christ, which we do together in faith and charity." [35] He expressed a general distaste for oral prayer, days of fast and abstinence, and holy days. Doni's dying weaver mentioned Scripture little, but its importance was taken for granted throughout the confession.

The confession read like the thought of a layman attempting to understand for himself the mysteries of faith and salvation, exactly as Doni described the anonymous weaver. From the viewpoint of existing theological positions, it was eclectic, containing strands which might be identified as Catholic, Zwinglian, Lutheran, Calvinist, or even a trace of Anabaptism. If Doni's statement about communicating the message to the *fratelli* can be taken at face value, Doni may at this time have been part of a conventicle, i.e., a group of laymen who met to discuss religious issues, read from Scripture, or to listen to reports from Protestant Europe.

What religious paths did the vernacular authors follow after mid-century? Lando did not live long enough to be faced with making a decision on his religious beliefs. Only his books suffered. They were put on the *Index* in 1559 but continued to be reprinted and sold despite the prohibitions. One or more copies of the *Sacra Scrittura* appeared in a Neapolitan book shop in 1565. [36]

The spirit of renewal and reform of post-Trent Italy caught up some of the vernacular authors. Luigi Tansillo wrote devotional works in reparation for earlier lascivious works. Others who had deserted the monastery returned to the religious life. Devotional writings became a mainstay of the publications of some of the Venetian printers who earlier had specialized in Aretino's racy stories. The *poligrafo* Girolamo Muzio became a dedicated but intemperate heretic hunter. Renewed, re-invigorated Catholicism claimed some of the vernacular authors by conviction — and compelled others through the *Index* and Inquisition to change their ways and thought.

Tridentine Catholicism did not satisfy all the vernacular authors after 1550, but still they did not opt for Protestantism. Doni continued to dream of a reformed Catholicism and expressed his dreams in the form of utopias. In 1552 he described a "New World," a primitive utopian city-state inspired by More's *Utopia*. [37] All the citizens of the

---

[35] "Io confesso che la cena del Signore è una santa memoria & ringratiamento della morte & della passione di GIESU CHRISTO, la quale noi facciamo insieme in fede et in charita; della quale si debbono mandar via tutti quegli che sono infedeli." *Lettere*, 51-51v.

[36] Salvatore Bongi, *Annali di Gabriel Giolito de' Ferrari da Trino di Monferrato, stampatore in Venezia* (Roma, 1890), I, lxxxv-ci.

[37] See Paul F. Grendler, "Utopia in Renaissance Italy: Doni's 'New World'", *Journal of the History of Ideas*, XXVI, n. 4 (1965), 479-494. The utopia is in Doni's *I Mondi del Doni*, Libro Primo. In Vinegia per Francesco Marcolini, MDLII, 90-99.

"New World" lived peaceable lives without private property or social institutions. It was an attempt by Doni to criticize the social abuses and moral vices of *Cinquecento* Italy by protraying a primitive, natural, good society. His New World utopia contained an undefined, vague religion presided over by priests. The citizens worshipped every seventh day in a great temple, as well as every morning and evening. Religion played a role in his natural utopian community but Doni did not elaborate on its features. The whole tone of the utopia implied a rational, naturalistic religion more typical of the seventeenth century.

Then in 1564 Doni constructed a utopian religious order to reform the Church in Italy. In each of thirteen Italian cities a large circular temple worthy to be a cathedral should be built. All should be constructed on the same design, with a high altar in the center with a depiction of the Calvary scene, and twelve side chapels, one for each apostle, placed around the circumference of the church. The church in Rome was the most important of the thirteen. To each temple were attached a bishop, twelve canons (one for each chapel), and thirteen priests to assist bishop and canons in reading daily mass and the office at the high altar and chapels. In Rome a cardinal protector assisted by twelve bishops presided. By Doni's count, the Order consisted of a cardinal, twenty-four bishops, and 313 canons and priests, "all learned and admirable."

Doni decreed strict rules of conduct and dress for the members of the order. Before admission, every character stain had to be eliminated. After entry, upon the commission of a notable crime or sin, a member was placed in penance and, at the second offence, expelled. The canons were to dress in a clear purple habit, and the priests in "honorable" black. But the members of the order were not to be restricted by monastic rules or forced to live in poverty. All were free to come and go as they pleased, to study, to ride, and to do anything characteristic of gentlemen. Learning was the path of advancement. When death depleted the ranks, the vacant places were to be filled by the most learned friars and priests. After reading and disputing before the Holy See, the Pope and bishops would select the new members. The entire order would be at the disposal of the Church, prepared to defend the Church and the papacy in disputes or in any other way. [38]

More's *Utopia* possibly suggested the setting of the thirteen temples and uniform clothing, or perhaps the Jesuits suggested the idea of a reformed religious order. In any case, Doni's reformed religious order was an extension of his belief in a Church led by a reformed monasticism.

One would like to believe that Doni finally found religious peace in old age, but the evidence indicates that he did not. Doni may have begun to doubt that an afterlife existed. [39] In a poem of 1567 on man's

---

[38] *La Zucca del Doni Fiorentino* ... In Venetia Appresso Fran. Rampazetto, ad instantia di Gio. Battista, & Marchio Sessa fratelli, MDXLV, 270-273v.
[39] *La Zucca*, 296v.

fate, Doni repeated the conventional words of comfort, that man should throw himself on God's mercy, but it seemed a solution of form rather than belief. The last two lines expressed his pessimism :

> And cry, at the end life is a sorrow,
> A fatal use, a living loss. [40]

I would like to summarize briefly the religious views of these free-lance authors. Initially they were caught up in the spirit of renewal along the lines of Scripture and faith, the movement which scholars usually call Evangelism. This lasted until the mid-1550's. At this point they began to lose their identity, going in different directions — to a sincere Tridentine Catholicism in some cases. Interestingly, in very few cases that have come to my attention did they opt for Protestantism. Some of them retained their vague, unrealized hope in a form of utopian religion. In this way Doni is a precursor. Giordano Bruno and Tommaso Campanella are the only Italian successors to Doni. In his utopian *City of the Sun* (1602) Campanella included a syncretic religion composed of elements of Christianity, Eastern religions, sun-worship, and his own peculiar kind of naturalism.

The religious history of Baroque Italy is another story, very little studied. I have simply tried to describe some of the religious turmoil, restlessness, and excitement of *Cinquecento* Italy in crisis, through the world of the free-lance authors, Aretino and his followers.

---

[40] "Et grida, al fin la Vita è un'affanno,
    Un utile mortale, un 'vivo danno."
Fredi Chiappelli, "Un poema inedito e sconosciuto di Anton Francesco Doni," *La Rassegna della letteratura italiana*, 58, Serie VII, n. 4 (Oct.-Dec. 1954), 567.

UTOPIA IN RENAISSANCE ITALY: DONI'S "NEW WORLD"

During the Renaissance authors of widely varying backgrounds wrote utopias. In the fifteenth and sixteenth centuries certain features of the utopias remained constant, but their aims varied as widely as their authors. One of those utopias, which seemed externally to fit easily within the framework of the Renaissance utopia but actually differed in important ways from all its fellows, was the "New World," contained in *I Mondi* (1552) of Anton Francesco Doni (1513–1574). After a short discussion of the general characteristics of the Renaissance utopias, this study will focus on Doni's "New World" in order to determine in what ways it fitted within the pattern of Renaissance utopias, and how it differed.

Although Plato's suggestions in the *Republic* and the *Laws* for a well-governed city, social regulation, and educational reform were the ultimate roots of all Renaissance utopias, the practical starting point for the Renaissance was the abstract city models of the *Quattrocento* architects. These utopias exhibited two fundamental characteristics of the Renaissance utopia: a city plan of geometrical regularity, and regimentation of the lives of the inhabitants for the sake of the city as a whole. Leon Battista Alberti's *De re aedificatoria* (written in 1452, published in Latin in 1485 and in Italian in 1546) listed plans and ideas for an organic city in which the inhabitants could live in peace. His plans went beyond architecture to encompass social considerations, as he planned asylums for the poor, and separated different social classes from each other. More complete was the utopia of Antonio Averlino, called Filarete (c. 1400–1466), the architect of the Sforza castle at Milan. Filarete's plan for a perfect city, named *Sforzinda* for his patrons, was in the shape of a regular eight-pointed star with streets leading from the eight city gates located between the points of the star to the center of the city. Filarete placed the various shops and crafts in specified areas of the city, and regulated the color of dress and value of jewelry permitted to the nobility of *Sforzinda*. He devised social regulations for the schools and prisons with a communal utilitarian aim in view. However, Filarete's *Sforzinda,* the earliest complete Italian utopia, remained in manuscript until the twentieth century, and probably had no influence on other utopias.[1]

[1] Luigi Firpo, "La città ideale del Filarete," in *Studi in memoria di Gioele Solari* (Torino, 1954), 11–59.

The Journal of the History of Ideas, © 1965.

480

With *The Best State of a Commonwealth and the new Island of Utopia* (1516) of St. Thomas More, the Renaissance utopia acquired moral purpose. More's *Utopia* was part of his action program as a Christian humanist to renovate contemporary society. It was based on the idea that men were not hopelessly corrupt; given the proper external conditions, men could attain the good society. More investigated the social evils of the day, and found that sin, especially pride, was at the root of human evils. His *Utopia* was an elaborate social structure (whose details are too well-known to need reiteration) for the purpose of subjugating sin. More wrote the *Utopia* as an example and model in order to educate European rulers.[2]

Doni had a hand in bringing More's *Utopia* to vernacular readers in Italy. In 1548 an Italian translation of More's work by Ortensio Lando was published in Venice without the name of publisher or translator. Doni wrote the dedicatory letter, praising the courageous, God-fearing More and his book. The *Utopia* of More contained, in Doni's opinion, ". . . excellent customs, good arrangements, wise rules, holy admonishments, sincere government, and royal men. Then, well composed are the cities, the offices, justice, and the works of mercy. . . ."[3]

As widely known as More's *Utopia* was the utopian land of the Garamanti in the *Relox de principes* (written c. 1518, printed in 1529) of the Spanish humanist Antonio de Guevara (c. 1480–1544). Guevara, a Franciscan bishop at the court of Charles V, wrote the *Relox de principes* as a Christian humanist handbook for princes. Early in the book, Guevara interpolated the story of the "barbarous people called Garamanti" as an example to princes. As Guevara nar-

---

[2] St. Thomas More, *Utopia*, ed. Edward Surtz, Yale Edition of the Works of St. Thomas More (New Haven and London, 1964). See J. H. Hexter, *More's Utopia: the biography of an idea* (Princeton, N. J., 1952), 58, 73–83, 93.

[3] "Voi troverete in questa repubblica, ch'io vi mando, ottimi costumi, ordini buoni, reggimenti savj, ammaestramenti santi, governo sincero e uomini reali; poi ben composte le città, gli officj, la giustizia e la misericordia . . ." Doni's dedicatory letter to Gerolamo Fava, n. d., n. pl., *La republica nuovamente ritrovata, del governo dell' isola Eutopia, nella qual si vede de nuovi modi governare Stati, reggier Populi, dar Leggi à i senatori, con molta profondità di sapienza, storia non meno utile che necessaria. Opera di Thomaso Moro Cittadino di Londra*. In Vinegia, MDXLVIII, pp. [3–5]. The catalogues of the British Museum and the National Central Library of Florence mistakenly attribute the translation to Doni. In 1561 Francesco Sansovino wrote that More's *Utopia* was ". . . tradotta dalla latina del Moro da Hortensio Lando." *Del governo dei regni et delle repubbliche . . . di Francesco Sansovino*. In Venetia . . . MDLXI, p. 184, as quoted in Giovanni Sforza, *Ortensio Lando e gli usi ed i costumi d'Italia nella prima metà del Cinquecento*, Memorie della R. Accademia delle Scienze di Torino, Serie II, LXIV, n. 4 (1914), 5, fn. 2. Doni corroborated this evidence by the fact that he never claimed the 1548 translation as his.

rated the story, Alexander the Great, in the midst of conquering the world, heard of the Garamanti and commissioned his ambassadors to threaten them with destruction if they did not submit to his power. But the Garamanti neither fled nor offered resistance. Alexander came to see for himself, and an old man was commissioned by the Garamanti to explain themselves and to create an example for future princes.

After rebuking Alexander as a tyrant, the old man explained how the Garamanti lived short, happy lives with few goods and laws, without enemies, and in continual peace and love. They lived under seven laws which contained "all virtue and resistance to vice." The first law established that there should be no more than seven laws because new ones caused people to forget the good old customs. The second law decreed that they should adore no more than two gods, one for life and the other for death, because one god served dutifully was worth more than a thousand served "jokingly." All had to dress alike because variety of dress generated madness and scandal, according to the third law. The fourth law ruled that no woman could bear her husband more than three children, because a large number of children made the father desirous of goods, and this anxiety gave birth to every vice. If women bore more than three children, the excess were sacrificed to the gods. The fifth law forbade lying. Liars were decapitated because one liar was "enough to ruin a people." The sixth law ordered that all had to inherit equally. All had an equal amount of goods because the desire for goods gave rise to great jealousies and scandals. The seventh and final law decreed that no woman could live more than forty years and no man more than fifty years. At these ages they were sacrificed to the gods. The reason was again moral; human beings became vicious if they knew that they could live indefinitely. With the aid of these laws, the Garamanti possessed all things equally, ate and drank temperately, avoided struggles among themselves, and carried no arms because they had no enemies.[4]

Like More's *Utopia*, Guevara's land of the Garamanti influenced Doni directly. In Part I of *I Marmi* (1552) written within six months of *I Mondi*, Doni included a dialogue in which the characters mentioned a book containing "healthy laws" (*legge sante*), and began reading from the imaginary work. These healthy laws were six of the seven laws of the Garamanti. Following Guevara's order, Doni closely paraphrased the laws, omitting only number six, and commented briefly, approving them.[5] Doni probably learned of the Garamanti

---

[4] *Comienca el primero libro del famossimo emperadoi Marco Aurelio con el Relox de principes nuevamente annadido: compuesto por el muy reverendo y magnifico señor don Antonio de Guevara . . .* (Barcelona, 1532), chs. 32–34, pp. 55v–59v.

[5] A. F. Doni, *I Marmi*, a cura di Ezio Chiorboli, 2 vols. (Bari, 1928), I, 26–27.

482

through the Italian translation of Guevara's work by Mambrino Roseo, *Institutione del prencipe christiano*, which had at least eight editions from 1543 to 1584.[6]

Two other Italian utopias followed in the second half of the sixteenth century. Nearest in time if not in spirit to Doni's New World was *La Città Felice* (1553) of the Platonic philosopher Francesco Patrizi da Cherso (1529–1597). *La Città Felice* was an aristocratic utopia modeled on Plato, Aristotle, and the Venetian state. Rejecting egalitarianism, Patrizi organized the city into a rigid caste system which separated irrevocably the warriors, magistrates, and priests from the peasants, artisans, and merchants, who served their masters. The upper caste lived in peace, virtue, and wisdom, as they progressed toward the "supercelestial waters," a vaguely defined Platonic perfection. In short, *La Città Felice* was a utopia for philosopher-kings.[7] Later in the *Cinquecento* the utopia assimilated the heightened religious emphasis of the Catholic Reformation. In *La Repubblica Immaginaria* (written between 1575 and 1580, unpublished until the twentieth century) of Ludovico Agostini (1535–1612), parallel civil and religious governments closely supervised the physical and spiritual welfare of the people. Agostini, a lawyer and administrator of the papal city of Pesaro, dictated a highly regulated life for the citizens of the imaginary republic, including a specified daily routine, stabilized occupations, and communal concern for the poor. The dominating feature of his utopia was the close religious supervision exercised by the bishop and parish priests, who tried hard to root out vice and to stimulate communal devotion in terms reminiscent of the decrees of the Council of Trent. At the same time the civil government used overseers and spies to supervise the crafts, solve family quarrels, check crime, and direct the lives of the inhabitants in very minute ways.[8] Agostini's imaginary republic suggests a Catholic version of Calvinist Geneva superimposed on the typical Renaissance utopia.

I Mondi was printed in April 1552. The dialogue which utilized material from Guevara was in Part I of *I Marmi*, with a dedicatory letter of 25 October 1552.

[6] The pages describing the Garamanti in Roseo's edition were a faithful translation without omissions, although placed in a different section of the book. *Institutione del prencipe christiano, tradotto di Spagnuolo in lingua Toscana per Mambriano Roseo de Fabriano*. Nuovamente Stampato, & con somma diligenza correto. In Venetia per Bernardin De Bindoni Mediolanensis Anno Domini MDXLV, pp. 8–13v.

[7] *Utopisti e riformatori sociali del Cinquecento: A. F. Doni—U. Foglietta—F. Patrizi da Cherso—L. Agostini*, a cura di Carlo Curcio (Bologna, 1941), xv–xvi, 122–142.

[8] *La repubblica immaginaria di Ludovico Agostini*, a cura di Luigi Firpo (Torino, 1957). See also Luigi Firpo, *Lo Stato ideale della Controriforma. Ludovico Agostini* (Bari, 1957).

The Renaissance utopias had in common a rational, even geometrical, organization of the physical environment and a highly regimented life for the inhabitants. The details varied from the slave society of Patrizi to equality of property in More and Guevara, but the common purpose of these utopias was to hold up societies with moral and social reform as examples for sixteenth-century rulers. All of the above-mentioned utopian authors, with the exception of Filarete, were respected and highly placed men of existing society. All wrote with the hope of persuading rulers to effect needed reforms. The path of reform would be from above; this was indicated by the authoritarian governmental structure of all the utopias. These authors had enough confidence in existing authority (although More entertained doubts about the nobility) to address petitions of reform to rulers, and they had enough optimism concerning the nature of most men to expect that they could be improved, morally and socially, through a better environment and authoritarian direction.

Doni was influenced by the rational organization and regimented life of the utopias of More and Guevara, but differed in background and suppositions from other utopian authors. The son of a Florentine scissors-maker, Doni became a monk and priest at the monastery of the *Annunziata* in Florence, only to leave in 1540 for a wandering career, living by his pen and wits in northern Italy. Skilled in music and literature, he was singularly unskilled in enlisting patrons. After travel in Lombardy and participation in Academies in Piacenza and Florence, he settled in Venice in 1547 to earn his living as a *poligrafo*, a prolific, vernacular author for the presses of Marcolini and Giolito. Blessed with acute observation and the ability to write quickly without need of correction, Doni wrote eighteen major works and many lesser ones. With Aretino, Lodovico Domenichi, Ortensio Lando, Nicolò Franco, Francesco Sansovino, and others, Doni produced the popular vernacular literature of the Italian Cinquecento—tales, plays, moral fables, travel literature, satires, poetry, literary criticism, letters, pornography and burlesques. From his first published work in 1543 through 1611, 78 printed editions of his works appeared, including French, Spanish, and English translations.[9] In 1555 he left Venice. After more wandering, he retired to live in semi-seclusion in Monselice, a few miles from Venice, and died in 1574.[10]

Doni matured in a period of crisis in Italian life, as Italy lost its political independence, suffered economic decline, underwent religious

[9] For a complete bibliography of Doni's works, see Cecilia Ricottini Marsili-Libelli, *Anton Francesco Doni scrittore e stampatore*, Biblioteca Bibliografica Italica, Vol. 21 (Firenze, 1960).

[10] On Doni's life, see my unpubl. diss. (Wisconsin, 1964), "Anton Francesco Doni: Cinquecento Critic," 91–143.

unrest, and changed artistically from Renaissance to Mannerism. Doni's writings were shaped by the mood of crisis, and he reflected it in several ways. He gave voice to a prevailing feeling of discouragement by writing about the restlessness and unhappiness of contemporary life. In a dialogue with autobiographical elements in *I Marmi* (1552–53), a character named *Inquieto*, "the restless one," narrated the story of his life. *Inquieto* told how he had ventured into the world with his father's wealth and blessing and, at first, enjoyed himself among friends and pleasures. But he very soon found this manner of life boring and withdrew to his books and solitary thought. His friends, however, dragged him out into the world again; and there, like a chameleon, he for a time unwillingly joined in the activities of others. Escaping his friends, he wandered in far countries until he returned to his native Florence in search of a useful and pleasing way of life. *Inquieto* commented that at this point he was 37 years of age (at the time of writing *I Marmi*, Doni was 39), rich, lettered, but very unstable. *Inquieto* tried many modes of life—the monastery, merchant life, and so on—but nothing satisfied him. In his torment *Inquieto* climbed the hill to the church of *San Miniato,* overlooking Florence, and there mused about the people below. How many confused, ribald, ignorant, unhappy, unsatisfied people struggled below! How many good men were tormented in prison, how many fathers could not provide for their sons, how many children were forced to enter the monasteries, how many monks wanted to leave the monasteries! He pondered: in a hundred years of effort, what will the rabble have accomplished? Nothing. The tiny people far below were a cage of madmen engaged in useless activities while the world remained unchanged. They had so many crafts when only a few things were necessary. They produced a multitude of inventions, extravagances in dress, and modes of living—which profited little. *Inquieto* concluded his discourse with a plea to Doni (personified as another character in the dialogue) for help because he was unable to understand himself. But Doni told *Inquieto* that his discourse had been so lengthy that he had lost the thread of the argument. He had no advice to offer.[11]

The discourse of *Inquieto* was typical of Doni. Underlying Doni's description of restless man was a pessimistic view of human nature. Man was weak, his physical existence hung on a thread, and his fragile intellect fought a losing battle against his restless appetites. Unlike earlier Renaissance authors (Pontano, for example, and Machiavelli), who thought that man could oppose Fortune, Doni thought that man could only accept resignedly what Fortune dealt, and that

[11] *I Marmi*, II, 205–211.

the world generally did not favor the just or the worthy. Man could only drift with the world, accepting whatever happened to him until the blank end.[12]

Doni questioned *Cinquecento* values. He rejected humanist learning which prepared man for the active, civil life, in favor of ignorant withdrawal from affairs.[13] Religion was no solution for man's ills. Doni, the renegade monk, paid only occasional lip service to religious ideals, usually at the end of free, critical passages, and his writings abounded in anti-clericalism.[14] Doni termed the esteemed literary figures of his lifetime (Ariosto, Bembo, Bernardo Tasso, Claudio Tolomei, and others) pedants who slavishly followed Petrarchan rules in their compositions.[15] In his *Pistolotti Amorosi* (1552) Doni mocked Neo-Platonic love treatises and the Petrarchan love vocabulary.[16]

Doni was at his sharpest in social criticism. In acute dialogues, particularly in *I Mondi,* he condemned the distorted division of wealth which granted to *signori* [17] the power to exploit the poor. Why do the *signori* have much and I nothing?, he asked. They ride fine horses, and I walk; they are richly dressed, but only a shift covers my nakedness. How did they get so wealthy? Why are matters so out of balance? [18] Doni supplied his own answers and remedies. The *signori* had not earned their place or their wealth; they and their ancestors had robbed the poor, and now they lived in lustful luxury. Doni wished that "everyone would eat bread earned by his own sweat." [19] Mocking the wealthy, Doni suggested that "four yards of earth" were enough for any man.[20] He used several literary devices

[12] *I Mondi del Doni,* Libro Primo. Jn Vinegia per Francesco Marcolini, Con Privilegio MDLII, pp. 16–17; *La Zucca del Doni Fiorentino* . . . In Venetia, Appresso Fran. Rampazetto . . . (in fine: MDLXV), pp. 145–146v, 165, 209–209v, 254–256v, 288–292, 296v. *La Zucca* was first printed in 1551. The 1565 ed., and all subsequent editions also include *Pitture del Doni Academico Pellegrino* . . . In Padova, Appresso Gratioso Perchacino, 1564.

[13] *La Zucca,* pp. 64v–67v.

[14] For an example of Doni's equivocation on religion, see *La Zucca,* p. 296v, where, in the midst of rejecting life after death, Doni inserted a brief, unconvincing clause to the effect that he was speaking of "mortal man" only, and not his soul.

[15] *I Marmi,* I, 160, 184, 186; *La Zucca,* pp. 213v–215v.

[16] *Pistolotti Amorosi del Doni* . . . In Vinegia Appresso Gabriel Giolito de Ferrari e Fratelli MDLII, pp. 9, 13v, 31v–34, 36v–37, 92–95.

[17] For Doni, *"signori"* meant a ruling class based on birth, wealth, and political power (nobility, wealthy merchants, and princes) rather than the narrow meaning of "gentlemen."

[18] *I Mondi,* pp. 19v–23v.

[19] ". . . vorrei che ogni persona mangiassi il pane del suo sudore." *I Mondi,* 21.

[20] *I Mondi,* 59.

to criticize the social structure. He compared the proud *signore* to the humble ass, much to the advantage of the latter.[21] In a satirical dialogue, Jove mixed souls and bodies, so that the soul of a loutish peasant was placed in the body of a signore—and no one could detect the change.[22] Doni also condemned legists, doctors, and scholars who cheated or robbed both rich and poor, and soldiers who knew only how to kill and ruin.[23]

As an alternative to his pessimistic view of man in the *Cinquecento*, Doni evoked the golden age of the past, the Age of Saturn in classical mythology, in which men had lived in primitive perfection. In the distant past, men had lived in peace in a primitive, natural society. Every individual had worked a small piece of earth; each man "lived from his own just sweat and did not drink the blood of the poor."[24] Men had lived thoughtlessly like children; they had gone about unclothed without shame because purity dwelt in the land. Everyone had aided his neighbor. But age by age, men had acquired vices, cheated each other for money, and fought in bloody wars, as the world sank to its vicious sixteenth-century state.[25]

Doni longed for a return to a simple, primitive, good life. In his *Le Ville* (1566), one of his last writings, he described in simple but effective style the life of a family of country peasants. In the early dawn the father arose, said a *Pater Noster,* and began the new day guided only by the stars as his clock. The happy family watched their crops ripen as their own lives matured free of vices. The rest of the world labored like ants to sustain some king or emperor, but these peasants lived peacefully on the green floor of the earth. In the last lines, Doni expressed the wish to leave the noise of palaces to flee to a solitary villa where he could live in repose.[26] Doni fulfilled his desire in the last decade of his life, when he withdrew to the tranquility of a hilltop castle in tiny, rural Monselice, where he mixed writing and gardening.

Wit, satirist, and bitter critic of the social structure as well as of

[21] *Il Valore de gli Asini.* Dell'Inasinito Academico Pellegrino. In Vinegia, Per Francesco Marcolini, MDLVIII. The first edition appeared in 1553.

[22] *I Mondi,* pp. 54v–55v.

[23] For criticism of legists, see *La Zucca,* pp. 72–72v; of scholars and legists, see *Inferni del Doni Academico Pellegrino.* Libro Secondo de Mondi. In Vinegia per Francesco Marcolini nel MDLIII, 78–80, 151, 156; of doctors, see *Inferni,* 123, and *I Marmi,* II, 143; of soldiers, see *La Zucca,* 293v–294, and *Inferni,* 217.

[24] ". . . viveva del suo giusto sudore e non beveva del sangue de' poveri." *I Marmi,* I, 267.

[25] *I Marmi,* I, 267–273; II, 141–143; *I Mondi,* 26–26v.

[26] *Attavanta Villa di M. Anton Francesco Doni Fiorentino* tratta dall'autografo conservato nel Museo Correr di Venezia (Firenze, 1857), 74–79.

religious, educational, and literary norms of his time, Doni, an "adventurer of the pen" of low social origins, approached the utopian form with a different point of view than Filarete, Alberti, More, Guevara, Patrizi, and Agostini. Doni's New World completed his indictment of the Italian world of the *Cinquecento*. Doni's critical but satirical attitude was apparent at the beginning of his utopian dialogue. The dialogue constituted the major part of the sixth of the seven worlds of *I Mondi*—the *Mondo de' Pazzi* (world of the madmen) narrated by two speakers named *Savio* (Wiseman) and *Pazzo* (Crazyman). In the introductory discourse,[27] *Savio*, playing on the meanings of *pazzia* and *saviezza* in a way reminiscent of Erasmus' *Praise of Folly,* commented that he was not certain whether his words ought to be called crazy or wise, because the world had little certainty on the subject. Thus, his readers could call "this New World" he was about to describe either *pazzo* or *savio,* as they pleased; neither did Savio mind if they called it a "hermaphroditic world" (90).

To illustrate his point, *Savio* narrated a satirical tale based freely on the biblical Flood. After the waters receded, a powerful stench which maddened men remained. Seeing the madness which affected the whole world, astrologers gathered together in a small, closed room to pool their wisdom. After long study, they emerged intent on leading men from madness to wisdom. But the people of the world continued in their crazy ways. The wise astrologers attempted in vain to regulate and halt the madness: because the *pazzi* were more numerous they soon overcame the *savi*. The *pazzi* forced the *savi* to act, against their will, like the *pazzi,* so that soon all were *pazzi.* The narrator, *Savio,* clearly speaking for Doni, concluded that although one could construct a "wise" world, it would, he suspected, soon become a "crazy" world. If there was such a thing as wisdom in the world, it could not prevail (90–92).

In this satirical, self-mocking vein, Doni began his dialogue on the perfect city. By way of contrast, Thomas More began his *Utopia*

---

[27] All of the modern editions of Doni's New World omit the introductory discourse with the tale of the astrologers, missing the self-mockery and cynicism with which Doni began his utopia. The New World dialogue is available in the following twentieth-century editions: *Le più belle pagine di Anton Francesco Doni* (Milano-Roma, 1932), 78–85; *Utopisti e riformatori sociali del Cinquecento,* 3–15; *Scritti scelti di Pietro Aretino e di Anton Francesco Doni* Classici italiani, vol. 37 (Torino, 1951), 475–490. Secondary accounts of Doni's New World have been very brief. See Luigi Firpo, *Lo Stato ideale della Controriforma,* and his "L'utopia politica nella Controriforma," in *Quaderni di Belfagor,* I (Contributi alla storia del Concilio di Trento e della Controriforma) (Firenze, 1948), 84. Also Carlo Curcio, *Dal Rinascimento alla Controriforma: contributo alla storia del pensiero politico italiano da Guicciardini a Botero* (Roma, 1934), 120–129, and his *Utopisti e riformatori,* viii-xii. References in the text are to the first edition (1552) of *I Mondi.*

with two gentlemen, on a mission to Antwerp, meeting a stranger who narrated his visit to a strange land. The other utopias had similar sober introductions. Doni manifested a different spirit with an introduction that mocked his own "wise" new world.

Savio and *Pazzo* began to narrate a vision shown them by Jove and Momus. For the most part, *Savio* explained the structure of the New World, while *Pazzo* added interpretative comments or prodded *Savio* with questions. In the vision, the two gods led *Savio* and *Pazzo* to a great city, the only city in a province the size of Lombardy, Tuscany, or the Romagna. The city's walls were built in the form of a star. In the center of the city was a very high temple, "higher than the cupola [of the cathedral] of Florence by four or six times." [28] The temple had a hundred doors from which, "like the rays of a star," a hundred streets radiated out to the hundred gates of the city. Thus, Doni's new city was star-shaped like the *Sforzinda* of Filarete.

A high degree of uniformity characterized the life of the city. On every street were two related crafts; for example, on one side of a certain street were all the tailors and on the other were cloth shops. The pharmacists worked on one side of a street, with the hospitals and doctors on the other. Shoemakers cobbled across the way from tanners, bakers labored across the street from the mills, and women spun thread on one side of a street while the weavers toiled on the other side. The hundred streets held two hundred different crafts (although Doni did not enumerate all of them), with each artisan specializing in his own craft and no other. The craftsmen did not sell their products, but produced them for the people of the city. If anyone had need of something, he went to the street of the craft which produced the desired article, as to the street of the tailors for a coat, and the article was made for him (95).

The same kind of specialization marked the lives of the peasants who lived outside the city. The rest of the province produced food to feed the city. Each part of the earth was "fruitful by its nature," so that the peasants planted only the crop (wheat, hay, vines, etc.) suitable to a particular patch of ground, and no other crop. These one-crop lands were cultivated by peasants who also specialized. Each group of peasants cultivated only one crop in order that in a few years they would know "the nature of the plant." With this experience they produced miraculous harvests (94v–95).

The utopian uniformity of the star city continued in every aspect of the lives of the inhabitants. This was common to all of the Renaissance utopias, but Doni went beyond the other utopian authors in the completeness of his uniformity. At mealtimes the people went to

[28] ". . . qui nel mezzo dove io fo questo punto, sia un tempio alto, grande come è la cupola di Fiorenza quattro o sei volte." *I Mondi,* 94v.

the streets of the inns, where they all ate the same few, simple dishes in equal, moderate quantity. All lived in homes furnished exactly alike, in extreme simplicity. All wore uniform clothing in colors which corresponded to their ages. Children up to ten years wore white, young adults aged eleven to twenty wore green, those between twenty-one and thirty dressed in peacock blue, those from thirty-one to forty years of age wore red, and after forty black was worn. Moreover, these were the only colors used in the city (95–95v). When one of the inhabitants was ill, he went to the street of the hospitals, where knowledgeable physicians had medicines to cure any disease within an hour. All the aged and infirm were cared for, without favor or discrimination, in the hospitals (95v). On the other hand, children born deformed were thrown into a well in order that no deformities should exist in the New World. All would be "beautiful, good, healthy, and fresh" (96). In Doni's words, everything from birth to death went according to one line; life in the star city did not depart from the rule (95v). Doni, who described man's life in the *Cinquecento* as restless and unhappy, proposed in his new world a uniform life according to one rule, that of perfect equality.

As he continued to explain the complete equality of the star city, his social and moral criticism of the *Cinquecento* became more evident. The star city held women, as well as goods, in common. The city had one or two streets of women who were possessed in common. Doni explained through *Savio* that there were three good reasons for this. First, social distinctions would be wiped out. Since women were used in common, the inhabitants never knew who their parents were (95v). Honored families and noble houses would be extinguished.[29] Secondly, holding women in common eliminated moral evils and social disturbances. Since marriage did not exist, social and moral problems surrounding marriage in the *Cinquecento* would be eliminated. There were no angry families, contested dowries, challenged honors, tumultous marriages, adulteries, cuckoldries, and murders in the New World. Third, as Doni the moralist gave way to Doni the cynical wit, holding women in common eliminated the heartbreak of unrequited love and loveless matches. No love difficulties occurred in the New World. Because love was nothing more than the privation of the loved object, the appetites that arose from the absence of the beloved were cancelled immediately (96v–97).

In his star city Doni eliminated the *Cinquecento* social and economic structure which he had criticized elsewhere. There was no noble class, existing idly on the labor of others in the New World. *Pazzo* worried about possible laziness, but *Savio* brought him up short with the New World dictum that "He who does not work does

[29] "... si sono spente le famiglie honorate, et le case nobilissime." *Ibid.*, 97.

not eat." [30] There were no distinctions between rich and poor because there was no money. The inhabitants lived by barter. Weights and measures, which were nothing more than means designed to torture (*straziare*) the people, did not exist. Notaries, procurators, lawyers, and "other intriguing thieves" disappeared because there were no deceiving merchants. Because all the needs of the citizens were met, robbery did not exist. In short, "Everything was in common, and the peasants dressed like those in the city, because everyone carried away the reward of his labor and took what he needed." [31]

The other utopias also criticized Renaissance society, but Filarete, Alberti, More, Patrizi, and Agostini all constructed alternative societies. Doni simply tore down the existing society. This is evident from what was missing from Doni's New World. In contrast to the other Renaissance utopias, Doni's star city lacked a governmental structure, means for defense, and a program of education. The New World had no way to enforce the simple, primitive way of life that Doni outlined. There were no police, laws, or courts in the city. He assumed that there would be no crime because all of man's necessities were provided, and his desires either satisfied or blunted. Doni indicated a minimal direction in the city—that the great temple housed one hundred priests, with each priest having charge over one of the hundred streets of the city, and that the eldest priest was the "head of the land." But Doni did not elaborate what sort of direction the priests exercised over the streets, or in what way the eldest priest was the head of the city. Rather, in the same sentence he stressed equality; even the oldest priest had nothing more than the other inhabitants of the city (95).

What would the inhabitants of the star city do if they were attacked by another city, asked *Pazzo?* In answer, *Savio* stated that the star city had neither offensive nor defensive weapons because no other country or city should wish to attack the city. Doni turned the issue into another criticism of the *Cinquecento* mentality. The people of the star city lacked the "pomps, fashions and tournaments" which moved others to anger and useless aggression (97–97v).

Neither did Doni, in contrast to More or Campanella, provide an educational curriculum for the New World. As the children grew, they were taken away from their mothers and raised in common. When they were old enough to learn, they studied, or learned a craft, according to the natural tendency of each child (95v). However, Doni wrote nothing more about education. Doni, who placed scholars

[30] "Chi non lavora non mangia adunque." *Ibid.*, 97.

[31] "Tutto era commune, et i contadini vestivano come quei della città, perche ciascuno portava giù il suo frutto della sua fatica, & pigliava cio che gli faceva bisogno." *Ibid.*, 96.

in hell in his *Inferni* (1553), had little faith in educating men for either knowledge or virtue. Instead of developing an educational curriculum, Doni insisted upon a close tie between the arts and physical life. For example, poets in the star city performed other tasks, like fishing and hunting, in order that their writings should be close to nature. After working all day, the people came to the temple every evening to hear music. Painters and sculptors filled the land with their creations (98).

All the other Renaissance utopias placed heavy emphasis on religion, although the type of religion varied. Doni left the religious features of his New World vague. The people of the star city celebrated every seventh day as a feast day on which they all went to the temple and remained there "with great devotion" the entire day. But Doni did not indicate whether the people prayed or practiced religious rites in the temple. Similarly, all visited the temple every morning before beginning work, and again before sunset in order to "make a feast of their work" (96). But again, Doni did not elaborate how the people made a feast of their work. It is very unlikely that Doni, the renegade monk who criticized clerics, would lay any store by religion in the New World. Indeed, he came close to denying an after-life. When one of the inhabitants died, the body was treated "as a piece of coarse meat (*carnaccia*), no longer a man [but] a cadaver, and not a thing from something else. It was placed in earth in order to return to the earth something that had consumed so much time of earth. It was treated like an ordinary thing, like a natural accident." [32] The statement was not overtly unorthodox because it mentioned only man's body. Moreover, at the end of the New World dialogue, Doni added a brief Christian coda. But the tone of his remarks concerning burial, taken in the context of a primitive, natural new world in which marriage was eliminated and the deformed child dropped into a well, argued for materialism. Doni's materialist remarks in the New World were similar to comments in his later writings, the *Pitture* of 1564 and *La Lumiera* of 1567, in which he more openly suggested materialism and the rejection of a future life. [33]

Treating death as a natural accident also had beneficial social implications. Since funerals were eliminated, the financial expenses of death did not ruin the survivors. It made no difference if a widow

[32] ". . . mettilo là senza troppi *funus*, et senza menarlo atorno a processione, a farlo vedere vestito d'oro o di seta, ma come un pezzo di carnaccia, (non piu huomo, cadavero, & non cosa da qualche cosa) si metteva la in terra a rendere alla terra quello ch'egli haveva consumato tanto tempo della terra: & come cosa ordinaria si stimava come accidente naturale." *Ibid.*, 98.

[33] *La Zucca*, 296v; and Fredi Chiappelli, "Un poema inedito e sconosciuto di Anton Francesco Doni," *La Rassegna della letteratura italiana*, a. 58, serie VII, n. 4 (Oct.–Dec. 1954), 561–568.

remarried or if she did not. A dead man who had no property did not leave a will and testament for his heirs to struggle over (98v).

To summarize the message of Doni's utopia, *Savio* and *Pazzo* gave free rein to their enthusiasm for the New World in their concluding discourses. How wonderful was this city in which goods meant nothing! Goods were not possessed and hoarded, but could go where they might. Men could live and die without suffering the pangs and troubles of inheritances. Vices and vanities were gone. The people of the star city had nothing in their houses but beds for sleep. What sorrow could men experience at death when they left only this? (98–98v).

For all intents and purposes, these impassioned words completed the dialogue, but Doni added an orthodox religious coda (99). *Savio* promised to speak again of the New World, but Doni never returned to the topic. In the following dialogue of *I Mondi*, *Savio* and *Pazzo* made brief inconsequential remarks on the possibility of the truth of dreams, and went on to other subjects (99v ff).

Thus, the New World dialogue brought to fruition Doni's many criticisms of the sixteenth century. He resolved man's restlessness by devising a way of life in which all lived according to a rule. He eliminated distinctions of wealth and nobility by eliminating possessions, money, and family life. In the star city, every man earned his bread by his own sweat. No princes ruled, but all worked together to provide for man's needs. By his running commentary in the New World dialogue, Doni pointed out how provisions of the star city checked social abuses and moral vices of men. He thus outlined the primitive natural society for which he longed.

Doni's New World differed from other Renaissance utopias by the greater social and economic equality which it adopted, and by its complete negativity. Only the Garamanti of Guevara lived in an equality that approached Doni's. More, for example, had equality of property, but also a governing elite and slaves. Doni swept aside all but an extremely rudimentary structure of society. He could not use a structured government or society because he felt that these were solely means to subjugate and cheat men. The extremely negative attitude toward the *Cinquecento* world came from Doni's very low opinion of man's nature. More, by way of contrast, held a more optimistic view of man. His prescriptions for reform in the *Utopia* were often based on ingenious appeals to man's reason, as binding the slaves with chains of gold in order to educate the utopians to reject gold. More also tried to foster a spirit of service to the city in a citizen militia, and retained the family.[34] For Doni, since man was susceptible, weak, and incapable of helping himself, the only way to improve him was to remove nearly all of *Cinquecento* civilization in order

[34] *Utopia*, 75, 82, 86, 107–111, 118–129.

to live in primitive simplicity. In the New World, men had no loyalty to spouse, family, city, or next world. The people of Doni's star city had all of their wants satisfied and avoided vice, but it was a life without aspiration. As *Savio* put it, what sorrow could men have at death upon leaving this kind of world? The primary purpose of the other utopias was didactic; Doni's purpose was destructive. More, Guevara, and Agostini were counselors to kings who attempted through their books and civil careers to persuade rulers to follow a more humane Christian policy. Doni, the low-born literary adventurer, hated the *signori*. His New World was a total rejection of the *Cinquecento*.

Finally, Doni's New World dialogue was designed for a lower level of the reading public than any of the other Renaissance utopias. By his own admission, Doni wrote for all kinds of men, low and high.[35] His star city dialogue was part of a book of satire and criticism for a popular audience. His tone was direct, earthy, and pragmatic. He emphasized for his readers the practical consequences of such features as the community of goods and women. He avoided the earnestness and high tone of other utopias.

Through the commercial success of *I Mondi*, Doni's ideas reached a large number of readers in the second half of the sixteenth century. *I Mondi* was printed in Italian in 1552, 1562, 1567, 1568, 1575, 1583, 1597, and 1606. French editions appeared in 1578, 1580 (twice), and 1583. If the number of extant copies is any indication, these were large printings. Expurgation of the star city dialogue was slight and did not diminish its message. In Italy, more editions of Doni's *I Mondi* appeared in these years than did editions of More's *Utopia*.[36]

Tommaso Campanella (1568–1639) knew of Doni's star city and was inspired by Doni's suggestion in the introduction to the dialogue that the *pazzi* would prevail over the *savi* to write a sonnet on the subject. In prison in 1601, the year prior to the composition of the *Città del Sole*, he wrote a sonnet, *Senno senza forza de' savi delle genti antiche esser soggetto alla forza de' pazzi* (Good judgment without force of the wise men of ancient peoples is to be subject to the force of madmen).

[35] *La Zucca*, 112–112v, 107v–108.

[36] More's *Utopia* was printed in Latin at Florence in 1519, translated into Italian in 1548, and printed in Latin again in Milan in 1620. Book Two of the *Utopia* was paraphrased in Italian in Francesco Sansovino's *Del Governo dei Regni et delle repubbliche* in 1561, 1567, 1578, and 1607. Sansovino's paraphrase omitted the closing discourse and changed a few words to conform to censorship. The 1519 Latin edition, the 1548 Italian translation, and the 1561 edition of Sansovino's work are scarce, indicating that they probably were not large printings. See R. W. Gibson, *St. Thomas More: A Preliminary Bibliography of his Works and of Moreana to the Year 1750*. With a Bibliography of Utopiana compiled by R. W. Gibson and J. Max Patrick (New Haven and London, 1961), 3–4.

The astrologers, having foreseen in a land
a constellation that maddened men,
took counsel to flee, later
to rule soundly the injured people.
Returning afterward to do their royal deeds,
they advised these madmen with well-chosen words
to live the old way, with good food and dress.
But everyone attacked them with kicks and blows.

So that the wise men were compelled to live
as fools, in order to avoid death,
because the greatest madman carried the royal burden,

they lived with good sense only behind closed doors,
in public applauding in deed and name
another's insane and wrong desires.[37]

It is generally agreed that the sonnet refers to Doni's dialogue of the star city.[38]

Although there are similarities between Doni's New World and the *Città del Sole* regarding social criticism and holding everything in common, there are also significant differences. But Campanella's *Città del Sole* is another Renaissance utopia with its own story. Like Doni's New World, it contains its own individuality within the rich genre of Renaissance utopias.

University of Toronto

[37]   "Gli astrologi, antevista in un paese
costellazioń che gli uomini impazzire
far dovea, consigliarsi di fuggire,
per regger sani poi le genti offese.

Tornando poscia a far le regie imprese,
consigliavan que' pazzi con bel dire
il viver prisco, il buon cibo e vestire.
Ma ognun con calci e pugni a lor contese.

Talché, sforzati i savi a viver come
gli stolti usavan, per schifar la morte,
chè 'l piú gran pazzo avea le regie some,
vissero sol col senno a chiuse porte,
in pubblico applaudendo in fatti e nome
all'altrui voglie forsennate e torte."

Tommaso Campanella, *La Città del Sole e Poesie* (Milano, 1962), 76. Luigi Firpo, *Ricerche Campanelliane* (Firenze, 1947), 255, dates the sonnet in the second half of 1601.

[38] The lone dissenter is Romano Amerio, who affirms that the sonnet was autobiographical, that Campanella referred to the madness he feigned in order to live. The two interpretations are not mutually exclusive, as the sonnet could refer to Doni's dialogue as well as contain a reflection on Campanella's own lot. See *Opere di Giordano Bruno e di Tommaso Campanella*, La Letteratura Italiana, vol. 33 (Milano-Napoli, 1956), 799, footnote.

V

Five Italian Occurrences of Umanista, *1540-1574*

DESPITE the repeated use of the term 'humanist' by modern scholars, few references to the term have been located in the fifteenth and sixteenth centuries. Campana has found nine Italian uses of the term in manuscript and printed sources from 1512 to 1588. In addition he has noted two sixteenth-century French uses, one English reference, and four appearances in the Latin text of the *Epistolae obscurorum virorum*.[1] Paul O. Kristeller has located the word in a letter of 1490 by the rector of the University of Pisa, in sixteenth-century university documents of Bologna and Ferrara, in John Florio's Italian-English dictionary of 1598, and in a Spanish document of the late sixteenth or early seventeenth century.[2] Eugenio Garin adds an example from a document of the *Studio di Pisa* of 1525.[3] This short article will contribute five additional vernacular uses of *umanista* in Italy between 1540 and 1574.

Campana and Kristeller agree that *umanista* denoted one who was involved in the teaching or study of the disciplines known in the Renaissance as the humanities. Campana has argued that, in its original sense, *umanista* qualified a person 'as a public or private teacher of classical literature, of the chair of *humanitas* or *umanità*.' He also points to a later, secondary use of the term, as a student of classical learning who was not necessarily also a teacher. This second use of *umanista* was current in 1515 and 'securely established' in 1544.[4] Kristeller argues that the term *umanista* originated in the latter half of the fifteenth century 'in the slang of university students and gradually penetrated into official usage.' *Umanista* signified the teacher or representative of the *studia humanitatis*, defined by Kristeller as 'grammar, rhetoric, history, poetry, and moral philosophy, and the study of each of these subjects was understood to include the reading and interpretation of its standard ancient writers in Latin and, to a lesser extent, in Greek.'[5]

---

[1] Augusto Campana, 'The Origin of the Word Humanist,' *Jour. of the Warburg and Courtauld Inst.*, IX (1946), pp. 60–73.

[2] *Renaissance Thought: the Classic, Scholastic, and Humanistic Strains* (New York, 1961), p. 160, n. 61.

[3] *Medioevo e Rinascimento, studi e ricerche*, 2nd ed. (Bari, 1961), p. 7 n.2.

[4] P. 66.

[5] Pp. 111, 10. Kristeller's views are repeated in his *Eight Philosophers of the Italian Renaissance* (Stanford, Cal., 1964), pp. 149–156, and elsewhere.

318

For Garin, humanism was essentially a new vision of man on earth which matured in men of action outside the schools as well as in scholars and teachers. It was an approach to man as a participant in the *vita civile*, to man who is dedicated to a life of service to city and family, and who accepts earthly values. Garin's definition of humanism puts heavy emphasis on philology and history, but he does not exclude speculative philosophy, including Florentine Platonism.[6] In the 1525 reference, he found *umanista* and *Phylosopho* to be in close proximity but not, however, interchangeable.[7]

Of the five uses of *umanista* that I have found, the first appearance, chronologically, occurs in a letter of October 5, 1540, by Francesco Sansovino (1521–83). The son of the sculptor Jacopo Sansovino, Francesco spent most of his life in Venice as an author, translator, editor, and printer, bringing to the vernacular reading public well over 100 works. He is probably best known for his many historical works.[8] Despite his ultimate literary career, his father sent Francesco to Padua to study law. Francesco soon discovered that he did not like law, and much preferred literature and good times. The conflict between father and son reached a crisis in September 1540 when Jacopo cut off his son's allowance. Francesco wrote to Pietro Aretino, asking him at first for money (unsuccessfully) and then begging him to intercede with his father. In a letter of October 5, 1540, Sansovino lamented that his father had abused him because he wished to enter the *Academia* where 'not only do they treat the profession of the humanists but ours as well through the declamations that continually are given there' (. . . se non mi si dicessi che l'aver io voluto entrar nell'Academia dove sono de più infimi di me, e dove non solo si tratta della profession de gl'umanisti, ma della nostra ancora per le declamazioni che continuamente vi si fanno).[9]

---

[6] For Garin's view, see *Italian Humanism, Philosophy and Civic Life in the Renaissance*, tr. by Peter Munz (Oxford, 1965), pp. 1–17; *L'educazione in Europa (1400–1600), problemi e programmi* (Bari, 1957), pp. 30–31; *Medioevo e Rinascimento*, pp. 6–7, and elsewhere.

[7] *Medioevo e Rinascimento*, p. 7, n. 2.

[8] The most complete source on Sansovino's life and works is E. A. Cicogna, *Delle iscrizioni veneziane raccolte da E. A. C.* (Venezia, 1834), IV, 31–91. See also Giovanni Sforza, 'Francesco Sansovino e le sue opere storiche,' *Memorie della R. Accademia delle Scienze di Torino*, serie II, XLVII (1897), 27–66; and Guido Pusinich, 'Un poligrafo veneziano del cinquecento,' *Pagine Istriane*, VIII (1910), 121–130, 145–151.

[9] The letter, with six others from Sansovino to Aretino, is in *Lettere scritte al signor Pietro Aretino da Molti Signori . . . Divise in due libri* (In Vinegia, Per Francesco Marcolini, MDLI), I, 328 ff., as cited in Cicogna, p. 81, with the quotation. Here the quotation is cited from the critical edition, *Lettere scritte a Pietro Aretino emendate per cura di Teodorico Landoni* (Bologna, 1873), I, pt. 2, p. 209.

The first point to note is that Sansovino spoke of the 'profession of the humanists.' However, one cannot ascertain exactly what this was. Sansovino differentiated the profession of the humanists from 'our' profession, viz., the profession of Sansovino and Aretino. This, of course, was authoring vernacular literature. As early as 1536 Sansovino had written Petrarchan sonnets.[10] In 1540 he published some *capitoli* in a collection which included Aretino and Lodovico Dolce. Since Sansovino's name occurred on the title page with his more distinguished elders, and the work was reprinted in 1541, he had achieved some professional success in literature and could identify himself with Aretino.[11] It is not likely that 'our' profession would be the legal profession. Aretino was not a lawyer, and Sansovino did not refer to himself as a lawyer in the letter. Neither did Sansovino use the editorial 'we' at any point in the letter.

The *Academia* to which Sansovino referred was the *Accademia degli Infiammati*,[12] founded in 1540, but it is difficult to pinpoint which declamations of the *Infiammati* would be included in the profession of the humanists. In the beginning the subject matter of the *Accademia* included many branches of learning. The academicians read Homer, Theocritus, Vergil, Horace, and other poets, and they heard lessons in theology, philosophy, and the liberal arts, presumably studying Latin and Greek as well as the vernacular. Under the principate of Sperone Speroni (begun in 1542) the *Infiammati* excluded theology, laws, and medicine, in order to study philosophy and to a lesser extent literature, exclusively in the vernacular.[13] It is clear from Sansovino's reference that *umanisti* had a learned profession and that it was not that of professional authors of vernacular literature, but it is not clear with which branch or branches of learning he associated humanists.

The next reference occurs in 1549 in a work of Lodovico Domenichi

[10] Pusinich, 'Un poligrafo veneziano,' pp. 125, 128.

[11] *Capitoli del S. Pietro Aretino, di M. Lodovico Dolce, di M. Francesco Sansovino, et di altri acutissimi ingegni* ([Venezia] Per Curtio Navò e fratelli, MDXL). Sansovino's *capitoli* are on ff. 34–35^v, 41–53^v.

[12] The *Accademia degli Infiammati* endured until ca. 1550, and Sansovino was listed as a participant in 1542. See Michele Maylender, *Storia delle Accademie d'Italia* (Bologna, 1929), III, 266–270.

[13] Count Fortunato Martinengo, one of the earliest members and perhaps a founder, stressed the eclectic nature of the early months of the *Infiammati* in contrast to the more specialized program under Speroni. See *Quattro libri della lingua Thoscana di M. Bernardino Tomitano* (In Padova. Appresso Marcantonio Olmo. MDLXX), I, 6–10. Also see Maylender, III, 269.

(1515–64). Born in Piacenza and living subsequently mostly in Venice and Florence, Domenichi was another popular vernacular translator, editor, and author who wrote plays, dialogues, and *facezie*.[14] In his *La nobiltà delle donne* (1549) Domenichi advised neither *Astrologi* nor *Humanisti* to marry. ('Io veramente non consiglierei mai ne gli Astrologi, ne gli Humanisti, che prendessero moglie.')[15] After disposing of the astrologers, Domenichi elaborated his reasons for counseling humanists not to marry. He did this with a page of amusing abuse on the theme that while humanists successfully pursued their studies in schools, at home they were failures as husbands and fathers. While the *popolo de grammatici* preached 'with terrible cries' Homer and Vergil in their schools, at home they suffered the anger of their wives.[16] The second speaker agreed. 'Men draw a nice fruit from studies and letters'; they criticize in school the deeds of Venus and Mars but later in bed 'verify in act' the fables of the gods. The first speaker resumed: 'these half men' generate monster children.[17] He continued: philosophers make poor spouses because they spend half their nights contemplating Ideas and separate substances, imagining a Utopia or a republic of Plato, and searching the 'crystalline heaven.' They dispute with the friars whether simple fornication is a sin, and after nine months they father a monster. By way of contrast, in the following page the same speaker advised that *dottori leggisti* and *medici* might take wives.[18]

[14] On Domenichi's life, see A. Salza, 'Intorno a Lodovico Domenichi,' in *Rass. Bibl. della Lett. Ital.*, VII (1899), 204–209.

[15] *La nobiltà delle donne di M. Lodovico Domenichi* (In Vinetia Appresso Gabriel Giolito di Ferrarii. MDXLIX), f. 89ᵛ. It was reprinted in 1551 and 1554. This reference is also noted in my article, 'The Rejection of Learning in Mid-*Cinquecento* Italy,' *Studies in the Renaissance*, XIII (1966), 238 n. 33.

[16] Al popolo de grammatici suol le piu volte avenire, che mentre eglino con terribili grida predica Homero o Virgilio alla sua scuola . . . fa prova in casa sua dell'ira & dell'armi della moglie (ff. 89ᵛ–90).

[17] Bel frutto traggono dunque gli huomini dagli studi & dalle lettere: poi che dichiarando essi nelle scuole i furti di Venere & di Marte, altri nel letto suo verifica in atto queste favole tali . . . . Aggiungesi che questi mezzi huomini ingenerano le piu volte figliuoli stropiati [sic] & poco meno che mostri (f. 90). In my previous reference to these lines, 'The Rejection of Learning,' p. 239, n. 38, *gli huomini dagli studi & dalle lettere* were seen (incorrectly I now believe) as the subject of the sentence.

[18] Stanno i philosophi tutta la notte a vegghiare, mangiano poco, mentre ch'abbracciano la moglie, mentre si reputano prodi & valorosi guerrieri nelle battaglie amorose, stanno allhora contemplando le idee, & le sostanze separate; imaginansi la Utopia o una republica di Platone; cercano il cielo cristallino; disputano co i frati se la semplice fornicatione è peccato; & cosi avviene che dopo i nove mesi ne nasce poi qualche mostro, o cosa contrafatta (f. 90). See also f. 90ᵛ.

Clearly humanists were neither astrologers, legists, nor medical men. Nevertheless, for Domenichi humanist was a broad term which seemed to include both grammarians and philosophers who had contact with the classics in schools. The grammarians taught Homer and Vergil in schools. The philosophers studied Plato, and the most likely place for the philosophers to dispute with the friars would be an academic locale. In each case Domenichi contrasted their scholarly activity with their behavior at home with their wives and noted the baleful results.[19] His use of *umanisti* seems to support Campana and Kristeller on the academic ties of humanists. On the other hand, Domenichi included philosophers (who were not just moral philosophers but metaphysicians and Platonists as well) within the term humanist. On this point Domenichi's passage may support Garin.

The third use of *umanista* comes from Sansovino again, in 1554. After the crisis of 1540, Sansovino bowed to his father's wishes and completed his law education. He may have practiced law for a short period, but then he devoted himself to the life of a Venetian *poligrafo*. However, in 1554 he published his *L'avvocato*, a dialogue concerning the path to follow in order to become a successful lawyer in Venice. Sansovino was not being facetious or hypocritical; the work was one of several practical guides he wrote. A better-known example was his *Secretario*, which presented useful advice on how to be a good secretary, including a lengthy discussion of the manner of writing letters for every occasion.

In the *Avvocato*, an older man explained to a young boy who wished to become a lawyer the path that he must travel. His education should begin as soon as he can understand letters, and he should study hard 'to make himself a good humanist, that is, experienced in the things of the Latin language.' (Io voglio adunque che subito che 'l fanciullo è capace di lettere, che si procuri con ogni diligenza e con ogni studio di farlo buon umanista, cioè pratico nelle cose della lingua latina. . . .)[20] The boy should learn from good teachers, not from pedants.

---

[19] Connecting grammarians and philosophers are the lines dealing with the 'nice fruit' that men draw from studies and letters, and *questi mezzi huomini* who generate monster children. 'These half men' may have referred to the grammarians who preceded, the philosophers who followed, or meant men generally who studied the classics.

[20] *L'Avocato dialogo nel quale si discorre tutta l'Auttorità che hanno i Magistrati di Venetia. Con la pratica delle cose giudiciali de Palazzo.* (In Vinegia, Appresso Lelio Bariletto, & fratelli. 1566), f. 8ᵛ. Copy in Columbia University. The first edition was 1554, followed by editions of 1559, 1566, 1586, and 1606, all printed in Venice. (See Cicogna, IV, 71.) See also the critical edition, *Francesco Sansovino. L'avvocato e il segretario*, a cura di Piero Calamandrei (Firenze, 1942), p. 101. The following references are to the 1942 edition.

322

This instance of *umanista* is Campana's secondary use, that of a student of classical (Latin) learning. Where does Latin learning fit within the total educational program of the young aspiring lawyer? After becoming a *buon umanista*, the boy should study Greek so that he could read the noble authors of that language, and then mathematics and philosophy, especially moral philosophy. Then he went on to civil laws. These disciplines (Latin, Greek, mathematics, and moral philosophy) comprised for Sansovino *buone e belle lettere di umanità*. Three pages after the reference to *umanista*, the elder speaker discussed the signs by which a concerned father could tell if his son had the aptitude to be a successful lawyer. Sansovino, perhaps thinking of his own unhappy experience, stressed that the father should not push the boy into something he did not like. But if he did show an interest, was modest, virtuous, and hardworking, the boy should learn *buone e belle lettere di umanità* from a good teacher, and follow the outline previously given. (Comunemente si suole aver speranza del giovane modesto, e a cui piace la lode; e che vedendo il compagno trapassarlo in cose onorate s'adira; e che desiando perpetuo onore si schiva dall'ozio. Ad un figlio tale, voglio io che il padre sollecito faccia apprendere buone e belle lettere di umanità da buon precettore, e dovendo farsi avvocato osservi l'ordine ch'io vi dirò.)[21] Sansovino's *buone e belle lettere di umanità* is close to Kristeller's *studia humanitatis*.

To complete his education, Sansovino insisted that the boy should become an honest, virtuous man experienced in worldly affairs. He should acquire a knowledge of the habits and customs of men, and the 'actions of the world.' One learned this through maturity and experience, and Christ was a better teacher than Aristotle, Cicero, or Seneca. Indeed, natural philosophy based on the ancient philosophers was of no value. All the rest of the above (Latin, Greek, mathematics, moral philosophy, knowledge of worldly affairs, and virtue), however, were necessary to the *vita civile*.[22] In this program the essential first step was to become a good humanist, i.e., skilled in Latin.

The fourth use of the word comes from Giovanni Andrea Gilio da Fabriano (fl. 1550–80), in 1564. An ecclesiastic born in Fabriano, Gilio

[21] *L'avvocato*, pp. 102, 104.

[22] *Ibid.*, pp. 109–110. Tutte queste cose e altre ch'io lascio addietro per ora, e che son necessarie alla vita civile, si apprendono da quei notabili autori, i quali per la cognizione delle cose nobili e belle aggiunsero lume al chiarissimo e splendido lume della eloquenza. *Ibid.*, pp. 110–111.

was prior of a monastery in Ascoli Piceno and active in the diocese of Camerino in 1579. He was the author of five works and a translation, including a discourse on the various words to designate 'city,' published in 1564.[23] In the middle of an effort to trace the development from *civium unitas* to *civitas* to *città*, Gilio broke off his discussion with the comment that he had gone as far as he wished to go in this question, and 'I will leave such a quarrel to the humanists.' He then stated his conclusion as the commonly accepted opinion. (. . . sia però come voglia, che io non intendo di far sopra cio questione; ma lascerò tal lite a gl'humanisti, dicendo solo, che a me piace l'Etimologia, che civitas detta sia civium unitas per le diffinitioni, che communemente gli sono date.)[24]

For Gilio, *humanisti* were experts in etymology with particular competence in Latin. The degree and specialization of expertise is difficult to determine. He may have meant that humanists were generally competent in the field of language as any scholar or teacher would be. Or Gilio may have meant specialists who composed large tomes on minute points. He obviously did not call himself a humanist, but his own detailed discussion of *città* and *civitas* demonstrated that he possessed enough confidence in his own ability to correct Leonardo Bruni. Gilio's use of *humanisti* fits within Campana's definition of a Latin scholar but lacks reference to an academic locale.

Finally, Gilio took a disdainful attitude toward humanists, implying that they were inclined to carry their scholarly quarrels beyond the point that a sensible man would go. Similarly, in 1545 or 1546, Benedetto Varchi blamed the low opinion in which humanists were held on the tendency of fifteenth-century men of letters to quarrel over matters of little importance or not in doubt.[25]

The fifth occurrence of *umanista* comes from Sansovino in 1574. In that year he published his translation of Jacopo Filippo da Bergamo's chronicle of history from Creation to 1490. Sansovino continued the

[23] Gilio composed religious works published in 1550, 1563, and 1573; a work of poetry in 1580; and a translation of a life of St. Athanasius in 1559. These were published in Venice, with the exception of the *Dialogi* cited below. See Filippo Vecchietti, *Biblioteca Picena o sia notizie istoriche delle opere e degli scrittori Piceni* (Osimo, 1796), V, 91–93.

[24] *Due Dialogi di M. Giovanni Andrea Gilio da Fabriano. Nel primo de' quali si ragiona de la parti Morali, e Civili appertenenti à Letterati Cortigiani . . . Nel secondo si ragiona de gli errori de Pittori circa l'historie . . . Con un discorso sopra la parola Urbe, Città, Colonia, Municipio, Prefettura, Foro, Conciliabolo, Oppido, Terra, Castello, Villa, Pago, Borgo, e qual sia la vera Città* (In Camerino per Antonio Gioioso. MDLXIIII), f. 126.

[25] Campana, 'Origin of the Word Humanist,' pp. 64–65.

chronicle with his own *Sopplimento* which narrated Italian and European events through early 1574. In the *Sopplimento* Sansovino interpolated sections on famous men of learning, the arts, and politics. In one of these he wrote that 'Lazaro Bonamico was a famous humanist.' Sansovino continued with a short description of Bonamico. He gave a new understanding to Cicero and read for a long time at Padua. Bonamico liked to play cards all night but still managed to go to school in the morning for his lecture. (Lazaro Bonamico da Bassano fu famoso huomanista. [sic] haveva impedita la lingua, con tutto ciò davasi nuovi sensi alle cose di Cicerone & d'altri che fu tenuto maraviglioso. Lesse lungamente in Padova, dove anco si morì. Ma sopra tutto si dilettava estremamente del giuoco a carte chiamato a trappola, al quale attese qualche volta le notti intere, non mancando poi la mattina alle scuole del suo solito officio nella lettura.)[26]

Bonamico (1479–1552) was a well-known teacher at Padua and champion of Latin against the vernacular. Born in Bassano, he taught in Bologna and became an avid Ciceronian with Jacopo Sadoleto at Rome. After the sack of Rome, Bonamico moved to Padua, where he was appointed to read Latin and Greek at the *Studio di Padova* at the handsome salary of 300 gold *scudi*.[27] His works were few and only published posthumously, but he acquired fame as a teacher of Latin eloquence.[28] In Speroni's 'Dialogo delle lingue' Bonamico was the speaker who argued for Latin and, to a lesser extent, Greek, against the *volgare*. For Bonamico, the vernacular was corrupted Latin, and the Italian loss of Latin as a spoken language was as serious as the loss of political liberty.[29]

This occurrence of *umanista* is a clear example of the humanist as a teacher of Latin. Sansovino named Bonamico as a humanist, mentioned that he interpreted Cicero, and taught in the schools at Padua. Speroni

---

[26] Sansovino's *Sopplimento* has a separate title page dated 1574 within the *Cronica Universale* but the paging is continuous. *Della Cronica Universale del Mondo chiamata gia sopplimento delle croniche Parte Terza. Tratta da diversi scrittori Latini & Volgari, & aggiunta di nuovo al sopplimento, da M. Francesco Sansovino. Nella qual si contengono tutte le cose avvenute dall'anno 1490. fino al presente 1574. cosi in Italia come fuori, & per tutte l'altre Provincie* (In Venetia, MDLXXIIII), in *Sopplimento delle croniche universali del Mondo di F. Iacopo Filippo da Bergamo. Tradotto nuovamente da M. Francesco Sansovino* (In Venetia, MDLXXV), f. 702 (misnumbered 704). It was reprinted in 1581 in Venice.

[27] *Opere di M. Sperone Speroni degli Alvarotti* (Venezia, 1740), I, 166.

[28] Bonamico's works included *Carmina* (1572), *Epistolae, Orationes*, and *Concetto della lingua latina per imparare insieme la grammatica e la lingua di Cicerone* (1562).

[29] *Opere di Speroni*, I, 166–201. On Bonamico see Giuseppe Toffanin, *Il Cinquecento*, 6th ed. (Milano, 1960), pp. 16–18, 32 n. 24.

verified that he was a well-paid teacher of Latin and Greek, and a champion of Latin. Moreover, Sansovino's use of *umanista* in 1574 was the same as his earlier uses.

It is difficult to come to conclusions when the evidence consists of five examples, but the following is tentatively offered. Four of the references are clearly tied to Latin, and in 1574 Sansovino names as a humanist a champion of Latin. Domenichi's reference does not exclude the possibility that the humanist was a Latin teacher or scholar. Four of the references relate humanists to schools or to a profession. Gilio's example does not, although a school or university would be a logical place to find an etymologist. Sansovino's 1554 reference clearly links the humanist to the *studia humanitatis*. Domenichi's reference involves some part of the *studia humanitatis* (teaching Homer and Vergil) but also includes philosophers. Finally, two of the citations are uncomplimentary. On the whole, these five Italian uses of *umanista* support the conclusions of Campana and Kristeller.

These five occurrences were in no way the product of a systematic search. Indeed, I came upon them by chance. Undoubtedly other examples will be found to broaden our knowledge of the meaning of *umanista* in fifteenth- and sixteenth-century Italy.

UNIVERSITY OF TORONTO

VI

THE CONCEPT OF HUMANIST
IN CINQUECENTO ITALY

Much scholarly discussion on the meaning and significance of Italian Renaissance humanism has ensued in the past twenty-five years. The works of Hans Baron, Eugenio Garin, and Paul Kristeller demonstrate the important role that the understanding of humanism plays in the interpretation of the Renaissance. These as well as other interpretations involve the understanding of such terms as *studia humanitatis* and *vita civile* because these terms meant much to Renaissance man and were often discussed in the fifteenth and sixteenth centuries. Scholars often employ two other terms as well: humanist and humanism. The latter is a nineteenth-century coinage not yet located in a Renaissance context. Scholars today either use these terms in a general way or define them carefully within the context of their discussions, and do not rest their argument on Renaissance definitions of these terms.

«Humanist» (*umanista* and more commonly *humanista* in the Cinquecento) originated in the Renaissance, and by the second half of the Cinquecento appeared reasonably often and had a fairly clear meaning for Italians. The purpose of this article is to examine the use and understanding of the term humanist in the second half of the Cinquecento with six occurrences and a discourse on humanists, hitherto unnoted.

Two scholars, Augusto Campana and Kristeller, agree that *umanista* denoted one who was involved in the teaching or study of the *studia humanitatis*. Campana has argued that in its original sense, *umanista* qualified a person « as a public or private teacher of classical literature, of the chair of *humanitas* or *humanità* ». He also points to a later, secondary use of the term, as a student of classical learning who was not necessarily also a teacher [1]. Kristeller argues that the term *umanista* originated in the latter half of the fifteenth century « in the slang of university students and gradually penetrated into official usage ». *Umanista* signified

---

[1] Augusto Campana, « The Origin of the Word Humanist », *Journal of the Warburg and Courtauld Institutes*, IX (1946), 66.

the teacher or representative of the *studia humanitatis*, defined by Kristeller as « grammar, rhetoric, history, poetry, and moral philosophy, and the study of each of these subjects was understood to include the reading and interpretation of its standard ancient writers in Latin and, to a lesser extent, in Greek »[2]. Kristeller adds that individual humanists were interested in other disciplines as well. For Garin, however, a humanist was one who shared the outlook of Renaissance humanism, which is seen as a new vision of man on earth to be found in men of action outside the schools as well as in scholars and teachers. Man was a participant in the *vita civile*, one who dedicated his life in service to city and family, and who accepted earthly values. Garin's definition of humanism puts heavy emphasis on philology and history, but he does not exclude speculative philosophy, including Florentine Platonism[3]. Hence, for Garin a humanist might engage in any activity but was disposed to view man in a certain way.

Campana has located nine Italian uses of humanist in manuscript and printed sources from 1512 to 1588 which support his argument. Kristeller has located the word in a letter of 1490 by the rector of the University of Pisa, and in sixteenth-century university documents of Bologna and Ferrara. In addition, these two scholars have found nine English, French, German, and Spanish references. Garin, on the other hand, adds an example from a document of the *Studio* of Pisa of 1525 in which *umanista* and *Phylosopho* were in close proximity but not interchangeable[4].

I have located five additional occurrences, and noted them in a previous article[5]. In 1540 the Venetian author Francesco

---

[2] *Renaissance Thought: the Classic, Scholastic, and Humanistic Strains* (New York, 1961), pp. 10, 111. Kristeller's views are repeated in other works.

[3] For Garin's view, see *Italian Humanism, Philosophy and Civic Life in the Renaissance*, tr. by Peter Munz (Oxford, 1965), pp. 1-17; *L'educazione in Europa (1400-1600), problemi e programmi* (Bari, 1957), pp. 30-31; *Medioevo e Rinascimento, studi e ricerche*. 2nd ed. (Bari, 1961), pp. 6-7.

[4] Campana, « The Origin of the Word Humanist », pp. 60-73; Kristeller, *Renaissance Thought*, p. 160, n. 61; Garin, *Medioevo e Rinascimento*, p. 7, n. 2. Cf. Marcel Françon, « Humanisme », *Renaissance Quarterly*, XXI (1968), 300-303.

[5] Paul F. Grendler, « Five Italian Occurrences of *Umanista*, 1540-1574 », *Renaissance Quarterly*, XX (1967), 317-325.

Sansovino (1521-83) used the term to refer to an undesignated learned profession. Lodovico Domenichi (1515-64), an author of popular literature, used the term in a book of 1549 to mean grammarians and philosophers who had contact with the classics in schools. Since he included metaphysicians and Platonists within the term his reference supported Garin. In 1554 Sansovino used humanist to refer to a young student of classical Latin. This was the first step in the *studia humanitatis* which led, in the end, to an educated man who lived the *vita civile*. Giovanni Andrea Gilio da Fabriano (fl. 1550-80) in 1564 called humanists those who were expert in etymology with particular competence in Latin. Finally, Sansovino named Lazzaro Bonamico (1479-1552), a champion of Latin who taught at Padua and interpreted Cicero, as a humanist in 1574. On the whole, these references supported the view of Campana and Kristeller.

The first three new occurrences are in the correspondence of the papal nuncio to Venice, Monsignor Giovanni Antonio Facchinetti (1519-91) who later became Pope Innocent IX. Born in Bologna, Facchinetti was nuncio from May 1566 to the end of June 1573. An experienced papal diplomat who served as vicar to Cardinal Alessandro Farnese in Avignon, and governor of Parma after the death of Pier Luigi Farnese, Facchinetti was « molto literato » according to the Venetian ambassador, and his correspondence shows him to have been an able and energetic nuncio [6]. Writing to Rome on August 31, 1566, Facchinetti reported on his inquiry with the Holy Office in Venice concerning Publio Francesco Spinola who was in a Venetian prison. He had learned that the prisoner was « a Milanese, a poet, a humanist, and unfrocked ». (« Egli è un milanese, poeta, humanista e sfratato »). Facchinetti added that Spinola had been in prison for 28 months, was a relapsed heretic because he had abjured heresy more than once in Milan but that he continued to hold various heretical opinions. The zealous nuncio wished to examine his case further because « if anyone can have information on heretics, certainly this man would because as a

---

[6] *Nunziature di Venezia*, VIII (Istituto Storico Italiano per l'età moderna e contemporanea, Fonti per la Storia d'Italia, 65), a cura di Aldo Stella (Rome, 1963), IX-X.

humanist he read to many here in Venice and associated with many here and elsewhere » [7].

Christened Francesco but adding the Latinized Publio, Spinola was born in Como c. 1520, although later considered a Milanese. After leaving an unidentified religious order and being exiled from Milan, he lived in Bergamo, Brescia, Venice, and Padua, often attached to noble households. On several occasions he taught: in 1560 he began the academic year in Brescia where he interpreted *Pro Milone* and other works of Cicero, and in the following year he supervised the literary education of the sons of the Venetian noble, Leonardo Mocenigo. Then, in or about 1562, he taught the son of the Venetian printer Gabriel Giolito while he worked for four months as a corrector for his press. All his published works were in Latin: in 1558 he completed and published a Latin translation of the psalms begun by Marco Antonio Flaminio; his collected poetry was published in 1563; and in 1562 his method for the correction of the Julian calendar. In July 1564 he was arrested for heresy, and, refusing to recant, he was executed by drowning on January 31, 1567 [8].

Concerned with the role which humanists could play in the spread of heresy, Facchinetti returned to the subject in a letter of May 24, 1567, and used « humanist » again. He reported to Rome that due to « the contagion of heresy being born of these humanists and schoolmasters », the Holy Office had resolved to publish a decree enforcing religious loyalty on them [9]. Ever fearful of the expansion of ecclesiastical jurisdiction, the Venetian government protested but in the end the nuncio arrived at an arrangement satisfactory to Rome. He reported in January 1569 that schoolmasters (omitting reference to humanists), would not be able to teach letters, music, arithmetic, or anything

---

[7] *Ibid.*, p. 100. « Et se alcuno può haver notitia d'heretici è verisimile che costui l'habbia perché come humanista ha letto a molti qui in Vinetia et praticato con molti e qui et altrove ».

[8] Pio Paschini, « Un umanista disgraziato nel Cinquecento: Publio Francesco Spinola », *Nuovo archivio veneto*, N. S., XXXVII (1919), 65-186.

[9] *Nunziature di Venezia*, p. 220. « Nascendo la contagione dell'heresia da questi humanisti et mastri di scuola, il tribunale dell'Inquisitione era venuto in risolutione di publicare il decreto ch'io mando qui inchiuso ».

else in Venice, publicly or privately, without examination and approval by the Patriarch [10].

Facchinetti called Spinola a humanist, noted that as a humanist he read to many people, and therefore wished to regulate humanists and schoolmasters. The third reference probably indicates that humanists, like schoolmasters, taught [11]. Since Spinola did teach, as well as comment on Cicero and publish exclusively in Latin, the teaching material of Spinola as a humanist was probably Latin literature. But, it must be added, if Spinola was a humanist because he read and taught the Latin classics, his intellectual interests were not limited to this. He also composed Latin poetry [12], had enough knowledge of mathematics to write on the problem of the calendar, and had a religious interest strong enough to translate the Psalms and to die for his beliefs.

The next occurrence of *humanista* is in a treatise on the education of a prince written in 1571 by Girolamo Muzio (1496-1576) [13]. Born in Capodistria of humble parentage, Muzio made a successful career in the service of many noble houses and as a prolific author of poetry, courtly literature, history, and religious polemic. For the tutor of a young prince Muzio rejected *letterati*, philosophers, medical and legal scholars, and mathematicians, before considering professors of the humanities. These he also rejected because they had a tendency to tyrannize their young charges in their schools [14]. Printed in the margin

---

[10] *Ibid.*, p. 481.

[11] When the nuncio spoke of humanists and schoolmasters, he saw them as similar insofar as heresy emanated from both and he wished to regulate both. Although he did not mention regulation of humanists as such when he returned to the subject in January 1569, it is possible that humanists were included in the decree as teachers of letters.

[12] Facchinetti probably differentiated humanist from poet, as his first statement described Spinola as Milanese, poet, humanist, and unfrocked monk. Since Milanese, humanist, and unfrocked monk refer to different aspects of existence, then poet should also mean a distinct activity.

[13] *Avvertimenti morali del Mutio Iustinopolitano* (Venice, 1572). Some copies carry 1571 as the date. It was not reprinted. Cf. Paolo Giaxich, *Vita di Girolamo Muzio Giustinopolitano* (Trieste, 1847).

[14] *Avvertimenti*, p. 4. « Nè a professori di studii di humanità è da dare cotale impresa, che (per non ne dir altro) essi essendo usati signoreggiare i teneri fanciulli nelle schuole ... ».

as a guide to the content, was *Humanisti*, along with *Philosofo*, *Medici*, *Leggisti*, and *Mathematici*. Muzio went on to cite from antiquity a « maestro di schuola » and a « maestro di lettere latine » who tyrannized their pupils. He concluded that he preferred an honest man of good habits who was experienced in the « things of the world », and who was « accustomed to practice with men and in courts », to any man of learning for the prince's tutor [15].

Whoever added the marginal note — probably the author or an unknown editor — identified a humanist as a professor of the humanities who taught children in a school. The more interesting point is that Muzio did not want a humanist to tutor the young prince because, as he later explained, he wished the boy to be taught « things » not « words ». Muzio was not completely opposed to books, but wanted the boy to learn from them heroic examples and moral doctrines rather than grammatical details [16]. He exhibited a hostility toward humanists to be found in some other Italians in the middle and second half of the sixteenth century [17].

Another use of humanist was by Mambrino Roseo da Fabriano (c. 1500-c. 1584), a prolific historian and translator [18]. In a history of the period 1513-1559, first published in 1562, which was part three of Giovanni Tarcagnota's *Istorie del mondo*, Roseo discussed the damage to scholars wrought by the *Index of Prohibited Books* issued by Paul IV in 1559. Every citizen had to take both Latin and vernacular books to the Inquisition, and Roseo opined that the *Index* was very injurious to the booksellers. Further, no learned man of any profession — doctors, legists, and humanists — was spared this harm [19]. Here humanists were

---

[15] *Ibid.*, p. 5.

[16] *Ibid.*, p. 18.

[17] See Paul F. Grendler, *Critics of the Italian World, 1530-1560: Anton Francesco Doni, Nicolò Franco, and Ortensio Lando* (Madison, 1969), pp. 136-161.

[18] For Roseo, see Romualdo Canavari, « Sulle opere di Mambrino Roseo da Fabriano », in *L'assedio di Firenze di Mambrino Roseo di Fabriano*, ed. Ant. Dom. Pierrugues (Florence, 1894), pp. XI-XLIX; and Francesco Ant. Soria, *Memorie storico-critiche degli storici napolitani* (Naples, 1781-82), pp. 531-33.

[19] *Delle istorie del mondo, parte terza. Aggiunte da M. Mambrino Roseo da Fabriano alle istorie di M. Giovanni Tarcagnota* (Venice, 1585), p. 603. « Fu estimato il danno di questi libri nuovi di librari con i vecchi, che ogni

members of a learned profession comparable to legists and doctors, but Roseo did not elaborate.

A use of humanist in a similar context appeared in the first edition of the *Piazza universale* (1585) of Tommaso Garzoni (March 1549-June 8, 1589). From Bagnacavallo, he studied law and logic at Ferrara and Siena, and later philosophy and theology, taking the habit of the Lateran Congregation of the Canons Regular at the monastery of Santa Maria di Porto in Ravenna in 1566. His major works include the *Piazza universale*, *Teatro de' vari e diversi cervelli* (1583), *L'hospidale de' pazzi* (1586), and *Sinagoga de gl'Ignoranti* (1589). They are storehouses of information on his period and enjoyed great popularity, appearing in many editions, including Spanish, Latin, German, and English translations [20]. The *Piazza universale* is a discussion of all of man's professions including that of the *librari*. The booksellers belonged to a noble profession because, among other reasons, they were always in the company of literate and virtuous persons: theologians, jurists, doctors of medicine, humanists, and so on [21]. As with Roseo, a humanist was a member of a learned profession, comparable to a legal or medical scholar.

In the 1587 edition of the *Piazza universale*, Garzoni added a « Discorso de gli Humanisti », the most extensive discussion

---

cittadino, così volgari, come Latini portava alla casa della inquisizione, di grandissima importanza: ne fu niuno litterato di qualunque professione, che fosse da questo danno essentato, medici, legisti, & umanisti, e d'ogni sorte ». The book appeared in 1562, and was reprinted in 1573, 1580, 1585, 1592, and 1598, always in Venice. The passage remains unaltered in the editions examined (all except 1562 and 1580).

[20] On Garzoni, see Girolamo Ghilini, *Teatro d'huomini letterati* (Milan, 1633), I, 416-17; Jean Pierre Niceron, *Mémoires pour servir à l'histoire des hommes illustres dans la République des lettres* (Paris, 1736), XXXVI, 59-65; Benedetto Croce, « Pagine di Tommaso Garzoni », in *Poeti e scrittori del pieno e del tardo Rinascimento*. 2nd ed. (Bari, 1958), pp. 208-20; and Giuseppe Cochiara, *Popolo e letteratura in Italia* (Turin, 1959), pp. 54-56.

[21] *La piazza universale di tutte le professioni del mondo* (Venice, 1585), p. 846 (sig. GGG 7 v). The signature is added because the pagination is often erroneous. « Per un'altra ragione si dice, che la professione de' Librari sia molto nobile, perché sempre sono in compagnia di persone letterate, & virtuose, di Teologi, di Dottori di legge, di Medici, d'Humanisti, & di molti scientiati ». This quotation occurs in all the other Italian editions. See n. 22.

454

yet found in the fifteenth and sixteenth centuries [22]. He began by noting that he had tried to embrace all the professions in his book but his attention had been drawn to his previous omission of the humanist, one of the most noble and honored. Garzoni added that he had originally sought to include the humanist under four other professions: grammarian, rhetorician, historian, and poet. But he had become convinced that a humanist is more than this, or rather, a compound of all these. The humanist must have complete knowledge of the disciplines which are the foundation of the profession of *humanità*. In addition, he has lesser knowledge of all the liberal arts, such as mathematics and moral philosophy, and has at his command the principles of all knowledge. In sum, Garzoni continued, the true humanist knows Latin and Greek, and can easily write in both oratory, poetry and prose. He knows every author [23] and from the professorial chair (*cathedra*) can interpret them worthily. Of such perfection or not far from it were Lazzaro Bonamico, Romolo Amaseo, Francesco Robortello, Carlo Sigonio, Fulvio Morato, and others. Garzoni warned against the error and presumption of those who dabbled in the beginning elements of grammar, and then, having taught these principles, arrogantly wished to be called humanists. They profaned the honored name of humanist, they were the reason that the world failed to distinguish between the true and false humanist, and spoke unfavorably of the profession. Garzoni attributed the above definition of the true humanist to Fabio Paolini who was then teaching in Venice, and who had recited in the library of St. Mark an oration concerning the perfect *doctor humanitatis* at the beginning of the academic year.

The five named as humanists and Paolini were scholars of classical Latin and Greek, teachers of the humanities in uni-

---

[22] The first two editions, 1585 and 1586, did not contain the discourse on humanists. Garzoni added it as the 155th and last discourse to the third edition, 1587, and it was then enlarged from 32 lines to 66 lines in five subsequent Italian editions of 1589, 1592, 1595, 1599, and 1601, before disappearing in Italian editions of 1610, 1617, 1638 and 1665, (although it was still listed in their Table of Contents). For the text of the discourse see the Appendix.

[23] Whether Garzoni meant the Latin and Greek classics or all authors is not clear.

versities and similar centers of learning, and authors who wrote
on rhetoric, history, and poetry. Lazzaro Bonamico was a well-
known teacher at Padua and champion of Latin against the
vernacular. Born in Bassano, he taught at Bologna, and later
was appointed to read Latin and Greek at the *Studio* in Padua.
His few works were published posthumously but he acquired
fame as a teacher of eloquence. In Sperone Speroni's *Dialogo
delle lingue* Bonamico was the speaker who argued for Latin and,
to a lesser extent, Greek, against the vernacular. Francesco
Sansovino also called Bonamico a *humanista* in 1574 [24]. Romolo
Amaseo (1489-1552) was an esteemed author, scholar, and teacher
of the humanities. He held the chair of Greek at Padua, and also
taught rhetoric, poetry, and the humanities at Bologna and
Rome. Author of Latin orations and translator of Xenophon
and Pausanias into Latin, he strongly identified the humanities
with antiquity, stressing archeology and linguistics in their
study. Like Bonamico, he argued that Latin was the only suitable language for the humanities, although Pietro Bembo maliciously pointed out that he taught the vernacular privately [25].

Francesco Robortello (Udine 1516-Padua 1567) studied at
Bologna, held the chair of eloquence at Lucca and Pisa, taught
at Venice, and then succeeded Bonamico at Padua where he
remained with the exception of a short period of teaching at
Bologna from 1557-60. He tried to ascertain the laws of poetry
of the ancients in order to teach them to contemporaries. This
resulted in his complete commentary on Aristotle's *Poetics* (1548),
the first of its kind, which ushered in the age of literary criticism
in the second half of the Cinquecento. His other works, all in
Latin, included a treatise on writing history (1548), *De artificio
dicendi* (1567), *De vita et victu populi Romani* (1559), orations,
and *Variorum locorum annotationes* (1549) [26]. Carlo Sigonio (c.
1520-84) of Modena was a famed historian of antiquity and the
Italian middle ages as well as a scholar of classical philology.

---

[24] For information on Bonamico and Sansovino's reference, see Grendler, « Five Occurrences », pp. 323-24.
[25] Rino Avesani, « Romolo Quino Amaseo », *Dizionario biografico degli
italiani* (Rome, 1960), II, 660-666.
[26] Giuseppe Toffanin, *Il Cinquecento*. 6th ed. (Milan, 1960), pp. 474-79;
Enciclopedia Italiana, XXIX, 519.

456

After studying Greek at Modena and further pursuing his studies at Bologna and Pavia, he taught at Modena from 1546 to 1552, Venice from 1552 until 1560, Padua from 1560 until 1563, and then at the *Studio* of Bologna until his death. A pioneer in legal and institutional history, Sigonio used library and archival sources extensively. All of his many works were written in Latin [27]. Fulvio Pellegrino Morato [28] (c. 1500-48) taught *umane lettere* at the court of Ferrara for many years. His publications were in the vernacular as well as in Latin, and included his Latin *Carmen* (1534), a *rimario* of Dante and Petrarch (1528), and a vernacular treatise on the significance of colors (1535). He was also the father of Fulvia Olimpia Morata (1525-55), a Protestant exile known for her Latin poetry and epistles.

Finally, Garzoni attributed the distinction between the true humanist and the grammatical pedant with a smattering of knowledge to Fabio Paolini (Udine c. 1535-Venice 1605). Paolini took degrees in both philosophy and medicine at Padua, but also studied the humanities and Greek under Robortello and Antonio Riccobono. In Venice he first practiced medicine, then c. 1580 became a teacher of eloquence and poetry, lecturing on Cicero's *De Oratore*. From 1589 until his death he held two teaching posts: interpreting Greek at the library of St. Mark, and reading Latin to the members of the *Collegio de' Notai*. He also discoursed on Greek and Arabic medical writers privately in his home. His publications included a commentary on *De Oratore* (1587), a Latin translation of Aesop's fables (1587), commentaries on Vergil (1589), Thucydides (1603), Avicenna (1609), Hippocrates (1604), and a medical work, *De viperis* (1604). The oration to which Garzoni referred exhorted young men to study humane letters and was published as *De doctore humanitatis* in Venice, 1588. Garzoni may have heard the lecture or had access to a manuscript copy [29].

---

[27] *Enc. Ital.*, XXXI, 761.

[28] His name is sometimes spelled Moreto, Moretto, or Moretti. On Morato, see Luigi Ughi, *Dizionario storico degli uomini illustri ferraresi* (Ferrara, 1804), II, 79; *Dizionario enciclopedico italiano*, VIII, 78.

[29] I have been unable to locate a copy of this work. On Paolini, see Gian-Giuseppe Liruti, *Notizie delle vite ed opere scritte da' letterati del Friuli* (Udine, 1780), III, 352-72.

Garzoni's « Discorso de gli Humanisti » appeared in the above form only in the 1587 edition; in 1589 it was enlarged by a 34-line insertion which praised Giovanni Paolo Gallucci (or Galluzzi), 1538 - c. 1621, of Salò. After listing Bonamico, Amaseo, Robortello, Sigonio, and Morato as humanists, the expanded version stated that Gallucci should be included in this group. Not content with grammatical studies in Latin, Greek, and Italian, as demonstrated in his compendium of grammar [30], Gallucci also toiled in logic and rhetoric as evidenced by his *De formis enthymematum* (1586). The insertion continued to name Gallucci's works in various fields: his *De iis, in quibus pueri et adolescentes Veneti erudiendi sunt, ut optime suam Rempublicam administrare valeant* (1586) in moral philosophy, *De usu tabularum* (1586) in natural philosophy, *Theatrum mundi et temporis* (1589) and a commentary on *Joannis Hasfurti ... de cognoscendis et medendis morbis ex corporum coelestium positione* (1586) in mathematics [31]. The versatile Gallucci also translated Albert Dürer's *Della simmetria dei corpi umani* (1591), and possessed a good Latin style as shown by his translation of the *Introductio in symbolum fidei* (1587) of the Spanish religious writer Luis de Granada. Gallucci was able to use spheres, astrolabes, and many other kinds of astrological instruments, and did the woodcuts for his *Theatrum* and translation of Dürer. He also took time from his own studies in order to teach others, and Garzoni opined that this was the true idea of a tutor of the humanities and a man useful to the world. Gallucci was in the process of demonstrating all the doctrines useful to men in a treatise on raising children which he was then writing [32]. The insertion ended there as the original text resumed with the warning against grammatical dabblers.

Gallucci was celebrated in his lifetime as a mathematician, astrologer, and cosmographer who followed the astronomical

---

[30] *La piazza universale di tutte le professioni del mondo* (Venice, 1589), p. 957. The text of the insertion praising Gallucci gave brief titles or descriptions of his works; one can identify them from Giuseppe Brunati, *Dizionarietto degli uomini illustri della Riviera di Salò* (Milan, 1837), pp. 70-72. However, there is no information on a grammar compendium.

[31] The title indicates, however, that this was a book on astrological medicine.

[32] No notice of this work has come to light.

458

system of Regiomontanus [33]. In addition to the works mentioned, he wrote other treatises in mathematics, astronomy, astrology, and medicine, composed Latin poetry, and translated several works from Spanish and Latin into Italian. He does not resemble the five humanists named by Garzoni in the 1587 version. In short, a man, the bulk of whose scholarly writing was in astronomy and astrology, was termed a humanist, although the insertion did not use the term humanist. As far as the expanded version of the « Discorso de gli Humanisti » was concerned, a humanist was any man of learning who did some work in the *studia humanitatis*, whatever his major scholarly activity.

The authorship of the insertion is unclear. Either Garzoni added the Gallucci material or else it was inserted by an unknown hand in the 1589 edition, possibly after Garzoni's death that June. The edition itself provides no help. It does not list the month of printing, presents no information that a second party prepared it, and the introductory material is exactly the same as in the 1587 edition.

Because of inconsistencies when compared with the 1587 version and other discourses in the *Piazza universale*, it is unlikely that Garzoni wrote the insertion. First, its structure differed from the 1587 edition. In the earlier version, the term humanist was discussed generally with a definition, examples, and an attribution to a source, Paolini, but not with a detailed list of the books of, and extensive praise for, one man. Second, in the 1587 version Garzoni clearly identified the humanist as a scholar and teacher of *humanità*, by which he meant an expert in grammar, rhetoric, history, and poetry, with lesser competence in the rest of the liberal arts, mentioning mathematics and moral philosophy. The insertion added logic, natural philosophy, astrology, painting, religion, and skill with astrological instruments. This was a very eclectic group of intellectual interests, several of which were never included in either the *studia humanitatis* or the liberal arts during the Renaissance. Third, while Bonamico, Amaseo, Robortello, Sigonio, and Morato resembled one another in scholarly interests and careers, they were unlike Gallucci.

---

[33] Lynn Thorndike, *History of Magic and Experimental Science* (New York, 1941), V, 158-60; VI, 60.

Finally, Garzoni's choice of examples was logical and consistent when he discussed other professions. At the beginning of the « Discorso de gli Humanisti », he wrote that previously he had sought to include humanist under grammarian, rhetorician, historian, and poet. In these discourses, Garzoni proceeded as in the 1587 version of the discourse on the humanist. He defined the term by means of Cinquecento treatises, discussed classical examples — which he could omit with the humanist because it was not a profession in the ancient world — and then listed Quattrocento and Cinquecento examples, whom modern scholars recognized as grammarians, rhetoricians, etc. He named Ludovico Dolce, Pietro Bembo, Giulio Camillo, Francesco Alunno, and Francesco Sansovino as modern grammarians; all wrote treatises on vernacular grammar [34]. The Renaissance rhetoricians included Bartolomeo Cavalcanti, Celio Calcagnino, Girolamo Mascher, Cyprianus Soarez, and Cristoforo Barzizza — all of whom wrote on rhetoric [35]. The historians included Leonardo Bruni, Flavio Biondo, Platina, Sabellicus, Collenuccio, Machiavelli, Guicciardini, Giovio, and many others [36]. The poets were Pontano, Vida, Ariosto, Bernardo and Torquato Tasso, Annibale Caro, Pietro Bembo, Claudio Tolomei, Girolamo Benivieni, and others [37]. Garzoni did not include in these four groups anyone so different as Gallucci, nor — to pick three random groups — men known principally as theologians, legists, or astronomers [38]. Each of these received its own discourse. While Garzoni did not differentiate between Latin and vernacular grammarians, rhetoricians, historians, and poets, he had a clear and accurate idea of these disciplines and the men who practiced them. For these reasons, it is very unlikely that Garzoni wrote the insertion concerning Gallucci. Because its purpose was to praise Gallucci rather than to discuss the humanist, it is of little value for the present analysis.

---

[34] *La piazza universale di tutte le professioni del mondo* (Venice, 1601), p. 86.
[35] *Ibid.*, pp. 277-83.
[36] *Ibid.*, pp. 357-59.
[37] *Ibid.*, p. 931.
[38] Incidentally, there is no mention of Gallucci in the discourse on astronomers and astrologers. *Ibid.*, pp. 369-91.

460

These occurrences show that in the second half of the Cinquecento a humanist was a teacher and scholar of the humanities
who often held a university position. He was a professional
whose scholarly activity was based on the study of Latin and
Greek antiquity. Because the humanities were the foundation
of all knowledge, the humanist was a key figure who elucidated
basic principles.

There are two minor points. First, the humanist's learned
activities were not restricted to the humanities. Several of the
six men named as humanists had strong interests in other fields
as mathematics and religion, and Garzoni pointed out that the
humanist should be acquainted with disciplines outside the
studia humanitatis. Second, there was criticism of humanists in
the second half of the Cinquecento. Muzio did not want humanists to serve as instructors for a young prince because they
were classroom tyrants and, by implication, were unacquainted
with « things of the world ». Garzoni warned against false
humanists who had only a smattering of grammar. Gilio thought
that humanists were quarrelsome, and Domenichi satirically
pointed out that while humanists successfully pursued their
studies in school, at home they were failures as husbands and
fathers — again implying that humanists were inept in the real
world [39].

Neither Garzoni's discourse nor the other occurrences mentioned involvement in the *vita civile*. Garzoni omits moral philosophy as one of the primary humanities, and the careers of
the humanists he named confirm this. Moral philosophy was
the humanity most closely allied to the active life because it
dealt with man's relations with other men. The humanists named
by Garzoni wrote influential works in rhetoric, history, and
poetry, but not in moral philosophy. Similarly, they played
little or no role in the state nor did they comment on current
politics and recent history. Sigonio came nearest to active involvement by serving a prince for a limited time and writing a
history of Bologna to 1256. The humanists were seen as professional scholars in disciplines unrelated to the active life.

---

[39] Grendler, « Five Occurrences », pp. 319-23.

With the notable exception of Venice, the ideal of the *vita activa e politica* declined in the Cinquecento [40]. Spanish rule and the growth of absolutist princes necessarily reduced the civic involvement of many Italians. The references to humanist and the humanities in the second half of the sixteenth century support this view. Sansovino, a Venetian, was the only writer noted by Campana, Kristeller, Garin, or myself, who linked a humanist to the *studia humanitatis*, and it, in turn, to the *vita civile*.

The Cinquecento humanist was clearly a professional teacher and scholar whose activities were usually limited to the classroom and study. The definition of Campana and Kristeller is essentially correct. But until more and earlier Quattrocento occurrences of humanist are located, this definition should be restricted to the sixteenth century, especially to the period after 1540 [41]. One hesitates to apply humanist in its Cinquecento meaning to such a figure as Leonardo Bruni who was both a classical scholar and political activist, but never held a university position. After 1540 Gilio did call Bruni, and Benedetto Varchi did term Bruni, Valla, Filelfo, Pontano, Poggio, and others, humanists, i. e., professional men of learning. But this meant that sixteenth-century Italians saw the above figures in the light of their own views, not that Bruni et al., looked at themselves in this way, nor that contemporaries viewed them thus. This is not to say that there were no Quattrocento humanists nor that Italians of that century had no conception of the humanist. In order to understand Renaissance humanists and humanism, the scholar needs to penetrate as much as possible the intellectual, political, and social background. Since Italy changed greatly from the Quattrocento to the Cinquecento, one should be cautious about applying the term with an identical meaning in both centuries [42].

---

[40] Hans Baron, « Secularization of Wisdom and Political Humanism in the Renaissance », *Journal of the History of Ideas*, XXI (1960), 144-45; Grendler, *Critics of the Italian World*, pp. 142, 146-48, 167-70.

[41] The earliest reference located to date is 1490 (by Kristeller) while Campana has found four references from 1512 to 1523/4, and five from 1544 to 1595.

[42] I wish to thank Professor Kristeller for his careful reading of this paper. The fact that I differ somewhat from him does not diminish the value of his comments nor my gratitude.

APPENDIX

This is the text of Garzoni's discourse from *La piazza universale di tutte le professioni del mondo* (In Venetia, Appresso Gio. Battista Somasco, 1587), pp. 956-57, from the Biblioteca Apostolica Vaticana copy. Some accents have been added.

DE GLI HUMANISTI
Discorso. clv.

Io pensava d'haver in questo mio libro abbraciato, e compreso tutte le professioni, & massimamente le più illustri. Ma mi hanno fatto avertito alcuni letterati, ch'io haveva escluso l'Humanista, professione fra le altre nobilissima, & honoratissima. Il quale però io mi credeva haver compreso parte sotto li Grammatici, parte sotto i Rhetori, parte anco sotto gli Historici, & ultimamente se pur vi restava alcuno sotto 'l genere de' poeti. Ma mi dicono, che l' Humanista è un non sò che di più, ò per dir meglio un composto di tutti questi. & che quattro sono come le fondamenta di essa professione d' Humanità: delle quali tutte bisogna ch' habbi intera cognitione quest'artefice: & che per ornamento poi sia tinto di tutte le altre arti liberali, come delle Mathematiche, della Filosofia morale, e finalmente c' habbi li principij d'ogni cognitione, acciò che occorrendo, da per sè possa cavar dalli fonti istessi delle scienze, e servirsi al suo bisogno, non altrimenti che li professori stessi di ciascun'arte. Et voglio insomma che quello sia il vero Humanista, qual sappia, & possa ne l'una, e l'altra lingua cioè latina, e greca, ne l'una & l'altra maniera d'oratione, verso dico, e prosa scriver commodamente. Intender bene ogni scrittore, & in cathedra poter ogni autore acconciamente, e con dignità interpretare. Tali, o poco lontani da questa perfettione dicono esser stati i Lazari Bonamici, i Romoli Amasei, i Robortelli, i Sigonii, i Moretti, & altri di questa schiera. Là onde si scuopre manifesto l'errore, e la presontione d'alcuni, che quando a pena sono tinti de' primi elementi di grammatica, & insegnano que' principij per non dir pedantarie si arrogano questo nome, & vogliono esser chiamati Humanisti, profanando con la loro prosontione questo nome honoratissimo, dando anco con le lor macchie, & vitii il più delle volte occasione al mondo, che non distingue tra vero, e simulato Humanista di parlar, e sentir sinistramente di questo nome. Autore di tal openione, e difinitione dell' Humanista vero è il Paolini, che legge hora in Venetia, qual nel principio di studio[a] quest'anno hà recitato nella libraria di San Marco una oratione de perfecto Doctore Humanitatis, & in essa hà dimostrato, che tale deve esser il buono, e perfetto Humanista, quale habbiamo detto.

---

[a] Text: stustio

VII

THE ENIGMA OF "WISDOM" IN PIERRE CHARRON

WHEN he attempted to provide a "guide to human wisdom" in *De la Sagesse* (1601) to complement his religious exhortations, *Les Trois Veritez* (1593) and the *Discours Chrestiens* (1600, 1601), Pierre Charron warned that his thought was not for the multitudes. He would have been surprised at the popularity of his works and the subsequent controversy whirling about his head to this day. With the addition of Jean Daniel Charron's challenging interpretation on his relative, [1] the debate is certainly to be re-opened. This discussion will focus on J. D. Charron's study and on other recent works on Charron and his era.

The traditional interpretation of Charron sees him as the disciple of Montaigne who dogmatized the sceptical elements of the *Essais*, separated fideist religion from rationalist ethics, and "taught the *libertins* to do without God." J. D. Charron argues that *Sagesse* was a perfectly orthodox attempt to convert Protestants and rationalists by providing a common basis of understanding on a natural level in the hope that the naturally perfected man would embrace God. He was, claims J. D. Charron, "the first to put into practical and teachable use the humanist culture he had inherited from the ancients (p. 105)". The argument rests upon a good account of Charron's life and an analysis of the *Petit Traicté de la Sagesse*, Charron's outline and defense of his position.

The author emphasizes Charron's important role in the French Church and is able to reconcile contradictions between La Rochemaillet's contemporary account of Charron's life and subsequent biographers. He suggests that Charron was already a priest and canon in Montpellier before receiving a *Docteur in utroque jure* in 1571 to

---

[1] Jean Daniel Charron, *The "Wisdom" of Pierre Charron: An Original and Orthodox Code of Morality,* Univ. of North Carolina Stud. in the Romance Lang. and Lit., No. 34 (Chapel Hill, N. C., 1960).

validate a previous degree from Orleans or Bourges, spoken of by La Rochemaillet but undocumented. Scholars who see in Charron the dissembling rationalist have a difficult time explaining his vow and earnest efforts to enter the monastery in 1589. J. D. Charron suggests that he may have made this vow as a result of the great plague in Bordeaux in 1585, or that he may have wished for release from worldly cares in order to devote himself to his program of furthering the counter-reform by writings directed to the non-believers.

The argument from Charron's thought is less convincing. Although the *Petit Traicté* outlines *Sagesse* and is relatively free of contradictions, it lacks the richness and complexities of the larger work. It was of less historical importance than *Sagesse,* as it appeared in only fifteen editions to sixty-one of *Sagesse. Sagesse* was the inspiration of *libertins,* and only it was placed on the Index by the Church (Decretum of December 16, 1605).

There are difficulties in J. D. Charron's interpretation. Exactly how does the wise man, naturally perfected, receive God's grace and worship Him? According to Charron, he worships in the spirit only. "That God will be served in spirit: and that that which is outwardly done is rather for ourselves than for God; for human unity, and for edification than for divine verity: *Quae potius ad morem quam ad rem pertinent* (Which rather belong to manners and customs than to the thing itself)." [2] With these statements, Charron is not far from the man-centered, non-sacramental religion of the Enlightenment. For the above statements and Charron's comments on the natural origins of the faith of most believers, he was attacked as a subverter of religion.

In addition, there is the problem of the wise man who follows nature, or the light of God in his reason, and is above all the laws. Charron had boundless confidence in the ability of the wise man who followed his reason (once freed of corrupting passions) to solve all of life's problems. J. D. Charron believes that Charron meant Christian conscience for natural law, not the spark of participation in the wisdom of the world of the Stoics. However, questions of orthodoxy arise when Charron equated natural law in men with the perfection of human nature in its natural state. When Charron spoke of "those original seeds

---

[2] *Of Wisdome Three Bookes, written in french by Peter Charron,* trans. Samson Lennard, 4th ed. (London, 1640), Bk. II, ch. 5, p. 300.

of goodness", or that "men are naturally and originally good" (*Sagesse,* II, 3), he was slipping into Pelagianism. When Charron is checked against the decrees of the Catholic Church in the sixteenth century condemnation of Baius, or the writings of Aquinas (S. T. I-II, q. 109, a. 1-10), one sees why Charron's contemporaries were very uneasy about his teachings. Charron was aware of the importance of grace, particularly in his second edition of *Sagesse,* but the relationship between nature and grace was always ambivalent.

Richard H. Popkin in *The History of Scepticism from Erasmus to Descartes,* 1960, emphasizes the importance of Charron in the counter-reformation attack on the Calvinists, using the scepticism of Sextus Empiricus. The method as practiced by Gentian Hervet, Charron, Juan Maldonat, Cardinal du Perron and others, was to doubt systematically the individual and rational Scriptural interpretations of the Calvinists while holding to an implicit fideism in regard to the true religion. As Hervet explained it, scepticism destroyed the proofs of reason so that faith alone led to religious truth. (Popkin, p. 69.) J. D. Charron may be correct in affirming that Charron was not a complete disciple of the sceptical Montaigne, but Popkin argues that Charron's use of Pyrrhonian doubt directly anticipated Descartes.

That Charron relied on Neo-Stoicism a great deal has been pointed out by Sabrié, Wilhelm Dilthey, and Eymard [3]. As Justus Lipsius and Guillaume Du Vair formulated Neo-Stoicism, the classical Stoic concept of Universal Reason, which dwelt in man through his individual reason, was another way of describing God and natural law. Neo-Stoicism gave war-weary Frenchmen confidence that they could do what was right in the midst of religious strife by emphasizing reason at the expense of creed, revelation, and authority. The description in Charron of the free man who does his duty, the wise man who is above the laws but obeys them in order to conform to the customs of the land, the emphasis on subduing the passions, and the concern with Destiny, Chance, Fate, and Providence, are evidences of Charron's heavy debt

---

[3] J. B. Sabrié, *De l'humanisme au rationalisme, Pierre Charron (1541-1603) l'homme, l'oeuvre, l'influence* (Paris, 1913). Wilhelm Dilthey, *Weltanschauung und Analyse des Menschen seit Renaissance und Reformation, Gesammelte Schriften* II. Band (Stuttgart, 1957), pp. 263-264, et al. Julien Eymard, "Le Stoicisme en France dans la 1er Moitié du XVIIe Siècle, Pierre Charron, Le Stoicisme Chrétien, Guillaume du Vair", *Etudes Franciscaines.* Vol. II, December, Paris: 1951.

to Lipsius, Du Vair, and Seneca, his most quoted source [4]. It can be strongly argued that Charron used natural law in the Stoic rather than in the Christian sense.

Some scholars have concluded from his ethics that Charron was teaching a separation of rationalist morality from religion. In his discussion of justice, for example, he recognized divine justice, and a "pliable and political justice". The former was too antiquated and absolute to do any service to the world, but the latter made "profit and probity" go hand in hand. The wise man should be guided by worldly justice because it accommodated itself to the necessities of life and the weakness of mankind. (*Sagesse*, III, 5.) The virtue of prudence was interpreted in the same "pliable" sense. Eugene F. Rice, Jr., in his widely-noted study, *The Renaissance Idea of Wisdom*, 1958, [5] argues that medieval speculative wisdom became in the Renaissance secularized, humanized, and moralized, and that Charron completed the process. For Charron, Rice argues, "Wisdom is an autonomous and naturally acquired moral virtue".

In his otherwise excellent account of the reception of *Sagesse*, J. D. Charron omitted the condemnation of *Sagesse* as "Machiavellian". Many of the solutions to moral problems proposed by Charron have seemed to his contemporaries and to scholars as the subordination of morality and religion to politics. Dagens has shown how *Sagesse* was considered a "*livre d'état*" by Nonce Buffalo, President Jeannin of the Sorbonne, St. Barthélemy, Gabriel Naudé, and others. Dagens believes that Charron was a sincere Christian, but Cherel treats Charron as an "indecisive Christian", and Mosse considers him a casuist [6].

---

[4] Heinrich Teipel, *Zur Frage des Skeptizismus bei Pierre Charron* (Elberfeld, 1912), has compiled a list, using all of Charron's works, of authors cited and the number and character of the references. The reliance upon the Stoics is overwhelming apparent.

[5] Eugene F. Rice, Jr., *The Renaissance Idea of Wisdom*, Harvard Historical Monographs, XXXVII (Cambridge, Mass., 1958). See also Hans Baron, "Secularization of Wisdom and Political Humanism in the Renaissance: Rice's *Renaissance Idea of Wisdom*", *JHI*, XXI (1960), 131-150, and Richard H. Popkin, *Renaissance News*, XII (1959), 265-269 (Book Review of Rice, *The Renaissance Idea of Wisdom*).

[6] Jean Dagens, "Le Machiavelisme de Pierre Charron", *Studies aangeboden aan Gerard Brom* (Utrecht, 1952), pp. 56-64. Albert Cherel, *La Pensée de Machiavel en France* (Paris, 1935), pp. 105-106. George L. Mosse, *The Holy Pretence: a study in Christianity and reason of state from William Perkins to John Winthrop* (Oxford, 1957), pp. 20-21.

THE ENIGMA OF "WISDOM" IN PIERRE CHARRON

Although most of Book III and part of Book II of *Sagesse* deal with political matters, no extensive treatment of Charron as a political philosopher has appeared. An alternative thesis to "Machiavellianism" could, I think, be worked out. If Charron does separate religion and morality, the *sage* would have to rely upon his reason alone to organize the state and to determine the roles of the king, citizens, and constitution. If the wise man viewed all worldly affairs in the light of Pyrrhonian scepticism, why could he not construct a theory of the state based solely on his own rational conclusions similar to Hobbes's *Leviathan?*

It is evident from these differing interpretations of Pierre Charron that he is one of the keys to our understanding of how the Renaissance gave way to the seventeenth century. Undoubtedly, the discussion will continue.

UNIVERSITY OF WISCONSIN

VIII

Pierre Charron: Precursor to Hobbes

THE POLITICAL philosophy of Thomas Hobbes is rightly considered as marking the end of one era in political theory and the beginning of a new one. Formerly, men had sought and found a guide to political conduct in a basic principle upon which the order of well-being of the state depended. Hobbes broke with the past by postulating the state as simply a rationalization of the needs of men. He analyzed man's psychology and relied on his own observation and ratiocination to establish the best possible state commensurate with mankind's situation, but his supreme emphasis on force and authority left no room for the older constitutional, religious, and traditional safeguards of the citizen. This was the price that Hobbes willingly paid to achieve a secure state during the English Civil War.

Hobbes was unique for his time in his ruthless delineation of the modern state. His method and conclusions, however, were strikingly anticipated in a similar historical situation, the French Wars of Religion, by the French Neo-Stoic Pierre Charron (1541-1603). Hobbes was extremely loath to admit that his ideas were anything less than original even when the similarity to Aristotle and the kinship of Bacon and Descartes were pointed out by his critics. Nowhere did Hobbes acknowledge the existence of Charron, nor have scholars uncovered any intellectual relationship. Yet the two political philosophers are strikingly similar and a historical connection between them is very likely.

In the course of his writings, chiefly *De la Sagesse*,[1] the French cleric attempted to resolve the difficulties of the political situation by the reformulation of the fundamentals of the state. His political writing was not merely a plagiarization of Bodin, Justus Lipsius, and others,[2] nor an example of the acceptance of Machiavelli.[3] He utilized the Neo-Stoic synthesis of Christianity and

---

[1] *De la Sagesse, trois livres par Pierre Charron, Parisien, Chanoine theologal et Chantre en l'eglise de Codom* (Paris, 1601). Textual references in this paper are to *Of Wisdom: Three Books*, trans. George Stanhope, 3rd ed. (London, 1729).

[2] J. B. Sabrié, *De l'humanisme au rationalisme, Pierre Charron (1541-1603), l'homme, l'oeuvre, l'influence* (Paris, 1913), pp. 258-261.

[3] Albert Cherel, *La Pensée de Machiavel en France* (Paris, 1935), pp. 105-106.

rationalism to reconcile the discordant elements of the state, and adapted the whole to the political realities of the emerging modern world of the late sixteenth and early seventeenth centuries. For Charron, as well as for Hobbes, man's autonomous reason became the sole arbiter of his conduct. Charron rationalized the state as the sole means of "providing barriers about the restless souls of men" for the sake of order, peace, and security for all. He used the Stoic analysis of man's psychology to determine the foundations of the state and its principles of operation. The result was a state very similar to the Leviathan, although Charron has not been noticed by historians of political theory. In him a union of Catholic theology and Renaissance moral philosophy produced a non-Christian political philosophy which was well adapted to political realities and is immediately akin to Hobbes.

Pierre Charron, with Justus Lipsius, Guillaume DuVair, and for a time Montaigne, was an adherent of Renaissance Neo-Stoicism. This compound of classical Stoic thought and Christianity attracted French intellectuals by its call to duty and emphasis on the inner man. In classical Stoic thought, Universal Reason dwelt in Nature. Man could have a knowledge of Nature by sensory representations. From these he derived concepts, and finally through reflection, wisdom or participation in Universal Reason. If man understood and followed the laws of Nature, he was living his life in accordance with Universal Reason, as Universal Reason dwelt in his soul through his reason. When a man had successfully quelled his passions, his clear reason could apprehend Nature and he would live rationally, moderately, and dutifully.[4]

Justus Lipsius in his commentaries on the Stoics reconciled them with Christianity. He identified Stoic Universal Reason with the Catholic doctrine of Natural Law, and Stoic Destiny with God's unknown Providence. The Scholastics had taught that Natural Law could be discovered by the use of "right reason."

---

[4] On sixteenth-century Neo-Stoicism, see Léontine Zanta, *La Renaissance du Stoicisme au XVIᵉ siècle* (Paris, 1914); Jason Lewis Saunders, *Justus Lipsius: The Philosophy of Renaissance Stoicism* (New York, 1955); Justus Lipsius, *Two Bookes of Constancie*, trans. John Stradling, ed. with introd. Rudolf Kirk (New Brunswick, N.J., 1939); Guillaume DuVair, *The Moral Philosophie of the Stoicks*, trans. Thomas James, ed. Rudolf Kirk (New Brunswick, N. J., 1951).

214

It was, however, supplemented by revelation to give men the knowledge for salvation. This use of reason to discover God's laws had been understood by the Stoics, Lipsius felt. He cited Stoic ethical theory and emphasis on the inner man as proof of their recognition of the Christian God. He taught that man could discover God for himself through the use of his passion-free reason. Since the world was ruled by Divine Providence, a knowledge of the world would yield knowledge of God's ways. If one could understand the ways of men and events, one would possess a secure knowledge of God without worrying about theological subtleties. God had implanted in man the rational faculty for the express purpose of discovering Him. The problem remained of freeing the intellect of the passions which clouded its judgment. Once this was accomplished, man could live a tranquil life attuned to God and men.

The Neo-Stoics did not reject revelation but they tended to make it superfluous. As Charron described the relationship between reason and revelation, the former was the foundation and the latter the roof (II, p. 700). Neo-Stoicism tended to emphasize reason at the expense of creed, revelation, and authority. For exhibiting such "naturalistic tendencies," the Catholic Church placed *Of Wisdom* on the Index in 1605.[5]

Such a philosophy could also provide a unique approach for Frenchmen attempting to find a new synthesis upon which to base the state. The traditional French unity of *"un roi, une foi, et une loi"* had disintegrated under the pressures of the civil wars. Francis Hotman, Pierre Du Belloy, Bodin, Robert Bellarmine, and the author of the *Vindiciae Contra Tyrannos* were among the theorists who sought to establish a stable political order by reconciling the "ancient constitution of the French people," the king's power, and God's sanction.

Charron had experienced at firsthand the uncertainties of the civil war. In the turbulent events of 1588-89 he had switched his allegiance from the king to the Catholic League, and then had returned to the monarch's cause. He tried to justify himself in a letter to the Sorbonne in April, 1589. The letter argued with force

---

[5] For an opposing viewpoint, see Jean Daniel Charron in *The "Wisdom" of Pierre Charron: An Original and Orthodox Code of Morality*, Univ. of North Carolina Stud. in the Romance Lang. and Lit., No. 34 (Chapel Hill, 1960), who argues that Charron was completely orthodox and misunderstood.

and linguistic vigor Belloy's divine right position, Bodin's concept of one sovereignty, respect for the legitimate authority, and passive resistance — all part of the *Politique* position.[6]

This letter was his only political venture until after years of reflection, he published his magnus opus, *Of Wisdom* (1601), as part of his complete Neo-Stoic world philosophy. In his *Trois Veritez* (1593) and in the *Discours Chrestiens* (1604) he discussed God and religion. In *Of Wisdom* he sought to guide man in his every human relationship, especially his political role. It contains Charron's mature political philosophy and embodies the new Neo-Stoic approach to politics.

If God's wisdom was to be known to man through his reason alone, of what need were the laws of constitution and Church? Neither the approbation of the Church nor constitutional sanction was necessary as the keystone of political order. The Neo-Stoic "wise man" needed merely to discover the "Natural Law" of society in order to bring the state into conformity with God's ways. By substituting a rational pragmatism for doctrinal and legal systems, men could achieve a stable political order. This is precisely what Charron attempted to outline.

The first prerequisite for political wisdom was a clear understanding of the world, its events, and man. Charron advised a worldly Pyrrhonism in order to understand objectively and evaluate the world of man, although this pre-Cartesian Pyrrhonism stopped short of questioning religion.[7] What did the wise man discover in the world around him? Man ought to be able to ascertain what the law of Nature (that is, of God) was in the world. But this was very difficult because man had rejected Nature and was encumbered with a variety of customs and practices. One easily saw that the most universal qualities of human nature were vanity, weakness, inconstancy, misery, and presumption. Life was nothing "but one unequal, irregular, and many-figured motion" like the "war of all against all" of Hobbes. By following Nature, a few men could approach God, but the majority were so corrupt

---

[6] *Qu'il n'est permis au subiet, pour quelque cause et raison que ce soit, de se liguer, bander, et rebeller contre son roy* in *De la Sagesse, trois livres par Pierre Charron,* ed. Amaury Duval, 3 vols. (Paris, 1827), III, pp. 349-358.

[7] For the relationship between Charron and Descartes, see Richard H. Popkin, *The History of Scepticism from Erasmus to Descartes* (Assen, Neth., 1960).

that they could not see "the footprints of Providence" (I, chs. 36-39, II, ch. 3).

Still, the rare man of wisdom whose human nature was preserved uncorrupted, and the "fickle," "savage," and "deformed" mob had to live together in mutual order. Charron agreed with his Neo-Stoic mentors, Justus Lipsius and DuVair, and placed his hope for worldly harmony in the secular state rather than a Christian world society. The state was "the band of all society . . . the vital spirit . . . that enables . . . so many thousands of men to breathe as one, and compacts all nature together" (I, p. 504). From this basis Charron proceeded to describe the operations and principles of the state.

Charron granted to the prince Bodin's sovereignty and made the magistrates subject to it. But more important than the legal foundations of the ruler's power was the question of the maintenance of authority. As Charron put it: "The greatest thing this world can show is authority. This is the image of the divine power. . . . Nothing but authority can prevail with fools, to make any tolerable advances toward wisdom" (II, pp. 832-833). To assist the ruler in the exercise and maintenance of authority, Charron offered advice on nearly every phase of government — military affairs, administration, taxation, espionage, and the like.

The Christian moral virtues of prudence and justice were the guiding principles for the ruler, but in Charron's hands they were transformed into Machiavellian rules of statecraft. Because the world was not perfect, man had to practice prudence, "the knack of managing mankind." The ruler might "take all imaginable care of his own preservation," and "defend himself from harm so long as there are any honest shifts and decent remedies left" (III, p. 1425). Because men were so degenerate, Charron advocated a "pliable justice" when dealing with worldly affairs. He recognized natural or divine justice. Unfortunately, thought Charron, this justice was "antiquated and absolute, capable of doing very little service to the world as it now stands" (III, pp. 1216-17). Man in his present condition could not bear such a bright light. On the other hand, there was a worldly justice much more pliable and political. It accommodated itself to the necessities and weaknesses of mankind and condoned matters that natural justice absolutely condemned. So-called "political justice" attempted to make "profit and probity go hand in hand." Since this justice managed the world, the wise man must act realistically and rule his affairs prudentially in the light of "political justice" (III, ch. 5).

To bring the point home to his readers, Charron guardedly approved four examples of "political justice." The first example was the suspension of the ordinary process of law in order to do away with a criminal who was creating disorder in the kingdom. The second concerned checking the rising power of a potential rival to the throne. Here, the Duke of Guise, whom Henry III had had assassinated in 1588, was probably in Charron's mind. The third was the seizure of private property for the good of the state and finally, infringing on the rights of the subject to prevent diminution of the prince's own power (III, pp. 1033-39). Elsewhere in Book III Charron permitted the prince to practice hypocrisy, deceit, cajolery, and flattery when dealing with civil disturbances.

Yet, Charron assigned limits and conditions to the "public prudence" of the prince. "Prudential" measures were only permissible under strict conditions: (1) the "absolute necessity" of the public good, (2) use for defense only, and (3) accomplishment "in darkness," that is, moderately and discreetly in order to avoid arousing other interests and further disturbing the state (III, pp. 1022-25).

For his use of "prudence" and "worldly justice" Charron has been bitterly attacked as a "Machiavellian," both by his contemporaries and by subsequent scholars, or as a "casuist," in the pejorative sense, as one who attempted to make "reason of state" fit within the traditional Christian ethics.[8] Charron was neither a "casuist" nor a "Machiavellian" because there is a fundamental difference between the manner in which Charron and Machiavelli or William Perkins, the Puritan casuist, treated political realities.

The sixteenth- and seventeenth-century casuists were arguing from the theological positions. Whether the theorist was Catholic, Anglican, or Puritan, he attempted to reconcile Christian moral

---

[8] For a description of the contemporary attack on Charron, see Jean Dagens, "Le Machiavelisme de Pierre Charron," in *Studies aangeboden aan Gerard Brom* (Utrecht, 1952), pp. 56-64. However, Dagens does not consider Charron a "Machiavellian." Cherel, pp. 105-106, does. George L. Mosse, *The Holy Pretence: a study in Christianity and reason of state from William Perkins to John Winthrop* (Oxford, 1957), pp. 20-21, treats Charron as a "casuist," and comes very near to the judgment of Cherel.

218

precepts and "reason of state." Evil actions, admittedly necessary for survival in an evil world, had to be justified within the moral commandments of Christianity. Charron, with the tool of natural reason presented him by Neo-Stoicism, approached the problem from entirely new premises. Because the world and its affairs were radically separated from revealed religion and God, the moral commandments of Christianity were adhered to in a different manner. Charron's wise man worshipped God in the spirit alone, while depending solely on his reason to guide him through human difficulties (II, ch. 5). Because his passion-free reason was attuned to God manifested in Nature, the actions of a reasonable man were godly. No casuistic reconciliation was necessary. If he followed his reason, he would necessarily do the will of God without the strictures of the Church to remind him of his duty. For Perkins the Bible was the court of appeals which told man if he was acting in conformity with the moral law. Botero's prince was guided by the father-confessor, the representative of the Church.[9] Charron, on the other hand, relegated the world and its imperfect ways to Neo-Stoic reason so that any conflicts could be resolved with a clear conscience by rational man.

To call Charron an undercover "Machiavellian" is to ignore his entire career as an esteemed and active churchman in French ecclesiastical affairs.[10] One must also discount his other devout and orthodox Catholic publications, *Les Trois Veritez* and the *Discours Chrestiens*. He was simply trying to propound a reasonable and moderate theory of the state which would avoid the two extremes typified on one hand by Machiavelli and Guicciardini, and the fanatical primacy of religion in politics championed by the Huguenots and the Catholic League at the other extreme.

Charron's solution of man's problems was a compound of divine fatalism and human optimism. Since God acted through Providence and Destiny, why should man oppose necessity? A reasonable and benevolent God could hardly expect His creatures to act otherwise than to steer a moderate and prudent path through the tangled affairs of life. Yet, man's reason was a participant in Divine Wisdom and he could rest assured that his actions were

---

[9] Mosse, *op. cit.*, pp. 37, 52.

[10] See J. D. Charron, *op. cit.*, pp. 59-85, for an account of Charron's career in the Church, and his activities in the effort to implement the decrees of the Council of Trent in France.

just. In this way Charron was outside the framework of Christian casuistry. His line of reasoning led directly to the independent morality of the Enlightenment and to the rationalism of Hobbes.

This is best seen by examining Charron's analysis of civil war situations. When the prince, the constitution, and established religion conflicted, as was the case in the French civil wars, the citizen was faced with the difficult question of where his allegiance lay. Charron's resolutions of these conflicts indicate which elements he considered the necessary and inviolable foundations of the state.

What if the ruler behaved in a manner contrary to "the laws of God and Nature, acting contrary to the established religion of his country, the express commands of God, or the native liberty of men's consciences?" Men should not obey, but neither could they have recourse to "sinful violence" if there were no relief by law. If persuasion failed to sway the prince, the citizens could only flee or suffer their fate. Similarly, if the prince violated the rights and estate of the citizen, the latter yet must render honor, obedience, and prayers to the prince because all power stemmed from God. This was Destiny or God's Providence to be borne as one suffered floods or a barren year (III, pp. 1397-99).

Thus Charron eliminated two prime causes of disturbance in the state. The religious conscience of the subject and the citizen's individual rights were theoretically acknowledged but denied as justifications for active revolt, just as Hobbes denied them. The state could not be secure for either Charron or Hobbes if the individual were permitted to revolt on behalf of absolute rights or religious conscience.

The exact role of the constitution presented a more difficult problem for Charron which he never unequivocally resolved. Because it embodied the "wisdom of generations," it was a potent force for stability in the realm and should be upheld at all costs. If a usurper brushed aside the laws and customs of the state and forced his way into power, he was to be resisted by all available means including force. When the constitution was mocked, the constitutional trustees or those with the principal interest in the state, had to fight the usurper (III, pp. 1399-1401).

But Charron also limited his support of the constitution. Once the tyrant had secured the throne, men should "bear and submit as well as they can." Continued opposition would only provoke a civil war whose miseries would far outweigh the evil resulting from the tyrant. Perhaps dutiful submission would soften the tyrant's will and, if good will between the prince and his subjects could be established, reasonable government would result (III, pp. 1198-99). Moreover, the prince might alter the constitution in peacetime upon certain conditions of ". . . evident or absolute necessity, or else evident and very considerable advantage to the public . . ." if he proceeded cautiously and stealthily (III, pp. 1095-96).

Charron was forced into uncertainty concerning the role of the constitution by his own political premises. Formerly, the French constitution had possessed either religious or historical inviolability. The Huguenots had based the constitution on a covenant with God as in the *Vindiciae Contra Tyrannos*. The Catholic League argued that it depended upon the preservation of the religious establishment. Hotman's *Franco-Gallia* founded the constitution on the historical French nation. Charron denied these positions because he had removed creed and church from political affairs, and his observation of men had taught him well that tradition and custom were very relativistic. Neither religion nor history could be a strong enough argument for the inviolate preservation of the constitution. Charron dealt with it rationally and pragmatically, as he had dealt with all other political matters, in terms of whether its preservation would strengthen public authority or bring on a civil war.

The dread of civil war permeated Charron's political thinking as it did Hobbes's. It was the worst calamity that could befall a state and demanded every remedy. Like Hobbes, Charron's remedies — elimination of the constitution, and religious and individual rights — were always based upon his analysis of what man was and what could be done. Charron firmly resisted the impulse toward utopianism of every kind because utopianism prescribed rules and laws that the majority of men, the "deformed mob," could never attain. Christ was the greatest lawgiver because He took into account human infirmities (I, ch. 51). Neither would an equalization of property contribute immensely to the peace and order of the state. Order in the state was like music; if all the sounds were the same, how could there be harmony? The problem of poverty could be managed through governmental measures to relieve want and misery. The prince should promote trade and public works and tax the very wealthy (I, ch. 62, III, ch. 2).

In the final analysis, Charron's state was a pragmatic rationalization of existing political realities. The components of his state — king, magistrates, people, and ancient constitution — were autonomous. That is to say, there was no connecting link, no contract, no covenant, no inviolable law or tradition to bind the components of the state into an organic whole. They all subsisted autonomously under the principle of order which society must provide for man in his worldly state. Man's reason, his human "wisdom," was the court of final appeal when the various elements of the state were in conflict. This was the only means that Charron could see to reconcile the inherent tensions in the political speculation of his French predecessors. His political philosophy was an uneasy coalition of dissident factors and a stage on the path to more complete and rigorous secular political systems. Thus Charron sketched the outline of the rational state, the construct of man's reason.

The "mortal god," Thomas Hobbes's *Leviathan,* was the next major development toward the modern state. Like Charron, he wrote in a period of disintegrating traditional institutions. He was motivated by the same distrust of the people and was absolutely convinced of the necessity of constructing the state on the firmest basis possible.

Hobbes must have been aware of *De la Sagesse.* By 1640, at least four English editions were available.[11] Moreover, during his numerous sojourns in France (1610, 1629-31, 1634-36, 1640-51), Hobbes had his pick of about thirty French editions.[12] By 1634, six years before the writing and publication of his first major political work, *Elements of Law,* Hobbes was known in French intellectual circles as part of the group around Father Marin Mersenne in Paris. Here he formed a deep social and intellectual friendship with Gassendi who, in turn, possibly exercised great influence over Hobbes's thought. Gassendi greatly admired the writings of Charron, and credited him with giving him an understanding of *la sagesse profane* and *l'utilité du scepticisme.* It is likely that Hobbes was well acquainted with Gassendi's favorite authors, Charron, Lipsius, Montaigne, Seneca, Plutarch, and

---

[11] These are the translations of Samson Lennard printed in 1606, 1612, 1630, and 1640.

[12] Matthew Dreano, "Charron," *Dictionnaire des lettres françaises. Le seizième siècle,* ed. Georges Grente et al. (Paris, 1951), pp. 172-174, counts 49 French editions in the years 1601-1672. J. D. Charron, *op. cit.,* pp. 148-149, lists 28 editions in the years 1601-1646.

222

Cicero, and the whole stream of thought of which Charron was such a vital part.[13] Mersenne was also acquainted with Charron's writings. In his *Impiété des Deistes* (1624) he condemned Charron's political philosophy. In Mersenne's opinion, Christianity and "the best policy imaginable in the world" were in no way repugnant. But he thought that Charron's attempt to reconcile the two, despite praiseworthy intentions, was conducive to more evil than good. Mersenne hoped that someone else would prove that religion and *la policie* made a true harmony.[14] In reality, the only direction in which Charron's attempt could lead was that of Hobbes and seventeenth-century rationalism.

There are many similarities. Both Charron and Hobbes began with an explanation of man's psychology in terms of motion toward various objects. According to Hobbes, these appetites and aversions produced the passions which determined man's conduct.[15] Charron called the passions "violent motions of the soul," and explained man's personality as a war between reasons and the passions (I, chs. 14, 18, et al.). Both theorists deduced from man's condition the necessary steps to form a stable society. Hobbes abstracted from the wretched condition of man in his natural state to determine that the first natural right of man was self-preservation. All men desired by "necessity" what was good for them and contracted together to abandon the state of nature. They formed the state in accordance with necessary utilitarian principles which Hobbes termed the laws of nature.[16] In Charron's political philosophy the "laws of nature," or God manifested through reason, reputedly directed man. But Charron strongly advocated Pyrrhonian observation of the world to discover how to act in human affairs. He severed justice, prudence, and wisdom from God and, in the end, human reason alone constructed the state and led the prince.

The principles of politics derived from reason were much the same for the two theorists. Each sacrificed all for the sake of an orderly but authoritarian state. The necessity of a good army, a

---

[13] Richard Peters, *Hobbes* (London, 1956), pp. 22ff. Sabrié, *op. cit.*, pp. 444-447.

[14] Marin Mersenne, *L'Impiété des déistes, athées et libertins de ce temps, combatue & renversée de point par raisons tirées de la Philosophie & de la Théologie* (Paris, 1624), pp. 182-183, 194.

[15] Thomas Hobbes, *Leviathan* (New York, 1950), pp. 39-50.

[16] Thomas Hobbes, *De Cive or The Citizen*, ed. Sterling P. Lamprecht (New York, 1949), pp. 27-32.

sound fiscal policy, unequal taxation to relieve want and to avoid rebellion, the ways and means of dissolving factions, and the judicious use of civil punishment to engender fear in the populace were part of the advice tendered to Charron's prince and to the Leviathan. Neither granted to the citizen more than a semblance of civil rights. Charron explained that justice, property rights, constitutional rights, and the religious conscience had to be relinquished to strengthen civil authority and to avoid civil war. Hobbes granted absolute dominion over all men to the state.

When the Leviathan no longer provided protection for the subjects, the obligation of obedience was dissolved. If as a result of a civil or foreign war, or like cause, the sovereign power in the commonwealth was no longer exercised effectively, men had to protect themselves again, as the natural right to self-preservation required them to return to the state of nature. Soon they would give their allegiance to a new Leviathan. This tenet of Hobbes was anticipated by Charron's solution of the problem of what to do when a usurper attempted to take the crown. Charron advocated resistance until further opposition would only produce dissension without hope of victory. At this point the citizens ought to submit. Charron's pragmatic solution, which recognized political reality while ignoring constitutional and divine laws, was adopted by Hobbes and permeated his entire system. Each recognized the importance of public order and gave it primacy. Neither Hobbes nor Charron expected men to fight on in a righteous but losing cause as, for example, the lonely God-fearing magistrate of the *Vindiciae* would. The realistic appraisal and acceptance of political necessities characteristic of the Renaissance were essential ingredients in the philosophies of both Charron and Hobbes.

Still, Charron was not a complete rationalist. In his eagerness to avoid dissenting opinions, Hobbes defined the moral law in a manner which Charron could not have countenanced. When in *Behemoth* the question was posed regarding the individual's conscience and the king's command, Hobbes completely rejected the individual religious conscience. The state made all decisions in doctrinal matters and determined what was to be called theft, murder, and injury.[17] Charron had not permitted the sovereign to pronounce the moral law, but had promulgated "worldly jus-

---

[17] Thomas Hobbes, *Behemoth or The Long Parliament*, ed. Ferdinand Tönnies (London, 1889), p. 50. Hobbes, *De Cive*, p. 81.

tice," and had admonished the people to withhold their judgment on apparently unjust actions of the prince. The results were hardly different although Charron still held to a theological foundation of the moral code.

In essence, Hobbes merely sheered Charron's *morale indépendante* from its tenuous spiritual base. Charron's political philosophy was formulated by the wise man's godly reason, or Neo-Stoic nature. Man's reason was not yet theoretically independent of God, although it was autonomous in practice. Hobbes's concept of "right reason" had no connection, theoretical or otherwise, with the divine. As he stated it, reason was not an "infallible faculty," but simply the act of ratiocination of every man. It was not universal consent nor God's voice within man, but was still certain and true because it came from true principles, namely an analysis of human nature.[18] Hobbes built upon the same foundation (man's nature) as had his French predecessor, and his definition and use of the concept of reason in political philosophy carried *De la Sagesse* to a logical conclusion.

---

[18] Hobbes, *De Cive*, pp. 31-32.

The Roman Inquisition and the Venetian Press 1540–1605

The external history of the Index of Prohibited Books, that is, its list of authors and rules, is generally known, but the internal history is not. How effective in practice were the Index and its enforcing agent, the Roman Inquisition? When, and to what extent, were the decrees and prohibitions enforced? Why, or why not, were they enforced? By and large, answers to these questions are lacking for sixteenth-century Italy. In any attempt to answer these questions, a study of Venice is essential, because it was the largest Italian center for printing, producing perhaps half or more of all Cinquecento Italian books. Equally important, the Inquisition records in Venice are accessible to scholars and are reasonably complete.

The development in Venice of the Inquisition activity against heretical literature is the focus of this brief paper on a large subject.[1] In the 1540s the machinery for censorship was set up, but the level

[1] This is a revised version of a paper read at the 1972 meeting of the American Historical Association in a session jointly sponsored by the American Society for Reformation Research and the American Catholic Historical Association. Because it is a précis of a monograph in preparation, the documentation has been abbreviated. The two fundamental works on Venetian censorship are Horatio F. Brown, *The Venetian Printing Press, 1469–1800: An Historical Study Based upon Documents for the Most Part Hitherto Unpublished* (London, 1891; reprint Amsterdam, 1969); and Giovanni Sforza, "Riflessi della Controriforma nella Repubblica di Venezia," *Archivio storico italiano* 93, pt. 1 (1935): 5–34, 189–216; 93, pt. 2 (1935): 25–52, 173–86. Not concerned with Venice but of great interest are the documents printed by Antonio Rotondò, "Nuovi documenti per la storia dell'*Indice dei libri proibiti* (1572–1638)," *Rinascimento*, ser. 2, 3 (1963): 145–211; and John Tedeschi, "Florentine Documents for a History of the *Index of Prohibited Books*," in *Renaissance Studies in Honor of Hans Baron*, ed. Anthony Molho and John Tedeschi (Florence and DeKalb, Ill., 1971), pp. 577–605. Also see the recent survey of Rotondò, "La censura ecclesiastica e la cultura," in *Storia d'Italia*, vol. 5, *I documenti* (Turin: Einaudi, 1973), pp. 1397–1492. All sixteenth-century Indices are printed in Franz Heinrich Reusch, ed., *Die Indices Librorum Prohibitorum des sechzehnten Jahrhunderts* (Tübingen, 1886; reprint Nieuwkoop, 1961). Reusch analyzed the Indices in *Der Index der verbotenen Bücher: Ein Beitrag zur Kirchen- und literaturgeschichte*, 2 vols. in 3 pts. (Bonn, 1883–85; reprint Darmstadt, 1967). Unless otherwise indicated, all documents cited are to be found in the Archivio di Stato, Venice, including the Holy Office (Santo Uffizio) records. The following abbreviations are used: SU, Santo Uffizio; ASVa, Archivio Segreto Vaticano, Rome; Bu., Busta; F., Filza; R., Registro.

of prosecution was low. In the 1550s the Venetians started to become inquisitors, although they still resisted jurisdictional initiatives from the papacy. In the 1560s, climaxing in 1569–71, the Venetians prosecuted heretical books with as much zeal as even Pope Pius V could want. Over the next twenty years enforcement continued, but the fervor gradually waned, until the papacy and the Republic quarreled over books in 1596, as they disputed other matters in that decade.

Whoever sought to censor the Venetian press faced a formidable task, for the Adriatic city harbored one of the great concentrations of printers in the sixteenth century. To make a conservative estimate, Venetian bookmen[2] printed more than 8 million books (i.e., 8 million individual volumes) in the second half of the sixteenth century. This total was the result of about 8,150 editions, new and reprints, an average of 163 annually. These figures do not include pamphlets that did not receive imprimaturs. In any given year, fifty or more publishers produced at least one title, and about 500 publishers appeared on the title pages of Venetian books during the sixteenth century.[3] A Venetian pressrun varied according to the anticipated demand and whether the publishing firm was large or small. The

[2] Rather than attempt to distinguish among publisher, printer, and bookseller (an artificial distinction in any case, because one man or firm frequently did all three), the general term "bookman" is preferred. In the documents, *stampatore, libraio,* and *bibliopola* are used interchangeably and indiscriminately.

[3] The figures are arrived at in the following way. A new title or a substantially revised edition had to receive a governmental imprimatur (permission to print). These, for 1550–99, are recorded in Capi del Consiglio dei Dieci, Notatorio, R. 14–31 and F. 1–14. The average yearly total was seventy-one, giving an estimate of the number of new titles per year. Then, for every new title there were one or more reprints; Gabriel Giolito, for example, published 1.09 reprints for every original title (Salvatore Bongi, *Annali di Gabriel Giolito de' Ferrari da Trino di Monferrato, stampatore in Venezia,* 2 vols. [Rome, 1890–97; reprint Rome, n.d.], supplemented by Paolo Camerini, "Notizia sugli Annali Giolitini di Salvatore Bongi," *Atti e memorie della R. Accademia di scienze, lettere ed arte in Padova,* n.s., 51 [1934–35]: 103–238). If one multiplies 71 × 2.09 for the average yearly production of 148, and then × 50 for the half-century, one arrives at 7,400 editions, a conservative estimate, because publishers did not obtain an imprimatur for every title, especially in the 1550s and early 1560s. Possibly for every ten titles for which an imprimatur was granted, one title was published in first edition and subsequent reprint without an imprimatur. If the total number of editions for the half-century is increased by 10 percent in order to add the works published without imprimaturs, then the total for the half-century is approximately 8,150 editions (148 plus 15 × 50). Then, if the average press run was approximately 1,000 copies (see n. 4 below), over 8 million books were printed in the half-century. The count of *privilegi* (copyrights) by Brown, pp. 236–40, is inaccurate, and the count of editions by Ester Pastorello, *Tipografi, editori, librai a Venezia nel secolo xvi* (Florence, 1924), is underestimated by approximately 50 percent.

50

normal, average pressrun of a title of ordinary sales potential was about 1,000 copies; a major publisher with a title of assured high demand printed pressruns of 2,000 or 3,000.[4] Then reprints followed. Sixteenth-century Venice, a city of 125,000–190,000 people, produced an enormous number of books for an international market.

Neither church nor state in the Renaissance—or perhaps at any other time—believed in complete freedom of the press. The church was interested in doctrinal censorship, the state in political censorship, and both in moral censorship, that is, protecting public morality. The Riformatori dello Studio di Padova were charged by the government with press censorship, but in practice the Venetian press had a minimum of censorship until the 1540s. Then the Venetians made an important administrative move. For several years the papacy had pressured the Venetians to do something about heretics and heretical books within the Venetian dominion. The Venetians resisted the papacy until political miscalculation put them in an awkward position necessitating some gesture toward Rome. Throughout 1546 the Venetians looked benignly on the Schmalkalden League and England, although they stopped short of active support. The Republic's policy awakened openly voiced hopes among Italian philo-Protestants that the Republic would take an active role in the reform of the church. But Henry VIII and Francis I died in early 1547, and Charles V defeated the Schmalkalden League in April 1547, decisively changing the European political balance. As if to erase the memory of their sympathy for the Protestant cause, and to assure pope and emperor of their orthodoxy, the Venetians in the spring of 1547 established a new magistracy with particular competence in heresy, the Tre savi sopra eresia. Their task was to assist the Venetian Inquisition in every aspect of its activity.[5]

[4] There is no study of this aspect of the press, but a number of references support these figures: Ant. Aug. Renouard, *Annales de l'Imprimerie des Alde, ou Histoire des Trois Manuce et de leurs éditions* (Paris, 1834), pp. 270–76; Alberto Tinto, *Annali tipografici dei Tramezzino* (Venice and Rome, 1968), pp. 117–19; Paul F. Grendler, *Critics of the Italian World, 1530–1560: Anton Francesco Doni, Nicolò Franco, and Ortensio Lando* (Madison, Wisc., Milwaukee, Wisc., and London, 1969), p. 179; Lorenzo Campana, "Monsignor Giovanni della Casa e i suoi tempi," *Studi storici* 18 (1909): 465 (letter of July 28, 1548); SU, Bu. 159, "Acta S. Officij Venetiarum 1554–1555," pt. 5, fol. 27ʳ (August 23, 1555), pt. 2, fol. 24ʳ (January 10, 1555).
[5] Aldo Stella, "Utopie e velleità insurrezionali dei filoprotestanti italiani (1545–1547)," *Bibliothèque d'Humanisme et Renaissance* 27 (1965): 133–82; Sforza, pt. 1, pp. 194–96.

From that point the Venetian Inquisition consisted of six members, three clerical and three lay. The inquisitor, the patriarch (or his vicar), and the papal nuncio (or his representative) constituted the ecclesiastical component, the three Venetian nobles the civil component. It met every Tuesday, Thursday, and Saturday, month after month, year after year, with very few missed days. All six could be present at a trial, and at least one of the Tre savi had to be present for the proceedings to be valid, but only the three clergymen handed down the sentence. Then the three laymen authorized the execution of the sentence.

But there can be little doubt that the laymen regulated the tribunal's activity. If the clerical members were unaware of their sentiments, the tribunal could not function. The Inquisition could not issue a warrant for arrest without the concurrence of the three lay assistants, and it depended on the nobles for liaison with the government. If an inquisitor disregarded the views of the lay deputies, the government could press Rome for his removal, as it did, successfully, in the case of Fra Felice Peretti da Montalto (the future Sixtus V) in 1560. Indeed, the Tre savi were the government. They were selected from the most important members of the patriciate, men who were frequently Procurators of St. Mark and often were members of the Consiglio dei Dieci and Collegio. On the whole, however, those nobles who were more sympathetic toward Rome tended to be named to the Inquisition, while notorious antipapalists like Nicolò Da Ponte and Leonardo Donà were seldom selected.[6]

The Roman Inquisition, which Paul III viewed as a tribunal independent of local secular and ecclesiastical control but assisted

---

[6] The names of the Tre savi do not appear in the records of the Segretario delle voci (the magistracy which recorded officeholders), because they were not elected by the Senate or Maggior Consiglio but were appointed by the doge in consultation with the Collegio (his cabinet). But neither do the Tre savi appear in Collegio, Notatorio, the series which usually records Collegio appointments. Then in 1595 selection passed to the Senate, and from that date the Segretario delle voci, Elezioni del Senato documents contain the names. For the period 1547–95, a nearly complete list has been compiled from the SU trials themselves, as the Tre savi were normally mentioned. A comparison with the lists of those who held the highest offices (the Consiglio dei Dieci, the Savii Grandi, Savii di Terraferma, and the Procuratori di San Marco) shows how important those nobles who served as Tre savi were. Indeed, two patricians who acted as lay deputies to the Inquisition later became doge: Alvise Mocenigo (1570–77) and Nicolò Da Ponte (1578–85). Contemporary observers agreed that the lay deputies were "senatori principalissimi."

by the state, was a contradiction in terms unless church and state were in substantial agreement. In Venice, the level of inquisitorial activity, whether it prosecuted vigorously or half-heartedly, reflected the majority opinion of the ruling nobility.

From a slow start in the 1540s, when the nobility were little concerned with heresy and heretical books, Inquisition prosecution grew as the patriciate became Counter-Reformation minded. In the late 1540s, the Inquisition confiscated and burned books in fair quantity. In July 1548, for example, probably about 1,400 volumes were burned publicly.[7] (They were ordinarily burned in Piazza San Marco or near the Rialto Bridge.) The trials of this period, however, show a limited scope of prosecution. The Inquisition normally investigated only upon receipt of a denunciation; then it burned the books and fined the owner but did not investigate the religious opinions of the accused, even if he had Protestant books and was accused of Protestant ideas and associations.[8]

If book censorship is to be effective, some kind of list or index of banned titles is necessary. In January 1549 the Consiglio dei Dieci ordered the Inquisition to draw up such a list. The list or catalog was to include "all the heretical books," "other suspect books," and books "containing things against good morals." The list was completed and printed in May. But no sooner was it printed than the Venetians drew back. Nicolò Da Ponte led the opposition with the argument that in Rome itself no such index existed and every sort of book was sold publicly. The lay deputies were asking Venice to take stronger measures against heresy than the pope was taking in Rome, he argued. Another important senator opposed it because the catalog contained a work composed by a friend of his. By the end of June 1549 the battle was lost and the catalog was suppressed.[9]

Yet, in the next decade, the patriciate showed that it was no friend of the press and not immune from Counter-Reformation sentiment when it came down heavily on the large and important Hebrew printing industry of Venice. As early as 1548, zealots in Rome were concerned with the danger to the faith of Hebrew books, despite earlier papal encouragement of Jewish learning. Then

---

[7] Campana, "Giovanni della Casa," *Studi storici* 17 (1908): 267. Also see the comments of the Father Inquisitor for the years 1544–50 in SU, Bu. 12, Processo Padre Marin da Venezia, fol. 3^v (August 9, 1555).

[8] Two examples are SU, Bu. 13, Processo Antonio Brucioli (1548); SU, Bu. 7, Processo Francesco Stella (1549).

[9] Consiglio dei Dieci, Comune, R. 18, fols. 194^v–195^r (January 16, 1549); Campana, "Giovanni della Casa," pp. 272–74.

in September 1553 the Inquisition in Rome ordered the burning of the Talmud all over Italy. The Venetian government promptly followed suit. On October 20 the Consiglio dei Dieci ordered everyone—Jews, Christians, and bookmen—to give up all Talmuds. The secular government, not the Inquisition, enforced the order, with the result that, in the nuncio's words, "a good fire" burned in Piazza San Marco.[10] The Venetians burned the Talmud in October, before all parts of the papal state complied. In papal Urbino they were burned only in December, and nothing yet had been done in papal Ancona.[11] In 1554 the papacy modified the regulations to permit the holding of Hebrew books after corrections, but in Venice Jewish publishing stopped completely for ten years. The Venetians paid little or no attention to the economic losses to the city, as they joined other Italian clerical and lay rulers in persecuting Hebrew publishing.

The 1550s witnessed a prolonged effort by the papacy to get an Index adopted by the Venetians, while the bookmen fought tenaciously with the limited weapons at their disposal to stop them. In March 1555 Rome sent a new Index to the Venetian Inquisition. The bookmen were given three months to comment on it before it would go into effect. They availed themselves of the opportunity by presenting three protest memorials, in which they made several points: (1) Many authors had their *opera omnia* banned despite the fact that most of their books had nothing to do with religious matters. (2) The bookmen pointed out the financial losses that the book industry would suffer. (3) They argued that the church had tolerated the works of such pagan authors as Lucian for 1,400 years; such titles were of great importance to humanistic studies and should not be banned. (4) They again used the argument of 1549 that the Inquisition wanted to subject the bookmen of Venice to an Index not in effect in Rome. Rome heeded the protests, as it modified and then suspended entirely the 1555 Index.[12]

[10] Consiglio dei Dieci, Comune, R. 21, fols. 58^v–59^r (October 20, 1553); letters of Nuncio Ludovico Beccadelli of August 19, 26, September 23, October 14, 21, 1553, Venice, in *Nunziature di Venezia*, vol. 6, Istituto storico italiano per l'età moderna e contemporanea, Fonti per la storia d'Italia, no. 86, ed. Franco Gaeta (Rome, 1967), pp. 255, 258, 267, 274–75, 277.

[11] See the letter of Girolamo Muzio to Fra Michele Ghislieri of December 16, 1553, Pesaro, in *Lettere catholiche del Mutio Iustinopolitano* (Venice, 1571), pp. 185–86.

[12] SU, Bu. 156, "Librai e libri proibiti, 1545–1571," fols. [55^r–55^v, 60^r–62^v, 64^r–66^v], and Bu. 159, "Acta S. Officij Venetiarum 1554–1555," pt. 2, fol. 48^v, pt. 3, fol. 42^v, pt. 5, fol. 5^r–5^v.

54

Paul IV issued the next Index in early 1559. From January through March, the Venetian bookmen refused to obey. If they were to give up some of their books to be burned, they demanded financial compensation from the papacy. Nevertheless, the papacy discovered a weapon to enforce compliance. All the major Venetian publishers owned bookstores outside the Venetian state, usually all over Italy, including the papal dominion. The papacy threatened to seize the stores and their contents within the papal state. In the face of this threat, the bookmen began to comply. From April though August they made their submissions, offering inventories and some books to be burned. However, it appears that they did not give up all their prohibited books. From the inventories, it appears that they yielded the northern Protestant books but did not yet give up such Italian authors as Machiavelli and Aretino.[13] Also, at this point the Inquisition began to check at the customs house books imported from abroad.[14]

By 1560 the intellectual atmosphere had changed greatly. A generation of free, mocking, anticlerical authors had died or had found the climate uncongenial to their writing and had gone into retirement. Machiavelli's name was disappearing from books, and writers were noticeably more cautious. At the same time, a genuine religious revival under the leadership of a reformed papacy occurred.

The bookmen were businessmen attuned to the intellectual atmosphere. They clearly saw what was happening and reacted like good merchants: they began to publish more religious books and fewer titles of secular vernacular literature. (By secular vernacular literature is meant poetry, drama, collections of letters, dialogues on various topics, courtesy books, vernacular grammars, and vernacular classics like Dante, Petrarch, Boccaccio, and Ariosto. Into this group fall most of the works of the most popular and prolific sixteenth-century authors, like Pietro Aretino, Anton Francesco Doni, et al.) An analysis of the imprimaturs, that is, the government's permissions to publish new books, from 1550 through 1606, shows the changeover (see table 1).

[13] Letters of Cardinal Michele Ghislieri to the Venetian inquisitor Fra Felice Peretti of December 31, 1558, January 19, 25, 28, February 4, 11, 18, 25, March 4, 11, 1559, Rome, in SU, Bu. 160, "Dispacci ai Capi del Consiglio dei Dieci, 1500–1560," no pagination, organized chronologically; SU, Bu. 14, Processi Vincenzo Valgrisi et al., testimony of Valgrisi and other bookmen of August 9, 11, 14, 17, 19, 1559, September 1, 1570, no pagination. Some inventories are found in SU, Bu. 156, "Librai e libri proibiti, 1545–1571," fols. [72^r–72^v, 86^r–86^v, 88^r, 89^r–90^v]. Part of the Valgrisi testimony is printed in Sforza, pt. 2, pp. 175–77.

[14] For the Inquisition decree, see Brown, pp. 127, 213 (text), 364.

TABLE 1

IMPRIMATURS ISSUED FOR NEW TITLES, 1550–1606

| | SUBJECT MATTER (%) | | |
	Religious	Secular Vernacular Literature	Average Number of Imprimaturs per Year*
1550–54 ....13.1		32.7	55.2
1555–59 ....14.8		23.0	78.0
1560–64 ....23.2		22.2	87.0
1565–69 ....23.2		20.6	92.4
1570–74 ....22.7		18.0	88.6
1575–79 ....31.6		11.7	45.2†
1580–84 ....30.5		28.3	45.25‡
1585–89 ....33.3		21.3	81.4
1590–94 ....35.5		16.7	63.6§
1595–99 ....27.5		18.3	73.7**
1600–1604 ....30.0		20.0	79.2
1605–6 ....35.3		22.2	113.0

SOURCE.—Capi del Consiglio dei Dieci, Notatorio, R. 14–33 and F. 1–14.
* The average yearly total of imprimaturs, 1550–1606, was seventy-one.
† Great Plague of 1575–77.
‡ 1584 data missing.
§ Famine, 1590–91.
** 1595 and 1596 data missing.

From 1550 through 1559, secular vernacular literature accounted for approximately 27 percent of the new titles published, while religious titles accounted for approximately 14 percent. During the 1560s the figures altered as vernacular literature dropped and the number of religious books rose. Then from 1570 through 1606 the figures reversed: secular vernacular literature accounted for approximately 20 percent of the total and religious titles approximately 30 percent. In short, Italians were more interested in religious matters, and the bookmen supplied them the books. The majority of these religious titles were devotional works rather than theological or doctrinal, that is, inspirational treatises, meditations, books of sermons, hagiography, and the like, and the majority were in the vernacular. These were books for the average devout person, cleric and layman, rather than for professional theologians. The publishers simply switched from supplying a secular market to a comparable devotional one. There is no evidence that they lost money or that their presses were idled by the changeover.

The political climate changed as much as the intellectual atmosphere. For the Venetians, the major threat was from the Turks, and, to meet this threat, the Republic had need of papal assistance.

56

Indeed, because of the Turks, the Venetians were on friendlier terms with the papacy than at any other time in the century.

Both the growth of religiosity and the political situation inclined the Venetians toward a more militant Counter-Reformation posture. But probably the clinching reason was the discovery that Protestantism had made inroads among the younger members of the nobility. Between 1565 and 1569, eight nobles abjured heretical views.[15] Most of them fitted a pattern: they were young, acquainted with each other, and had developed heretical views under the tutelage of Protestant humanists and schoolmasters. These young nobles read Calvin's *Catechism* and *Institutes* and titles of Bernardino Ochino, Peter Martyr Vermigli, and Pier Paolo Vergerio.

The presence of a few Protestants among the younger nobility did not mean that there was any possibility of the city moving into the Protestant orbit, then or later. Not only was it too late politically for such a move, but more important, Venetian loyalties were fundamentally and traditionally Catholic. Nevertheless, the discovery of Protestantism among the nobility must have been disconcerting, for the Venetian elders always worried greatly about the moral and political training of their successors. In addition, like most princes and nobles of the century, the Venetians believed that religious division inevitably led to sedition; how much worse might the situation be if some of the dissenters were nobles? In the 1560s the Venetians fervently proclaimed their orthodoxy to the world[16] and

[15] SU, Bu. 20, Antonio Loredano and Alvise Malipiero, contains the abjurations of these two and Giacomo Malipiero, all in 1565; Bu. 20, Michele De Basili, Carlo Corner, and Venturino Dalle Modonette, has Corner's abjuration of 1565; Bu. 22, Francesco Emo, has his abjuration of 1567; Bu. 23, Silvestro, Cipriano, and Stefano Semprini, Andrea Dandolo, Marc'Antonio Canale, et al., contains the abjurations of Andrea Dandolo (1568), Marc'Antonio Canale (1568), and Alvise Mocenigo (1569). In addition, other nobles were accused but not questioned. The only study of these patrician heretics is Edouard Pommier, "La société vénitienne et la Réforme protestante au XVIᵉ siècle," *Bollettino dell'Istituto di storia della Società e dello Stato Veneziano* 1 (1959): 7–14. Pommier sees these heretical nobles as moved by "une sorte de dilettantisme religieux" (p. 10). Perhaps he underestimates the seriousness of their quest, for they developed their beliefs over several years of clandestine activity. Some of them considered following Andrea Da Ponte, brother of future doge Nicolò, to Geneva. And the anguish revealed in the testimony of Marc'Antonio Canale appears to be deeper than what one would expect from a dilettante.

[16] In 1562, for example, the government reacted angrily to French court gossip which reported that Protestant preachers enjoyed large audiences in Venice. The Consiglio dei Dieci dispatched an indignant letter denying the allegations and affirming that the city was *cattolicissima* (Consiglio dei Dieci, Secrete, R. 7, fol. 88ʳ–88ᵛ, August 7, 1562). Nevertheless, at that time Venetian nobles and commoners gathered at the Fondaco dei tedeschi and elsewhere to be taught by Protestants.

took the necessary steps to make the reality conform to the image. While the new censorship decrees of the 1560s did not present the discovery of local heresy as their justification (such an admission would have been acutely embarrassing), it is hard to escape the conclusion that the two were linked.

In the 1560s, church and state cooperated to enact new censorship legislation. A number of decrees erected various tedious legal hurdles before an author or publisher could obtain the necessary license to publish a book. These regulations were not new, but they were more extensive and better enforced. The government tightened the inspection of imported books at the customs house, giving the Inquisition power to have a man on the spot to inspect the books. All this was summarized in an omnibus law of the Consiglio dei Dieci of June 28, 1569.[17]

For its part, the Tridentine Council issued a new authoritative Index of Prohibited Books with extensive rules for authors and publishers. The Venetian government accepted this Index along with all the other Tridentine decrees without a murmur in 1564, but the bookmen ignored it. Then with the passage of the law of June 28, 1569, the Inquisition began to enforce the Tridentine Index. The tribunal demanded inventories and the consignment of prohibited titles. The inquisitor's men began making personal visits to the shops and storehouses of the bookmen. These visits were new; in the past the Inquisition had no such authority. From 1569 through 1571, the inquisitor's men systematically visited the Venetian bookstores. Catching some of the bookmen unprepared, they found and confiscated a large number of prohibited volumes, this time Italian books of Machiavelli and Aretino as well as nonreligious titles of northern Protestants. The Holy Office burned the books and warned or fined twenty-two bookmen, assessing fines of from a few ducats to fifty, depending on their guilt or ability to pay.[18]

In addition, all through the 1560s and early 1570s there were a number of trials in which individual bookmen or others were denounced for having prohibited titles. The Inquisition in this way caught and punished—almost always with fines—a number of people.

The parallel civil court, the Esecutori contro la bestemmia, also burned books in the late 1560s. Like the Inquisition, in March 1568

---

[17] Consiglio dei Dieci, Comune, R. 29, fols. 30ʳ–31ʳ.
[18] SU, Bu. 156, "Librai e libri proibiti, 1545–1571," fols. 6ʳ–9ᵛ, 15ᵛ–34ʳ (August 9, 18, 23, 25, 28, 30, September 6, 13, 18, 20, 27, October 2, 5, 8, 11, 15, 24, 1571).

58

it appointed an official, a former printer, to visit bookstores and to spy on bookmen, and he cooperated with the Holy Office.[19] The Esecutori also fell on the Jews again. Hebrew publishing had resumed in 1563, although the Talmud was still banned, under the condition of prepublication censorship. But in 1568 the Esecutori arrested a number of Jews and several of their Christian printers for publishing volumes lacking the proper corrections. The Esecutori confiscated well over 15,000 volumes and imposed fines of over 2,200 ducats, to be paid to the Arsenal. Venetian Jews who had commissioned the books had to pay most of the fines, up to 500 ducats per individual. The civil tribunal assessed much heavier fines than did the Inquisition.[20]

Yet there were limits to the Venetian acceptance of the war against heresy. The Venetian government demonstrated very little sympathy for the bookmen and the Jews, but it did protect the German Protestant scholars at Padua. Of a total of 1,000–1,500 students in any given year, the Germans, by far the largest group of foreigners, numbered from 100 to 300. Most were Protestants, and a good number of the French scholars there were Huguenots. As scholars and students, these foreign Protestants brought prohibited books into the Venetian territory and were customers for the prohibited titles of Erasmus, Melanchthon, and others. The papacy wanted to keep Protestant scholars and their books out of Padua, but the Venetians turned a deaf ear for reasons of politics, economics, and prestige: (1) They hesitated to offend German princes by turning away German students. (2) They did not wish to lose the 25,000–30,000 ducats that the Germans spent annually on food, accommodation, clothing, books, and other expenses. (3) The Venetians believed that the greater the number of scholars, especially foreign ones, the greater the reputation of the university.[21] The papacy tried to answer these arguments, and the Venetian government agreed that every scholar had to make a profession of

[19] Esecutori contro la bestemmia, Bu. 56, Notatorio Terminazioni, R. 1561–1582, fol. 38ᵛ (March 7, 1568); SU, Bu. 25, Processo Girolamo Calepin, testimony of Alvise Zio, the Esecutori official, of March 20(?), 1568, no pagination.

[20] Esecutori contro la bestemmia, Bu. 56, Notatorio Terminazioni, R. 1561–1582, fols. 41bisʳ–47ᵛ (September 22, 24, 27, October 29, 1568).

[21] Biagio Brugi, *Gli scolari dello Studio di Padova nel Cinquecento, con un'appendice sugli studenti tedeschi e la S. Inquisizione a Padova nella seconda metà del secolo XVI*, 2d ed. rev. (Padua and Verona, 1905), esp. pp. 71–100; letter and memorial of Nuncio Giovanni Antonio Facchinetti of September 14, 1566, Venice, *Nunziature di Venezia*, vol. 8, ed. Aldo Stella (Rome, 1963), pp. 105–9.

faith before receiving his degree. But the law was not enforced, and Rome knew it.

The first, small sign that the high-water mark of book burning had been reached and that potential for disagreement existed occurred in the early 1570s over what at first glance might be considered an insignificant issue: exclusive papal permission to print canonical and liturgical works. In its concluding decrees of 1563, the Council of Trent authorized the papacy to revise and promulgate Catholicism's two most important devotional manuals, the Roman Breviary and the Missal, as well as the Tridentine Catechism and the Index. As the revised editions were completed, the papacy promulgated them, forbidding the use of many older ones. In order to ensure accuracy, the papacy authorized exclusive printing rights to the press of Paolo Manuzio in Rome for all of Catholic Christendom. Manuzio printed the first editions of these texts and then sold rights to other printers across Europe.

These exclusive privileges provoked intense, prolonged disputes which heralded future conflict. The reason is obvious: the market was enormous. Every priest or religious had to have a breviary; a Missal was necessary for the celebration of every single mass. In addition, pious laymen and women used breviaries or simplified offices. In short, while humanist texts earned prestige, the Roman Breviary and the Missal paid the bills. Publishers in Protestant lands were similarly dependent on the Psalter.[22]

The controversy over the exclusive privilege for the reformed Little Office of Our Lady (Officium Beatae Mariae Virginis nuper reformatum) illustrates the nature and results of these disputes.[23] As

[22] See the important articles of Robert M. Kingdon, "Patronage, Piety, and Printing in Sixteenth-Century Europe," in *A Festschrift for Frederick B. Artz,* ed. David H. Pinckney and Theodore Ropp (Durham, N.C., 1964), pp. 19–36, and "The Plantin Breviaries: A Case Study in the Sixteenth-Century Business Operations of a Publishing House," *Bibliothèque d'Humanisme et Renaissance* 22 (1960): 133–50.

[23] SU, Bu. 156, "Librai e libri proibiti, 1545–1571," fols. 9^v–10^v, 12^r–15^v, 19^r–20^r, 37^v–47^r (testimony of various bookmen of August 18, 21, 23, 25, 28, 30, 1571, January 3, 31, July 26, 29, 31, August 9, October 30, 1572); letters of Nuncio Facchinetti of July 26, August 2, 9, 23, October 25, November 15, 29, 1572, Venice, in ASVa, Segretario di Stato, Venezia, F. 12, fols. 40^v–41^r, 43^r–43^v, 46^r–47^r, 56^r, 98^r–98^v, 119^v–120^r, 129^v–130^r; letter of Venetian Patriarch Giovanni Trevisan of November 1, 1572, Venice, in ibid., fol. 100^r. For final resolution of the conflict, see the papal letter of January 27, 1573, authorizing Luc'Antonio Giunti to print the Little Office notwithstanding the previous exclusive privilege granted to Paolo Manuzio (see the letter in the following copy of the Little Office: Biblioteca Apostolica Vaticana, Barb. C. I. 24, *Officium Beatae Mariae Virginis nuper reformatum Pij V. Pont. Max. iussu editum,* Venetiis Apud Iunctam, Permittente Sede Apostolica, MDLXXXI, Sigs. +i^v–+ii^r).

the title suggests, it is a smaller office consisting of psalms, hymns, and prayers, for the most part in honor of Mary. It was used not only by many monks and nuns, but also by laymen and laywomen and even children. The Aldine press of Venice won the exclusive Venetian privilege, and it was sanctioned by the Venetian Senate. The Aldine press quickly began to capitalize on the privilege by printing 20,000 copies in seven or eight months in 1572. The other bookmen were acutely unhappy and began to contravene the exclusive privilege. This provoked a controversy which lasted for two years; it was finally resolved by personal negotiation between the Venetian ambassador and the pope.

Rome defended the exclusive privilege by arguing that only in that way could she ensure accuracy, and the Venetian printers were not above carelessness or adding unauthorized material. Rome also argued that since the original printers had had heavy expenses in preparing the new editions, they deserved to be rewarded. The Venetian bookmen saw the issue as acutely financial. Some smaller printers pleaded that the printing and sale of the Little Office and similar books meant the difference between success and starvation.

At first unsympathetic and unconcerned for the bookmen, the government eventually responded when the dispute would not go away. At first a few nobles, like the anticlerical Nicolò Da Ponte, supported the bookmen, and eventually the majority did. When the nobility eventually supported them, they justified their stance on economic and jurisdictional grounds. These motives should not be overemphasized, because it took a long time for the government to bestir itself. Moreover, the government came to the defense of the bookmen only when it was apparent to everyone, including the papal nuncio, that profit, not piety, was at the bottom of the dispute. The disputes over the Breviary, Little Office, Missal, and Catechism ended in 1573 with the victory of the bookmen. The papacy sanctioned the violation of the exclusive privilege, a minor defeat in comparison with the successful enforcement of the Index of Prohibited Books.

The disputes demonstrated that papal regulation of the Venetian press had reached a plateau. From 1573 until the early 1590s, the Index was strongly enforced on the surface. Certainly very few prohibited books were published. But there are many signs that there was a great deal of violation in the sale and importation of prohibited titles. Certain kinds of heretical and prohibited books could be found without difficulty if one knew where to look.

Humanistic works by northern Protestant authors like Melanchthon, Protestant editions of the Bible like that of Antonio Brucioli, the works of Erasmus, Italian titles like the works of Aretino and Machiavelli, titles of Ochino, Calvin's *Catechism,* and a few works by Luther could be purchased at Venetian bookstores if the customer knew where to look. Some bookstores, like the firms of Francesco and Giordano Ziletti, made a practice of selling these books under the counter.[24]

Scholars in the humanities particularly resented and disobeyed the regulations of the Index and Inquisition. Northern humanists, many of them Protestants, wrote a great deal and very well in these disciplines. Italian humanists who obeyed the Index had little or no access to much northern scholarship. Since it was practically impossible to obtain from the Inquisition permission to hold these titles, many disobeyed the laws and tried to be discreet about it. They seldom fell into the hands of the Holy Office unless they were flagrant violators. To cite a case of 1580, one monk was not denounced for heretical books and opinions until he had been in the monastery for six years, had tried repeatedly to persuade his fellow monks to accept heretical views, and showed himself to be an irascible and tactless man.[25] It is a reasonable assumption that others, less outspoken and contentious, held heterodox religious books without being disturbed.

Throughout the 1570s and 1580s Venetian bookmen continued to smuggle prohibited books from Germany and Switzerland into Venice. On their regular journeys from the Frankfurt bookfairs, they acquired prohibited works, especially in Basel, and brought them into Venetian territory. Then the bookmen found a way of eluding the Inquisition check at the customs house.[26] One can only speculate on how they did it. Bribery, of either the customs officials or the Inquisition agents, is a possibility, although the dedication of the latter appears to have put them beyond bribery. False title pages were a common device. Most likely, the sheer cumbersomeness of the process, involving several people and minute lists of titles,

[24] For examples, see the following trials: SU, Bu. 25, Girolamo Calepin (1573); Bu. 37, Giovanni Battista Sanudo (1574); Bu. 37, Bartolomeo de Sabio (1574); Bu. 38, Fra Leonardo (1574); Bu. 50, Guidone Simottini (1583); Bu. 59, Gioachino Brugnoli (1587).

[25] SU, Bu. 47, Fra Clemente Valvassore (1580–82).

[26] See the following trials: SU, Bu. 49, Francesco Ziletti and Felice Valgrisi (1582), Bu. 50, Bonifacio Ciera, Luc'Antonio Giunti, Melchiorre Scoto, and Antonio Bragia (1583).

62

generated shortcuts and carelessness that defeated the inspection. Noting or copying the titles of hundreds of books is a tiresome process. Probably the habit developed of not looking at all the books; perhaps the Inquisition agent only examined those at the top of the bale. The written lists were possibly not done carefully, or the Inquisition agent accepted a list already prepared by the bookman, who falsified it if necessary. Once the bookmen were through customs, the Inquisition found it practically impossible to trace the books.

But focusing solely on the known violations gives a one-sided view of these two decades. In 1559, and again in 1569–71, the Inquisition found and destroyed large quantities of prohibited titles, thus asserting its will on the book industry and driving commerce in prohibited titles underground. In the 1570s and 1580s, the tribunal's task was to hold traffic to a low level. The Inquisition used customs checks, bookstore visitations, and denunciations to do this. Once it learned of a violation, the tribunal questioned witnesses and made arrests; sometimes it located the guilty party and contraband titles, and other times it did not. Given the size and scope of the book trade and the limited Holy Office resources, total enforcement was not possible, nor was it necessary. The Holy Office realized that it did not need to catch each violator or to destroy every prohibited title to be effective. Rather, it aimed at keeping prohibited titles out of the hands of the vast majority of the reading public by maintaining enough pressure to hold the traffic down to an acceptable level. The evidence of the trials suggests that the Holy Office achieved this goal, for while a range of prohibited titles appeared in these trials, they were discovered in single copies rather than in quantity. As long as banned titles could not be printed in Venice, and the clandestine traffic was kept within bounds, the tribunal with the aid of time gradually diminished the stock of prohibited titles.

As the century waned, the Venetians argued that the press was in economic decline. In 1588 the government told the nuncio that the number of Venetian presses had declined from 120 to seventy, and in 1596 the bookmen lamented that the number had fallen to forty.[27] Significantly, the Venetians attributed the decline of the local press to the growth of the Vatican and other Roman presses.

[27] The documents do not state at what date there were 120 presses (letter of Nuncio Girolamo Matteucci of April 2, 1588, Venice, in ASVa, Segretario di Stato, F. 26, fol. 181ᵛ; petition of the bookmen of May 3, 1596 to the Venetian government and forwarded to Rome in ASVa, Fondo Borghese IV, 224, fol. 117ʳ).

The available documentation does not support the Venetian view. The number of presses in operation at a given moment is unknown, but reliable statistics on the number of imprimaturs issued for new or substantially revised titles are available. Using the period 1550–74 as the base, during the plague of 1575–77 the number of imprimaturs dropped to 50 percent of the previous figures and remained at this low level through 1584. Then, for the period 1585–1605, the number of imprimaturs rose to 95 percent of the base period.[28] These figures do not include the unchanged reprints for which an imprimatur was not needed, but it is unlikely that the reprint figure was different. Thus, despite the Index and the gradual demise of such publishing giants as the Aldine press and Giolito, Venetian publishing quantitatively declined, but only modestly. Nevertheless, the Venetians constantly stressed the economic decline of the press in their disputes with Rome.

What had changed was the Venetian attitude toward the jurisdictional prerogatives of church and state.[29] To put it succinctly, the Venetian government was now determined to enlarge its control over the religious, moral, and social lives of its citizens, and this could only occur at the expense of the papacy. The battle over the 1596 Index illustrated this new sensibility.

The Venetians in 1596 did not object to the papacy's right to censor books, nor did they object to the titles listed in the Index. They did object very strenuously to the new rules which were appended.[30] One of these gave local ecclesiastical authorities the power to prohibit other titles not on the Index which they judged to be heretical or immoral. Another rule decreed that the bookmen had

[28] See table 1.

[29] Gaetano Cozzi, *Il doge Nicolò Contarini: Ricerche sul patriziato veneziano agli inizi del Seicento* (Venice and Rome, 1958); Aldo Stella, *Chiesa e stato nelle relazioni dei nunzi pontifici a Venezia: Ricerche sul giurisdizionalismo veneziano dal XVI al XVIII secolo,* Studi e testi, no. 239 (Vatican City, 1964); William J. Bouwsma, *Venice and the Defense of Republican Liberty: Renaissance Values in the Age of the Counter Reformation* (Berkeley and Los Angeles, 1968); also see Martin J. C. Lowry, "The Church and Venetian Political Change in the Later Cinquecento" (Ph.D. diss., University of Warwick, 1970–71).

[30] The rules and the concluding concordat are summarized by Brown, pp. 144–52. The struggle over the Index is discussed by Mario Brunetti, "Schermaglie veneto-pontificie prima dell'Interdetto: Leonardo Donà avanti il Dogado," in *Paolo Sarpi e i suoi tempi: Studi storici* (Città di Castello, 1923), pp. 124–33. However, there is more information available than what Brown and Brunetti uncovered. The chief sources are Collegio, Esposizioni Roma, R. 6, fols. 112ʳ–170ᵛ, passim; Senato, Deliberazioni Roma, R. 11, fols. 67ᵛ–113ʳ, passim; Senato, Dispacci da Roma, F. 37, fols. 202ʳ–409ᵛ, passim, and F. 38, fols. 32ʳ–33ᵛ, for the ambassador's letters; ASVa, Segretario di Stato, Venezia, F. 32, fols. 293ʳ–351ʳ, passim, for the nuncio's letters.

to swear an oath before the bishop and inquisitor that they would obey the new Index and would not knowingly admit into the guild anyone suspected of heresy. The Venetians, led by Leonardo Donà and Giacomo Foscarini, objected above all to the oath as encroaching on civil jurisdiction.

The dispute was heated, but in the end the papacy agreed to the Venetian conditions. A concordat was signed and issued with the new Index. The oath was revoked and other rules modified. The concordat of 1596 was a clear victory for the bookmen and the Venetians. While it did not touch the list of prohibited titles or the guidelines for expurgation, it substantially restricted in practical ways papal and inquisitorial control of the book trade. Moreover, the concordat provided the jurisdictional platform from which Paolo Sarpi and the Senate might expand state control of censorship in the future. The fight over the Index and the resultant concordat were the logical result of a slow growth of Venetian solicitude for the press and the Republic's growing insistence that she, rather than the papacy, should rule the moral and, to a growing extent, the spiritual lives of her citizens. Finally, the Index dispute contributed to the strained relations between the two which led to the Interdict conflict of 1606–7.

Probably more prohibited materials entered Venice in the period 1590–1605 than in any previous decade since the implementation of the Tridentine Index in 1569. Gone were the days of surprise inspections of bookstores. The outbreak of the Interdict conflict provided little or nothing new in such areas as clandestine book importation but accentuated or increased the tendencies already evident by providing greater public support, even approbation, for violations and violators. The clandestine traffic became for all intents and purposes open, and the Inquisition could do little or nothing about it. This state of affairs continued for a few years after the Interdict until Venetian-papal relations regained their former equilibrium.

This study suggests several conclusions. The Index and Inquisition became effective when the Venetian patriciate decided to support them. This took a number of years and the joining together of political and religious motives. But once the ruling class made its decision, neither economic and jurisdictional reasons nor the pleas of the bookmen moved it. Once supported by the Venetian government, the censorship was very effective. Prepublication censorship ensured that very few banned titles were printed in Venice. Halting the clandestine importation of prohibited titles and the resale of older banned volumes was more difficult, but again the Inquisition had notable success. For the vast majority of the reading population, the banned books were unavailable. But for the determined few, enough loopholes existed so that any title could be found if the reader was willing to bear the necessary difficulty, risk, and cost. Weighing the exact impact of the Index and Inquisition on Italian intellectual life is beyond the scope of this study, but a precise understanding of the availability of prohibited titles would be part of this assessment. With the passage of time, state support for the Index waned. Just as a combination of circumstances generated this support earlier, so jurisdictional, political, and, to a lesser extent, economic motives eroded it in the 1590s. Banned titles still could not be printed in Venice, but it became easier to acquire those printed abroad. Eventually, in the seventeenth century, the fervor of the Counter-Reformation cooled to the point that even some prohibited titles of the previous century were reprinted in Venice.[31]

[31] Between 1628 and 1633, Marco Ginammi published Machiavelli's *Discourses,* which he attributed to "Amadio Niecollucci," and six of Aretino's religious titles, attributed to "Partenio Etiro."

X

THE *TRE SAVII SOPRA ERESIA* 1547-1605: A PROSOPOGRAPHICAL STUDY

The purpose of this study is to examine the membership of the *Tre Savii sopra Eresia* from its inauguration in 1547 to the eve of the interdict. Fighting heresy and, at the same time, guarding lay jurisdiction were very important political matters to the Republic. Consequently, the leaders of the state chose the *Savii sopra Eresia* with care. This study offers a list with political biographies of the 117 nobles known to have served as assistants to the Holy Office in this period. It shows that the majority of the *Savii sopra Eresia* were the most powerful patricians of the period, the leaders of the Venetian state. The data compiled may be of use to scholars analyzing the Venetian political system.[1]

I

On April 22, 1547, the Venetian government issued a decree:

« Noi Francesco Donato Doge di Venezia, etc. Conoscendo niuna cosa esser più degna di Principe Christiano che l'esser studioso della relliggione e difensore della fede cattolica, il che etiam m'è commesso per la Commissione Nostra Ducale et è stato sempre istituito dalli Maggiori Nostri, e però ad honore della Santa Madre Chiesa havemo elletti in questi tempi, col Nostro Minor Consiglio, Voi dilettissimi Nobili nostri Nicolò Tiepolo Dr., Francesco Contarini, e mess. Antonio Venier Dr., come quelli che siete probi, discreti e cattolici uomini e diligenti in tutte le attioni vostre, e massimamente dove conoscete trattarsi dell'honore del Signore Iddio; e vi commettemo che dobbiate diligente-

1. In order to conserve space without sacrificing the data of Part II, the introduction and supporting documentation in Part I has been much abbreviated. I hope to return to the subject of the Venetian constitution and the concentration of political power in a future study. I thank Dr. Martin Lowry for showing me some of his research and for reading this paper. Fellowships from the American Council of Learned Societies and the Canada Council made my research possible.

mente inquirere contro gl'eretici che si trovassero in questa Città, et etiam admettere querele contro alcuno di loro che fossero date, et essere inseme col Rev.^{mo} Legato e Ministri suoi, col Rev. Patriarca Nostro e Ministri suoi e col Venerabile Inquisitore dell'heretica pravità, sollecitando cadauno di loro in ogni tempo et in ogni caso che occorrerà alla formatione dei processi; alla quale etiam sarete Assistenti; et etiam procurando che siano fatte le sentenze debite contro quelli che saranno conosciuti rei; e di tempo in tempo ne avviserete tutto quello che occorrerà, perché non vi mancheremo d'ogni aiuto e favore secondo la forma della Promotione Nostra, etc. »[2]

Doge Donà's decree cited historical precedent and his ducal commission to guard the faith for the appointments. The earliest documented notice of the establishment of a magistracy to investigative heresy comes from Doge Marino Morosini's *promissione ducale* of 1249:

« Ad honorem autem Dei et sacrosante matris Ecclesie et robur et defensionem fidei catholice studiosi erimus cum consilio nostrorum Consiliariorum vel maioris partis quod probi et discreti et catholici Viri eligantur et constituantur super inquirendis hereticis in Veneciis. Et omnes illos qui dati erunt pro hereticis per dominum Patriarcham Gradensem, Episcopum Castellanum vel per alios Episcopos provincie ducatus Veneciarum, a Grado videlicet usque Caputaggeris, comburi faciemus de consilio nostrorum consiliariorum vel maioris partis ipsorum ».[3]

The similarities between the two documents demonstrate that the Venetians in 1547 were aware of historical precedent. The *promissione ducale* of 1249 first states that the doge with his *Consiglieri* should elect an unspecified number of « probi et discreti et catholici viri » to investigate heresy in Venice. Then it promises that the doge and his *Consiglieri* would burn those that the Patriarch of Grado, the Bishop of Castello, or other bishops from the Venetian Dominion found guilty of heresy.[4]

2. The decree is printed by G. SFORZA, *Riflessi della Controriforma nella Repubblica di Venezia,* in « Archivio Storico Italiano », 93 (1935), pt. I, pp. 195-196.
3. *Promissione del Doge Marino Morosini 1249,* a.c. di A. TORNIELLI, Venezia 1853, p. 26.
4. Pope Nicholas II in 1451 suppressed the patriarchate of Grado and the

Despite medieval precedents, the decree of April 22, 1547, established a new magistracy, the *Tre Savii sopra Eresia*.[5] The decree stated that the doge with his *Minor Consiglio* (the doge meeting with his six Ducal Councillors) would choose the lay deputies. But it did not establish the electoral procedure nor the length of service for the *Savii sopra Eresia*. Constitutionally, the Venetians linked the office to the ducal *promissione*. Hence, when they wished to change the election procedure or terms of office, they waited for an interregnum, and then altered the *promissione*.

The Venetians refined the electoral procedure on June 5, 1554, in the interregnum between the death of Doge Marcantonio Trevisan (May 31) and the election of Francesco Venier (June 11). The doge would propose names and the *Consiglieri* would vote for them; the successful candidates had to receive the approval of at least four of the six *Consiglieri*. Those elected could not refuse the office under pain of 100 ducats, and the term was set at two years.[6]

diocese of Castello in order to create the new patriachate of Venice, naming St. Lorenzo Giustiniani the first patriarch of Venice.

5. For a brief summary of the medieval Inquisition in Venice, see GRENDLER, pp. 35-36. (Please see the list of ABBREVIATIONS in Part II for many citations used in this study). Also, the Archivio della Curia Patriarcale, Venezia, contains 33 *causae* for the period 1461 through 1558 in its *Repertorium Criminalium Sanctae Inquisionis*. The majority dealt with the occult, but there were also heresy trials in 1461, 1468, 1473, 1510, 1512, 1514, 1525, and. 1526.

6. « Circa 'l capitolo terzo della promissione ducal disponente, che per il ser.^mo Principe si habbi ad elegger boni, discreti, et Catholici homini sopra la inquisitione delli heretici co'l cons. delli conseglieri, over della maggior parte de quelli, sia dichiarito, et preso, che quelli, che saranno denominati per il serenissimo Principe sopra detta inquisitione s'habbiano a ballotar per li consiglieri, et non s'intendono rimasti se non haveranno al meno ballote quattro di essi consiglieri, et quelli, che saranno eletti non possano refutar sotto pena di ducati cento delli quali siano mandati immediate debitori a palazzo donde non possano esser depenati se non haveranno integramente satisfatto, li quali siano dell'arsenal nostro, et non stiano in detto officio più de anni doi ». Vote: 1289 di si, 72 di no, 37 non sinceri. The *Cinque Correttori della Promissione Ducale* who proposed the law were Priamo Da Lezze PSM (a strong contender for the ducal biretta), Marc'Antonio di Cristoforo Venier PSM (another strong contender), Tommaso di Alvise Contarini (PSM in 1557), Lorenzo di Alvise Priuli PSM (doge 1556-59), and Girolamo di Marin Grimani (PSM in 1560). All except Priamo Da Lezze had been *Savii sopra Eresia* in the past or would be in the future. A.S.V., *Maggior Consiglio, Deliberazioni,* reg. 28 (*Rocca*), 1552-1565, f. 41 v.

Two years later, the Venetians shifted the election from the *Minor Consiglio* to the larger *Collegio*. On June 7, 1556, in the interregnum between the death of Doge Francesco Venier and the election of Doge Lorenzo Priuli, the *Maggior Consiglio* approved the change. The election of the « savi sopra la inquisitione delle heretici » was of such importance, because it concerned the « servitio del Signor Dio », that it should proceed with greater solemnity, declared the preamble. Therefore, the doge would nominate two men for each vacancy, and the *Collegio* would elect one of them by majority vote. The noble could not refuse the office under penalty of 100 ducats. The elected patrician would serve for a period of not more than two years. He was then ineligible for re-election for a period of time equal to his service as lay deputy.[7]

With the revision of 1556, the *Tre Savii sopra Eresia* became, in effect, a sub-committee of the *Collegio*, the governing council of greatest importance in the Venetian system. The decree further applied to the lay deputies the principle of *contumacia* (ineligibility) under the same terms applied to other very high offices, as the *Savii del Consiglio*. This emphasized the importance with which the leaders of the Republic endowed the magistracy of the *Tre Savii sopra Eresia*.

7. « La elettione delli savi sopra la inquisitione delli heretici della quala parla il capitolo terzo della promission Ducal, et la parte della correttione di esso presa in questo conseglio del 1554 à dì cinque Zugno è di tale importantia trattandosi del servitio del Signor Dio, che è conveniente, che la se faccia ancor con maggior solennità di quella, che fin hora è stato deliberato. Però sia preso, che ogni volta che si havevà à far elettione di detti savij, il Serenissimo Principe se ne havevà à far tre, ne habbia à denominar sei, se due, quattro, et se uno, due, che habbiamo le qualità, che ricerca tal officio: ita che l'elettione sempre se facci con scontro, overo scontri, et li denominati poi siano ballotati nel collegio nostro. Et quelli che scaderanno più ballote delli altri passando la mità, siano rimassi non possano refutar sotto le pene statuti in detta parte del 1554 dovendo star in detto officio anni due, come in essa parte si contiene, ne possano esser reeletti, se non haveranno vacato altratanto tempo, quanto saranno stati in detto officio ». Vote: 1152 di si, 43 di no, 36 non sinceri. The *Cinque Correttori* who proposed this measure were Filippo Tron PSM, Francesco Contarini (probably Francesco di Zaccaria, one of the original lay deputies and PSM later in 1556), Stefano Tiepolo PSM, Nicolò di Antonio Da Ponte (doge 1578-85), and Vettore Grimani PSM. All five received votes in the 1556 ducal election. Da Mosto, p. 324. A.S.V., *Maggior Consiglio, Deliberazioni*, reg. 28 (*Rocca*), 1552-1565, ff. 58 r - 58 v.

The remarkable constitutional feature of the lay deputy post was the exclusiveness of its electoral procedure. Most other very high officials were chosen by means of an elaborate system of nomination followed by the vote of a large governmental body, such as the Senate or *Maggior Consiglio*. By contrast, a handful of men nominated and elected the *Tre Savii sopra Eresia*. Doge and *Collegio* probably felt that the Republic's goal of stamping out heresy and safeguarding lay jurisdiction would be best served by a very restrictive franchise which eliminated the possibility of *Savii sopra Eresia* elections becoming subject to the politicking of several hundred patricians. The attempt to concentrate power into a very few high offices was typical of Venetian political life in the middle years of the sixteenth century.

On April 8, 1595, in the interregnum between the death of Doge Pasquale Cicogna on April 5, and the election of Marin Grimani on April 26, the *Cinque Correttori* took the election of the *Savii sopra Eresia* out of the hands of doge and *Collegio* and gave it to the Senate. The new measure stated that the lay deputies should be chosen by the Senate according to the usual electoral pattern for other very important offices chosen by the Senate. Moreover, those elected to the post could immediately be taken from every other office except the *Collegio*, but including the eighteen offices recently reserved in the Senate law of July 25, 1593.[8] Nor could a

8. The Senate on July 21, 1593, and the *Maggior Consiglio* on July 25, 1593, passed a law designed to halt the continuous rotation of membership in important administrative committees elected by the Senate. According to the preamble, the constant change of faces in these « più principali et importanti officij » hampered their effectiveness. Therefore, the law decreed that those elected to eighteen important offices could not be substituted for, and could not depart the office before expiration of the normal terms, unless authorized by the *Maggior Consiglio*. The penalty for violation was 500 ducats. The eighteen offices were the *Conservatori del Deposito di Cecca, Proveditori in Cecca, Depositario in Cecca, Proveditori all'Arsenal, Sopra Proveditori alle Biave, Savii alle Acque, Cinque Savii sopra la Mercantia, Proveditori sopra l'Armar, Sopra Proveditori alle Pompe, Proveditori sopra le Artegliarie, Proveditori sopra le Fortezze, Proveditori sopra i Beni Inculti, Revisori delle Intrade de Publice, Regolatori sopra la Scrittura, Proveditori sopra i Monti, Proveditori sopra i Confini, Proveditori sopra i Feudi,* and *Proveditori alla Giustitia Vecchia.* The Senate vote was 138 di si, 6 di no, 12 non sinceri. The *Maggior Consiglio* vote was 666 di si, 40 di no, 145 non sinceri. A.S.V., *Maggior Consiglio, Deliberazioni,* reg. 32 (*Surianus*), 1588-1600, ff. 101 v-102 v. The 1595 law suggests

patrician refuse to serve without paying a penalty. An elected lay deputy served one year and then was ineligible for a period of time equal to his service in the office. While serving as a *Savio sopra Eresia* a noble could refuse every other post to which he was elected by the Senate. Finally, the law charged the doge to take particular care to ascertain that the lay deputies should be ready to assist in everything that took place in the Inquisition.[9]

The change in election procedure reflected the growing belief of the leaders of the state that civil jurisdiction had to be protected against clerical encroachment. Some patricians felt that the previous doge, Pasquale Cicogna, had failed to choose lay deputies mindful enough of lay prerogatives. And two clamorous cases of Dominion inquisitors meddling in political affairs had alarmed the leadership. The clause in the new law charging the doge to make sure that the *Savii sopra Eresia* were ready to assist in « everything » (« tutte quelle cose ») that went on in the Inquisition bespoke the desire for closer supervision.[10] Finally, the law was a small sign that

that the office of *Savio sopra Eresia* was more important than the eighteen, although not as important as the offices that comprised the *Collegio*.

9. « Essendo il carico delli Savj sopra la Inquisizione dell'Eresia di somma importanza, et tale, che non cede a qualsivoglia altro importantissimo della Repubblica Nostra: Si deve provedere, che siccome per l'adietro la elezione di essi soleva esser fatta nel Collegio Nostro & per nominazione prima del Serenissimo Principe, ballotazione poi di esso Collegio, justo la Parte di questo Conseglio, 1556. 7 Zugno, ove sia fatta con più maturità: Però L'anderà Parte, che de caetero la elezione delli tre Savi sopra la Eresia sia fatta per scrittino del Conseglio Nostro de' Pregadi, secondo il solito delle altre elezioni più principali, che si fanno in detto Conseglio; potendo esser tolti d'ogni luogo, Conseglio, et Offizio, etiam continuo, et con pena et etiam di cadauno dei diciotto Offizi ultimamente riservati per la Parte di questo Conseglio de' 25. Luglio 1593. accetto quei del Collegio Nostro. Nè possino li eletti rifiutar sotto tutte le pene contenute nella Parte delli rifichenti Ambasciare a Teste Coronate. Dovendo star per anno uno, et haver contumacia di tanto tempo, quanto saranno stati: et per quel tempo, che staranno, possino rifiutar ogni altro Offizio solito darsi per il Conseglio Nostro de' Pregadi, al quale fossero eletti; et il Serenissimo Principe debbi haver cura particolare, che alli tempi debiti siano fatti le loro elezioni, sicchè sempre possino esser impronti a ridirsi, per assister a tutte quelle cose, che sono tenuti nel Tribunal dell'Inquisizione ». Vote: 1107 di si, 20 di no, 24 non sinceri. A.S.V., *Maggior Consiglio, Deliberazioni*, reg. 32 (*Surianus*), 1588-1600, ff. 127 v-128 r. There is another copy in A.S.V., *Santo Uffizio*, busta 154, *Sommari di leggi e decreti relativi all'Inquisizione*.

10. Three of the *Cinque Correttori* who proposed the change — Marin di Giro-

the Senate was regaining a little of the power lost to higher executive councils in the past decades. The election of the *Tre Savii sopra Eresia* remained in the hands of the Senate for the duration of the period investigated.

The office of *Savio sopra Eresia* had political as well as constitutional significance. The post of lay deputy went only to nobles of mature age, vast experience, and political weight. The biographies of the *Savii sopra Eresia* listed in Part II show this, and make possible some generalizations about the careers of patricians who reached the inner ring of the great offices.[11] The following table analyzes the age at which ninety-one patricians, who served as lay deputy, won their initial election to one of the great offices.

TABLE ONE

Age upon First Winning Election as Ducal *Consigliere*, *Savio Grande*, Council of Ten, or *Zonta* [12]

Age 40-49	Age 50-54	Age 55-59	Age 60-64	Age 65-74
20.9%	19.8%	29.7%	17.6%	12.1%
(19 patricians)	(18)	(27)	(16)	(11)

The median age was fifty-six.

Table One clearly shows how much age and experience meant in the Venetian political system. It also points out how

lamo Grimani, Leonardo di Giovanni Battista Donà, and Giacomo di Alvise Foscarini — were major contendors for the ducal *corno*. The other two were Giovanni Paolo di Sebastiano Contarini and Luca Michiel. All were procurators. Foscarini was elected a lay deputy for the first time in December 1594, just a few months earlier. Contarini was elected a *Savio sopra Eresia* in 1597 and 1602, Donà in 1604. The other two never served as lay deputies. Since public opinion held Grimani to be sympathetic to the papacy and ecclesiastical preroga-tives, one wonders if relinquishing ducal nomination of lay assistants to the Senate was part of the price that he had to pay for his victory. For further detail on the 1595 law, see GRENDLER, pp. 214-220.

11. For convenience, *Consigliere*, *Savio Grande*, Council of Ten, and *Zonta* are collectively abbreviated as the « great offices ».

12. The table is based on the 91 patricians (of the 117 listed in Part II) whose birth dates are secure enough to determine the age of entry into the great offices. Naturally, those lay deputies who did not win election to the great offices are omitted.

many years it took to climb the ladder of public office. An ambitious patrician began with entry to the *Maggior Consiglio* between the ages of eighteen and twenty-five, and arrived at the inner circle thirty-five to forty years later — if he were among the lucky few.

On the average, patricians first served as *Savii sopra Eresia* five years after they initially entered the great offices. Indeed, fifty-eight per cent of the lay deputies were sixty years of age or older when first elected *Savio sopra Eresia*.

TABLE TWO

Age upon Initial Election as *Savio sopra Eresia* [13]

Age 40-49	Age 50-54	Age 55-59	Age 60-64	Age 65-69	Age 70-87
5.3%	13.7%	23.2%	20%	17.9%	20%
(5)	(13)	(22)	(19)	(17)	(19)

The median age was sixty-one.

That the *Savii sopra Eresia* were at their initial election five years older, on the average, than nobles entering the great offices for the first time follows from the election procedure. Doge and *Collegio* usually chose those patricians who had proven through service in the great offices that they possessed the experience, discretion, and political weight expected of leaders of the Republic. In other words, they often chose themselves.

The patricians who climbed the diplomatic ladder to high office became *Savii sopra Eresia* ten to fifteen years earlier than other patricians, just as they tended to reach the great offices a decade or more earlier. The youngest *Savii sopra Eresia* were the diplomats Domenico di Barbon Morosini, elected lay deputy in 1553 at the age of 45, and Paolo di

13. The table is based on the 95 patricians (of the 117 listed in Part II) whose birth dates are secure enough to determine the age, at least within a year more or less, of initial service as a *Savio sopra Eresia*.

Stefano Tiepolo, elected lay deputy in 1569 at the age of 46.[14] But advanced age was the norm. The oldest was Tommaso di Alvise Contarini, the brother of Cardinal Gasparo, who was elected a lay deputy in 1575 at the age of 87. The bulk of the patricians who served as *Savii sopra Eresia* were in their sixties when first elected. At times all three *Savii* were men in their seventies, especially in the 1560s when a relatively small group of nobles monopolized the office. For example, in 1565 seven patricians filled the office: Paolo di Marin Corner who was c. 77, Melchiorre di Tommaso Michiel PSM, c. 76, Matteo di Marco Dandolo PSM who was between 70 and 75, Girolamo di Marin Grimani PSM, c. 65, Giulio di Zorzi Contarini PSM, c. 65, Alessandro di Alvise Bon, 61, and Alvise di Tommaso Mocenigo (the future doge), who was a mere « youngster » of 58.

The preference for very old and experienced men changed slightly in the last five years before the interdict. In 1600, a year of several elections, Alvise di Bernardino Belegno at the age of 61, Giovanni di Agostino Bembo (the future doge) age 57, Francesco di Marco Giustiniani age 59, Nicolò di Zorzi Contarini PSM, c. 65, Alessandro di Alvise Bon, 61, and Nicolò di Zuanne Donà (a third future doge) age 61, were elected *Savii sopra Eresia*. For all but Giustiniani, this was the first election to the post. In the following year, three men in their seventies were elected. But the slight preference for younger men continued with the election in 1603 of Antonio di Marc'Antonio Querini at the age of 49, plus the elections of Francesco di Zaccaria Bernardo at the age of 52 and Antonio di Girolamo Lando at the age of 51, in the following year. Since several of these younger nobles were notably antipapal, their election probably manifests the militant lay jurisdictionalism of the Venetian patriciate in these years. That is, the Senate elected them because they were staunch defenders of civil jurisdiction rather than because they were relatively young for the post.

14. Possibly Antonio di Giovanni Canale (1567-1650) was elected lay deputy in 1598 at the age of thirty-one. But such a young *Savio sopra Eresia* would be so unusual that the identification may be mistaken.

The *Savii sopra Eresia*, with a few exceptions, came from the inner ring, the thirty to forty patricians — one to two percent of the total — who won the lion's share of the great offices and dominated the government. Patricians who were already procurators, or soon would be elected procurators and doges, served with the Holy Office. Winning one or more previous elections as *Consigliere, Savio Grande*, member of the Council of Ten or its *Zonta* (until 1582-83), was the most important qualification for lay deputy.

Yet, some of these great office holders possessed qualities that made them slightly more likely to be elected and re-elected *Savio sopra Eresia.* A reputation for learning helped to win election as lay deputy. A number of patricians were listed as « dottori ». They had authored books and/or were held by contemporaries to be learned: Nicolò di Francesco Tiepolo (one of the original *Savii sopra Eresia* of 1547), Marc'Antonio di Cristoforo Venier (also 1547), Nicolò di Antonio Da Ponte (first elected in 1562), Federico di Polo Valaresso (1568), Giacomo di Michele Foscarini (1571 and often re-elected), Francesco di Zuanne Andrea Venier (1580), and Paolo di Giovanni Paruta (1596). Others owned fine libraries and collections of antiquities: Federico di Francesco Contarini (first elected lay deputy in 1589 and often re-elected) and Girolamo di Cristoforo Da Mula (1597).

Those patricians who had served as resident ambassadors to the papacy frequently were elected *Savii sopra Eresia* after completing their tours of duty. Twelve of the twenty-three nobles who held the Roman residency became *Savii sopra Eresia*.[15] Clearly the leaders of the Republic believed that Roman experience was useful in Inquisition matters.

---

15. They were Giovanni Antonio di Giacomo Alvise Venier (ambassador to the papacy 1544-46 and lay deputy in 1549), Nicolò di Antonio Da Ponte (ambassador 1546-48 and 1550-53, lay deputy in 1562 and 1564), Matteo di Marco Dandolo (ambassador 1548-50, lay deputy 1565), Domenico di Barbon Morosini (ambassador 1553-55, lay deputy in 1553 and 1557), Alvise di Tommaso Mocenigo (ambassador 1557, lay deputy 1562, 1565, 1568-69), Girolamo di Alvise Soranzo (ambassador 1560-62, lay deputy 1568-69), Paolo di Stefano Tiepolo (ambassador 1565-67 and 1572-75, lay deputy 1569-70), Giovanni di Francesco Soranzo (ambassador 1570-72, lay deputy 1574 and 1592), Antonio di Nicolò Tiepolo (ambassador 1575-78, lay deputy 1580), Leonardo di Giovanni

Conspicuously absent from the ranks of the *Tre Savii sopra Eresia* were some powerful patricians who were close relatives of noble prelates. A law barring the *parenti* of ecclesiastics from the office has not been found.[16] Nevertheless, no member of the families well known for ecclesiastical connections became *Savio sopra Eresia*. The Grimani of Santa Maria Formosa and the Barbaro of Santa Maria Mater Domini together almost made the Patriarchate of Aquileia into a family benefice; no member of these two families ever became *Savio sopra Eresia*.[17] For example, Marc'Antonio di Francesco Barbaro (1518-95), who had a distinguished career as ambassador (to England, France, and Constantinople), became procurator, and was considered learned, was obviously the type of powerful patrician who would normally be elected *Savio sopra Eresia*. But he was not, probably because he was the brother of one patriarch of Aquileia and the father of a second.[18] No member of the Trevisan family was a lay deputy, probably because the Benedictine Giovanni Trevisan was Venetian patriarch from 1559 until 1590. The Corner of Ca' Grande held many bishoprics, including the rich see of Padua almost continuously between 1524 and 1630. They produced no *Savii sopra Eresia*. Paolo di Marin Corner (c. 1486-1580), who served as lay deputy from 1562 through 1567, was not a close relative. The closest relative of a high prelate to serve as lay deputy was Tommaso di Alvise Contarini (1488-1578), who served with the Inquisition in 1575, thirty-three years

Battista Donà (ambassador 1580-83 as well as several extraordinary legations to Rome, lay deputy in 1604), Paolo di Giovanni Paruta (ambassador 1592-95, lay deputy 1596), Giovanni di Iseppo Dolfin (ambassador 1595-97, lay deputy 1602). For the list of residents in Rome, see ALBÈRI, Serie II, Vol. 3, pp. vii-viii.

16. Sagredo notes a decree of June 10, 1574, barring *papalisti* from election to the *Savii sopra Eresia*, but provides no citation or further information. A. SAGREDO, *Leggi venete intorno agli ecclesiastici sino al secolo XVIII*, in « Archivio Storico Italiano », Ser. III, no. ii (1865), p. 104.

17. Girolamo di Marin Grimani (c. 1500-70), who served as lay deputy 1560-62 and 1565-67, and his son Almorò di Girolamo (1539-1611), who was a *Savio sopra Eresia* in 1605, were from the San Luca branch and not closely related to the Grimani of Santa Maria Formosa.

18. Marc'Antonio di Francesco Barbaro is the subject of C. YRIARTE, *La vie d'un patricien de Venise au seizième siècle*, Paris 1874. Also see LOGAN, pp. 31-33, 77-78, 298-299, 308-311.

after his brother, Cardinal Gasparo Contarini (1483-1542), had died.

While *papalisti* did not became *Savii sopra Eresia*, a good number of staunch supporters of papal aims and clerical interests were elected, and sometimes re-elected again and again, to the Inquisition. Several patricians proved themselves to be « protectors of ecclesiastical rights » and « devoted to the Holy See » in the judgment of nuncios assessing their performance: Giulio di Zorzi Contarini (first elected 1553 and often re-elected), Girolamo di Marin Grimani (1560 and subsequently), Paolo di Marin Corner (1562 and subsequently), Matteo di Marco Dandolo (1565), Lorenzo di Agostino Da Mula (1567), Antonio di Andrea Bragadin (1571), Alvise di Benedetto Zorzi (1573 and subsequently), Giovanni di Francesco Soranzo (1574 and 1592), Pasquale di Gabriel Cicogna (1577 and subsequently), and Federico di Francesco Contarini (1589 and later).

It is hardly surprising that from the mid-1550s until the mid-1590s doge and *Collegio* elected to the Inquisition stern opponents of heresy and men sympathetic to religion. Like all other European rulers, the Venetian nobility believed that heresy was an offense against God and a threat to the civil order.[19] The perilous times required that state and church make common cause. These years marked the height of the Counter Reformation in Venice.

After 1595, when the right of electing *Savii sopra Eresia* passed from *Collegio* to Senate, men with different views began to be elected more often. They were still leaders of the state, men from the inner circle of great office holders, but they were not friends of Rome. As the seventeenth century opened to the clamor of heated church-state jurisdictional wrangling, strong defenders of lay rights, men known for their hostility to papal claims, were elected *Savii sopra Eresia*. Besides, heresy was no longer a real threat in Venice, despite papal fears fostered by increased Venetian political and economic contact with Protestant states. When Pope Paul V

19. GRENDLER, pp. 28-29.

threw down the jurisdictional gauntlet in December 1605, the Republic responded by electing Leonàrdo Donà doge in January 1606. The political and religious climate had changed a great deal since the 1560s, and the magistracy of the *Tre Savii sopra Eresia* showed the change.

II

Below are the lists of all the patricians who held the office of *Savio sopra Eresia* from 1547 through 1605.

For 1547 through 1592, the names have been compiled from the Inquisition trials themselves: A.S.V., *Santo Uffizio*, buste 7-69. The transcripts of the interrogations and other documents normally listed those in attendance: the inquisitor, the patriarch or his vicar, the nuncio or his auditor, and one, two, or all three of the *Savii sopra Eresia*. For two or three years after 1547, the documents sometimes noted the *Savii sopra Eresia* generically rather than by name; thereafter, they scrupulously listed the names. The names omit patronymics but include useful abbreviations denoting distinctions: « Pro » for Procurator of St. Mark, « K » for a knighthood bestowed by a foreign prince, and « Dr » for a university doctorate.[20] The abbreviations aid identification. After 1556, periodic brief notations of lay deputy elections can be found in A.S.V., *Collegio, Notatorio*. But because they are incomplete, they have been used only occasionally, to check a name or to supplement the *Santo Uffizio* listings in 1593, 1594, and the first six months of 1595, when no Inquisition trials are extant.

After April 8, 1595, the names of the lay deputies are taken from A.S.V., *Segretario alle Voci, Elezioni dei Pregadi*, reg. 6 (1588-1600), ff. 131 v - 132 f, and reg. 7 (1600-1606), ff. 104 v - 105 r. This source makes it possible to determine when a lay deputy began his term, but it is seldom clear how much of the year's term he completed. The names cannot be

20. The same abbreviations are found in *Segretario alle Voci* records.

checked against the trials because of the gap in the trials from 1593 until 1616.

Compiling the names of the lay deputies from the trials themselves makes it possible to determine that a patrician actually served. In the following pages the names of the lay deputies are listed under a given year, along with information on repeated service (second year, third year, etc.). But determining the day and month of a lay deputy's initial and concluding assistance at Inquisition trials has not been done, because the information gleaned would not have been worth the substantial effort involved. There are two exceptions. The appearance at Inquisiton meetings of those fiery opponents of Rome, Nicolò di Antonio Da Ponte (1562 and 1564) and Giovanni di Bernardo Donà (1573), was so surprising that the precise dates of their very brief service as *Savii sopra Eresia* have been given in the notes. Generally speaking, the lay deputies were remarkably faithful in attendance. Such patricians as Giulio di Zorzi Contarini (first appearing in 1553), Girolamo di Marin Grimani (1560 and subsequently), and Giacomo di Michele Foscarini Dr (1571 and later) not only served year after year, but conscientiously appeared every Tuesday, Thursday, and Saturday throughout their terms.

The vast majority of the patricians chosen *Savii sopra Eresia* came from the inner circle of the most powerful office holders of the Republic. To show this, brief political biographies are appended to each deputy's name. First, the patrician is identified with the aid of the Barbaro genealogies and other sources. Then the highlights of his political career — procuratorship, ducal elections contested, a few important diplomatic and administrative posts held — are given.[21] Most important of all, each patrician's elections to the highest

---

21. A useful list of procurator elections and other events is found in R. Mo-rozzo della Rocca and M. F. Tiepolo, *Cronologia veneziana del Cinquecento,* in *La Civiltà veneziana del Rinascimento,* Firenze 1958, pp. 197-249. A list of the *Luogotenenti del Friuli* is found in *Relazioni dei rettori veneti in Terraferma,* Vol. I, *La Patria del Friuli (Luogotenenza di Udine),* a.c. dell'*Istituto di Storia Economica di Trieste,* Milano 1973, pp. lx-lxi. A list of the *Podestà* and *Capitani del Padova* is found in *Ibid.,* Vol. IV, *Podestaria a Capitanato di Padova,* Milano 1975, pp. l-li, liv-lv.

offices below procurator and doge — *Consigliere, Savio del Consiglio, Consiglio dei Dieci*, and, until the winter of 1582-83, its *Zonta* of fifteen members — are listed. Finally, wherever possible the footnotes discuss each lay deputy's actions and attitudes bearing on the Inquisition, the papacy, and church-state relations.

The election timetable and terms of office need a little explanation. The six Ducal Councillors (one from each of the *sestieri* of the city) were elected by the *Maggior Consiglio* at staggered intervals throughout the year, either three at a time, or one or two, as vacancies occurred. They served eight-month terms, and then underwent a period of ineligibility (*contumacia*) of eighteen months before they could again be elected *Consigliere*.

The *Savii Grandi* (or *Savii del Consiglio*) were elected by the Senate every three months to serve six-month terms. At the end of December, three *Savii Grandi* were elected to serve from January 1 through June 30 of the following year; on March 30, three more were elected to serve from April 1 through September 30; at the end of June, another three were elected to serve for six months from July 1 through December 31; and at the end of September, another three were elected for the period October 1 through the end of March of the succeeding year. Single vacancies occurring throughout the year, when a patrician died or left for another post, were filled immediately with a special election. After serving his term, a patrician was ineligible for re-election as *Savio Grande* for six months. However, during the Cyprus War, the government — citing the need for good advisors during the war — eased the ineligibility attached to the *Savii Grandi*. Those who served the full six-month term were ineligible for only three months; those who served less than three months were ineligible only for a period of time equal to their term in office.[22] The shortening of *contumacia*

22. A.S.V., *Maggior Consiglio, Deliberazioni*, reg. 30 (*Angelus*), 1566-1577, ff. 67 r-67 v, November 26, 1570. The vote showed much opposition: 823 di si, 311 di no, 65 non sinceri. The Senate passed the law on November 24: 144 di si, 16 di no, 7 non sinceri. Whether the measure was ever repealed is not known.

made it easier for powerful patricians to monopolize the office of *Savio Grande*.

The Council of Ten were elected by the *Maggior Consiglio* in August and September to serve one-year terms commencing October 1. They were then ineligible for one year. Members of the *Zonta*, who were nominated by the *Consiglio dei Dieci* and elected by the *Maggior Consiglio*, also served twelve-month terms beginning on October 1. A constitutional anomoly made the office very attractive: because it was considered a temporary office rather than a fixed part of the government, it did not carry the penalty of *contumacia*. It was possible for a patrician to sit in the *Zonta* and participate in the deliberations of the *Consiglio dei Dieci* continuously for a period of years.[23] Some did.

The practice of « reserving the place » (« è riservato il luogo ») also helped powerful patricians to maintain their positions in the highest councils. If an elected patrician was unable to take his seat because he was absent from the city in the service of the Republic, the *Consiglieri* might ask the *Maggior Consiglio* to elect another. But the original place was reserved for the absent electee. When he returned to the city, he entered the office at the first ordinary vacancy and served a full term.[24] Later the returning noble did not have to wait for a vacancy, but took his seat within three days of his return.[25] Presumably the noble elected in his absence gave up his seat. Even though the *Consiglieri* had to take each request for a reserved place to the *Maggior Consiglio* for approval, they were frequent.

In the political biographies below, the successful elections to the great offices are listed in short form. The date of the

---

23. LOWRY, pp. 285-286.
24. A.S.V., *Maggior Consiglio, Deliberazioni*, reg. 28 (*Rocca*), 1552-1565, ff. 90 v - 91 r, January 8, 1559 m.v. The law referred specifically to *Savii Grandi* and *Savii di Terraferma*.
25. To cite one example among many, the *Maggior Consiglio* approved reserving the place of « Conseglier di Venetia del sestier Dorso Duro » won by Giacomo di Alvise Foscarini until completion of his duties as *Proveditore Generale di Candia*. In the meantime, another would be elected. A.S.V., *Maggior Consiglio, Deliberazioni*, reg. 30 (*Angelus*), 1566-1577, f. 142 v, March 24, 1575.

initial election to one of the four offices is given within parentheses; subsequent elections are simply counted. For example, Nicolò di Francesco Tiepolo Dr in the decade 1540 through 1549 was elected *Consigliere* twice (the first time in 1543), *Savio Grande* nine times (the first in 1542), to the Council of Ten once (in 1541, his initial election to that office), and to the *Zonta* five times (the first in 1541). A patrician elected to an office, but then declared ineligible (*cazzado*), has not been counted. The dates indicate the year in which a patrician was elected to an office, although the term might run into the following year. For example, a patrician elected *Savio Grande* on September 30, 1544, is listed under 1544, although he would not complete a full term until the end of March 1545. But those elected at the end of the year (e. g., December 30, 1559), are listed under the following year to coincide with the actual term of office. All dates have been changed to modern style.

It would have been very difficult to find out exactly how much of a term in office a partician served, because of the continuous movement from office to office in the Venetian system. No sooner did the *Maggior Consiglio* finish electing the members of the Council of Ten when they had to hold new elections to replace patricians chosen for embassies abroad, governorships in the *Terraferma*, *Savii Grandi*, and other posts. In some years, few, if any, of the original ten remained the full twelve months. The most important thing was that a noble commanded the support to win election to the very high offices of *Consigliere, Savio Grande, Consiglio dei Dieci*, and its *Zonta*. The number of his successful elections demonstrated his political weight.

Because of gaps in the *Segretario alle Voci* records, several sources have been used to compile the list of offices. The sources for the lists of *Consiglieri*, 1541-1610, are as follows: A.S.V., *Segretario alle Voci, Elezioni del Maggior Consiglio*, reg. 2 (1541-1552), ff. 1 v - 4 v; *Ibid., Serie Mista*, reg. 12 (ex 15), (1550-1573), ff. 60 v - 61 v; *Elezioni del Maggior Consiglio*, reg. 5 (1570-1577), ff. 4 v - 8 v. (I am grateful to Martin Lowry for showing me his notes on this *registro*). *Raccolta dei*

Consegi dal 1576 fino 1580, ms. Bibl. Marc., Cod. It., cl. VII, 829
(= 8908), *passim*; *Raccolta dei Consegi dal 1581 fino 1587*, ms. Bibl.
Marc., Cod. It., cl. VII, 830 (= 8909), *passim*; A.S.V., *Elezioni del
Maggior Consiglio*, reg. 7 (1587-1595), ff. 1 v - 4 v; *Ibid.*, reg. 8 (1595-
1602), ff. 1 v - 4 v; *Raccolta dei Consegi dal 1601 fino 1605*, ms. Bibl.
Marc., Cod. It., cl. VII, 833 (= 8912), *passim*; *Raccolta dei Consegi
dal 1606 fino 1610*, ms. Bibl. Marc., Cod. It., cl. VII, 834 (= 8913),
passim.

For the *Savii Grandi* 1540-1610: A.S.V., *Segretario alle Voci, Elezioni dei Pregadi*, reg. 1 (1531-1554); reg. 2 (1554-1559); reg. 3 (1559-
1567); reg. 4 (1568-1577); reg. 5 (1578-1587); reg. 6 (1588-1600);
reg. 7 (1600-1606); reg. 8 (1607-1613). The *Savii del Consiglio* lists
are always the first in the *registri*. I wish to thank Martin Lowry for
providing me his lists of *Savii Grandi* for 1572 through 1592.

For the *Consiglio dei Dieci* 1540-1610 and *Zonta* 1540-1582: A.S.V.,
Consiglio dei Dieci, Comuni, reg 13, f. 205 r; *Raccolta dei Consegi
dal 1541 fino 1545*, ms. Bibl. Marc., Cod. It., cl. VII, 822 (= 8901),
passim; *Raccolta dei Consegi dal 1546 fino 1550*, ms. Bibl. Marc., Cod.
It., cl. VII, 823 (= 8902), *passim*; A.S.V., *Segretario alle Voci, Serie
Mista*, reg. 12 (ex 15), (1550-1573), ff. 1 r - 10 r; *Segretario alle Voci,
Elezioni del Consiglio dei Dieci e Zonta*, reg. 13, ff. 1 r - 6 r; reg. 14
(1574-1597), ff. 4 r - 22 v. (I am indebted to Martin Lowry for most
of the lists from 1540 through 1592). *Raccolta dei Consegi dal 1595
fino 1600*, ms. Bibl. Marc., Cod. It., cl. VII, 832 (= 8911), *passim*;
Raccolta dei Consegi dal 1601 fino 1605, ms. Bibl. Marc., Cod. It., cl.
VII, 833 (= 8912), *passim*; *Raccolta dei Consegi dal 1606 fino 1610*,
ms. Bibl. Marc., Cod. It., cl. VII, 834 (= 8913), *passim*.

ABBREVIATIONS

A.S.V.	Venezia, Archivio di Stato
A.S.Vat.	Città del Vaticano, Archivio Segreto Vaticano
Bibl. Marc.	Venezia, Biblioteca Nazionale Marciana
C	Consigliere
CX	Consiglio dei Dieci
Correr	Venezia, Museo Civico Correr
K	Cavalierato
PSM	Procuratore di San Marco
SG	Savio Grande
Z	Zonta
ALBÈRI	*Le relazioni degli ambasciatori veneti al Senato*, a.c. di E. ALBÈRI, 15 voll., Firenze 1839-1853.

BARBARO A.S.V.   MARCO BARBARO, *Arbori dei Patritii veneti*, 7 voll., mss. in A.S.V.

BARBARO Bibl. Marc.   MARCO BARBARO, *Arbori dei Patritii veneti*, mss. Bibl. Marc., Cod. It., cl. VII, 925-928 (= 8594-8597).

« B.S.V. »   « Bollettino dell'Istituto di Storia della Società e dello Stato Veneziano »

CICOGNA   E. A. CICOGNA, *Delle iscrizioni veneziane*, 6 voll., Venezia 1824-1853.

COZZI   G. COZZI, *Il doge Nicolò Contarini: Ricerche sul patriziato veneziano agli inizi del Seicento*, Venezia-Roma 1958.

DA MOSTO   A. DA MOSTO, *I Dogi di Venezia nella vita pubblica e privata*, Milano 1966.

D.B.I.   *Dizionario biografico degli Italiani*, Roma 1960-1979.

GRENDLER   P. F. GRENDLER, *The Roman Inquisition and the Venetian Press, 1540-1605*, Princeton, N. J. 1977.

LOGAN   O. M. T. LOGAN, *Culture and Society in Venice 1470-1790: The Renaissance and Its Heritage*, London 1972.

LOWRY   M. J. C. LOWRY, *The Reform of the Council of Ten, 1582-3: An Unsettled Problem?* in « Studi Veneziani », *13* (1971), pp. 275-310.

Nunziature VI   *Nunziature di Venezia*, Vol. VI (1552-1554), a. c. di F. GAETA, Istituto Storico Italiano per l'età moderna e contemporanea. Fonti per la Storia d'Italia, Roma 1967.

Nunziature VIII   *Nunziature di Venezia*, Vol. VIII (1566-1569), a. c. di A. STELLA, Roma 1963.

Nunziature IX   *Nunziature di Venezia*, Vol. IX (1569-1571), a. c. di A. STELLA, Roma 1972.

Nunziature XI   *Nunziature di Venezia*, Vol. XI (1573-1576), a. c. di A. BUFFARDI, Roma 1972.

SENECA   F. SENECA, *Il Doge Leonardo Donà: la sua vita e la sua preparazione politica prima del Dogado*, Padova 1959.

STELLA   A. STELLA, *Chiesa e stato nelle relazioni dei nunzi pontifici a Venezia. Ricerche sul giurisdizionalismo veneziano dal XVI al XVIII secolo*, Studi e testi, 239, Città del Vaticano 1964.

X

TRE SAVII SOPRA ERESIA

1547 Francesco di Zaccaria Contarini d. 1558, K PSM 1556, ambassador to Ferdinand, King of the Romans 1534-36, and to Charles V 1540--41. received votes in ducal elections of 1553 and 1556; BARBARO Bibl. Marc., vol. 1, f. 272 v; DA MOSTO, pp. 314, 324.
1540-49: C - 2 (1544); SG - 3 (1544); CX - 3 (1544).
1550-58: SG - 7; CX - 1.

Nicolò di Francesco Tiepolo Dr d. 1551, associate of Contarini, Giustiniani and Querini in youth, diplomat[26]; BARBARO A.S.V., vol. 7, p. 83.
1540-49: C - 2 (1543); SG - 9 (1540); CX - 1 (1541); Z - 5 (1541).
1550-51: SG - 1; CX - 1; Z - 1.

« Antonio Venier Dr », probably Marc'Antonio di Cristoforo Venier Dr d. 1566, PSM 1554, diplomat[27]; BARBARO A.S.V., 7, 241.
1540-49: C - 2 (1544); SG - 4 (1541); CX - 3 (1541); Z - 1 (1549).
1550-55: C - 1; SG - 3; CX - 1.

26. Probably born between 1480 and 1485, Tiepolo was an associate of Tommaso (Father Paolo) Giustiniani (1476-1528), Vincenzo (Father Pietro) Querini (c. 1479-1514), and Gasparo Contarini (1483-1542) at the time of their spiritual self-examination, 1510 to 1512. There is a large literature on the trio, too extensive to list here. Pope Julius II conferred the doctorate of arts from Padua on Tiepolo in 1507. Tiepolo enjoyed the reputation of being a learned man, and he wrote vernacular poetry. Some of his poems are found in *Rime di diversi*, ms. Bibl. Marc., Cod. It., cl. IX, 203 (6757), ff. 24 r - 27 v, 80 v, 101 r - 102 r, 130 r - 133 v; and *Ibid.*, ms. Bibl. Marc., Cod. It., cl. IX, 213 (6881), ff. 31 r - 34 r. He married in 1522. His political career included *podestà* at Brescia in 1525, ambassador to Charles V, 1530-32, to the Congress of Nice in 1538, and again to Charles V in 1541, the year after he reached the great offices.
27. Barbaro lists no «Antonio Venier Dr » of the appropriate age or political stature to be this initial lay deputy. None of the three listed by Barbaro, Antonio di Piero (1493-1554), Antonio di Zuanne (1507-71), and Antonio di Zuan Francesco (1507-79), was designated as « Dr », and none of them reached the great offices between 1540 and 1560. Moreover, Barbaro provides no additional information on them, suggesting that they had no political careers worth mentioning. BARBARO A.S.V., 7, 227, 229, 234.
« Antonio Venier Dr » is probably Marc'Antonio di Cristoforo Venier Dr, because he is almost always listed as « Dr » in A.S.V., *Segretario alle Voci,* in *Maggior Consiglio, Deliberazioni,* and other documents, and because of his political stature. Probably born c. 1480-85, Venier married in 1516, reached the office of *Savio di Terraferma* in 1522, and then had a long diplomatic career including ambassadorships to England 1522-26, to Clement VII 1531-33, an ambassadorship extraordinary to Julius III 1549-50, and other charges. Upon his election as procurator, Nuncio Ludovico Beccadelli described him as a « gentilhomo di grandissima reputatione et dotto ». *Nunziature* VI, 236, June 10, 1553. Venier received votes in the ducal election of 1553, and was one of the leading candidates for doge in 1554. DA MOSTO, 320; *Nunziature* VI, 356, 357, 361. It is not known why he ceased to hold high office after 1555.

1548 Alvise di Galeazzo (detto Imperiale) Contarini K d. 1555, diplomat [28];
BARBARO A.S.V., 2, 487.
1540-49: CX - 3 (1544).
1550-55: C - 1 (1551); CX - 2.

Francesco di Francesco Longo d. 1566 [29]; BARBARO A.S.V., 4, 301.
1540-49: C - 1 (1547); CX - 3 (1544); Z - 4 (1543).
1550-59: C - 1; Z - 6.

Lorenzo di Alvise Priuli 1489-1559, S. Stae branch, diplomat and governor of several cities, K PSM 1551, received votes in ducal election of 1553, Doge 1556.
DA MOSTO, 323-25.
1540-49: C - 1 (1544); CX - 1 (1548).
1550-55: C - 3; SG - 3 (1551); CX - 1; Z - 1 (1554).

1549 Alvise di Galeazzo Contarini K (second year).

Francesco di Francesco Longo (second year).

Giovanni Antonio Venier, probably Giovanni Antonio di Giacomo Alvise Venier, c. 1477-February 2, 1550, K diplomat, including ambassador to France 1530-32, to Charles V 1535-38, to Rome 1544-46, and ambassador extraordinary to Charles V in 1541; BARBARO Bibl. Marc., 4, 175 r.
1540-49: SG - 2 (1545); CX - 1 (1547 but replaced).

1550 Alvise di Galeazzo Contarini K (third).

Lorenzo di Alvise Priuli (second).

Bernardino (or Bernardo) di Marco Venier, PSM 1557, d. 1559, received votes in ducal elections of 1556 and 1559; BARBARO Bibl. Marc., 4, 169; CICOGNA, 6, 63; DA MOSTO, 324, 330.

---

28. In 1552 some clergymen levelled charges against Fra Marin Valier, the Franciscan inquisitor of Venice from c. 1542 to 1551. The accusations included consorting with heretics such as Piero Paolo Vergerio, and visiting prostitutes by night. Members of the *Collegio* hastened to defend Fra Marin. The nuncio noted that one of his defenders was « un Contarino, consiglier, ch'è stato longo tempo al tribunale dell'heresia... ». This was Alvise di Galeazzo Contarini, who served as lay deputy all or part of the years 1548 through 1551, and was elected *Consigliere* on July 12, 1551. The Holy Office exonerated Fra Marin; probably his noble birth and his post as personal chaplain of Pietro Loredan, who became doge in 1567, helped. *Nunziature* VI, 73, March 19, 1552; A.S.V., *Segretario alle Voci, Serie Mista*, reg. 12 (ex 15), f. 60 v.

29. Francesco di Francesco Longo was one of the three *Esecutori contro la bestemmia* who in 1553 recommended to the *Consiglio dei Dieci* the destruction of the *Talmud* because of its « quante blasphemie et maledicentie ». A.S.V., *Consiglio dei Dieci, Comuni*, reg. 21, ff. 56 r, 58 v (October 2, 18, 1553). Also see GRENDLER, 90-93. Francesco di Francesco Longo should not be confused with Francesco di Antonio Longo (d. 1584), friend of nuncios and prominent great office holder from 1577 until 1584. M.J.C. LOWRY, *The Church and Venetian Political Change in the Later Cinquecento*, Ph. D. thesis, University of Warwick, 1971, pp. 351-353; LOWRY, 295.

1540-49: C - 2 (1542); CX - 1 (1548).
1550-59: C - 1; CX - 2; Z - 1 (1556).

1551 Alvise di Galeazzo Contarini K (fourth).

Antonio di Girolamo Dandolo d. 1553; BARBARO Bibl. Marc., 2, 50.
1540-49: CX - 1 (1541).
1550-53: C - 2 (1550); CX - 1; Z - 1 (1551).

Andrea di Antonio Marcello 1484-1556, received votes in ducal election
of 1553; BARBARO A.S.V., 4, 483; DA MOSTO, 314.
1540-49: C - 3 (1542); CX - 3 (1541); Z - 6 (1541).
1550-56: C - 1; CX - 2; Z - 4.

Bernardino di Marco Venier (second).

Bernardo di Nicolò Zorzi 1482-January or February 1566 [30]; BARBARO
Bibl. Marc., 4, 240.
1550-59: CX - 2 (1555); Z - 1 (1559).
1560-66: C - 2 (1562); SG - 5 (1560); CX - 3; Z - 3.

1552 Antonio di Girolamo Dandolo (second).

Andrea di Antonio Marcello (second).

Melchiorre (or Marchio) di Tommaso Michiel c. 1489-April 26, 1572 [31],
PSM 1558, K 1560 from Pius IV.
BARBARO A.S.V., 3, 125.

30. As *Capo del Consiglio dei Dieci*, Zorzi authorized the Venetian printing of the Pauline *Index* in July 1559. As *Savio sopra Eresia* a month later, he approved the punishment of several printers who had refused to obey the 1559 *Index*. GRENDLER, 122, 124.

31. Only Nicolò Da Ponte in his generation enjoyed a more successful political career than Melchiorre Michiel. At the beginning of his ascent up the ladder of offices, Michiel used his wealth to surmount age qualifications. In 1524, while about five years short of the required forty for Senate election, Michiel offered 400 ducats for the right to speak in the Senate. In 1527 he was elected *Avvogadore* extraordinary with a donation of 2,200 ducats. Many other offices, especially governorships and military posts, but few diplomatic charges, followed. Michiel was elected *Proveditore Generale* and superintendant of the cavalry in Dalmatia in 1539, Captain of Famagusta (Cyprus) in 1540, Captain of Brescia in 1550, of Padua in 1553, and supreme commander at Corfù in 1558. His climb up the ladder of great offices followed a classic pattern: first elected *Savio di Terraferma* in 1538, *Zonta* of the Council of Ten in 1545, Council of Ten in 1547, *Savio Grande* in 1551, and *Consigliere* in 1552. From this date he divided his time between *Savio Grande* and the *Zonta,* serving in one or the other for the rest of his life except when absent from the city. He sat in the highest councils of the Republic from 1545 until his death in 1572, a period of twenty-eight years. Only the ducal « corno » eluded him; he received votes in the elections of 1556, 1559, and 1567, but never came close to election. Michiel served as one of the lay deputies almost as often as he did in the great offices: in 1552, 1557, 1560, 1562-65, 1567, and 1570. Despite years of service with the Inquisition in the crucial years of the implementation of the Counter-Reformation, his views on church and state are unknown. CICOGNA, 4, 13-15; ALBÈRI, Serie II, vol. 2, p. 2; DA MOSTO, 324, 330, 334.

1540-49: CX - 1 (1547); Z - 4 (1545).
1550-59: C - 3 (1552); SG - 7 (1551); CX - 2; Z - 6.
1560-69: SG - 9; Z - 7.
1570-72: SG - 4; Z - 2.

Bernardino di Marco Venier (third).

1553 Giulio di Zorzi Contarini PSM c. 1500 - c. 1578, Conti del Zaffo
branch, not closely related to other Contarini who were *Savii
sopra Eresia*[32],
PSM 1537; BARBARO A.S.V., 2, 515.
1550-59: SG - 1 (1559).
1560-69: SG - 3
1570-77: SG - 6; Z - 1 (1572).

Andrea di Antonio Marcello (third).

Domenico di Barbon Morosini K 1508 - January 9, 1558, diplomat
and scholar[33], BARBARO A.S.V., 5, 324.
1550-59: SG - 1 (1556); CX - 3 (1552).

---

32. In dire need of funds, the Republic sold procuratorships in 1537. Contarini purchased his with a loan of 14,000 ducats to the state. PAOLO PARUTA,
Historia vinetiana divisa in due parti, In Vinetia, Appresso Domenico Nicolini, MDCV, 653. Those who purchased procuratorships seldom won election
to the great offices. Contarini did, when he reached the appropriate age (late
fifties and sixties), demonstrating that he was politically powerful as well
as wealthy. The Barbaro genealogies state that Contarini died in 1575; elections
to the *Savii Grandi* in 1576 and 1577 show that this death date is mistaken.
When he did die (c. 1578), he left an estate of 150,000 *scudi*. STELLA, 137.
    Contarini defended clerical persons and interests. For example, in June
and July 1559, Zuanne di Bernardo Donà asked the Senate to take immediate
action to force Patriarch Vincenzo Diedo (1556-59) to pay 2,000 ducats in
taxes owed the Republic. Diedo asked the *Collegio* for a delay, and the
Collegio agreed. But when Giulio Contarini, then *Savio Grande*, urged the
Senate to accept postponement, the senators made so much noise that Contarini was forced to sit down. A few days later, Diedo, despite previous
pleas of poverty, paid part of his debt. ZUANNE LIPPOMANO, *Delle historie
vinitiane dall'anno MDLI all'anno MDLXIII divise in dieci libri scritte da
Zuanne Lippomano fo di Alessandro,* ms. Correr, Cicogna 2558, p. 474,
July 20, 1559.
    Contarini served as lay deputy to the Holy Office in 1553, 1555, 1559-62,
1565-67, and 1570-71, more often than anyone else. Very faithful in attendance,
he was present during many of the politically delicate trials of young Venetian
nobles in the 1560s. GRENDLER, 134-138. Nuncio Giovanni Antonio Facchinetti
(the future Innocent IX) found him to be a « caldo protettore della immunità
e giuriditione ecclesiastica » and « acerrimo defensore delle cose della fede in
cotesto S. Uffitio ». He noted Contarini's « ardente zelo per conservatione
dell'honor di Dio et della sua molta devotione verso questa S. Sede ». The
papacy twice commended him in 1566, the second time for his aid in the
successful effort to extradite to Rome the accused heretic Guido Giannetti
da Fano. NUNZIATURE, VIII, 46-47, 49 (quotes), 96, 102.

33. Morosini served as ambassador to Ferdinand, King of the Romans, 1544-46,
to Charles V 1550-52, and to popes Julius III, Marcellus II, and Paul IV
from mid-1553 through 1555. He was *podestà* at Verona in 1546-47 and a

Bernardino di Marco Venier (fourth).

Maffeo di Giacomo Venier c. 1490/1510-1557; BARBARO Bibl. Marc., 4, 167.
    1540-49: CX - 1 (1549).
    1550-57: CX - 2.

Catarino di Piero Zeno 1497 - January 9, 1560, ambassador extraordinary to Constantinople 1549-51; BARBARO Bibl. Marc., 4, 224.
    1540-49: C - 1 (1548); CX - 1 (1546); Z - 2 (1546).
    1550-59: C - 2; CX - 1; Z - 2.

1554 No names. The few extant Inquisition trials suggest that this was a year of little activity.

1555 Giulio di Zorzi Contarini PSM (second).

Andrea di Giacomo Renier d. 1560; BARBARO Bibl. Marc., 4, 60.
    1550-59: C - 2 (1555); CX - 2 (1552); Z - 3 (1552).

Francesco di Anzolo Sanudo K 1494-1556, ambassador to Urbino 1538, to Ferdinand, King of the Romans, 1539, lieutenancy in Friuli 1552; CICOGNA, 2, 112-14.
    1550-59: SG - 1 (1551); Z - 3 (1551).

Maffeo di Giacomo Venier (second).

1556 Alvise Foscarini, probably Alvise di Andrea c. 1490 - December 2, 1560 [34], successful merchant, father of Giacomo (see note 83).

Riformatore dello Studio di Padova in 1552. According to the birth date given by Barbaro, Morosini reached the great offices in his mid-forties, a very young age. Those who climbed the diplomatic ladder tended to reach the great offices at a younger age than others. However, the birth date could be incorrect. Contemporaries held Morosini to be very learned and especially knowledgeable about Plato. Having obtained permission from Paul III to hold Lutheran books, Morosini, from the imperial court, in August 1550 asked for a renewal in order to write a refutation of heresy. The response is unknown; neither has a treatise come to light. The papacy normally refused such permissions at this time.

    Upon Morosini's appointment to Rome, Nuncio Ludovico Beccadelli wrote the papacy that Morosini was a « gentilhomo da bene et di bonissime lettere et costumi et molto stimato, et credo che Sua Santità ne rimarà ben satisfatta: è un di quelli ch'al presente assiste al tribunale dell'heresia ». NUNZIATURE, VI, 230, letter of May 20, 1553. In the summer of 1555, the Venetian Inquisition asked the Congregation of the Holy Office to ameliorate the 1554/55 *Index*. Morosini, still ambassador to the papacy, conducted the negotiations, but his views do not emerge from the letters. CICOGNA, 4, 459-60; PIO PASCHINI, *Venezia e l'inquisizione romana da Giulio III a Pio IV*, Padova 1959, p. 51, GRENDLER, p. 100.

34. Although Cicogna quotes an inscription stating that Foscarini died in 1563 at the age of 72, this is not correct. Barbaro gives December 2, 1560, as the death date, and A.S.V., *Segretario alle voci, Serie Mista*, reg. 12 (ex 15), f. 6 r, confirms that he died at about this time. Foscarini may have been pro-papal. On July 28, 1558, Foscarini, then *Capo del Consiglio dei Dieci*, joined with Girolamo di Marin Grimani, a powerful noble considered to be a « protector of ecclesiastical things » by the nuncio. Together Foscarini and

BARBARO Bibl. Marc., 2, 136 r.
CICOGNA, 2, 408-09.
1540-49: CX - 1 (1549).
1550-59: CX - 4; Z - 1 (1557).
1560: C - 1; CX - 1.

Pietro (Piero) Sanudo, probably Pietro di Benedetto c. 1500 - c. 1573 [35], *podestà* at Bergamo 1548, lieutenancy in Friuli 1557, captain at Padua 1569-70.
BARBARO Bibl. Marc., 4, 95 v; CICOGNA, 6, 564-65.
1560-69: C - 1 (1568); SG - 6 (1562); CX - 1 (1569); Z - 1 (1565).
1570-73: C - 1 (?); SG - 3; Z - 1.

Bernardo di Nicolò Zorzi (second).

1557 Alvise di Andrea Foscarini (second).

Melchiorre di Tommaso Michiel (second).

Domenico di Barbon Morosini K (second).

1558 Andrea Barbarigo, probably Andrea di Gregorio c. 1500 - December 1570 [36]; BARBARO Bibl. Marc., 1, 67 v; *D.B.I.*, 6, 55-56;

Grimani proposed to the *Consiglio dei Dieci* that the heretic Giovanni Bernardino Bonifacio, the Marchese d'Oria, be extradited to Rome. The motion lost. A.S.V., *Consiglio dei Dieci, Secrete*, reg. 6, f. 193 v.

An alternate, but unlikely, identification is Alvise di Nicolò Foscarini (1507-67) elected to the *Consiglio dei Dieci* in 1553, but not to any other great offices. BARBARO Bibl. Marc., 2, 135 v.

35. Barbaro states that Sanudo died in September 1572. However, « Piero di Benedetto Sanudo » was elected *Savio Grande* on March 14, 1573 (A.S.V., *Segretario alle Voci, Elezioni dei Pregadi*, reg. 4, f. 4 v) and perhaps *Consigliere* on May 3, 1573 (*Segretario alle Voci, Serie Mista*, reg. 12 (ex 15), f. 62 v, but the patronymic is difficult to read). Less likely identifications are the much less prominent Pietro di Zuanne Battista Sanudo (c. 1506-68, elected to the *Consiglio dei Dieci* in 1567) and Pietro di Bartolomeo Sanudo, elected to the *Consiglio dei Dieci* in 1561, but otherwise unidentified.

36. Andrea di Gregorio Barbarigo, the grandson of Doge Marco Barbarigo (1485-86), was a wealthy man who used his money to procure offices early in his career. Later he held a number of administrative posts and one important governorship, at Padua 1555-57. He received some votes in the ducal election of 1567, and was the candidate of many in 1570 because he was a weak man. The nuncio reported that some patricians preferred the « tractable » and « very timid » Barbarigo instead of the stronger Alvise di Tommaso Mocenigo. « Ma nell'intrinseco molti ne son alieni, et specialmente la giovintù, perché egli [Mocenigo] è severo et acerrimo custode dell'osservanza delle leggi, et per questo alcuni credono che questa dignità possa cedere in huomo più trattabile et facile, tra' quali si nomina il clar.mo Andrea Barbarigo gentilhuomo di coscienza, timoratissimo et da bene... ». NUNZIATURE IX, 269, May 6, 1570. The nuncio's comment shows that, while strong-willed men were frequently elected to the great offices, so were timid souls. How many patricians often elected to the highest councils were simply timorous nonentities? In any case, Barbarigo came close, but Alvise di Tommaso Mocenigo was elected doge in 1570. DA MOSTO, 334, 339.

Barbarigo appears to have been on good terms with the nuncio, and he

1550-59: SG - 1 (1559); CX - 3 (1553); Z - 2 (1558).
1560-69: C - 3 (1562); SG - 9; CX - 3; Z - 7.
1570: C - 1; SG - 1.

Andrea di Giacomo Renier (second).

Pietro di Benedetto Sanudo (second).

Bernardo di Nicolò Zorzi (third).

1559 Andrea di Gregorio Barbarigo (second).

Giulio di Zorzi Contarini PSM (third).

Girolamo Morosini, probably Girolamo di Vettore [37] d. 1566; Barbaro Bibl. Marc., 3, 159.
1560-66: C - 1 (1566); CX - 1 (1563); Z - 1 (1562).

Andrea di Alvise Sanudo c. 1495 - September 1574, entered *Maggior Consiglio* in 1514 with donation to the state, purchased *provveditore* in Cyprus in 1516 with donation of 500 ducats, received votes for doge in 1559. Barbaro Bibl. Marc., 4, 93 v; Cicogna, 2, 133; Da Mosto, 330.
1550-59: C - 1 (1558); CX - 1 (1558); Z - 1 (1558).
1560-69: C - 2; CX - 6; Z - 4.
1570-71: C - 1; CX - 1.

Pietro di Benedetto Sanudo (third).

Bernardo di Nicolò Zorzi (fourth).

1560 Giulio di Zorzi Contarini PSM (fourth).

Girolamo di Marin Grimani K, PSM c. 1500 - early 1570, PSM 1560, San Luca branch of the Grimani, and not closely related to the several patriarchs of Aquileia and cardinals of the S. Maria Formosa branch. Very wealthy, father of Marino (1532-Doge 1595-1605) and Procurator Almorò (1539-1611), served with the Inquisition 1560-62 and 1565-67 [38]; Barbaro Bibl. Marc., 2, 182 r.

had a financial interest in church properties. Stella, p. 7 n. 13. On November 20, 1568, Barbarigo, Lorenzo di Agostino Da Mula (see note 45) and Girolamo di Marin Grimani (note 38) asked the nuncio to persuade Rome to allow some grain to be sent from Ravenna for « certe povere monache ». Nunziature VIII, 462-463.

37. A less likely identification is Girolamo di Cristoforo Morosini (d. 1564) who did not hold any great offices. Barbaro Bibl. Marc. 3, 160 r.

38. Grimani's very successful political career was probably the result of many relatives and supporters (« numerosissimo parentado ») and wealth. He was not a diplomat; his diplomatic experience consisted only of journeys to Rome as ambassador .extraordinary to congratulate newly elected pontiffs in 1555, 1560 (at which time Pius IV conferred the *cavalierato* on him), and 1566. He received votes in the ducal elections of 1556 and 1559. In 1567 he was one of the three major candidates, but after many ballots the lesser known Pietro Loredan was elected. (Da Mosto tends to see Loredan as a minor figure. This is not wholly accurate. While he never won a procuratorship or election

1540-49: SG - 7 (1544); CX - 4 (1542); Z - 5 (1542).
1550-59: C - 3 (1551); SG - 6; CX - 2; Z - 5.
1560-69: SG - 8: Z -6.
1570: SG - 1.

Melchiorre di Tommaso Michiel K, PSM (third).

Girolamo di Vettore Morosini (second).

Andrea di Alvise Sanudo (second).

Bernardo di Nicolò Zorzi (fifth).

1561 Andrea di Gregorio Barbarigo (third).

Giulio di Zorzi Contarini PSM (fifth).

Girolamo di Vettore Morosini (third).

Pietro (Piero) Morosini. This is one of the following:
Piero di Battista d. 1570; BARBARO A.S.V., 7, 327.
1550-59: C - 3 (1553); SG - 2 (1555); CX - 2 (1556).
1560-69: C - 1; SG - 2; CX - 4; Z - 1 (1565).
Piero di Lorenzo d. 1564; CICOGNA, 2, 270.
1550-59: SG - 2 (1557); CX - 2 (1553).
1560-64: C - 1 (1561); SG - 1.

Piero di Zuanne Francesco CX - 1566, 1568.

to the *Savii Grandi*, Loredan was elected *Consigliere* in 1556, 1559, 1562, and 1565, to the *Consiglio dei Dieci* in 1551, 1558, 1562, 1564, and 1566, and to the *Zonta* in 1546 (?), 1550 through 1554, 1556, 1557, and 1561). DA MOSTO, 324, 330, 333-4; NUNZIATURE VIII, 298, 303-05, 308; LOGAN, 311.

Grimani consistently supported papal initiatives against heretics. When the papacy requested that Francesco Stella da Portobuffolè be extradited to Rome, Grimani, then *Consigliere*, proposed this to the *Consiglio dei Dieci* on May 27, 1558. The motion failed. But on June 4, Grimani and two *Capi del Consiglio dei Dieci*, Piero Morosini and Piero Venier, proposed a new motion of extradition that was carried. (Nevertheless, Stella was not extradited at this time; in 1561 the papacy tried again and may have succeeded. GRENDLER, 61.) On July 28, 1558, Grimani and Alvise di Andrea Foscarini moved that Giovanni Bernardino Bonifacio, the Marchese d'Oria, be extradited to Rome. The motion lost. A.S.V., *Consiglio dei Dieci, Secrete*, reg. 6, ff. 192 r, 193 v. When in July 1559 Zuanne di Bernardo Donà attacked Patriarch Vincenzo Diedo for failure to pay his taxes, Grimani defended the patriarch. He admitted, but minimized, the patriarch's culpability, and he begged for special consideration for the patriarch because of his office. Grimani also advised against irritating Paul IV, whom Diedo had called on for assistance. LIPPOMANO, *op. cit.*, pp. 472-473. Nuncio Facchinetti judged Grimani to be « devotissimo alla Sede Apostolica et protettore delle cose ecclesiastiche ». *Nunziature* VIII, 62, June 11, 1566; also p. 463, November 20, 1568. When Grimani asked the papacy for a favor involving taxes in Ravenna, the nuncio immediately and persistantly begged Rome for a favorable decision because Grimani « è d'incredibile auttorità qui ». *Nunziature* VIII, 475, December 29, 1568. Grimani opposed the papacy only on the question of Venetian taxation. In 1566 he stood with Nicolò Da Ponte to oppose a papal request that the mendicant orders be granted tax exemptions for their property. *Nunziature* VIII, 145.

Piero di Vettore CX - 1561 [39].

Andrea di Alvise Sanudo (third).

1562 Giulio di Zorzi Contarini PSM (sixth).

Paolo di Marin Corner (Cornaro) c. 1486-1580, PSM 1577, lay deputy
    1562-67 [40]; BARBARO A.S.V., 3, 111.
    1550-59: C - 3 (1553); CX - 4 (1552); Z - 5 (1551).
    1560-69: C - 3; CX - 3; Z - 6.
    1570-72: C - 1; CX - 1.

Nicolò di Antonio Da Ponte 1491-1585, PSM 1570, Doge 1578-85,
    strongly anti-papal [41]; BARBARO A.S.V., 6, 204.
    1540-49: CX - 1 (1548); Z - 2 (1546).

---

39. The documents fail to list a patronymic for the following great office
elections won by Piero Morosini: CX - 1549; SG - 1553, 1564.

40. Corner had financial interests in church properties. STELLA, 7 n. 13. On
December 6, 1567, the nuncio described Corner as « mio amico e servitore per
essere quasi in tutto il tempo ch'io sono stato qui intravenuto per uno de gli
assistenti al S. Offitio ». On the other hand, Corner would not support the
nuncio's attempt to claim a benefice for the recipient of the pope's choosing.
Nunziature VIII, 312, 318.

41. Nicolò di Antonio Da Ponte enjoyed one of the two or three most successful political careers of the century. This note will chronicle the highlights
of his political career, mention his wealth and learning, and discuss briefly his
anti-papal views.
Da Ponte was elected Savio agli Ordini in 1513 at the age of twenty-two,
three years short of the constitutional requirement of twenty-five. Many other
offices followed; indeed, he never lost an election in his early career. C. CAIRNS,
Domenico Bollani Bishop of Brescia. Devotion to Church and State in the
Republic of Venice in the Sixteenth Century, Nieuwkoop 1976, p. 24 n. 64.
He held various administrative posts in the Venetian Empire and went to the
Council of Trent as ambassador in 1542. Upon returning to Venice, he won
election in 1543 as Savio di Terraferma, the springboard to the great offices.
Two embassies to Rome, to Paul III in 1546 and to Julius III (May 1551
through early November 1553), confirmed his political stature. He rose to the
great offices in 1546, beginning with election to the Zonta. After 1553 he was
elected Savio Grande and to the Zonta with monotonous regularity. Only
absence from Venice, for example when serving as podestà at Padua in 1557
and 1558, and again as ambassador to the Council of Trent in 1561 and 1563,
removed him from the great offices. From 1546 until elected doge in 1578,
Da Ponte won 55 great office elections, more than any other patrician in the
period 1547 through 1605. He won a procuratorship in 1570 by defeating Paolo
di Marin Corner by the very slim margin of 8 or 9 votes of 1,200 cast. Nunziature IX, 321. He received votes in the ducal elections of 1559, 1567, and
1570, but was not a major candidate. He won in 1578, despite opposition to his
family. DA MOSTO, 330, 334, 339, 366-74; ALBÈRI, Serie II, vol. 3, pp. 142-146.
    DA MOSTO, 369, suggests that Da Ponte rose from poverty. However, his
amazing electoral success suggests both wealth and influence from the beginning
of his adult life. CAIRNS, op. cit., p. 24 n. 64. By the end of his life, contemporaries judged him to be very wealthy, estimating his net worth to be 150,000
ducats (DA MOSTO, 369), and his annual income to be 10,000 scudi. Letter of
Nuncio Lorenzo Campeggi of August 3, 1585, in A. S. Vat., Segretario di Stato,
Venezia, filza 10, f. 393 r. Other evidence confirms his wealth—which some

1550-59: C - 3 (1550); SG - 3 (1553); CX - 2; Z - 6.
1560-69: C - 3; SG -8; CX -3; Z - 8.
1570-78: SG - 10; Z - 6.

Girolamo di Marin Grimani K, PSM (second).

Melchiorre di Tommaso Michiel K, PSM (fourth).

thought had been gained through dishonest practices.

Da Ponte was a learned man. He received his doctorate in 1513, and as a young man often participated in public disputations in logic, philosophy, and theology. He won a *concorso* to substitute for Sebastiano Foscarini in the chair of philosophy at the *Scuola di Rialto* in 1521, and he held this position for two years. B. NARDI, *La scuola di Rialto e l'umanesimo veneziano*, in his *Saggi sulla cultura veneta del quattro e cinquecento*, a. c. di P. MAZZANTINI, Padova 1971, pp. 91-96. Da Ponte frequently interjected classical Latin phrases into his speeches in later life.

Da Ponte fought every papal jurisdictional initiative that came to his attention. He led the opposition against Nuncio Giovanni Della Casa's *Catalogo*, the first Venetian Index, in June 1549. Da Ponte successfully argued against the *Tre Savii* and the nuncio, and the *Catalogo* was suppressed. In August 1572 he and Doge Alvise Mocenigo objected to the exclusive papal privileges for the printing of the revised Tridentine breviary and missal. They believed that the privileges enriched papal printers and their Venetian partners, but excluded and impoverished the majority of Venetian printers. In December 1581 Doge Da Ponte again objected to papal privileges on the breviary and missal. GRENDLER, pp. 88, 177, 239.

In March 1581 the *Capi del Consiglio dei Dieci* demanded that the Venetian inquisitor leave the city because he had allegedly threatened to excommunicate Antonio Tiepolo and one of the lay deputies. Tiepolo sent word to the nuncio that Da Ponte was behind the threat, adding that it was an empty threat. The inquisitor stayed. Letter of Nuncio Alberto Bolognetti of c. March 11, 1581, in A.S. Vat., *Segretario di Stato, Venezia*, filza 22, ff. 99r-99v, 102r-102v. The next clergyman to fall victim to Da Ponte's wrath was not so fortunate. In March 1584 a visiting preacher condemned Venetian judicial corruption in his sermon at San Francesco della Vigna. Nobles in attendance denounced him to the *Capi del Consiglio dei Dieci*. Doge Da Ponte was enraged: never in my 93 years have I heard such things! The preacher fled, and the government forbade him to preach ever again in the Venetian state. A.S.V., *Collegio, Esposizioni Roma*, reg. 3, ff. 5 r - 6 v, March 14, 1584; and the letter of Nuncio Campeggi of March 17, 1584, in A.S. Vat., *Segretario di Stato, Venezia*, filza 25, ff. 87 v - 88 r. Da Ponte also challenged the papacy over benefices, excommunication, jurisdiction over Ceneda, and taxation of the clergy. *Nunziature* IX, 327; VIII, 97, 110, 113, 145, 407-08. Small wonder that nuncios feared and hated him. *Nunziature* IX, 45.

Da Ponte was not popular in Rome. The newly elected Pius V refused to receive him as one of the envoys sent to offer the Republic's homage in January 1566. Da Ponte had aroused the pontiff's ire when the latter had been Grand Inquisitor and head of the Congregation of the Inquisition. Moreover, Pius V doubted Da Ponte's orthodoxy. ALBÈRI, Serie II, vol. 3, pp. 143-44. Doubtlessly, he remembered that Da Ponte's younger brother, Andrea di Antonio (1509-85), was a fervent Protestant who in the 1550s had led a Venetian conventicle that included several young patricians. Andrea fled to Geneva in or about 1560. BARBARO A.S.V., 6, 204; GRENDLER, pp. 134-136. Da Ponte defended himself against Pius V's suspicions by proclaiming his hostility toward heresy. He claimed that he had argued for the death penalty for heretics in the

Alvise di Tommaso Mocenigo 1507-77, PSM 1566, Doge 1570, administrator and diplomat [42], lay deputy 1562, 1565, 1568-70; BARBARO Bibl. Marc., 3, 114 r.
1550-59: CX - 1 (1554); Z - 3 (1554).
1560-69: C - 1 (1563); SG - 8 (1560); CX - 2; Z - 3.
1570: SG - 1.

Andrea di Alvise Sanudo (fourth).

1563 Andrea di Gregorio Barbarigo (fourth).

Paolo di Marin Corner (second).

Melchiorre di Tommaso Michiel K, PSM (fifth).

Andrea di Alvise Sanudo (fifth).

Bernardo di Nicolò Zorzi (sixth).

Consiglio dei Dieci and as lay deputy to the Inquisition. STELLA, p. 14 n. 37.
 Even if Da Ponte favored severe measures against heresy, his life-long hostility toward the papacy makes his election as lay deputy surprising. The *Collegio* usually chose patricians more sympathetic to papal aims. However, Da Ponte spent very little time with the Inquisition. He served once in November 1562 at the trial of Nicolò Buccella, an Anabaptist. A. STELLA, *Dall'Anabattismo al Socinianesimo nel Cinquecento veneto. Ricerche storiche*, Padova 1967, p. 129 n. 31. Similarly, he served only one day in 1564. A.S.V., *Santo Uffizio*, busta 20, Francesco Lazzaro, testimony of September 7, 1564. Obviously, Da Ponte left the tribunal at the earliest opportunity. In addition to sources previously cited, see STELLA, pp. 12-16, 34-38.

42. Alvise di Tommaso (or Tomà) Mocenigo came from a very powerful branch of the Mocenigo family, the one that descended from Doge Tomà Mocenigo (1414-23) and produced brother doges Pietro (1474-76) and Giovanni (1478-86) as well as two or three procurators in every generation, including Alvise's father. Mocenigo was wealthy, and some patricians disliked him as doge for that reason. COZZI, p. 30 n. l. A chronicler stated that Mocenigo enjoyed annual income of 10,000 ducats, although he declared only 1,799 ducats in rents in the *decima* of 1566. DA MOSTO, 344. In his youth Alvise reportedly despised trade, preferring to read the lives of kings and emperors. His political career gave him ample opportunity to emulate the statesmen of the past. Beginning as *Savio agli Ordini* in 1532, he moved to Vicenza as captain in 1540, and reached *Savio di Terraferma* in 1544 at the relatively young age of 37. Ambassadorships to Charles V in 1546-48, to France in 1553, to the papacy 1557, to Maximillian II in 1564, and several governorships, followed. He won slightly fewer elections to the great offices than some other powerful patricians, probably because he was more frequently elected ambassador or governor. Nevertheless, he was elected procurator at the early age of 59, received votes in the ducal election of 1559, came close to winning in 1567, and succeeded in 1570. DA MOSTO, 330, 334, Nuncio Giovanni Antonio Facchinetti reported that Mocenigo shared Nicolò Da Ponte's views on church-state relations; hence, the nuncio disliked Mocenigo. *Nunziature* IX, 45, letter of April 16, 1569. Mocenigo stood with Da Ponte to defend the Venetian printers in 1572 (see note 41), but other evidence has not come to light. Mocenigo served frequently with the Holy Office in the 1560s, but did not win any commendations from Rome. On the other hand, the nuncio was happy at Mocenigo's election as doge because he judged that Mocenigo would vigorously prosecute the war against the Turks. The nuncio was correct. ALBÈRI, Serie II, vol. 4, p. 22; DA MOSTO, pp. 337-342.

1564   Paolo di Marin Corner (third).

Nicolò di Antonio da Ponte (second). He served only one day. See note 41.

Melchiorre di Tommaso Michiel K, PSM (sixth).

Andrea di Alvise Sanudo (sixth).

Bernardo di Nicolò Zorzi (seventh).

1565   Alessandro Bon, probably Alessandro di Alvise Bon, 1514-76, who purchased the PSM in 1571 with a loan of 20,000 ducats but never held a great office. BARBARO Bibl. Marc., 1, 157 v.

Paolo di Marin Corner (fourth).

Giulio di Zorzi Contarini PSM (seventh).

Matteo di Marco Dandolo K, PSM, 1495/1500 - July 29, 1570, PSM 1563, diplomat [43]; BARBARO Bibl. Marc., 2, 47 v.

---

43. Matteo di Marco Dandolo became a *Savio di Terraferma* in 1530, at the age of 36 or a little younger. He then passed to a series of ambassadorships: France 1540-42, ambassador extraordinary to Henry II in 1547, to Rome 1548-51, and to the Council of Trent in 1561. He was also governor of Padua in 1545. He received votes for doge in 1556, 1559, and came close to winning in 1567. His sister Zilia was the wife of Doge Lorenzo Priuli (1556-59). DA MOSTO, 324, 326, 330, 334, 339; for the 1567 election, also see *Nunziature* VIII, 298, 304; CICOGNA, 6, 640. For additional biographical material, see ALBÈRI, Serie II, vol. 3, pp. 335-336.

Nuncio Facchinetti described Dandolo as « molto cattolico et pio », and regarded his death as a great loss. *Nunziature* IX, 318, 321, letters of July 29, August 2, 1570. He seems to have been a tactful supporter of the Holy Office. In late January 1567, the nuncio asked for a public execution by burning of the relapsed and obstinate heretic Publio Francesco Spinola, arguing that a public execution would hearten the Catholics of Flanders and France, and disprove the Huguenot claim that Venice befriended Protestants. The « vecchi » agreed with him, but the *Savii di Terraferma* did not. Then Dandolo intervened: since the dispute might take weeks and months to resolve, during which time the heretic might escape, he recommended immediate drowning. The nuncio agreed, and Spinola was drowned. *Nunziature* VIII, 166-67, letter of February 1, 1567.

Two other contacts with churchmen shed a little more light on Dandolo's position on church-state relations. While ambassador to the papacy, Dandolo became acquainted with Ignatius Loyola. In September 1551 Loyola turned to Dandolo to relay assurances to the Republic about the teaching in Jesuit schools recently opened in Venice and Padua. Loyola informed Dandolo that Jesuit aims were spiritual and pastoral, and that the schools would avoid political matters. Presumably Dandolo relayed Loyola's pledge to members of the government, but his reply, if any, to Loyola, has not come to light. *Monumenta Ignatiana ex autographis vel ex antiquioribus exemplis collecta*, Serie Prima: *Sancti Ignatii de Loyola Epistolae et Instructiones*, III, Madrid 1905, letters 2086 and 2088, pp. 665-67; P. TACCHI VENTURI, *Storia della Compagnia di Gesù in Italia narrata col sussidio di fonti contemporanee*, Vol. II, parte 2, *Dalla solenne approvazione dell'Ordine alla morte del fondatore (1540-1556)*, Roma 1951, p. 377. When Patriarch Diedo came under attack in 1559 for failing to pay his taxes, he appealed to two curial cardinals for help. One of the cardinals wrote to Dandolo on behalf of the patriarch. Obeying the Republic's prohibition

1540-49: CX - 1 (1544).
1550-59: C - 3 (1551); SG - 4 (1556); Z - 1 (1559).
1560-69: C - 1; SG - 9; Z - 5.
1570: SG - 1.

Girolamo di Marin Grimani K, PSM (third).

Melchiorre di Tommaso Michiel K, PSM (seventh).

Alvise di Tommaso Mocenigo (second).

Marc'Antonio Mocenigo, not positively identified [44].

Marco Morosini, possibly Marco di Lorenzo (1513-69) of the Santa Maria Formosa branch; BARBARO A.S.V., 5, 381; or Marco di Orsatto (d. 1584); BARBARO A.S.V., 5, 336.

Bernardo di Nicolò Zorzi (eighth).

1566 Giulio di Zorzi Contarini PSM (eighth).

Paolo di Marin Corner (fifth).

Marco Morosini (second).

1567 Giulio di Zorzi Contarini PSM (ninth).

Paolo di Marin Corner (sixth).

Lorenzo di Agostino da Mula (Amulio) 1498/1502-1579, PSM 1570, pro-papal sympathies [45]; BARBARO Bibl. Marc., 3, 202 v.

---

against private communication with foreign powers, Dandolo turned the letter over to the *Capi del Consiglio dei Dieci*. Thus, he escaped Giovanni Donà's wrath, for the latter excoriated another patrician who failed to report a letter from Rome. These incidents suggest that churchmen did look upon Dandolo as a supporter of their aims, but that Dandolo behaved so cautiously and scrupulously that he escaped criticism from anti-clericals as Donà. LIPPOMANO, *op. cit.*, p. 468.

44. Possibly this is Marc'Antonio di Piero Mocenigo (1517-85) of the San Samuele branch of the family, and not closely related to Doge Alvise di Tommaso Mocenigo of the powerful S. Stae branch. BARBARO A.S.V., 5, 193. His great office elections were 1580-84: CX - 3 (1580); Z - 1 (1580). Yet, it would be unusual for a patrician to be elected lay deputy at the relatively young age of 48 and fifteen years before entering the great offices.

45. Lorenzo di Agostino Da Mula was elected to the *Tre Savii sopra Eresia* on October 23, 1567. A.S.V., *Collegio, Notatorio*, reg. 37, f. 36v. He had enough political weight to receive votes in the ducal election of May 1570. DA MOSTO, 339. Indeed, he would have been a strong candidate had he been in Venice at the time, in the opinion of the nuncio. *Nunziature* IX, 269.
Da Mula fits the pattern of a pro-papal noble. He supported the fight against heresy, maintained friendly relations with the nuncio, had a financial interest in church property, and was related (although not closely) to a noble who enjoyed high ecclesiastical preferment. Politically he favored the Holy League and opposed the French alliance.
The nuncio spoke favorably of Da Mula on several occasions. On April 3, 1568, Nuncio Facchinetti wrote: « Il clar.mo messer Lorenzo Da Mula, il quale è uno degli assistenti et dell'honor di Dio zelantissimo si trova di presente capo de' X, onde si può sperare qualche bene ». *Nunziature* VIII, 369. On August 17, 1569, the nuncio wrote: « Il clar.mo messer Lorenzo Da Mula è stato creato

1550-59: CX - 2 (1557); Z - 1 (1558).
1560-69: CX - 2; Z - 4.
1570-79: SG - 1 (1571); Z - 4.

Girolamo di Marin Grimani K, PSM (fourth).

Melchiorre di Tommaso Michiel K, PSM (eighth).

Marco Morosini (third).

Marco Venier, possibly Marco di Girolamo (1527-96), although a lay deputy only forty years old was very unusual; Barbaro A.S.V., 7, 230.

1568 Francesco di Marc'Antonio Bernardo 1514-1580?, art collector [46]; Barbaro A.S.V., 2, 17.
1560-69: SG - 2 (1567); CX - 2 (1565).
1570-79: C - 1 (1576); SG - 7; CX - 4; Z - 3 (1573).
1580: C - 1.

Lorenzo di Agostino Da Mula (second).

Alvise di Tommaso Mocenigo K, PSM (third).

Girolamo di Alvise Soranzo K c. 1495-April 11, 1569 [47]. He was not

proveditore in Candia...; partirà di qua presto et desidera haver la benedittione da N. S. [Pius V]. Questo è un gentilhuomo che nelle cause del S. Offitio non può esser né più accurato né più zelante, et se ci fosser molti de' suoi pari non laboraremus ». *Nunziature* IX, 112. Cardinal Michele Bonelli wrote back that Pius V « ha sempre havuto buonissimo concetto di questo gentilhuomo, et volentieri l'accompagna ancora con la sua santa benedettione... ». *Nunziature* IX, 116, August 24, 1569. Da Mula served in Candia until he became ill in November 1570. Upon his return the nuncio praised his « molto pietà ». *Nunziature* IX, 494, Aprii 28, 1571.

Da Mula spoke freely to the nuncio. When he and Federico di Polo Valaresso arrived for the day's meeting of the Holy Office, they informed the nuncio of current Venetian views about the proposed Holy League. Da Mula and Valaresso, « senatori del Consiglio de' X et assai principali », according to the nuncio, both favored the alliance, but the majority of the Senate would not yet take the advice of the « vecchi ». *Nunziature* VIII, 372-73, April 10, 1568. Da Mula had financial interests in church properties, according to Stella, p. 7 n. 13. Finally, Da Mula was a second cousin of Marc'Antonio di Francesco Da Mula (1506-72) who in 1561 converted his ambassadorship to the papacy into a cardinalate, thus provoking a storm of opposition in the Senate.

46. That this is Francesco di Marc'Antonio Bernardo is confirmed by A.S.V., *Collegio, Notatorio*, reg. 37, f. 86 r, May 5, 1568. He served until September 20, 1568, when he was elected captain at Padua. Girolamo di Alvise Soranzo replaced him. A.S.V., *Collegio, Notatorio*, reg. 37, f. 141 v. Bernardo was also captain at Verona, and he received some votes in the ducal election of 1578. In 1577 he was appointed to the commission charged with redecorating the ducal palace after the fire of that year. Bernardo had a large collection of antique marbles and medals. Logan, 187, 300 (Logan notes a will of 1589; this suggests that the death date given in Barbaro may be wrong); Da Mosto, 370.

47. Because he had to direct the family business, Soranzo did not enter public office until middle age. Late entry proved no handicap, for he was elected *Savio di Terraferma* in 1553, and to the great offices five years later when he

a close relative of brothers Giacomo and Giovanni di Francesco Soranzo. BARBARO Bibl. Marc., 3, 107 v.
   1550-59: SG - 2 (1558); CX - 1 (1558).
   1560-69: C - 2 (1563); SG - 3; CX - 2; Z - 3 (1565).

Federico di Polo Valaresso c. 1493-1572, scholar[48]; CICOGNA, 2, 70-71.
   1560-69: C - 2 (1566); SG - 4 (1563); CX - 2 (1567); Z - 6 (1562).
   1570-72: C-1; SG - 1; CX - 1.

1569 Andrea di Piero Badoer 1515 - September 11, 1575[49]; BARBARO Bibl. Marc., 1, 30 v.
   1560-69: SG - 4 (1567); CX - 3 (1564); Z - 2 (1567).
   1570-75: C - 2 (1570 ris., 1573 ris.); SG - 3; Z - 2.

Andrea di Gregorio Barbarigo (fifth).

Agostino Barbarigo, probably Agostino di Zuanne 1516-October 9, 1571, *Proveditore Generale da Mar* and second-in-command of Venetian forces at Lepanto, died of wounds. BARBARO Bibl. Marc., 1, 67 r; *D.B.I.*, 6, 50-52.
   1560-69: SG - 2 (1568); CX - 2 (1566).
   1570: SG - 1; CX - 1.

Alvise di Tommaso Mocenigo K, PSM (fourth).

Girolamo di Alvise Soranzo K (second).

Paolo di Stefano Tiepolo K 1523-85, PSM 1576, diplomat[50]; BARBARO

---

was in his early sixties. He also served in several administrative offices, was elected *podestà* at Verona in 1555 and Padua in 1563, served as ambassador to the papacy 1561-63, and received some votes for bishop of Verona and patriarch of Venice in 1559. ALBÈRI, Serie II, vol. 4, p. 66.

48. A. S. V., *Collegio, Notatorio*, reg. 37, f. 56 r, January 20, 1567 (mv), confirms that this is Federico di Polo Valaresso. He enjoyed a reputation for great learning and special competence in the ancient Greek authors. He served as *Riformatore dello Studio di Padova* in 1571, and in January of that year was named to a special commission to investigate financial and other problems concerning the military forces in Dalmatia. *Nunziature* IX, 425. He had a financial interest in ecclesiastical properties. STELLA, p. 7 n. 13. In 1568 Valaresso and Lorenzo di Agostino Da Mula informed the nuncio of government views about the proposed Holy League, as well as their own preference for it and dislike for the French alliance. *Nunziature* VIII, 372-373. But the nuncio never commented on Valaresso's religious views or his performance as lay deputy.

49. Badoer was governor at Feltre in 1552 and at Crema in 1553. He led Senate opposition to Venetian participation in the Holy League because he feared that the alliance would lead to greater Spanish hegemony in Italy. In 1573 he favored a separate peace with the Turk, and was sent to Constantinople to negotiate it. In July 1574 the Senate named Badoer and three other patricians to meet Henry III at the Venetian frontier and to accompany him into the city. *D.B.I.*, 5, pp. 98-99; *Nunziature* IX, 214 n. 1.

50. Tiepolo enjoyed a very distinguished diplomatic career. He began as ambassador extraordinary to Mantua in 1549; subsequently he was ambassador to Ferdinand, King of the Romans, 1554-57, to Spain 1558-62, to Rome 1565-68, and again 1572-75. He received votes in the ducal election of 1578. DA MOSTO,

A.S.V., 7, 84; Albèri, Serie II, vol. 4, p. 163.
1560-69: C - 1 (1568); CX - 1 (1569); Z - 1 (1569).
1570-79: C - 1 (*riservato*); SG - 5 (1571); Z - 4.
1580-85: SG - 6; Z - 2.

Federico di Polo Valaresso (second).

Andrea Venier, possibly Andrea di Lion (1514-?); Barbaro A.S.V., 7, 240.

1570 Giulio di Zorzi Contarini PSM (tenth).

Melchiorre di Tommaso Michiel K, PSM (ninth).

Alvise di Tommaso Mocenigo K, PSM (fifth).

Paolo di Stefano Tiepolo K (second).

Piero (Pietro) Venier, probably Piero di Zuanne 1489/95 - entered *Maggior Consiglio* 1514 - c. 1576, brother of Doge Francesco Venier (1554-56), received votes in ducal elections of 1559,

---

370. Lowry opines that Tiepolo was one of the chief targets of the reformers in the constitutional crisis of 1582-83. Lowry, 294-295.
    Observors considered Tiepolo to be pious and a friend of Rome. Certainly he was a valued contact for nuncios, and he was able to obtain ecclesiastical favors for dependents. Stella, 9, 39, 41 n. 73; Cozzi, p. 38 n. 2; Lowry, 294-295. Tiepolo also enjoyed the income from church lands and fought to retain it. Like their father before them, Tiepolo and his brothers received substantial revenues (« grossa entrata ») from lands leased from the monastery of Follina in Friuli. In October 1570 their income was threatened. The previous holder having died, the benefice passed to Cardinal Carlo Borromeo who announced his intention of cancelling the lease. Tiepolo informed the nuncio that he and his brothers were going to appeal Borromeo's decision to a Venetian civil court rather than to an ecclesiastical court. The nuncio immediately understood the danger involved and informed Rome. Borromeo might have canon law on his side, the nuncio wrote, but so many other Venetian nobles also enjoyed the financial fruits of church lands that the Venetian court would easily support Tiepolo and defy Rome. Should this happen, the nuncio foresaw a great loss to papal jurisdictional authority. He urged Rome to drop the matter. « ..et dico a V. S. ill.ma che molto ben *de iure* si diffenderia che questa causa potesse esser conosciuta da giudici ecclesiastici, ma ci sono tanti gentilhuomini vinitiani c'hanno di questi beni di Chiesa che faranno impedimento grandissimo, vedendo, se potranno esser convenuti per cause tali dinanzi a giudici ecclesiastici, che saranno costretti a restituire detti beni. Et io n'aviso perché se, fatta la citatione, l'avogadore s'oppone et la difficultà non venchi superata, si farà piaga alla giurisditione della Sede Apostolica... » *Nunziature* IX, 376-77, October 25, 1570. The papacy ignored him and supported Borromeo. As the dispute dragged on, the nuncio repeatedly begged Rome to let Tiepolo have his way. Since Tiepolo had helped the papacy to persuade the Republic to join the Holy League, why offend him now? « et diferisco perché il clar.mo messer Paolo Tiepolo in questa materia della lega si è portato benissimo et non gli vorrei dar disgusto alcuno... ». *Nunziature* IX, 382, 414-16, 418, 421, 487, 491 (quote), 503-04 (November 1, 1570, through May 19, 1571). Tiepolo probably prevailed, for in the *decima* of 1582 he and his brother Bernardo declared a joint annual income of c. 280 ducats from the Follina lands. Lowry, *Church and Venetian Political Change*, 363-64.

1567, and 1570; BARBARO A.S.V., 7, 231; DA MOSTO, 330, 334, 339.
1560-69: C - 2 (1564); CX - 3 (1563); Z - 2 (1566).
1570-75: CX - 4.

1571 Antonio di Andrea Bragadin 1510-91 [51], PSM 1585; BARBARO A.S.V., 2, 138; D.B.I. 13, pp. 663-64.
1560-69: CX - 1 (1569).
1570-79: SG - 4 (1571); CX - 5; Z - 1 (1572).
1580-89: SG - 6; CX - 1; Z - 2.
1590-91: SG - 2.

Giulio di Zorzi Contarini PSM (eleventh).

Giacomo (Jacopo) di Michele Foscarini Dr 1507-83, scholar [52]; BARBARO

---

51. Bragadin was a merchant who held a number of financial posts in the government and was governor at Brescia 1568-70. He received votes in the ducal elections of 1578 and 1585. DA MOSTO, 370, 378. In 1585 he favored a Spanish proposal that would have returned the Venetians to the international pepper trade. However, the government rejected the proposal for fear that it would draw the Republic into the Spanish political orbit. Bragadin was fervently Catholic, pro-papal, and philo-Spanish in the judgment of COZZI, p. 12 n. 1.

52. The « Jacopo Foscarini Dr » who served as lay deputy 1571-73, 1576-78, and 1580-81, was Giacomo di Michele Foscarini, not the more powerful and better krown Giacomo di Alvise (see note 83). The Inquisition records always add the suffix « dott. » or « Dr » or simply « D » to confirm that this is Giacomo di Michele. Giacomo Foscarini Dr was almost always present from 1571 through 1573 when the Holy Office punished many members of the book trade for violating the Tridentine Index. GRENDLER, pp. 162-168. Moreover, A.S.V., Collegio, Notatorio, records confirm that «Jacobus Fuscareno doct.» was elected a lay deputy on January 27, 1575 mv, and that « Giacomo Foscarini D » completed a term as Savio sopra Eresia on June 17, 1581. A.S.V., Collegio, Notatorio, reg. 42, f. 64 r; reg. 45, f. 89 v. The 1581 reference is particularly useful, for this is after the election of Giacomo di Alvise to a procuratorship (March 8, 1580). After 1580 the records clearly distinguish between « Giacomo Foscarini D » and « Giacomo Foscarini Pro ». Before 1580 the records in A.S.V., Collegio, Notatorio, and Segretario alle Voci usually, but not always, make a distinction between « Giacomo Foscarini Dr » and « Giacomo Foscarini ». The documents securely identify Giacomo di Michele as the winner of the great office elections noted above. But in five cases it is impossible to determine whether the winner was Giacomo di Michele or Giacomo di Alvise: CX - 1582; Z - 1570, 1571, 1579, 1580. After Giacomo di Michele's death in 1583, the problem disappears.

Foscarini combined a reputation for learning with political weight, a combination that won election to the Savii sopra Eresia reasonably often. He was a scholar reportedly learned in Aristotle, Greek, and logic. At the opening of the academic year at the Scuola di Rialto (November 5, 1524), Foscarini participated in a public dispute in logic. NARDI, La scuola di Rialto..., pp. 77-78, 96. On December 4, 1555, the Senate elected him to the chair of philosophy at the Scuola di Rialto; he held the post until replaced in February 1559. A.S.V., Segretario alle Voci, Elezioni dei Pregadi, reg. 2, f. 59 v. He was also elected Riformatore dello Studio di Padova in 1567, 1572, and 1576. Either Giacomo di Michele or Giacomo di Alvise received some votes in the ducal election of

A.S.V., 3, 528; CICOGNA, 2, 409.
1560-69: CX - 1 (1569); Z - 1 (1568).
1570-79: C - 1 (1577); SG - 1 (1574 *ris.*); CX - 2; Z - 2.
1580-83: C - 1.

Andrea Venier (second).

Piero di Zuanne Venier (second).

1572 Giacomo di Michele Foscarini Dr (second).

Vincenzo di Barbon Morosini 1511-88 [53], K PSM 1578; BARBARO
A.S.V., 5, 324 v; CICOGNA, 4, 457-58.
1560-69: C - 1 (1568); SG - 2 (1568); CX - 1 (1569); Z - 1 (1569).
1570-79: C - 3; SG - 8; CX - 2; Z - 4.
1580-88: SG - 8; Z - 2.

Nicolò Venier, probably Nicolò di Agostino [54] 1520/27 - enrolled
Maggior Consiglio 1545 - 1587, PSM 1580; BARBARO A.S.V., 7,
248 v.
1560-69: CX - 1 (1567).
1570-79: C - 3 (1570); CX - 4; Z - 1 (1577).

Piero di Zuanne Venier (third).

1573 Domenico Contarini, possibly Domenico di Francesco (1526-1601)
of the San Benedetto branch. BARBARO A.S.V., 2, 500.

Vincenzo Contarini, possibly Vincenzo di Francesco 1513-75.
BARBARO A.S.V., 2, 485.
1560-69: CX - 1 (1569).
1570-75: CX - 1.

Giovanni di Bernardo Donà 1510-91, defender of the laws of the
Republic and anti-clerical [55]; BARBARO A.S.V., 3, 318.

1578. DA MOSTO, 370. While *podestà* at Padua in 1574, Giacomo di Michele
arrested and tried for murder a Knight of Malta. The nuncio protested strongly
that the knight should be tried in an ecclesiastical court, but the Republic
disagreed, and the dispute dragged on. *Nunziature* XI, pp. 194-197 *et passim*.

53. Morosini was *rettore* at Bergamo in 1555 and Brescia in 1566, and ambassador extraordinary to Gregory XIII in 1572. He received some votes for doge
in 1578, and was a strong candidate in 1585. DA MOSTO, 370, 378-379; A. S.
Vat., *Segretario di Stato, Venezia*, filza 10, ff. 399 v, 403 r-403 v, August 10,
24, 1585. It is interesting that he first won election to all four of the great
offices within a twelve- to thirteen-month period. Despite thirty-two successful
elections to great offices, his political and religious views are unknown.

54. Venier received votes in the ducal elections of 1578 and 1585. DA MOSTO,
370, 378; A. S. Vat., *Segretario di Stato, Venezia*, filza 10, f. 393 v, August 3, 1585.

55. Giovanni di Bernardo Donà (Zuanne « Dalle Renghe » Donado as he is described in Barbaro and elsewhere) was famous for his many long speeches, his
strong anti-clericalism, and his ferocious attacks on those who violated laws of
the Republic.
    Giovanni di Bernardo came from the San Polo branch of the Donà, the same
branch that produced Nicolò di Giovanni Donà (1539 — elected doge 1618 —
d. 1618) who was also strongly anti-papal. Giovanni di Bernardo was not closely

1560-69: CX - 1 (1567); Z - 1 (1569).
1570-79: C - 2 (1572); SG - 4 (1570); CX - 4 Z - 4.
1580-89: C - 1; SG - 1; CX - 2.

related to Doge Francesco di Alvise Donà (c. 1470 — elected doge 1545 — d. 1553) or to future doge Leonardo di Giovanni Battista Donà (1536 — doge 1605 — d. 1612). Giovanni di Bernardo did not marry, according to Barbaro, had no heirs, and had no politically significant brothers. He enjoyed a reputation for eloquence, for he composed epigrams and poetry in Latin and the vernacular. He delivered the funeral oration for Doge Francesco Donà in 1553. After three elections as *Savio agli Ordini*, he entered the Senate in 1543 with an offer of 500 ducats to the treasury. This offer and the elections as *Savio agli Ordini* argue that Donà was wealthy. The twenty great office elections between 1567 and 1584 demonstrate that Donà had a successful but not distinguished political career. He was also elected *Savio di Terraferma* six times, and held administrative posts. But he never held any captaincies in the Venetian state nor any diplomatic posts. Indeed, it is hard to imagine the outspoken Donà implementing policies with which he disagreed or possessing any of the suppleness and duplicity necessary for diplomacy. Probably his denunciations of his corrupt colleagues and his long speeches made him unpopular with the majority of nobles. He did not reach the great offices until he was 57 years old and, more significantly, did not enjoy the uninterrupted electoral success afterward that patricians of his age and stature normally did. Despite his advanced years and probable wealth, he never became a procurator. In the ducal election of 1567 Donà opposed Alvise Mocenigo and helped to elect Pietro Loredan. Donà received some votes in the ducal elections of 1578 and 1585, but was not a strong candidate. DA MOSTO, 334, 370, 378.

The nuncio judged Giovanni di Bernardo to be « poco amico de' preti » and « huomo ordinariamente contrario all'ecclesiastici ». *Nunziature* VIII, 265 (August 23, 1567); IX, 91 (July 13, 1569). This was certainly true. But even stronger was Donà's belief in the integrity of the laws of the Republic and his zeal in denouncing violators.

Donà played a prominent role in the attempt to punish the guilty in most of the important cases of noble corruption in the 1550s and 1560s. In July 1559, when he was a *Savio di Terraferma*, Donà rose in the Senate to attack Patriarch Vincenzo Diedo for failing to pay 2,000 ducats in taxes owed the Republic. Speaking directly to Diedo, Donà denounced him in the strongest possible terms. He pointed out that while the patriarch claimed poverty, he had spent 900 ducats on a banquet honoring one of Paul IV's cardinal nephews. Donà exhorted the senators to ignore Diedo's relatives, to rise above their fears of Vatican influence, and to procede against « this hypocrite ». « Non temete la sua parentela, non vi spaventino le cose di Roma, ma con il solito vostro valore procedete contra questo hyppocrito... ». In another speech Donà called the patriarch « questo lupo rapace ». Diedo appealed to his friends in Rome who wrote supporting letters to members of the Venetian government. Nobles were bound by law to give such communications from agents of a foreign power to the *Capi del Consiglio dei Dieci*. When one of the recipients, Antonio Longo, a *Savio di Terraferma*, did not, Donà publicly attacked him, ridiculing Longo's claim that he was ignorant of the law. Throughout his fierce campaign to force Diedo to pay his debts, Donà stressed obedience to the laws and the corruption of the patriarch. LIPPOMANO, *op. cit.*, pp. 464-79, quotes on 470 and 476; COZZI, 29-30.

In 1567 the government intercepted coded Hebrew letters (which may have been counterfeit) giving the details of a plot by Jews in Constantinople and Venice to bribe Marin de' Cavalli, Venetian ambassador extraordinary to the Turk. The Senate chose Donà and three others to judge Cavalli, who was eventually found innocent. *Nunziature* VIII, 251, 260-61, 290, 388. In 1568 as *Capo del*

Giacomo di Michele Foscarini Dr (third).
Nicolò di Agostino Venier (second).
Alvise Zorzi, probably Alvise di Benetto Zorzi[56] 1515-93, PSM 1592;

Consiglio dei Dieci Donà secured a severe punishment for a noble found guilty of election fraud. The nuncio commented that others had done the same, but Donà was a stern upholder of the law. *Nunziature* VIII, 377.

Donà directed his heaviest fire against those nobles who used political office in order to win the rich rewards of ecclesiastical benefices. Donà led the Senate attack in 1560 and 1561 against Marc'Antonio Da Mula who, while ambassador to Rome, was first nominated bishop of Verona and then named cardinal. Donà accused him of intriguing for ecclesiastical preferment while serving the Republic, a violation of the law forbidding Venetians to accept rewards from foreign powers unless authorized by the Republic. *Cicogna*, 6, 613-14.

Sometimes Donà succeeded in halting the profitable church-state intrigue of his fellow nobles. In 1569 Bernardo Surian, brother of Michele who was ambassador to Rome, wished to become bishop of Sebenico. Giacomo Surian, another brother, was elected ambassador to Spain, and the Senate was about to grant him 1,000 scudi for travel expenses when Donà rose to speak. He opposed the election of Giacomo Surian and the grant of money on the grounds that the two brother ambassadors would successfully intrigue to obtain ecclesiastical preferment for the third brother, Bernardo. The Senate endorsed Donà's position by a single vote, although other considerations also moved some to vote against Surian. But then « tutti i buoni » and « tutti quei che hanno preti in casa » (in the nuncio's words) perceived that this was « una via indiretta a escludere dall'ambasciarie ». So they succeeded in overturning the motion; the Senate gave Surian his 1,000 scudi. Donà and his supporters fought back; they wished to pass a law forbidding any relative of a current ambassador from obtaining church benefices during the ambassador's tenure.

Throughout this dispute, the nuncio strongly urged the pope to give Bernardo Surian the bishopric that he desired, so that « this family (Surian) would not suffer and, more importantly, so that other nobles with church connections would not cool in their efforts to promote papal aims ». « acciò che questa famiglia non venisse a patire et, di più, gli altri gentilhuomini interessati con la Chiesa non si raffreddino a favorire le cose della Sede Apostolica ». *Nunziature* IX, 58, 77, 81, 91 (quote), 92, 111. But Pius V had heard disturbing things about Bernardo Surian; he had not resided in his parish (near Vicenza) and then had resigned it. The nuncio confirmed this, but urged the pontiff to bestow the bishopric on Bernardo for the sake of the political advantage to be derived in Venice and Rome. It would be money well spent. « ...la quale sarà, come io credo, certo bene impiegata ». *Nunziature*, IX, 101, 111 (quote). Pius V insisted that Bernardo Surian lacked the qualities of a good bishop and refused to give him the see of Sebenico. Moreover, because of the Senate opposition led by Donà, Giacomo Surian withdrew, and another noble was elected ambassador to Spain. *Nunziature* IX, 95, 99, 113.

Donà spent very little time with the Holy Office. He was elected to replace Vincenzo di Barbon Morosini on February 15, 1573, and was replaced upon becoming *Savio Grande* on July 1, 1573. A. S. V., *Collegio, Notatorio*, reg. 40, ff. 109 r, 156 v. Donà's name appeared only once in a trial, in A. S. V. *Santo Uffizio*, busta 34, Alessandro Mantica, document of May 29, 1573. Finally, in GRENDLER, p. 45 n. 57, I mistakenly opined that this lay deputy « Zuan Donado » might also be Giovanni di Benedetto Donà. « Zuan di Benedetto » does not exist.

56. Alvise di Benedetto was *Proveditore Generale* in Corfù in 1571 and captain at Padua. He should not be confused with Alvise di Paolo Zorzi, a prominent opponent of Rome and pamphleteer at the time of the interdict. In 1579 Nuncio

BARBARO A.S.V., 7, 424.
1570-79: C - 1 (1578); SG - 6 (1572); Z - 4 (1572).
1580-89: C - 3; SG - 6; Z - 2.
1590-93: C - 1; SG - 3.

1574 Francesco di Marc'Antonio Bernardo (second).

Giovanni Alvise Bragadin, probably Giovanni Alvise di Marco 1516-76, brother of Marcantonio, the martyr of Famagusta [57]; BARBARO Bibl. Marc., 1, 179 r; *D.B.I.*, 13, 680-81.
1570-76: C - 1 (1576); Z - 2 (1572).

Vincenzo di Francesco Contarini (second).

Domenico di Piero Duodo 1513-96, PSM 1592; brother of Francesco PSM 1587, received votes for doge in 1595.
BARBARO Bibl. Marc., 2, 94 v; DA MOSTO, 386.
1560-69: Z - 1 (1569).
1570-79: C - 3 (1571); CX - 3 (1570); Z - 2.
1580 - 85: C - 1; CX - 3.

Giovanni (Zuanne) di Francesco Soranzo K 1520-1603, PSM 1596, papal supporter [58]; BARBARO A.S.V., 3, 50.

Alberto Bolognetti described Alvise di Benetto as « senatore di grandissima autorità e molto favorevole alle cose della Chiesa. A. S. Vat., *Segretario di Stato, Venezia*, filza 19, f. 234 r, as cited by LOWRY », *Church and Venetian Political Change...*, 365. In 1588 when Leonardo Donà opposed asking the pope to create more Venetian cardinals, Zorzi spoke in favor of the request. He argued that Venetian nobles could serve two masters (the Republic and the church) and that noble cardinals were useful to Venice. GRENDLER, pp. 30-32. But Zorzi could be found on the other side as well. In 1586 and 1587 the Senate fought Sixtus V over whether Patriarch Giovanni Trevisan should be allowed to channel the revenues from the abbey of San Cipriano di Murano to two young relatives. Leonardo Donà opposed the pope, condemning the power and wealth of the clergy as a threat to the liberty of the Republic. Zorzi supported Donà. LOWRY, *Church and Venetian Political Change...*, 265-271.
    The elections of Alvise Zorzi on July 1, 1573, Giovanni di Francesco Soranzo on January 7, 1574, and Francesco Bernardo and Domenico Duodo on February 15, 1574, are confirmed by A. S.V., *Collegio, Notatorio*, reg. 40, ff. 156 v, 223 v, 252 v. Giacomo Gussoni is also noted as elected on July 1, 1573, but I have not found his name in Inquisition documents.
57. From a branch of the family with only modest wealth and connections, Giovanni Alvise was destined for second-level administrative posts and naval commands. However, the heroic death of his brother Marcantonio, the commander of Famagusta flayed alive by the Turks in 1571, probably won great public esteem for his near relatives. Giovanni Alvise immediately rose to the great offices, but his death, possibly from the plague, cut short his career.
58. Giovanni di Francesco Soranzo was ambassador to Spain 1562-64 and to Rome 1570-72, as well as ambassador extraordinary to Spain in 1573 and to Rome 1581-82. Leonardo Donà took the last appointment as a personal affront. *Seneca*, pp. 142-146. Soranzo was also *podestà* at Brescia 1577-78 and was chosen with Andrea di Piero Badoer, Giacomo di Alvise Foscarini, and Giovanni Michiel to escort Henry III into Venice in July 1574. *Nunziature* XI, 214 n. 1. Soranzo was a influential *vecchio*. COZZI, pp. 35-36 n. 4. He strongly

1569: C

1570-79: C - 2; SG - 3 (1573); Z - 2 (1572).

1580-89: C - 1; SG - 2; CX - 1 (1580).

1590- 99: C - 2; SG - 6.

1575 Giovanni Alvise di Marco Bragadino (second).

Tommaso di Alvise Contarini PSM 1488-1578 [59], PSM 1557, Madonna Del Orto branch, brother of Cardinal Gasparo 1483-1542. Barbaro A.S.V., 2, 466; Cicogna, 2, 241-242.

1549: C.

1550-59: C - 1; SG - 5 (1551).

1560-69: SG - 4; CX - 1 (1568); Z - 3 (1563).

1570-75: SG - 2; Z - 4.

Vincenzo di Francesco Contarini (third).

Domenico di Piero Duodo (second).

defended the *Consiglio dei Dieci* at the time of the constitutional reform of 1582-83. Lowry, pp. 291-292, 294.

Soranzo was the brother of Giacomo (1518-99; PSM 1575) who held several diplomatic posts including an ambassadorship to the papacy 1562-65. However, in 1584 the *Consiglio dei Dieci* convicted Giacomo of passing state secrets to Francesco de' Medici, Grand Duke of Tuscany, in the hope of obtaining a cardinalate. The *Consiglio dei Dieci* stripped him of his procuratorship and confined him for life to Capo d'Istria. Giacomo was permitted to return to Venice after two years, but his political career was finished. Giovanni Soranzo was implicated in his brother's misdeeds but not tried. Albèri, Serie II, vol. 4, pp. 123-126. Still, his political career languished for a decade. He held no great office between 1583, when he was elected *Savio Grande*, and 1592, when he was elected *Consigliere* and *Savio Grande*. Thereafter, he won *Savio Grande* elections in 1594, 1595, 1596, 1597, and 1598, another term as *Consigliere* in 1596, and crowned his political comeback with a procuratorship in 1596.

Like his brother, Soranzo supported papal causes and was a useful ally to nuncios. In 1576 Rome informed a new nuncio that he could count on Giovanni Soranzo's help. Stella, p. 9. For examples of Soranzo's usefulness to the papacy, see Cozzi, pp. 35-36 n. 4. Upon his election as lay deputy, Giovanni Soranzo assured the nuncio that he was the pope's servant. « È stato posto adesso per assistente nel Santo Officio della Inquisitione il chiarissimo messer Giovanni Soranzo, fratello del chiarissimo messer Giacomo, del quale scrissi un'altra volta. Questo messer Giovanni dice che è gran servitore et molto affettionato a V. S. ill.ma et rev.ma et ha voluto che io gliene faccia fede, come fo per la presente ». Letter of Nuncio Giambattista Castagna of January 16, 1574, in *Nunziature* XI, 130.

59. Another source reports that Tommaso di Alvise Contarini died on December 15, 1578, at the age of 97, healthy in mind and body until the moment of death. Contarini was *podestà* at Verona in 1540-41, and held a few other administrative posts. He received votes in the ducal elections of 1556, 1559, 1567, 1570, and 1578, but was never a strong candidate. Da Mosto, 324, 330, 334, 339, 370. In March 1571, when the other procurators appointed Contarini to investigate an alleged mishandling of funds at a monastery, the nuncio called him a « gentilhuomo pieno d'integrità et alieno dal suspetto delle brutture ». *Nunziature* IX, 469.

Gasparo Venier, possibly Gasparo di Sebastiano 1531-99; BARBARO
A.S.V., 7, 246.
1598: CX.

1576 Giovanni Alvise di Marco Bragadino (third).

Tommaso di Alvise Contarini PSM (second).

Domenico di Piero Duodo (third).

Giacomo di Michele Foscarini Dr (fourth)[60].

1577 Pasquale di Gabriel Cicogna 1509-95, PSM 1583, Doge 1585[61]; BAR-
BARO Bibl. Marc., 1, 245 r; DA MOSTO, 375-383.
1570-79: C - 4 (1572 and twice *luogo riservato* in 1574); CX -
2 (1577); Z - 1 (1579).
1580-85: C - 2; SG - 5 (1580); Z - 1.

Giacomo di Giacomo Emo d. 1596, PSM 1584, rector at Brescia 1569,
podestà at Padua 1571-73[62]; BARBARO A.S.V., 3, 397.
1560-69: CX - 1 (1569); Z - 2 (1567).
1570-79: C - 3 (1570); CX - 2; Z - 4.
1580-81: C - 1; Z - 1.

Giacomo di Michele Foscarini Dr (fifth).

Andrea Gradenigo, probably Andrea di Alvise 1509-77.
BARBARO A.S.V., 4, 71.
1569: CX
1570-75: C - 1 (1575); Z - 4 (1570).

Alessandro di Alessandro Gritti d. 1582, PSM 1578, strong candidate
for doge 1578; BARBARO A.S.V., 4, 181; DA MOSTO, 370-71.
1560-69: C - 2 (1566); CX - 4 (1561); Z - 1 (1564).
1570-79: C - 2; SG - 9 (1572); CX - 3; Z - 8.
1580-82: SG - 2; Z - 2.

Giovanni Battista Mocenigo, probably Giovanni Battista di Andrea
1527-94[63]; BARBARO Bibl. Marc., 3, 114 r.

60. Confirmed by A. S.V., *Collegio, Notatorio*, reg. 42, f. 64 r, January 27, 1575 mv.
61. Cicogna held a number of military and administrative positions including
posts at Candia and Corfù, the lieutenancy of Friuli, and *podestà* at Treviso and
Padua in 1577. He reached the great offices in 1572, but was not elected regu-
larly until the late 1570s. His election as doge was unexpected, because Vincenzo
di Barbon Morosini was the favorite. A. S. Vat., *Segretario di Stato, Venezia*,
filza 10, ff. 393 v, 395 v, 399 v, 403 r - 403 v. Popular opinion held Cicogna to be
a saint and associated him with a miracle. Upon his election as doge, the nuncio
judged him to be an admirer of the ecclesiastical order: «E huomo di età di
settantasei anni, di gran prudenza, et bontà, et amatore dell'ordine Ecclesiastico
à quello che ho potuto comprendere ne' ragionamenti, che sino qui hò havuto
seco ». A. S. Vat., *Segretario di Stato, Venezia*, filza 10, f. 414 r, August 19, 1585.
62. Why Emo no longer served in the great offices after 1581 is not known.
He received votes for doge in 1578 and was a major candidate in 1585. DA
MOSTO, 370, 378; A. S. Vat., *Segretario di Stato, Venezia*, filza 10, ff. 393 v, 399 v.
63. Giovanni Battista di Andrea Mocenigo was not an important figure. But he

Nicolò di Agostino Venier (third).

1578 Pasquale di Gabriel Cicogna (second).

Sebastiano Contarini, probably Sebastiano di Dionisio 1521-89 [64], Sant'Antonin and Porte Dell'Arco branch; BARBARO A.S.V., 2, 491.
    1570-79: C - 1 (1577); CX - 2 (1574).
    1580-89: C - 2; CX - 4.

Giacomo di Giacomo Emo (second).

Giacomo di Michele Foscarini Dr (sixth).

Marco di Nicolò Grimani PSM [65] d. 1583, PSM 1576, *capitano* at Padua 1567-69, received votes in ducal election of 1578; BARBARO A.S.V., 4, 133; DA MOSTO, 370.
    1560-69: CX - 1 (1565); Z - 1 (1569).
    1570-79: CX - 1; Z - 4.
    1580-81: Z - 2.

Giovanni Battista di Andrea Mocenigo (second).

Domenico di Marc'Antonio Priuli 1522-85, nephew of brother doges Lorenzo (1556-59) and Girolamo (1559-67), rector of Verona 1578; BARBARO Bibl. Marc., 4, 12 r.
    1570-79: C - 1 (1577); CX - 2 (1573).
    1580-84: C - 1; CX - 3.

Nicolò di Agostino Venier (fourth).

1579 Andrea di Francesco Bernardo 1518-91, *podestà* of Padua 1584-85, Dalla Nave branch [66]; BARBARO A.S.V., 2, 19.
    1570-79: CX - 3 (1572).
    1580-89: C - 2 (1582); CX - 2.
    1590: C.

Marco di Nicolò Grimani PSM (second).

Domenico di Marc'Antonio Priuli (second).

Gasparo Renier (Rhenerio), probably Gasparo di Girolamo 1511-80, rector at Brescia 1567-68, *podestà* at Padua 1573; BARBARO A.S.V., 6, 413.

---

was the brother of Giovanni di Andrea (1531-98; PSM 1595) who was powerful. The brothers were in the direct line of a branch of the Mocenigo that produced four doges and many procurators in the fifteenth and sixteenth centuries.

64. The documents with patronymics confirm that Sebastiano di Dionisio Contarini was elected *Consigliere* in 1577 and 1587. In addition, no other Sebastiano Contarini of the appropriate age is apparent.

65. The Grimani and Priuli elections are confirmed by A.S.V., *Collegio, Notatorio*, reg. 43, f. 146 v, October 19, 1578.

66. Andrea di Francesco Bernardo was not the son of Francesco di Marc'Antonio Bernardo, collector of antiquities.

1569: CX; Z
1570-79: C - 2 (1572); SG - 2 (1570); CX - 2; Z - 5.

1580 Andrea di Francesco Bernardo (second).

Sebastiano di Dionisio Contarini (second)[67].

Giacomo di Michele Foscarini Dr (seventh).

Marco di Nicolò Grimani PSM (third).

Domenico di Marc'Antonio Priuli (third).

Antonio di Nicolò Tiepolo K 1526-82, diplomat[68], son of Nicolò di
Francesco, one of the original *Savii sopra Eresia* of 1547.
BARBARO A.S.V., 7, 83.
1570-79: CX - 1 (1572).
1580-82: SG - 1 (1580); CX - 1.

Francesco di Zuanne Andrea Venier 1515-81, Aristotelian scholar[69].
BARBARO A.S.V., 7, 236.
1570-79: C - 1 (1577); CX - 2 (1573).
1581: C - 1.

1581 Sebastiano di Dionisio Contarini (third).

Giacomo di Giacomo Emo (third)[70]

Giacomo di Michele Foscarini Dr (eighth).

Antonio di Nicolò Tiepolo K (second).

Nicolò di Agostino Venier PSM (fifth).

1582 Sebastiano di Dionisio Contarini (fourth).

Vido (Vito) di Piero Morosini 1513-91, San Zuanne Novo branch,
lieutenancy in Friuli 1569, received votes in ducal election of
1585; BARBARO A.S.V., 5, 308; DA MOSTO, 378.
1570-79: C - 1 (1575); CX - 1 (1579).

67. Election confirmed by A.S.V., *Collegio, Notatorio*, reg. 44, f. 183 r, November 3, 1580.

68. The election of Tiepolo as lay deputy is confirmed by A.S.V., *Collegio, Notatorio*, reg. 44, f. 183 r. Tiepolo was ambassador to Spain 1564-67, *bailo* at Constantinople 1573-76, and ambassador to Rome 1576-78. He was also ambassador
extraordinary to Spain 1571, to Portugal 1572, to Tuscany 1579, and governor
of Brescia in 1582. ALBÈRI, II, vol. 4, pp. 243-244. After this distinguished
diplomatic career, Tiepolo could probably have looked forward to regular election
to the great offices and other honors. But he died at the relatively young age
of 56. STELLA, 36, states that Antonio Tiepolo was « notoriamente devotissimo
(come tutta la sua famiglia) alla Sede Apostolica ». However, evidence of his devotion to Rome has not been found, and he was not a close relative of Paolo di
Stefano Tiepolo.

69. Venier authored *I discorsi sopra i tre libri dell'anima d'Aristotele*, Venezia
1555, and *Discorsi sopra i due libri della generazione & corruttione d'Aristotele*,
Venezia 1579. He was one of the twelve *Conservatori* of the *Accademia degli
Uniti* in 1551. CICOGNA, 3, 321.

70. The elections of Emo, Foscarini, Tiepolo, and Venier as lay deputies are
confirmed by A. S. V., *Collegio, Notatorio*, reg. 45, f. 89 v, June 17, 1581.

1580-89: C - 3.
1591: CX.

Nicolò di Agostino Venier PSM (sixth)[71].

1583 Agostino Barbarigo, probably Agostino di Lorenzo[72] 1514-87, PSM 1585; *D.B.I.*, 6, 49-50; BARBARO A.S.V., 1, 171.
1570-79: C - 1 (1577); CX - 2 (1575).
1580-87: C - 2; CX - 1.

Vido di Piero Morosini (second).

Nicolò di Agostino Venier PSM (seventh).

1584 Agostino di Lorenzo Barbarigo (second).

Giacomo di Giacomo Emo PSM (fourth).

Piero Morosini[73].

Vido di Piero Morosini (third).

Piero Pisani, probably Piero di Sebastian 1529-92.
BARBARO Bibl. Marc., 3, 256 r.
1570: CX.
1580-89: C - 2 (1583); CX - 1.
1590: CX.

Giovanni Battista Querini, probably Giovanni Battista di Pietro 1510-96. BARBARO Bibl. Marc., 4, 52 r.
1570-79: CX - 2 (1573); Z - 3 (1576).
1580-89: C - 2 (1585); CX - 3; Z - 1.
1590-96: CX - 2.

1585 Giacomo di Giacomo Emo PSM (fifth).

Piero Morosini (second).

---

71. Confirmed by A.S.V., *Collegio, Notatorio*, reg. 45, f. 89 v, June 17, 1581.

72. Barbarigo enjoyed a youthful reputation as a skilled logician; his mature political career included many administrative, financial, and judicial posts in Venice, but no governorships or other positions outside the city. He received votes in the ducal election of 1578, and was a major candidate in 1585. DA MOSTO, 370, 378; A.S. Vat., *Segretario di Stato, Venezia*, filza 10, f. 393 v, August 3, 1585. Probably this is the Agostino Barbarigo who in 1566 sought the bishopric of Curzola and Stagno in Dalmatia held by his late brother Pietro. The *Collegio* supported his candidature with the papacy on the grounds that he had two daughters in need of dowries, and that he had advanced to his late brother the funds to purchase ecclesiastical offices. However, Pius V would neither appoint him nor give him his late brother's benefices. *Nunziature* VIII, 142-43, 146-47, 149-51, 157, 163-64, 168, 210, 216. This may also be the Agostino Barbarigo who in 1581 persuaded the *Consiglio dei Dieci* to ban all commedies in Venice. G. COZZI, *Appunti sul teatro e i teatri a Venezia agli inizi del Seicento*, « B.S.V. », 1 (1959), p. 188.

73. This could be Piero di Vido Morosini (d. 1585), Piero di Lunardo (d. 1591), or, less likely, Piero di Zuanne (1542-84). BARBARO A.S.V., 5, 308-09. « Piero Morosini » was elected *Consigliere* from the *Sestiero di Santa Croce* in 1578 and 1582.

Giovanni Battista di Pietro Querini (second).

1586 Zaccaria di Paolo Contarini 1522-1602 [74], PSM 1599.
    BARBARO A.S.V., 2, 455.
    1577: CX.
    1580-89: C - 1 (1589); SG - 2 (1585); CX - 2.
    1590-99: C - 1; SG - 7; CX - 1.
    1600: CX.

Domenico di Piero Duodo (fourth).

Piero Morosini (third).

Vido di Piero Morosini (fourth).

Giovanni Battista di Pietro Querini (third).

1587 Zaccaria di Paolo Contarini (second).

Domenico di Piero Duodo (fifth).

Vido di Piero Morosini (fifth).

Giovanni Battista di Pietro Querini (fourth).

1588 Domenico di Piero Duodo (sixth).

Giacomo di Giacomo Emo PSM (sixth).

Alvise Foscari, probably Alvise di Ferigo 1521-98, a direct descendant
    of Doge Francesco Foscari 1423-57; BARBARO Bibl. Marc., 2,
    130 v.
    1570-79: CX - 1 (1579); Z - 1 (1577).
    1580-89: C - 1 (1588); SG - 2 (1587); CX - 2; Z - 1.
    1590-98: C - 2; SG - 4.

Giustinian Giustiniani (Zustignan Zustiniani), probably Giustinian di
    Giovanni 1507-96 [75], San Zuanne Bragora branch; BARBARO A.S.V.,
    7, 460.
    1578: CX.
    1580-89: C - 2 (1586); SG - 2 (1588); CX - 3.
    1590-96: SG - 5; CX - 2.

Pietro Marcello, probably Pietro di Antonio 1521-96, PSM 1595, po-
    destà at Rovigo 1574 and captain at Padua 1586; BARBARO Bibl.
    Marc., 3, 40 r.
    1580-89: C - 1 (1584); CX - 3 (1581).
    1590-96: C - 2; CX - 2.

74. Contarini was rector at Bergamo and Brescia, captain at Padua 1594-95, and
served as ambassador extraordinary to Rome in 1590 and 1592. He received votes
in the ducal election of 1595. DA MOSTO, 386. In 1577 he persuaded the Senate
to continue its decree banning actors from the city. COZZI, *Appunti sul teatro...*,
p. 188.

75. CICOGNA, 5, 666, gives his dates as 1525-96. Giustiniani held the lieutenancy
in Friuli, and was *podestà* at Treviso and at Padua in 1593. He was related by marriage to the Barbaro-Grimani and Corner-Pisani family groups whose members
held many ecclesiastical offices. LOGAN, 31; LOWRY, 296, 305 n. 138.

Vido di Piero Morosini (sixth).

Giovanni Battista di Piero Querini (fifth).

1589 Andrea di Francesco Bernardo (third).

Federico di Francesco Contarini PSM 1538-1613, PSM 1571, San Luca branch, collector and antiquarian, papal supporter [76]; BARBARO A.S.V., 2, 440.

Vido di Piero Morosini (seventh).

Giovanni Battista di Piero Querini (sixth).

1590 Andrea di Francesco Bernardo (fourth).

Federico di Francesco Contarini PSM (second).

Alvise di Ferigo Foscari (second).

Vido di Piero Morosini (eighth).

1591 Sebastiano Barbarigo, probably Sebastiano di Francesco 1518/20-1598, De Candia branch, received votes in ducal election of 1595; BARBARO A.S.V., 1, 185; DA MOSTO 386.
1587: C.

Federico di Francesco Contarini PSM (third).

76. The wealthy Contarini became a procurator in 1571 when the Republic needed money for the Cyprus War. In exchange for an interest-free loan of 20,000 ducats to be repaid over a period of fourteen years, he obtained the high honor. *Nunziature* XI, 430; A. S. V., *Maggior Consiglio, Deliberazioni*, reg. 29 (*Angelus*), 1566-1574, f. 70 v, January 13, 1570 mv. Contarini collected antiquities and paintings, and participated in many cultural and artistic enterprises in the city. LOGAN, passim; M. T. CIPOLLATO, *L'eredità di Federico Contarini: gli inventari della collezione e degli oggetti domestici*, in « B.S.V. », 3 (1961), pp. 221-253. The Republic deputized Contarini and two others to organize the festivities for Henry III's visit in 1574. LOGAN, 186.
  Contarini strongly supported the educational aims of the Jesuits and was definitely pro-papal. In his frequent service as lay deputy (1589-94, 1598, and 1610), he supported several papal initiatives. In 1590 he aided the negotiations between the Holy Office, Rome, and Venice which resulted in the excision of passages offensive to the other rite in Latin and Greek religious books. G. FEDALTO, *Ricerche storiche sulla posizione giuridica ed ecclesiastica dei Greci a Venezia nei secoli xv e xvi*, Firenze 1967, pp. 104-107, 138-144. In January 1593, he played a key role in persuading the government to extradite Giordano Bruno to Rome. V. SPAMPANATO, *Vita di Giordano Bruno con documenti editi e inediti*, I, Messina 1921, pp. 760-761. The nuncio considered him to be « very pious », « of good character », and « always favorable to ecclesiastical things ». In 1593, and again in 1595, the nuncio asked the pope to send Contarini letters of commendation for his work on the Holy Office, but cautioned secrecy, for Contarini would be ruined if it were learned that he was partial to the papacy. Rome sent the letters. A.S.Vat., *Segretario di Stato, Venezia*, filza 30, ff. 59 r - 59 v; filza 31, ff. 72 v - 73 r, 88 r (February 27, 1593, May 24 and June 9, 1595). They were first noted by G. COZZI, *Federico Contarini: un antiquario veneziano tra Rinascimento e Controriforma*, in « B.S.V. », 3 (1961), pp. 195-197, the fundamental study on Contarini. As late as 1610, the nuncio wrote of Contarini: « Egli però è gentilhuomo di buona mente, et, per quello che può, aiuta il Santo Officio ». Letter of Nuncio Berlinghiero Gessi of December 25, 1610, as quoted by P. SAVIO, *Per l'epistolario di Paolo Sarpi*, in « Aevum », 14 (1940), p. 68.

Alvise di Ferigo Foscari (third).

Piero di Antonio Marcello (second).

Giacomo Renier, probably Giacomo di Andrea 1529-1616, PSM 1598, held many administrative and financial posts; received votes in ducal election of 1615; BARBARO Bibl. Marc., 4, 60 r; CICOGNA, 5, 393; DA MOSTO, 415.
>   1590-99: C - 1 (1595); CX - 3 (1592).
>   1600-09: CX - 1.

1592 Sebastiano di Francesco Barbarigo (second).

Vincenzo Capello, probably Vincenzo di Domenico 1522-1604. BARBARO A.S.V., 2, 274.
>   1590-99: C - 2 (1595); CX - 1 (1595).

Federico di Francesco Contarini PSM (fourth).

Alvise di Ferigo Foscari (fourth).

Giacomo (Jacopo) Marcello, probably Giacomo di Andrea[77] 1530-1603. BARBARO Bibl. Marc., 3, 41 r.
>   1580-89: CX - 2 (1583).
>   1590-99: C - 2 (1590).
>   1601: C.

Francesco da Molin, probably Francesco di Zuanne 1540-1611, K PSM 1604, diplomat[78]; BARBARO Bibl. Marc. 3, 131 r.
>   1590-99: SG - 4 (1597); CX - 1 (1596).
>   1600-09: C - 1 (1602); SG - 8.
>   1610-11: SG - 2.

Tommaso Morosini, probably Tommaso di Almorò 1534-97, *podestà* at Padua 1594-95; BARBARO Bibl. Marc., 3, 166 v.
>   1580-89: CX - 2 (1587).
>   1590-97: C - 2 (1592); CX - 2.

Giovanni Battista di Piero Querini (seventh).

Giacomo di Andrea Renier (second).

Giovanni di Francesco Soranzo K (second)[79].

77. In 1578 the government chose Giacomo Marcello and three other patricians to plan the redecoration of the ducal palace after the fires of 1574 and 1577. They devised a scheme based on Venetian history for the hall of the *Maggior Consiglio*; various artists executed it. LOGAN, 187-189. Marcello also possessed a large library. F. SANSOVINO and G. STRINGA, *Venetia città nobilissima, et singolare...*, Venetia 1604, p. 257 v.

78. Francesco di Zuanne da Molin was ambassador to Spain in 1599, ambassador extraordinary to Rome in 1605, *Riformatore dello Studio di Padova* in 1608, and was again elected lay deputy to the Inquisition on September 7, 1607. CICOGNA, 5, 128, 597; 6, 60. He is not the anticlerical diarist Francesco di Marco da Molin.

79. Giovanni Soranzo returned to the post of lay deputy in the same year that he returned to the great offices, eight years after he was accused of passing secrets to foreign powers. See note 58.

1593 Federico di Francesco Contarini PSM (fifth) [80].

Vincenzo di Domenico Capello (second) [81].

Giovanni Battista di Piero Querini (eighth).

1594 Federico di Francesco Contarini PSM (sixth) [82].

Giacomo di Andrea Marcello (second).

From December 11, 1594, probably until mid-July 1595 :

Giacomo (Jacopo) di Alvise Foscarini K PSM 1523-1602, PSM 1580 very powerful officeholder [83]; BARBARO A.S.V., 3, 552.

80. Because of the gap in Holy Office trials from 1593 until 1617, one must use A.S.V., *Collegio, Notatorio*, and whatever other sources that might help, to find the names of the *Savii sopra Eresia* until April 8, 1595, when the election procedure changed. As noted earlier, the lay deputy elections in A.S.V., *Collegio, Notatorio*, are probably incomplete. For Federico di Francesco Contarini's service with the Holy Office in 1593, see COZZI, *Federico Contarini...*, 195-196, and A.S.Vat., *Segretario di Stato, Venezia*, filza 30, ff. 59 r - 59 v.

81. Giovanni Battista di Piero Querini replaced Vincenzo di Domenico Capello who was elected a *Consigliere*. A.S.V., *Collegio, Notatorio*, reg. 55, f. 86 r, July 12, 1593.

82. On December 11, 1594, Federico Contarini and Giacomo Marcello completed their terms with the Holy Office, and were replaced by Giacomo Foscarini PSM and Nicolò Gussoni. A.S.V., *Collegio, Notatorio*, reg. 56, f. 173 r.

83. Giacomo di Alvise, rather than Giacomo di Michele Foscarini, also may have won the following great office elections in which the documents fail to list a patronymic: CX - 1582; Z - 1570, 1571, 1579, and 1580.

Foscarini first became prominent as a naval commander. As *Proveditore Generale* in Dalmatia he fought Adriatic pirates in 1571. *Nunziature* IX, 421. In 1572 the *Consiglio dei Dieci* appointed Foscarini commander of the Venetian forces in the war against the Turk; he replaced Sebastiano Venier who had found collaboration with Don John of Austria difficult. R. CESSI, *Storia della Repubblica di Venezia*, I, Milano e Messina 1968², pp. 136-139. Thereafter Foscarini occupied a prominent position in Venetian political life. In July 1574 the Republic chose Foscarini and three others to meet Henry III at the frontier and to accompany him during his state visit. *Nunziature* XI, 214 n. 1. Foscarini was sent as ambassador extraordinary to congratulate newly elected pontiffs in 1585, 1590, and 1591, and to Clement VIII upon papal acquisition of Ferrara in 1598. He received the *cavalierato* from Henry III and Sixtus V.

After reaching the great offices in 1572, or a year or two earlier, Foscarini served as *Savio Grande* every year until his death. He also held many administrative positions and special appointments. He played a key role in the financial policy of the Republic at the end of the 1590s, advancing proposals that Nicolò di Zan Gabriel Contarini disliked. COZZI, pp. 65-67. Foscarini was rich; see LOWRY, *Church and Venetian Political Change...*, 347-348. From the early 1590s until his death, Foscarini was co-leader of the government with Leonardo Donà.

Foscarini may have received votes in the ducal election of 1578, and he definitely did in 1585. In the latter election, the nuncio wrote that Foscarini wanted the ducal crown, but withdrew because of objections raised against him in the *Maggior Consiglio*. A.S.Vat., *Segretario di Stato, Venezia*, filza 10, f. 395 v, August 3, 1585. In 1595 Foscarini, Leonardo Donà, and Marin di Girolamo Grimani contested the election, won by Grimani after a very long conclave apparently filled with intrigue. Da Mosto states that Grimani won when Donà broke an agreement to support Foscarini and threw his votes to Grimani. DA MOSTO,

1570-79: C - 1 (1575);   SG - 1 (1572);   CX - 1 (1577).
1580-89: SG - 10.
1590-99: SG - 11.
1600-02: SG - 3.

Nicolò Gussoni, probably Nicolò di Marco 1539-1599 or 1600. Ponte di Noal branch, rector at Bergamo and captain at Padua 1593-94.

370-71, 378, 386-87. The nuncio, on the other hand, wrote that Donà would have won if he had engaged in the « usual intrigues » (« havesse fatto li soliti brogli »). Cozzi, p. 35 n. 1.

One wonders why Donà threw his votes to Grimani, who was conservative and generally sympathetic to the church. (Marin was the son of Girolamo di Marin Grimani, c. 1500-1570, who had been lay assistant to the Holy Office 1560-62 and 1565-67, and was considered « very devoted » to the papacy). Possibly the agreement reached in the interregnum to alter the electoral procedure of the lay deputies played a role. As noted in part I, the *Cinque Correttori* (Donà, Foscarini, Grimani, Giovanni Paolo Contarini, and Luca Michiel) revised the *promissione ducale* in order to transfer election of the lay deputies from doge and *Collegio* to the Senate. Observors interpreted the change as a means to ensure that stronger defenders of lay jurisdiction would be elected. It is tempting to speculate that Donà threw his votes to Grimani in exchange for Senate control over the election of the *Savii sopra Eresia*.

However, this is only speculation; other political or personal reasons may have influenced Donà. Strong political rivals, as Foscarini and Donà surely were, do not normally help each other to win the supreme office. One would also like to know what the nuncio meant when he said that Donà declined to engage in « li soliti brogli ». In any case, Foscarini failed to cap his illustrious carrer with the ducal *corno*.

Nuncios viewed Foscarini as favorably inclined toward the church and papacy. In 1580 the nuncio wrote that the papacy could count on Foscarini. Cozzi, pp. 94-95. In the late 1590s, Foscarini sought to reopen the Jesuit school in Padua. Cozzi, *Federico Contarini...*, p. 200. At his death the nuncio wrote that Foscarini had been « the most reverent toward the papacy »; he feared for the future now that Donà controlled the affairs of the Republic. Cozzi, pp. 94-95.

Nevertheless, there were limits to Foscarini's support of the papacy, especially in the 1590s. In 1600 the Republic chose Foscarini and Donà to defend against strong papal objections the diversion of the Po River at Goro. The documents in A.S.V., *Collegio, Esposizioni Roma*, reg. 9 and reg. 10, show that they carried out their charge. During the heated discussions with the nuncio over the Clementine Index in the summer of 1596, Leonardo Donà spoke eloquently and often against the papal demand that members of the book trade must swear an oath before bishop and inquisitor that they would obey the Index. Foscarini spoke less often, less eloquently, and less belligerently. But his message was the same. Doge Marino Grimani, *Savio Grande* Nicolò Gussoni, and other unidentified members of the *Collegio* also defended lay jurisdiction over the book trade. For Foscarini's speeches, see A.S.V., *Collegio, Esposizioni Roma*, reg. 6, ff. 124 r (July 12), 136 r-136 v (August 9), and 164 r (September 6, 1596). For the whole dispute and additional bibliography, see GRENDLER, pp. 266-273.

Foscarini may have been sympathetic to « cose ecclesiastiche », but he probably was neither so ardent nor open as others, such as Federico di Francesco Contarini and Giovanni di Francesco Soranzo. Moreover, the political climate had changed so much since the 1560s, 1570s, and 1580s, that even a patrician sympathetic to the papacy had to modify his position if he wished to maintain his influence. Whatever his private views, Foscarini balanced his duties to church and Republic in such a way as to enjoy a long and illustrious political career.

Barbaro A.S.V., 4, 205.

1587: CX.

1590-99: C-1 (1597); SG-10 (1591); CX-1.

In conformity with the revision of the *promissione ducale* approved by the *Maggior Consiglio* on April 8, 1595, the Senate now elected the *Tre Savii sopra Eresia* for one-year terms. However, it is seldom clear how much of the year's term with the Holy Office individual patricians served.

1595 July 13: Giustinian di Giovanni Giustiniani (second).

Vincenzo di Giacomo Gussoni 1539-99, San Vidal branch; Barbaro A.S.V., 4, 206.

1594: SG.

July 22 Alvise Mocenigo, probably Alvise di Francesco 1532-98, San Lio branch; Barbaro A.S.V., 5, 201.

1590-98: SG-2 (1595).

1596 (modern style) January 4: Pietro di Antonio Marcello PSM (third).

February 14: Nicolò Gradenigo K, probably Nicolò di Bortolo 1546-1620, Rio Marin branch, not closely related to Vincenzo di Bartolomeo Gradenigo.

Barbaro A.S.V., 4, 101.

Francesco Giustiniani, probably Francesco di Marco[84] 1541-1604, held many administrative posts.

Barbaro A.S.V., 7, 476; Cicogna, 4, 673.

1595: CX.

1600-04: C-1 (1603); SG-2 (1601); CX-1.

April 19: Bernardo di Girolamo Zane 1536-1610, *podestà* at Brescia brother of future patriarch[85]; Barbaro A.S.V., 7, 324.

1590-99: C-1 (1594): CX-3 (1590).

1607: CX.

September 6: Giovanni Battista di Piero Querini (ninth).

October 2: Vincenzo di Bartolomeo Gradenigo K 1540-1600, ambassador to Emperor Rudolf II 1587-90, captain at Padua 1591-

---

84. His brother Girolamo di Marco (1547-1632, PSM 1616) was a firm, but moderate supporter of Venetian resistance to the papacy during the interdict. Cozzi, p. 103.

85. Matteo di Girolamo Zane (1545-1605) after a long diplomatic career including ambassadorships to Portugal and Spain 1579-84, to Vienna 1584-87, to Constantinople 1591-94, and to other courts, was elected Venetian patriarch on January 28, 1600. His election did not please Clement VIII who preferred Giovanni di Iseppo Dolfin (note 97). The pope insisted that Zane come to Rome for formal examination. The Senate eventually agreed, under conditions that preserved Venetian prerogatives, and pope and patriarch went through the motions of an examination. See G. Benzoni, *Una controversia tra Roma e Venezia all'inizio del '600: la conferma del patriarca*, « B.S.V. », 3 (1961), pp. 121-138.

93, ambassador extraordinary to France 1594[86].
BARBARO A.S.V., 4, 100; CICOGNA, 5, 126.
1590-99: C - 2 (1594); SG - 7 (1590), one *riservato*; CX - 1 (1595).

December 30: Andrea di Giovanni Dolfin PSM 1540-1602, PSM 1573[87], San Salvador Riva dall'Ferro branch, banker and reputedly very wealthy; BARBARO A.S.V., 3, 270.
1601: SG.

December 30: Paolo di Giovanni Paruta PSM 1540-98, PSM 1596, historian and diplomat[88]; ALBÈRI, II, 4, DD. 357-58.
1590-98: C - 2 (1594 *riservato*, 1595 *riservato*); SG - 3 (1590).

1597 January 22: Giovanni Paolo di Sebastiano Contarini PSM 1519-1602[89], PSM 1594, San Felice branch; BARBARO A.S.V., 2, 468.
1578: CX; Z.
1580-89: C - 1 (1584); CX - 1.
1590 - 94: C - 2; CX - 1.

January 22: Giovanni di Andrea Mocenigo PSM 1531-98, PSM 1595, S. Giovanni Crisostomo branch, lieutenancy in Canaa; BARBARO A.S.V., 5, 186.
1590-93: C - 3 (1590 plus two *riservati*).

June 26: Alvise di Ferigo Foscari (fifth).

September 6: Girolamo di Cristoforo Da Mula PSM 1540-1607, PSM 1573 with loan of 16,000 ducats to the state. He was known for his fine library. BARBARO Bibl. Marc., 3, 203 r; CICOGNA, 2, 363; SANSOVINO and STRINGA, *Venetia...*, p. 257 v.

1598 January 21: Antonio Canale, possibly Antonio di Giovanni 1567-1650, PSM 1632, wealthy, held many administrative posts and received

86. Gradenigo sympathized with the Jesuits and was devoted to the papacy, according to G. COZZI, *Paolo Paruta, Paolo Sarpi e la Questione della sovranità su Ceneda*, « B.S.V. », 4 (1962), p. 207 n. 72.

87. Dolfin purchased a procuratorship with a loan to the state of 20,000 ducats. On his wealth, see COZZI, p. 30 n. 2, p. 354; B. PULLAN, *The Occupations and Investments of the Venetian Nobility in the Middle and Late Sixteenth Century*, in *Renaissance Venice*, a. c. di J. HALE, London 1973, pp. 390-391.

88. Paruta was ambassador to Rome 1592-95 and ambassador extraordinary to Clement VIII in 1598; he also undertook other diplomatic missions. He was named public historiographer in 1579, and was elected *Savio di Terraferma* in 1582. His fame as an historian and philosopher, his successful legation to Rome, and especially his election to a procuratorship clearly indicated that Paruta had risen to the inner ring of governing patricians. Indeed, he was elected procurator (December 27) and *Savio sopra Eresia* (December 30) almost simultaneously. But death at the relatively young age of 58 prematurely ended his career. The bibliography on Paruta is far too large to list here.

89. Contarini was one of the *Cinque Correttori* who proposed the law of 1595 that transferred the election of the *Savii sopra Eresia* from doge and *Collegio* to the Senate.

votes in ducal election of 1646 [90]; *D.B.I.*, 17, 637-638; BARBARO A.S.V., 2, 222.

Vincenzo di Giacomo Gussoni (second).

April 28: Vincenzo di Domenico Capello (third).

Federico di Francesco Contarini PSM (seventh).

1599 January 3: Bertucci di Zuanne Bondumier (or Bondimier) PSM 1523-1602, PSM? [91]; BARBARO A.S.V., 2, 107.
1590-99: C - 3 (1592); CX - 3 (1591).
1601: CX.

March 11: Zorzi di Giacomo Gradenigo 1522-1607 [92], Dai Tolentini branch; BARBARO A.S.V., 4, 83.
1590-99: C - 2 (1596); CX - 1 (1594).
1600-07: C - 1; CX - 1.

March 11: Renier Foscarini, probably Renier di Michiel 1524-1606.
BARBARO Bibl. Marc., 2, 135 v.
1590-99: C - 2 (1595).
1601: C.

October 4: Andrea di Giovanni Dolfin PSM (second).
Giovanni Battista Bernardo, probably Giovanni Battista di Giovanni Battista 1536-1601; BARBARO Bibl. Marc., 1, 136 r.
1598: SG; 1600: C, SG.

1600 January 22: Alvise Belegno (Bellegno), probably Alvise di Bernardino 1539-1606, lawyer and poet, lieutenancy in Friuli 1593-94.
BARBARO Bibl. Marc., 1, 105 v; *D.B.I.*; 7, 555-556.
1590-99: C - 1 (1598); SG - 1 (1598); CX - 2 (1595).
1600-01: SG - 2.

February 4: Giovanni Bembo, probably Giovanni di Agostino 1543-1618, PSM 1601, Doge 1615, naval commander with a distinguished career, not a follower of Sarpi, compromise choice as doge in 1615 [93].
BARBARO Bibl. Marc., 1, 114 v; *D.B.I.*, 8, 119-122.
DA MOSTO, 413-420.
1590-99: C - 4 (1594, and all four were *riservati*).

---

90. A lay deputy only thirty-one years old is extraordinary; but Barbaro lists no other Antonio Canale of appropriate dates.

91. Although Bondumier was listed as a PSM when he won election as a lay deputy, I have been unable to confirm his procuratorship from other sources.

92. Barbaro lists his death date as 1604. However, he was elected to the *Consiglio dei Dieci* on May 16, 1607. *Raccolta dei Consegi dal 1601 fino 1605*, ms. Bibl. Marc., Cod. It., cl. VII, 833 (=8912), f. 71 (with patronymic).

93. After 1605 Giovanni di Agostino Bembo continued to be elected lay deputy to the Holy Office: July 28, 1609; September 13, 1610; July 21, 1611; July 6, 1612. A.S.V., *Segretario alle Voci, Elezioni dei Pregadi*, reg. 8 (1607-1613), ff. 104 v - 105 r.

1600-09: SG - 6 (1602); CX - 1 (1600).
1610-15: SG - 2.

April 13: Francesco di Marco Giustiniani (second).

October 4: Nicolò Contarini, probably Nicolò di Zan Gabriel 1553-1631, Doge 1630, strongly anti-papal.
1600-09: SG - 7 (1601), including two *riservati*; CX - 2 (1605).
1610: SG; for the rest of his political career, see Cozzi.

Nicolò di Zuanne Donà[94] 1539-1618, San Paolo branch, *podestà* in Capo d'Istria, *capitano* at Vicenza and Brescia (twice), and other posts, Doge for 34 days in 1618, strongly anti-papal.[95]
BARBARO A.S.V., 3, 313.
1590-99: C - 1 (1596); CX - 3 (1593).
1600-09: C - 1; SG - 4 (1603); CX - 2.

1601 February 8: Costanzo di Alessandro Loredano 1530-1612; BARBARO A.S.V., 4, 333.
1580-89: CX - 1 (1589).
1590 - 99: C - 3 (1593); CX - 3.
1609: C.

Giacomo di Alvise Foscarini K, PSM (second).

---

94. This is one of the very few times in which the patronymic of the patrician elected lay deputy is given: A.S.V., *Segretario alle Voci, Elezioni dei Pregadi*, reg. 6 (1588-1600), f. 132 r.

95. Nicolò di Zuanne Donà was the son of Zuanne di Nicolò Donà (1507-71), and not a close relative of either Giovanni di Bernardo (« Dalle Renghe ») Donà (see note 55) or Nicolò di Giovanni Battista Donà, brother of future doge Leonardo. Nicolò di Zuanne was a merchant, a collector of paintings, *Riformatore dello Studio di Padova* in 1611, and recipient of votes for doge in 1615 before winning the ducal *corno* (without having been a procurator) in 1618. He was wealthy, and considered avaricious and miserly. DA MOSTO, 415, 421-27. He was strongly anti-papal; Cozzi groups him with the fiery adversaries of Rome at the time of the interdict: Nicolò di Zan Gabriel Contarini, Francesco di Constantin Priuli, Agostino di Francesco Da Mula, Sebastiano di Gasparo Venier, and Alvise di Paolo Zorzi. COZZI, 140, 167 n. 1. The simultaneous election to the Holy Office of two patricians so hostile to papal jurisdictional claims as Nicolò di Zan Gabriel Contarini and Nicolò di Zuanne Donà (each elected lay deputy for the first time) shows how much Venetian attitudes toward the Inquisition had changed since earlier decades.
Nicolò di Zuanne Donà won the great offices listed above; the documents list his patronymic. However, there were four other patricians of the same name politically prominent at the time: Nicolò di Giovanni Battista Donà (1542-1614); Nicolò di Filippo Donà (1528-1604); Nicolò di Iseppo Donà (d. 1603 or 1604); and Nicolò di Agostino Donà (not located in Barbaro). In most cases the precise « Nicolò Donà » who won a great office election can be determined from the patronymic or by other means. Nevertheless, it is not clear which Nicolò Donà was elected *Savio Grande* in 1596, 1597, December 30, 1599, 1601, 1606, 1609, and 1610. Since Nicolò di Zuanne Donà was the most prominent of the five patricians of the same name active in these years, it is likely that he won several of the unidentified *Savio Grande* elections.

Benetto Erizzo, probably Benetto di Zuanne [96] 1530-c. 1609.
  BARBARO Bibl. Marc., 2, 104 r.
  1580-89: CX - 1 (1586).
  1590-99: C - 3 (1592); CX - 2.
  1600-09: C - 3.

April 28: Vincenzo di Domenico Capello (fourth).

1602 February 28: Giovanni di Agostino Bembo PSM (second).
  Giacomo di Andrea Renier PSM (third).

March 4: Giovanni di Iseppo Dolfin K, PSM 1545-1622, PSM 1598
  San Lio branch, diplomat, pro-papal, became bishop and cardinal [97];
  BARBARO A.S.V., 3, 273.
  1590-99: C - 1 (1596 *riservato*); SG - 5 (1591 *riservato*); CX -
  1 (1594).
  1600-03: SG - 3 (one *riservato*).

Giovanni Paolo di Sebastiano Contarini PSM (second).

December 3: Giovanni Paolo Gradenigo, probably Giovanni Paolo di
  Zuanne 1544-1607, *podestà* at Feltre and captain at Brescia; BAR-
  BARO A.S.V., 4, 72.
  1600-04: C - 1 (1601); CX - 3 (1601).

1603 March 8: Girolamo di Cristoforo Da Mula PSM (second).

May 10: Antonio Querini, probably Antonio di Marc'Antonio 1554-
  February 1608, San Polo branch, author of anti-papal tracts
  during the interdict [98]; BARBARO A.S.V., 6, 335.
  1600-08: SG - 1 (1606).

---

96. Benetto Erizzo was again elected lay deputy on August 19, 1606. A.S.V.,
Segretario alle Voci, Elezioni dei Pregadi, reg. 7 (1600-1606), f. 105 r.

97. Dolfin reached the office of *Savio di Terraferma* in 1582, and then embarked
on a diplomatic career. He was ambassador to France 1586-88, and to the papacy
1595-98; he also served as ambassador extraordinary to France 1594, to Spain
1598, and to France again in 1600. ALBÈRI, II, 4, 450. Dolfin returned from
his papal ambassadorship in 1598 bearing Clement VIII's approval and many
relics that helped him to acquire political influence and a procuratorship. Clement
VIII unsuccessfully favored him in the Venetian patriarchal election of 1600.
After the death of Giacomo di Alvise Foscarini, the nuncio (in January 1603)
considered Dolfin to be the Venetian leader most favorable to the papacy and
the only counterweight to Leonardo Donà. Nicolò di Zan Gabriel Contarini
disliked Dolfin for the same reasons and for his supposed intrigues to secure
ecclesiastical office. COZZI, 70, 77, 78, 86, 95, 99, 218-219. After suffering serious
reverses in Cyprus, Dolfin's father had tried to restore the family's fortune
through *terraferma* land investment. Giovanni possibly sought the same end through
ecclesiastical office. Clement VIII appointed Dolfin bishop of Vicenza in 1603
and conferred the cardinal's hat in 1604. Dolfin resigned his bishopric in 1606
in favor of a relative and moved to Rome. B. PULLAN, *Service to the Venetian
State: Aspects of Myth and Reality in the Early Seventeenth Century*, in « Studi
Secenteschi », 5(1964), pp. 129-132.

98. After election as *Savio agli Ordini*, the traditional starting point for youthful
patricians destined for the great offices, Querini abandoned public life for ten

1604 February 3: Francesco Bernardo, probably Francesco di Zaccaria 1552-
1612, Riva dei Schiavoni branch, *podestà* at Padua in 1602[99];
BARBARO A.S.V., 2, 21.
1600-09: C - 2 (1600).

Antonio Lando, probably Antonio di Girolamo 1553-1618, K PSM
1613, *podestà* at Padua 1605-06 and at Brescia 1609-10[100]; BAR-
BARO Bibl. Marc., 2, 209 v.
1599: CX.
1600-09: C - 1 (1602); CX - 2.

April 20: Costanzo di Alessandro Loredano (second).

Giovanni Donà, probably Giovanni di Piero 1526-1612, not a close
relative of the other Donà.
BARBARO Bibl. Marc., 2, 84 v.
1580-89: CX - 1 (1587).
1590-99: SG - 4 (1592); CX - 4.
1600: SG.

July 13: Vincenzo di Domenico Capello (fourth).

October 2: Leonardo di Giovanni Battista Donà K, PSM 1536-1612,
PSM 1591, Doge 1606, strong defender of lay jurisdiction and
leader of the Republic in 1590s and early years of the seventeenth century[101].

years of study. He returned to a series of administrative posts. In 1597 he
finished second in the Senate balloting to fill the vacant archbishopric of Candia.
Immediately before and during the interdict controversy, Querini served in the
Collegio as *Savio di Terraferma*. A friend of Paolo Sarpi, Querini authored several
tracts defending Venice and attacking the papacy during the interdict. On Jan-
uary 31, 1608, Querini was again elected lay deputy, but died in February.
A.S.V., *Segretario alle Voci, Elezioni dei Pregadi*, reg. 8 (1606-1613), f. 104 v;
CICOGNA, 2, pp. 279-281; COZZI, 57, 71-75, 98-100, 104-105, 107-108, 119-120.
    It is less likely, but possible, that this Antonio Querini was Antonio di
Nicolò Querini (1534-1616), of the Alla Pietà branch. He was not politically
prominent at this time. BARBARO A.S.V., 6, 317.

99. Francesco Bernardo was again elected *Savio sopra Eresia* on April 8, 1606;
October 3, 1608; and October 2, 1610. A.S.V., *Segretario alle Voci, Elezioni dei
Pregadi*, reg. 7 (1600-1606), f. 105 r; reg. 8 (1606-1613), ff. 104 v - 105 r.

100. Lando was *provveditore generale* in Friuli during the war against imperial
troops in 1617-18. He received votes in the ducal elections of 1615 and 1618.
CICOGNA, 1, 178; COZZI, 84, 162-166; DA MOSTO, 415, 422.

101. Donà's most important offices included ambassador to Spain 1570-73, *podestà* at Brescia 1578-80, ambassador to Rome 1581-83, and *provveditore generale*
in Friuli 1593. He went on many special diplomatic missions: ambassador
extraordinary to the papacy in 1585, 1589, 1590, 1591, 1592, 1598, and 1605;
ambassador extraordinary to Emperor Rudolph II in 1577 and to Constantinople
in 1595. For his political career, views, and additional bibliography, see SENECA
and COZZI, *passim*.
    Donà's election to the Inquisition, like those of Nicolò di Zan Gabriel Con-
tarini, Nicolò di Zuanne Donà, and Antonio di Marc'Antonio Querini, was
another sign of heightened Venetian jurisdictional militancy in these years.

1570-79: C - 1 (1578); SG - 2 (1577); CX - 2 (1576).
1580-89: C - 4 (one *riservato*); SG - 4; CX - 3.
1590-99: SG - 9.
1600-05: SG - 6.

1605 January 19: Almorò di Girolamo Grimani PSM 1539-1611, PSM
1603, San Luca branch [102]; BARBARO A.S.V., 4, 134.
1590-99: C - 1 (1593); CX - 2 (1590).
1608: C, CX.

April 23: Girolamo di Cristoforo Da Mula PSM (third).

Leonardo Mocenigo, probably Leonardo di Marc'Antonio 1550-1615,
PSM 1615, San Samuele branch, strongly antipapal [103]; BARBARO
A.S.V., 5, 193.
1597: CX.
1600-09: C - 1 (1603); CX - 3.

September 2: Girolamo Giustiniani probably Girolamo di Marco
1547-1632, PSM 1616, anti-papal [104]; BARBARO A.S.V., 7, 476.
1600-09: C - 1 (1605); SG - 2 (1607); CX - 2 (1600).
1610: SG.

November 19: Alessandro Zorzi, probably Alessandro di Paolo 1540-
1618, strongly anti-papal, received votes in ducal election of 1615.

However, one wonders how much time Donà spent with the Holy Office, for he
was elected to so many other offices at this time, including *Proveditore alle Biave*
on the same day. SENECA, 245 n. 1.

102. Almorò was the son of Girolamo di Marin Grimani PSM who was pro-
papal and frequently a lay deputy in the 1560s. Doge Marin Grimani (1532 —
doge 1595 — 1605) was his brother. He married Angela di Andrea Morosini,
sister of Doge Marino's wife Morosina Elisabetta di Andrea Morosini. Like his
father and brother, Almorò was wealthy; he declared an annual income of 3449
ducats from rents in 1582. DA MOSTO, 385. But his views on church-state relations
are unknown.

103. Leonardo was the son of Marc'Antonio di Piero Mocenigo who may have
been a lay deputy in 1565. Leonardo was captain at Padua in 1600. While governor of Brescia during the interdict, Leonardo so vigorously enforced the laws
of the Republic against those who sought to follow Rome that he earned the
hatred of the clerical party in the city. After the interdict, the nuncio several
times identified Mocenigo as a follower of Sarpi and « no friend of priests ».
COZZI, 123, 125-128; P. SAVIO, *Per l'epistolario di Paolo Sarpi*, in « Aevum », 10
(1936), p. 34. Mocenigo was again elected lay deputy on April 6, 1610, and
July 21, 1611. A.S.V., *Segretario alle Voci, Elezioni dei Pregadi*, reg. 8 (1606-
1613), ff. 104 v - 105 r. He received votes in the ducal election of 1615. DA
MOSTO, 415.

104. The brother of Francesco, who was a lay deputy in 1596 and 1600, Girolamo
received votes in the ducal election of 1615 and was one of the favorites in
1618. DA MOSTO, 415, 422-423. At the interdict he was anti-papal but moderate.
COZZI, 103; SAVIO, *Per l'epistolario di Paolo Sarpi* (1936), p. 33; CICOGNA, 3, 199.
He was again elected *Savio sopra Eresia* on March 30, 1609. A.S.V., *Segretario
alle Voci, Elezioni dei Pregadi*, reg. 8 (1606-1613), f. 104 v. BARBARO Bibl. Marc.,
4, 270 v, gives his dates as 1543-1623.

Barbaro A.S.V., 7, 423; Cozzi, 71, 103-105; Da Mosto, 415.
1587: CX.
1590-99: SG - 2 (1598); CX - 5.
1600-09: C - 1 (1600); SG - 5; CX - 2.
1610: C.

Addenda. The following works came to my attention too late to use: Robert Finlay, *The Venetian Republic as a gerontocracy: age and politics in the Renaissance*, in « The Journal of Medieval and Renaissance Studies », 8 (1978), pp. 157-178; and William Archer Brown, *Nicolò Da Ponte: The Political Career of a Sixteenth-Century Venetian Patrician*, Ph. D. thesis, New York University, 1974.

The Survival of Erasmus in Italy

Relatively few copies of the innumerable sixteenth- and seventeenth-century printings of Erasmus survive today in the major Florentine and Venetian public libraries, not because Italians failed to respond to his message, but because the *Index librorum prohibitorum* condemned and the Inquisition destroyed large quantities of Erasmus' works. Italian Catholic reformers manifested an extraordinary hostility toward the Dutch humanist and vigorously suppressed his works, especially in the decades from the promulgation of the Pauline Index in 1559 to the appearance of the Clementine Index of 1596. We will examine some examples of the inquisitorial destruction of the Erasmian corpus and the reasons behind it in the first part of our study, and then we will list the current Erasmus holdings of five major Florentine libraries and the Venetian Biblioteca Marciana in the second part. This will necessarily be an introductory study, because of the inaccessibility or disappearance of much of the Italian Inquisition documentation, and because libraries in other Italian cities have not been surveyed.[1] Until very recently, scholars have largely ignored the Italian *fortuna* of Erasmus' works, their publishing history and possible readership.[2] Much remains to be done; indeed, the newest scholarship underlines how potentially rewarding this field might be. We hope that this analysis of the destruction and survival of Erasmus' works will aid the assessment of his posthumous Italian influence.[3]

Vatican circles began to lose patience with Erasmus in the mid-1520s. Some churchmen suspected that he shared Luther's views when he refused to condemn Luther forthrightly, and continued to publish devastating attacks on abuses of Catholic practices – attacks that seemed to damn the practice as much as the abuse. The Sorbonne condemnations of some passages and works of Erasmus in 1526, and later, lent prestigious theological weight to the case against him.

The movement against Erasmus gained momentum in the 1530s when Italian church leaders voiced the opinion that Erasmus' works had to be expurgated or banned if souls were to be saved. His old enemies led the assault. Count Alberto Pio da Carpi (1475-1550) published in Venice in 1531 a book listing the passages in Erasmus' corpus deserving correction or elimination.[4] Another old antagonist, Girolamo Aleander (1480-1542), had learned to fear Erasmus' works during his unsuccessful effort to halt the Lutheran heresy in Germany. Now as nuncio to the Venetian Republic in 1534, he discovered that the Venetian nobility was reading with gusto Luther's *Address to the German Nobility* and other Protestant works. He asked the Venetian government to suppress the books, but the leaders blandly informed him that they were not sure that all of them were heretical. Stung, Aleander strongly urged the papacy to compile a list of heretical books, and insisted that Erasmus' works be included.[5] Clement VII, as usual, did nothing, and died shortly thereafter.

Prominent leaders of the Catholic Reform movement, including men who might be expected to give Erasmus' works the benefit of the doubt, formally directed papal attention to the pernicious influence of part of the Erasmian corpus in the famous *Consilium de emendanda ecclesia* (1537). It advised the prohibition in schools for the young of the *Colloquia* and similar books lest they lead the uninformed into impiety. It further recommended that Paul III write to princes requesting them to establish some form of press censorship under the care of local bishops.[6] The recommendation of prohibition demonstrated a broadening disenchantment with Erasmus' works, for the authors of the *Consilium* comprised a cross-section of the most dedicated reformers in the hierarchy. Cardinal Gaspare Contarini chaired the commission, which included Aleander; Tommaso Badia who was Master of the Sacred Palace (the pope's theologian); the stern Gian Pietro Carafa; Gregorio Cortese; the model bishop of Verona, Gian Matteo Giberti; Reginald Pole; and Jacopo Sadoleto.[7]

The *Consilium* produced neither action against Erasmus' works nor any other discernible press censorship. Only after the collapse of the Ratisbon colloquy in 1541 had marked the failure of the policy of reconciliation, and the apostasy of Celio Secondo Curione, Bernardino Ochino, and Peter Martyr Vermigli in 1542 had demonstrated the deep Protestant penetration into the peninsula, did Italians move against heretical books. Not the papacy but city governments, with the advice of local clergymen, began to draft lists of prohibited books.[8] These city indices usually banned the opera omnia of a few northern heresiarchs (such as Bucer, Luther, and Melanchthon), all or some of the works of the Italian apostates, and a handful of the anonymous Protestant titles that enjoyed extensive Italian distribution in the 1540s. The city indices claimed local authority only, and probably generated no action, because governments provided little or no enforcement machinery.

A Sienese index of April 1548 became the first Italian index to include Erasmus, reportedly banning the 'greater part' of his works including the *Colloquia*.[9] Other city indices of the 1540s tolerated the Dutch humanist, although the Venetian *Catalogo*, an index printed in May 1549 and suppressed a month later, listed a title by a Paduan professor which turned out to be a work of Erasmus. This cost the Paduan anxious moments at the hands of the Venetian Holy Office a few years later.[10]

The papacy finally committed itself to preparing its own index at the end of the 1540s, when the Congregation of the Inquisition began to draft one. An inquisition commissioner in Venice wrote to Rome in June 1549 urging that the coming papal index include the works of Erasmus because they 'had opened the gate to all heresy.'[11] His remark suggested that, as churchmen began to combat Italian heresy in the 1550s, their judgment on Erasmus hardened. The authors of the *Consilium* had worried in 1537 that the *Colloquia* led uninformed young people into impiety, while this commissioner flatly asserted that Erasmus brought adults to the brink of heresy. Such militant leaders of the Catholic Reform movement and the fight against Protestantism as Carafa and Fra Michele Ghislieri (the future Pius V) had probably reached the same conclusion on Erasmus, and would shortly possess the power to implement their decision.

After several years' work, the Congregation of the Index tentatively promulgated the initial papal Index in the spring of 1555.[12] The first to enlarge significantly the principles of prohibition, it fathered a new family of indices. This one went beyond heresy in order to ban anticlerical works, antipapal titles, the Talmud, and necromancy. Earlier indices very occasionally did this, but the 1554/5 Index condemned many more including, for example, Dante's *De monarchia*, Lorenzo Valla's *De falso donatione Constantini* and *De libero arbitrio*, and Giambattista Gelli's *I capricci del bottaio*. This Index also initiated the practice of condemning the opera omnia of northern Protestant writers who were primarily scholars rather than theologians: that is, they firmly held Protestant convictions and usually had written at least one anti-Catholic tract, but the bulk of their work embraced such fields as law, medicine, and classical studies. The Erasmian corpus would suffer under both these policies.

The composition of the Congregation of the Inquisition during the pontificate of Julius III (1550-5) helps to explain the greater severity of the Index. The pontiff's initial appointees ranged from the moderate reformers Giovanni Morone and Reginald Pole to the stern Carafa. Morone and Pole soon withdrew, but Carafa remained, and Fra Michele Ghislieri joined the body as commissioner general of the Congregation. Although the membership continued to fluctuate, Carafa and Ghislieri were fixtures, and the sterner reformers dominated. The completed Index probably reflected a compromise that leaned toward the views of the severer reformers

who saw the faith threatened by a variety of sources, including Erasmus.

The Erasmus entry varies in the two surviving versions of the 1554/5 Index.[13] The Milanese edition banned his *Novum Testamentum Annotationes, Colloquia, Moriae encomium*, and the 'scholia in opera Divi Hieronymi,' that is, Erasmus' notes to his edition of the epistles of St Jerome in which he rebuked the contemporary church for abandoning the patristic ideal.[14] The Venetian text banned, in addition to the above, all the paraphrases of the New Testament, *Liber de sarcienda ecclesiae concordia, Enchiridion militis christiani, Modus orandi Deum, Exomologesis sive modus confitendi*, the preface to Hilary, and *Institutio Christiani matrimonii*.

The papacy had decisively turned against Erasmus, but did not yet destroy his books, because it hesitated to promulgate the Index. On 12 March 1555, the Venetian Holy Office gave the Venetian bookmen copies of the Index as well as three months in which to comment on it before it went into effect. The bookmen in three different statements severely criticized the Index. The Holy Office relayed their views to the Congregation in Rome which made some concessions and studied others. In the meantime, a succession of conclaves deprived the Congregation of papal leadership: Julius III died on 23 March 1555; Marcellus II succeeded him on 10 April only to die on 1 May; and Gian Pietro Carafa became pope on 23 May. Paul IV was not ready to promulgate an Index in this form, so eventually, on 28 September the Venetian Inquisition suspended it, no doubt with the approval of Rome. More than likely, the Milanese version suffered a similar fate. The Venetian Inquisition trials offer no evidence that the tribunal banned or destroyed Erasmus' works at this time.

Although the papacy withdrew the 1554/5 Index, Italian publishers recognized that the times had changed. The prohibition of several of Erasmus' works in the stillborn Index, and Carafa's accession to the papal throne, warned them that Erasmus' works would not circulate freely much longer. Attuned to the religious atmosphere, the bookmen abruptly halted the printing of Erasmus' works in 1555. Lorenzo Torrentino of Florence published Erasmus' edition of Cicero's *De officiis*, in 1554. Possibly a Venetian printing of *De constructione* also appeared in that year.[15] These were the last sixteenth-century Italian Erasmus printings to carry the author's name on the title page.[16] The bookmen stopped publishing Erasmus at the same time as they gave up on other prominent but suspect authors. They printed no more Machiavelli after 1554, issued the last edition of Pietro Aretino in 1557, and the last unexpurgated version of Boccaccio's *Decameron* in the same year. A publishing era had come to an end.

The 1554/5 Index created difficulties for one Paduan professor because he had translated a work of Erasmus and had printed it under his own name. Bernardino Tomitano (1517?-76) taught logic from 1539 to 1563, later medicine, participated in the Paduan literary academies, and basked in the praise of students and the Venetian Senate. He published as his own an *Espositione di Matheo evangelista* (Venice: Giovanni Griffio 1547); the Venetian *Catalogo* and both versions of the 1554/5 Index banned 'Thomitanus super Matthaeum.'[17] When he learned of the latter prohibition, Tomitano spontaneously went to the Venetian Holy Office

in May 1555, in order to exculpate himself. He testified that the work was his vernacular translation of Erasmus' *Paraphrasis in evangelium Matthaei*, done at the request of a third party who had borne the cost of publication. He could not remember much else about this benefactor, however. Tomitano then testified that the Venetian inquisitor of the late 1540s had approved its publication with minor corrections. The Holy Office called the former inquisitor who contradicted Tomitano: he had refused to approve the work because of its 'quibbling and very astute logic' (*logico caviloso et molto astuto*), but Tomitano had gone ahead and printed it anyway.[18]

Tomitano then swore to the Holy Office that he had never assented to Erasmus' doctrines. The tribunal accepted his disavowal, but ordered him to prepare an expiatory oration. Tomitano defended himself and attacked Erasmus in his oration – but not vehemently. Because Erasmus' works were earlier approved by the learned, read by everyone, and printed 'with the *privilegi* (copyrights) that ordinarily are given to good works,' Tomitano had been attracted to his works. But then he had begun to suspect that Erasmus' 'instability of mind' and 'brevity on the most important things' (an apparent reference to the humanist's tendency to ignore doctrine) stemmed from malice. And so on. Apparently the Holy Office was not satisfied with this half-hearted condemnation of Erasmus, and ordered Tomitano to try again. Tomitano wrote a second oration, published in 1556, which lauded religious orthodoxy and contained no ambiguous phrases. The Holy office did not question Tomitano again.[19] The 1559 Index again listed the translation of Erasmus as Tomitano's work, but the Tridentine Index cited it correctly.[20]

A Roman commission began work on a new index for Paul IV in 1556. As an interim measure, the Venetian Holy Office, with Fra Felice Peretti da Montalto (1521-90), the future Sixtus V, now inquisitor, forbade the sale of the *Colloquia* on 22 June 1557, a portent for the future.[21] The papacy printed and promulgated the new Index, usually called the Pauline Index, in January 1559. Its Erasmus entry was simplicity itself: it banned the opera omnia.[22]

While the Pauline Index condemned many more titles than its predecessors and added new categories of prohibitions, its greatest significance derived from the fact that the papacy, for the first time, unequivocally promulgated an index. Paul IV did not invite the bookmen to evaluate his index, he demanded immediate enforcement.

This index produced the first of the century's two massive waves of book-burning. On 18 March, the Saturday before Palm Sunday, the Venetian Inquisition burnt 10,000 to 12,000 volumes, and reported that more were accumulating.[23] The greater part of these probably came as a result of voluntary compliance of individuals and ecclesiastical institutions. A similar pattern emerged elsewhere. A contemporary historian, primarily describing Rome, estimated that every reader lost some books, and that humanists, legists, and medical scholars were particularly hard hit.[24] The judgment that humanists especially lost books suggests the destruction of many copies of Erasmus, for no humanistic library would lack his works.

The Venetian bookmen refused to obey the Index until the papacy found the lever to force compliance. All the major

Venetian publishers owned bookstores throughout Italy, including the papal state. The papacy simply threatened to seize the stores and their contents within its dominion. In the face of this potent economic threat, the Venetian bookmen began to comply. From April through August 1559 they offered inventories of the prohibited titles in their stores and some books to be burned. The inventory of the very large publisher Gabriel Giolito, dated 14 August 1559, listed twenty-nine prohibited titles, including the following of Erasmus: *De puritate tabernaculi s. ecclesiae christianae, Enchiridion militis christiani, Espositione di Matheo evangelista* (the Tomitano translation), *In Novum Testamentum annotationes, Modus orandi Deum, Moriae encomium, Precationes aliquot novae*, and possibly the *Exomologesis sive modus confitendi*. The inventory did not indicate the number of copies of each title.[25]

Neither Giolito nor the other Venetian bookmen offered complete inventories of the prohibited titles in their stores, but only a sampling in the hope that the Holy Office would be satisfied. The Holy Office might have pursued the bookmen further but for Paul IV's sudden death on 18 August. Inquisitor Peretti, whose zeal had severely tried the patience of the Venetian government, immediately fled. Enforcement of the Index halted in Venice and probably in the rest of the peninsula, permitting the bookmen to return to their old ways.

Pius IV did not issue a new index but awaited action by the Council of Trent. The fathers expressed a variety of views in general sessions at the end of January 1562, and then appointed a commission to draft a new index. The commission devoted months to the thorny task. In a letter of 3 February 1563, Anton Brus von Müglitz (d 1588), archbishop of Prague and chairman of the commission, summarized the discussion on Erasmus. The commission had by that date agreed to ban the *Moria, Colloquia*, some apologetical writings, and many letters, he wrote. They had so severely corrected other works that Erasmus would no longer acknowledge them. The archbishop affirmed that he and one or two other members had fought to save the entire corpus because the great humanist had given the world good editions of the Church Fathers and fought heresy. Moreover, he had always submitted to the judgment of the church and died a Catholic. But, Brus lamented, the majority endorsed the Pauline condemnation and felt that they granted Erasmus a great boon if they only expurgated him.[26]

When the Council ended before the Index commission could finish its task, it turned over the task to the papacy. Pius IV attempted to compromise the views on Erasmus expressed at the Council in the Tridentine Index, promulgated in the spring of 1564. It prohibited *Colloquia, Moriae encomium, Lingua, Institutio Christiani matrimonii, Epistola ... de interdicto esu carnium*, and the Tomitano translation of the *Paraphrasis in evangelium Matthaei*. Next, it permitted the *Adagia* in the expurgated version being prepared by Paolo Manuzio. Finally, it prohibited all the other works dealing with religious matters unless they were expurgated by the theological faculties of Paris or Louvain.[27]

The Tridentine Index appeared to provide a moderate solution to the Erasmus conundrum. In order that the Catholic world might continue to reap the benefits of the great humanist's learning, the pa-

pacy would excise the objectionable passages and make available all but six of the titles in expurgated form. Rome fulfilled part of this promise with the publication of the expurgated version of the *Adagia* (Florentiae: Apud Iuntas 1575). The Congregation of the Index had done the correction, although this version attributed both expurgation and authorship to Paolo Manuzio (1512-74). It relegated Erasmus to a brief notice in the prefatory material, while subsequent Italian printings of 1578, 1585, 1591, and 1609, always in Venice, completely avoided mentioning him.[28] The papacy next issued an expurgated version of *Apophthegmata* (first printing either Venetiis: Ex aedibus Manutianus 1577, or Venetiis: Ex Officina Damiani Zenari 1583) which also credited Manuzio with authorship. The 1583 printing, as well as subsequent ones of 1590 and 1604 (both Venice) and 1601 (Brescia), made no reference to Erasmus.[29]

But the papacy expurgated no other Erasmus titles and consistently refused permission to others to correct them. In response to an inquiry, the Master of the Sacred Palace in 1576 informed the inquisitor of Modena that preparing an expurgated version of *Apophthegmata* was out of the question. He should confiscate any copies that he found, for the papacy would not concede permission to hold any Erasmus titles.[30] Similarly, Rome in 1579 instructed the Venetian inquisitor that he must refuse all requests to hold expurgated versions of 'le cose d'Erasmo d'humanità.'[31] Consequently, the nine or ten printings of the expurgated versions of *Adagia* and *Apophthegmata* remain the only known Italian printings of Erasmus from the conclusion of the Council of Trent through the end of the seventeenth century.

Why did the papacy change its mind and abandon the expurgation of Erasmus? No doubt the magnitude of the task daunted the officials of the Congregation of the Index. They discovered from the few titles corrected in the 1570s and 1580s, notably Boccaccio's *Decameron* and Castiglione's *Courtier*, that even a single title required great expenditure of time and effort. The amount of labour required for the huge Erasmian corpus would be enormous, for what part of it failed to touch religious and moral issues?

The practical difficulties were great, but possibly not so significant as the spiritual objection to Erasmus. The leaders of the post-Tridentine church, and many other Italians, firmly believed that Erasmus had initiated the Protestant Reformation. Fra Francesco Panigarola (1548-94), the most popular preacher of the time, summarized the indictment against him: Erasmus was the fomenter of all modern heresies.[32]

Erasmus' enemies had denounced Erasmus as Luther's precursor many years earlier, but as late as Trent some prelates had pointed out Erasmus' contributions as well. However, as Europe increasingly divided into two armed doctrinal camps, a stark black historical portrait of Erasmus replaced the nuanced view of earlier years. The historian and political theorist Giovanni Botero (1543/4-1617) elaborated the case against Erasmus' books. Botero started his history of the German Reformation with Erasmus.

The perversion of the most noble province of Germany began with the impertinence, if not malice, of Desiderius Erasmus ... He was a man of varied intellect, quick with epigrams and tracts, of great and wide learning, easy and abundant of speech. Used maliciously, these talents produced most grave injury to the Christian religion. Besides the overflowing buffoonery of the Moria, *he composed among his first works a book of* Colloquia *in which he partly despised, partly doubted, the laws and ceremonies of the Church. He laughed at the theologians ... and mocked the regular clergy and the monastic life. He spoke of the religious and of sacred things with the same license and slander in his* Adagia *and in his other works. Diffused throughout the academies and schools of Germany (where they even read the* Colloquia *publicly), these books fell into the hands of every sort of person. And because man inclines more to evil than good, nothing made a greater impression on the souls of readers than the witticisms and epigrams with which he lacerated the lives and habits of holy persons and laughed at ecclesiastical ceremonies, chastity, and vows, and everything held pious by Christians and the simple. He set out then to censor the greater part of the Holy Fathers, to judge their works, and to write about the Gospels with the same freedom and license that others used with Cicero or Terence.* Erasmus, Botero continued, treated theological material humanistically, the humanities theologically, but his sophistry covered everything. Lutherans honoured him, and the Zwinglians considered him a confidant. Having destroyed the reputation of sacred things with laughter and derision, he prepared the road for Luther. After repeating old epigrams on the two (*Erasmus innuit, Lutherus irruit; Erasmus dubitat, Lutherus asseverat; vel Lutherus Erasmizat, vel Erasmus Lutherizat*), Botero proceeded directly into a discussion of the indulgence controversy and the events of 1517.[33]

Botero's portrait of Erasmus was not particularly vicious by the polemical standards of the century, but it completely ignored the positive side of Erasmus' program, 'the philosophy of Christ.' Panigarola, Botero, and probably most Italians could not judge Erasmus' books objectively because of their deep fear of heresy. They hated and feared religious discord not only for spiritual reasons, but because they believed that heresy inevitably led to war and devastation. With the examples of France and the Netherlands before their eyes, the vast majority of Italian rulers, clergymen, and laymen lent the Index and Inquisition strong support in order to guarantee Italian peace and security in a strife-torn world.[34] They preferred to keep Erasmus' books completely out of circulation in order to avoid the risk of heresy and war.

For all his vitriol, Botero did not accuse Erasmus of heresy. But he and probably most church leaders judged Erasmus' savage attacks on church abuses to be only a hair's-breadth short of the open heresy that inevitably followed. They argued with some plausibility that heretics began to break with Rome by criticizing the sins of the church, especially of her leaders. Panigarola offered scriptural justification for this view. He pointed out how Judas' betrayal of his master began with criticism of Mary Magdalen's annointment of the feet of Jesus with a costly ointment: 'Why wasn't this ointment sold for three hundred denarii and the money given to the poor?' (John 12:5) So also Luther, Calvin, and other heretics intending to leave the church initially feigned concern for clerical abuses, Panigarola asserted.[35] Panigarola's argument justified keeping Erasmus' books out of the hands of readers, for who had attacked the sins of the church and churchmen more effectively

than Erasmus, and with what consequences in northern Europe?

On the other hand, Panigarola's assumption that critics of the church intended to leave the fold ran the risk of silencing all critics, however well motivated. Sincere reformers could also present another argument, that allowing Erasmus' attacks on clerical sin to circulate only delayed the real reform of the church. Some dedicated churchmen were devoting their lives to stamping out the abuses which helped to bring on the Reformation, at times in the face of heavy opposition from political bishops and obstructive princes. They wanted to effect a genuine pastoral renewal at the local level. Indeed, much of the Tridentine disciplinary reform attempted to renew the parish, through bringing the sacraments and the catechism to laymen, improving the educational and spiritual level of the lower clergy, and much else. The pastoral renewal depended heavily on restoring lay respect for the clergy. How could this be done if readers had access to Erasmus' devastating and hilarious attacks on them?[36]

This combination of fear, caution, and hope helps to explain why the papacy tended to treat Erasmus as a heretic of the first class, that is, one whose opera omnia were banned. Because the papacy did not expurgate the bulk of the Erasmian corpus, most of his titles were canonically prohibited. The Venetian Holy Office trials demonstrate that this tribunal, and perhaps others, tended to follow the papal lead on Erasmus, especially in the 1570s. Inquisition officials preparing inventories of the contents of a bookstore or a private library usually marked the prohibited titles with a cross (+). Some of these surviving inventories so designated relatively innocent Erasmus titles, for example, *De conscribendis epistolis*. Similarly, the Venetian inquisitor often treated an Erasmus scriptural title as prohibited when questioning the owner.[37] This attitude accounted for the substantial destruction of Erasmus' titles in the years after Trent.

The enforcement of the Tridentine Index produced the second of the two large waves of bookburning in sixteenth-century Italy. The Index's Rule X authorized local inquisitions to inspect bookstores. When city governments permitted this, the inspectors found substantial numbers of Erasmus' works. In 1565 the Neapolitan Inquisition discovered about seven hundred banned volumes in a local bookstore, including eighty-six volumes of twenty-three different Erasmus titles, ranging from the style manuals through *Colloquia* (nine copies) to the New Testament. Only Pietro Aretino among the banned authors was better represented on the shelves of this bookstore.[38]

After a delay of several years, the Venetian government authorized the Inquisition to make surprise visits to the bookstores for the purpose of enforcing the Tridentine Index. In July and August 1570, the inspectors (members of the regular clergy deputized for the task) went in pairs from store to store. Index in hand, they examined the shelves, made inventories, and confiscated prohibited titles. Catching the startled bookmen off guard, they discovered thousands of prohibited books, including many, many copies of Erasmus.

Early in their tour, the inspectors visited the store of Vincenzo Valgrisi, publisher and bookseller.[39] Originally from France, Valgrisi came to Venice in or about 1531, and began to publish in 1540 under the sign 'nella bottega d'Erasmo' or 'ex officina Erasmiana.' However, in 1559 he dropped this for other, less provocative signs, most often simply 'appresso Vincenzo Valgrisio.' He located his establishment 'in Merceria, presso l'horologio di San Marco;' that is, near the head of the street which began under the fifteenth-century clocktower of Mauro Coducci on the north side of Piazza San Marco. The Merceria Orologio and the other streets connecting Piazza San Marco to the Rialto by way of the church of San Zulian harboured almost as many printing houses and bookstores in the sixteenth century as souvenir shops today. A medium- to large-sized publisher, Valgrisi issued at least 202 editions from 1540 through 1572, including Italian translations of *Colloquia* (1545 and 1549) and *Apophthegmata* (1546).

The inspectors found about seventy-five prohibited titles in Valgrisi's store, some of them in enough copies to reach a total of over 1,150 prohibited volumes.[40] Valgrisi had an abundance of Erasmus:

Adagia thirty-two copies

Apophthegmata thirty-two copies, thirty described as the Italian translation entitled *Proverbi* (Vinegia: Gabriel Giolito, 1550)[41]

'Cato': *Catonis disticha moralia* edited by Erasmus, twenty-eight copies

Joannes Chrysostomus commentarius in Pauli epistolas edited by Erasmus and the German Protestant humanist Wolfgang Musculus, six copies

Joannes Chrysostomus in Evangelium Matthaei one copy

Opera divi C. Cypriani six copies

Colloquia ten copies, two described as Italian translations

De conscribendis epistolis seventeen copies, ten specified as a Venetian printing

De copia verborum twenty-five copies

De immensa Dei misericordia concio two copies

Institutio christiani matrimonii four copies, three specified as the Italian translation *Ordinatione del matrimonio de christiani* (Vinetia: Francesco Rocca e fratelli 1550)

Moriae encomium one copy

Novum testamentum Greek and Latin, two copies

Opera omnia one copy (Basileae: Hier. Froben & N. Episcopius 1540)

Parabolae sive similia five copies

'Paraphrasis scripturae': six copies, as well as three copies of 'Paraphrasis'

Spongia adversus aspergines Hutteni one copy

Terentii comoediae ten copies, two described as edited by Erasmus and eight as edited by Erasmus and Melanchthon

The inventory also listed other Erasmus titles too briefly for identification: 'Apologia,' one copy; 'diversi opusculetti,' seven copies; 'Epistola,' one copy; and 'Oratio,' eleven copies.

The inspector had marked the vast majority of the Erasmus titles with a + signifying that he considered them to be prohibited. The tribunal assessed Valgrisi the relatively small fine of fifty ducats, but also confiscated the prohibited books.[42] Since eleven hundred volumes possessed a retail value of three to five hundred ducats, depending on their size and format, this was a substantial loss.

Although only Valgrisi's inventory survives in entirety from this inspection tour, other bookmen also lost Erasmus titles. Upon being tipped off that the inspectors were about to come, a small bookseller left some eighty banned titles in the care of a neighbour – who promptly informed

the Holy Office. The Erasmus titles included *Colloquia, Novum Testamentum, Parabolae*, and several other humanistic works such as his editions of Galen and Terence. Again the zealous inquisition officials marked as prohibited most of Erasmus' titles.[43]

The Holy Office ordered the prohibited books found in twenty-five or more bookstores burned publicly in Piazza San Marco in early September 1570. The number destroyed must have reached the thousands, for the tribunal often referred to titles found 'in quantity.' With the exception of a few titles of Italian apostates, such as Bernardino Ochino, the tribunal did not find Protestant religious works in the book stores. Instead, it uncovered large quantities of the works of Aretino, Machiavelli, Erasmus, and like authors. The short-lived enforcement of the Pauline Index in 1559, together with the Tridentine purge of the bookstores, probably accounted for the greatest part of the destruction of Erasmus titles in Venice and the rest of Italy.

In the first few years after Trent, the Inquisition also uncovered Erasmus' works in the libraries of heresy suspects, especially authors and humanist schoolmasters. The Holy Office of Adria, a small town close to the mouth of the Po within the Venetian Dominion, arrested the blind vernacular author Luigi Groto (1541-85), called il Cieco d'Adria, on suspicion of heresy in 1567. The tribunal discovered twenty-seven banned works in his library, including many by Erasmus. The Inquisition was particularly upset because the young people who read to Groto would also imbibe dangerous ideas from his library. After Groto abjured some Protestant beliefs, the tribunal sentenced him to penances and, presumably, confiscated his illicit books.[44]

While churchmen denounced Erasmus and inquisitions destroyed his books, a determined minority revered his memory and sought out his works. Nicolò Franco (1515-70), a prolific vernacular author, admired Erasmus. Just as Cicero was the wonder of his century, so 'the divine Erasmus' is the marvel of ours, he wrote in 1539. Franco endorsed 'the philosophy of Christ' and imitated Erasmus' thrusts against clerical abuses and church practices. When the Roman Inquisition tried him in 1569, for a pasquinade against Paul IV, Franco, in peril of his life, still condemned the Pauline Index ban of Erasmus on the grounds that the Dutch humanist had never been a heretic.[45]

Few so courageously affirmed their allegiance but many continued to seek out his books. After the purge of their stores in 1570, the Venetian bookmen established clandestine organizations to bring in from northern Europe banned titles in demand, including Erasmus' scriptural works. For example, a roving inquisition commissioner in 1582 found a Franciscan monk with a copy of Erasmus' Greek and Latin New Testament. The monk informed him that all the bookstores had it and told him where he had purchased his copy. The commissioner went incognito to the shop and asked for the title by name. The proprietor brought out an armful of banned scriptural titles including three different printings by Nikolaus Brylinger of Basel of Erasmus' New Testament. The Holy Office confiscated and destroyed them.[46]

Italian readers wanted Erasmus' scriptural works because they recognized that the biblical scholarship of Erasmus and such Protestants as Robert Estienne surpassed that of Catholic scholars. The Council of Trent acknowledged this as early as 1546 when it authorised the preparation of a new edition of the Vulgate that would meet the highest standards of Renaissance scholarship. But until the Clementine Vulgate of 1592 fulfilled the Tridentine decree, scholars and devout souls who wanted the best texts sought out those of Erasmus, Estienne, and other northerners. Indeed, it is likely that numerous clergy were among those who owned Erasmian scriptural works.

The humanistic portion of the Erasmian corpus also continued to attract readers. While dividing the corpus into distinct parts is an arbitrary exercise, the style manuals (*Adagia, Apophthegmata, De copia verborum, De conscribendis epistolis, Parabolae*) and the commentaries, editions, and translations of classical authors, were primarily humanistic. But the Index denied Italian readers access to most of these, as well as to works of northern Protestant humanists whose opera omnia had been prohibited. Perhaps no aspect of the Index irritated Italian scholars more than these prohibitions, so they ignored the Index and tried to escape detection.

They did not always succeed. In 1574 the Venetian Holy Office interrogated a lawyer and druggist, aged either seventy-four or eighty-four, whose humanistic library contained four prohibited works of Melanchthon, single works of Lefèvre d'Etaples, Simon Grynaeus, Christoph Hegendorff, Andreas Osiander, Sebastian Münster, and about fifteen works of Erasmus, including *Adagia, Apophthegmata, Bellum, Catalogus lucubrationum, De copia verborum*, and commentaries on several classical authors. He admitted purchasing most of his books from Venetian booksellers but would not (or could not) remember when or from whom. When the inquisitor admonished him that prohibited books fostered evil in their readers, he answered that this was true only if the reader's intention was bad. He probably alluded to St Paul's dictum, 'To all who are pure themselves, everything is pure; but to those who have been corrupted and lack faith, nothing can be pure ...' (Titus 1:15), a favourite humanist defence for reading pagan literature. Taking into account his age, the tribunal released the old man with a warning – but confiscated his prohibited books.[47]

The Inquisition also arrested in 1574 a Fra Leonardo, a Canon Regular (Augustinian) priest at the Venetian monastery of San Salvatore. The tribunal discovered in his library Erasmus' *Colloquia, De conscribendis epistolis, De copia verborum, De praeparatione ad mortem, Paraphrasis Joannem*, and *Querela pacis*. He also owned several banned Italian works. Fra Leonardo testified that his passion for 'l'arte oratoria' had led him to procure the books. When witnesses produced no evidence of heresy, the Holy Office sentenced him to penances and forbade him to preach for three years.[48]

Italian inquisitions destroyed an immense number of Erasmus volumes. Or to look at this fact from another direction, an astonishingly large number of copies of Erasmus' books circulated in Italy both before and after the appearance of the Counter-Reformation. This suggests that Erasmus' influence may have been greater than scholars have estimated. The virulence with which churchmen denounced Erasmus and destroyed his books offers another clue to his popularity, for if it had been slight, strong measures would have been unnecessary. Tracing the Italian *fortuna* of Erasmus from the 1530s through the next half-century or so

would be difficult, but might yield surprising results.[49]

The papacy never did expurgate the bulk of Erasmus' works, but finally authorized individuals to expurgate their own copies. The *Instructio* which prefaced the Clementine Index of 1596 permitted readers to correct their own copies of a title according to the directions issued by the theological faculties of Louvain and Paris many years earlier. Finally, in 1607, the first and only papal *Index Expurgatorius* appeared with instructions for the expurgation of but fifty titles, none of them by Erasmus.[50] A year later the papacy tacitly acknowledged its inability to complete an *Index Expurgatorius* and turned over the rest of the task to individual readers. It instructed the Venetian Holy Office that it might permit 'suitable and intelligent persons' to hold and expurgate 'suspect books' according to the expurgation guidelines issued with the 1596 Index. In particular they might hold 'libri d'humanità' if they cancelled out the names of heretics and their glosses.[51] With this the papacy all but abandoned its attempt to keep banned humanistic works of Erasmus and northern Protestants out of the hands of Italian scholars.

In effect, Rome encouraged readers to mutilate Erasmus' books. Obedient readers and librarians, especially those overseeing the libraries of ecclesiastical institutions, may have added at this time the ink erasures that disfigure some surviving copies of Erasmus. Still, those who wanted to read the books may have felt that a mutilated copy was better than nothing.

And Italians continued to remember and admire Erasmus. Gian Vincenzo Pinelli (1535-1601) was a Neapolitan noble who came to Padua in 1558 and stayed the rest of his life. Blessed with wealth and a great love of learning, he assembled one of the great libraries of his time, a collection of some 6,500 printed volumes and over 800 manuscripts. He begged his many northern European correspondents for news of the most recent publications. Nor did he forget the great men of learning of the past. A few months before his death, he wrote to Jacob Zwinger (1569-1610), professor of Greek at Basel and a Protestant, to ask if he could find for him an Erasmus autograph, because he wished 'to understand the real character of that good man.'[52] One hopes that his quest was successful.

However tenaciously individuals held on to their copies of Erasmus, persistent index condemnation over several generations doomed the greater part of the books. Venetian and other Italian bookmen smuggled in additional copies from northern Europe, but the number could not have begun to replace those destroyed. And when intellectual interests changed, readers no longer went to trouble and expense to procure Erasmus titles from abroad. The copies now found in the libraries of Florence and Venice are the remnants of a huge quantity of Erasmus' works once circulating in sixteenth-century Italy.

NOTES

1 The Holy Office records survive and are open to scholars in one major Italian city, Venice, and in several minor cities. The archives of the Roman congregations of the Index and Inquisition are housed in the Palazzo del Santo Uffizio, Piazza S. Uffizio 11, just outside the walls of the Vatican, now the home of the Congregation of the Doctrine of the Faith. However, scholars are denied access. The amount of surviving sixteenth-century material is problematical in any case, because of the razing of the Holy Office building by Roman mobs at the death of Paul IV in 1559, and the unfortunate destruction in 1815-17 of the bulk of the inquisitorial records taken to Paris by Napoleon Bonaparte.

2 The most important of the few and brief older studies are those of Croce and Cantimori: Benedetto Croce 'Sulle traduzioni e imitazioni italiane dell'*Elogio* e dei *Colloqui* di Erasmo,' first published in 1913, and reprinted in his *Aneddoti di varia letteratura* vol I (Naples 1942) 327-38; for additional information and bibliography on Croce's interest in Erasmus, see Beatrice Corrigan 'Croce and Erasmus: The *Colloquies* and the *Moria* in Italy' *Erasmus in English* 7 (1975) 21-5; Delio Cantimori 'Note su Erasmo e la vita morale e religiosa italiana nel secolo XVI,' first published in 1936, and reprinted in Armando Saitta ed *Antologia di critica storica* II *Problemi della civiltà moderna* (Bari 1957) 473-93. Nicola Badaloni recently summarized much of the older work in Badaloni, Renato Barilli, and Walter Moretti *Cultura e vita civile tra Riforma e Controriforma* (Bari 1973) 87-97. This small work is part of the multi-volumed *Storia della Letteratura Italiana* published by Laterza.

Important new scholarship with fresh information has recently appeared: Silvana Seidel Menchi 'Alcuni atteggiamenti della cultura italiana di fronte a Erasmo (1520-1536)' in *Eresia e Riforma nell'Italia del Cinquecento* (Florence and Chicago 1974) 71-133; and 'Sulla fortuna di Erasmo in Italia: Ortensio Lando e altri eterodossi della prima metà del Cinquecento' in *Schweizerische Zeitschrift für Geschichte* 24 (1974) 537-634. For a good overview of several aspects of the question, see Myron P. Gilmore 'Italian Reactions to Erasmian Humanism' in Heiko A. Oberman with Thomas A. Brady, Jr eds *Itinerarium Italicum: The Profile of the Italian Renaissance in the Mirror of its European Transformations* (Leiden 1975) 61-115. Also see his 'Anti-Erasmianism in Italy: The dialogue of Ortensio Lando on Erasmus' funeral' *Journal of Medieval and Renaissance Studies* 4 (1974) 1-14.

3 In general, Paul wrote part I and Marcella part II, but we have worked together throughout and acknowledge joint responsibility for the entire study. Marcella wishes to thank the Canada Council, and Paul the American Council of Learned Societies and

14

the Canada Council, for the support that made research in Italy possible. Together we thank Ron Schoeffel who first suggested this study and has taken a keen interest in it, and Sir Roger Mynors who gave it a careful reading.

4 Pietro Tacchi Venturi *Storia della Compagnia di Gesù in Italia* vol I, pt 1: *La vita religiosa in Italia durante la prime età della Compagnia di Gesù* (2nd ed enlarged, Rome 1930) 124-5

5 Letter of Aleander of 30 April 1534, Venice, in *Nunziature di Venezia* vol I (1533-1535) ed Franco Gaeta (Istituto Storico Italiano per l'età moderna e contemporanea. Fonti per la Storia d'Italia) (Rome 1958) 214

6 Cited from the Italian version in Massimo Marcocchi *La riforma cattolica: Documenti e testimonianze: Figure ed istituzioni dal secolo XV alla metà del secolo XVII. Saggio introductivo di Mario Bendiscioli* vol I (Brescia 1967) 486

7 Determining individual authorship of various parts of the *Consilium* is very difficult, in the opinion of Hubert Jedin, *A History of the Council of Trent* trans Ernest Graf. vol I (London 1957) 425-6

8 Franz Heinrich Reusch ed, *Die Indices Librorum Prohibitorum des Sechzehnten Jahrhunderts* (Tübingen 1886; rpt Nieuwkoop 1961) 136-42, prints the Lucca Index of 1545, the Venetian *Catalogo* of 1549, and most other sixteenth-century indices. In general, further discussion and documentation for some statements made in this article will be found in Paul's forthcoming monograph to be published by Princeton University Press. A brief synopsis appears in 'The Roman Inquisition and the Venetian Press 1540-1605' *Journal of Modern History* 47 (1975) 48-65.

9 An edict of the Sienese government, 9 April 1548, described in Paolo Piccolomini 'Documenti del R. Archivio di Stato in Siena sull' eresia in questa città durante il secolo XVI' *Bullettino senese di storia patria* 17 (1910) 26-7

10 See below.

11 'Nel catalogo sarà da ricordarsi delle opere di Erasmo, le quali hanno aperto la porta a tutta la heresia ...' Letter of Annibale Grisonio of 29 June 1549, Venice, in Archivio di Stato, Parma, Carteggio Farnesiano, Venezia, Filza 510/2, no 64, ff192-3. Consulted on microfilm at the Fondazione Giorgio Cini, Venice.

12 Although the surviving copies of the Index carry the date 1554, it was not sent to Venice until the spring of 1555. It is reproduced in Reusch *Indices* 143-75.

13 See Reusch *Indices* 156 for the Erasmus entry. In this article all Erasmus titles are given in a short title form based on van der Haeghen, *Bibliotheca Erasmiana.*

14 Roland H. Bainton *Erasmus of Christendom* (New York 1969) 132

15 These editions are noted in van der Haeghen, pt I, p 73 item 6 (hereafter abbreviated 73-6), 181-8; pt II, 21-13. van der Haeghen also lists the *De constructione* (pt I, 63-1) but without the printer's name. Our difficulty in locating in Florentine and Venetian libraries or standard bibliographical guides, such as the *British Museum Short-Title Catalogue of Italian Books*, Italian printings without publishers listed by van der Haeghen leads us to treat such entries cautiously.

16 van der Haeghen lists two post-1554 Italian printings of Erasmus, but the copies examined omit any reference to the Dutch humanist. The first of these is Aesop's fables as interpreted by Erasmus and others (Venetiis: D. Nicolinum 1563), cited by van der Haeghen, pt II, 5-2. The British Museum copy of this work (57 k 24, and listed in the *Short-Title Catalogue of Italian Books* on p 9, first entry) does not mention Erasmus anywhere. The *Index Aureliensis* 101.209 also lists this Aesop edition without noting an Erasmian contribution. The second post-1554 printing of Erasmus listed by van der Haeghen is an annotated edition of Cicero's *De officiis* and other works (Venetiis: Paulum Manutium 1559; van der Haeghen, pt II, 21-26). Again the British Museum copy (1385 b 23, and listed in the *Short-Title Catalogue of Italian Books* on p 176, entry 14) fails to mention Erasmus. Ant. Aug. Renouard *Annales de l'imprimerie des Alde ...* (Paris 1834; rpt Bologna 1953) p 178, mentions Paolo Manuzio's annotations on Cicero, but not Erasmus'. (We wish to thank Mr David M. Jones for examining these British Museum copies.) Only an expert in the textual history of Aesop and Cicero could determine whether or not these two editions contain any Erasmus contribution. Even if they do, those who prepared these editions for the press feared to mention Erasmus, further proof of the great humanist's disrepute after 1554.

17 Reusch *Indices* 139, 172

18 Archivio di Stato, Venice (hereafter ASV), Santo Uffizio (hereafter SU), Busta (Bu) 12, Padre Marin da Venezia, ff2r-v, his testimony of 9 August 1555

19 ASV, SU, Bu 11, Bernardino Tomitano (including an autograph copy of the first

oration, delivered to the Holy Office on 22 August 1555). Antonio Rotondò prints excerpts from the first oration in his 'La censura ecclesiastica e la cultura' in *Storia d'Italia*. V: *I documenti* (Turin 1973) 1435. Also see Luigi De Benedictis *Della vita e delle opere di Bernardino Tomitano: studio* (Padua 1903), and E. Riondato 'Bernardino Tomitano' *Enciclopedia filosofica* vol 4, pp 1228-30. We have not found a printed version of the 1555 oration; but see Menchi 'Sulla fortuna di Erasmo' 616-17. The second oration is *Oratione seconda de l'eccellente M. Bernardino Tomitano, alli medesimi signori* (no place, printer, or date, but with a dedicatory letter of 20 March 1556, Padua). There is a copy in the VM, Misc. 2380.-.5. There is a copy of the *Espositione letterale del testo di Matteo evangelista di M. Bernardin Tomitano* In Venetia, per Gio. dal Griffio. Nel 1547; Biblioteca Nazionale, Firenze, Gui. 11.7.56.

20 Reusch *Indices* 180, 259

21 ASV, Bu 156, a packet of miscellaneous material entitled 'Librai e libri proibiti, 1545-1571,' ff[56r-v]

22 Reusch *Indices* 185

23 Ludwig von Pastor *The History of the Popes* trans F.I. Antrobus et al. vol 14 (London 1924) 281, 482

24 *Delle istorie del mondo, parte terza: Aggiunte da M. Mambrino Roseo da Fabriano alle istorie di M. Giovanni Tarcagnota* (Venezia: Giunti 1585), bk VII, 603-04. The first edition was 1562.

25 ASV, SU, 'Librai e libri proibiti, 1545-1571,' f[88r]. Like almost all other inventories discovered in the Inquisition archive, this one is brief, the entries consisting of either author and a one- or two-word title, or perhaps only author or title. Place of publication, printer, and date are normally omitted. But with the aid of bibliographical guides, one can usually make a sure identification of the titles.

26 Franz Heinrich Reusch *Der Index der Verbotenen Bücher: Ein Beitrag zur Kirchen- und literaturgeschichte* vol I (Bonn 1883; rpt Darmstadt 1967) 320

27 'Desiderii Erasmi Roterodami Colloquiorum liber, Moria, Lingua, Christiani matrimonii institutio, De interdicto esu carnium, ejusdem Paraphrasis in Matthaeum, quae a Bernardino Tomitano in Italicam linguam conversa est. Caetera vero opera ipsius, in quibus de religione tractat, tamdiu prohibita sint, quamdiu a facultate theologica Parisiensi vel Lovaniensi expurgata non fuerint. Ada-

gia vero ex editione, quam molitur Paulus Manutius, permittentur; interim vero, quae jam edita sunt, expunctis locis suspectis judicio alicujus facultatis theologicae universitatis catholicae vel inquisitionis alicujus generalis, permittantur.' Reusch *Indices* 259.

28 These editions are noted and described in *Bibliotheca Belgica* new ed Marie-Thérèse Lenger. vol II (Brussels 1964), items E123 (with a very full description of the contents), E124, E127, E128, and E132, respectively. We have examined copies of the 1578 and 1591 printings in the Centre for Reformation and Renaissance Studies of Victoria University in the University of Toronto.

29 Renouard *Annales des Alde* p 224, describes the 1577 printing, and the *Bibliotheca Belgica*, E367, repeats this description although a copy had not been examined. The *Bibliotheca Belgica* also describes and gives locations for printings of 1583, 1590, and 1604 (E369, E370, and E373, respectively). We have examined in the Centre for Reformation and Renaissance Studies the 1583 printing as well as another one (Brixiae: In Aedibus Polycreti Turlini 1601) not noted by the *Bibliotheca Belgica*. This last one exactly repeats the title page and contents of the 1583 printing.

30 'Delli *Apophtegmi* d'Erasmo non si parla d'espurgatione, ma si levano tutti perché niun'opra d'Erasmo, sia qualsivoglia, si concede in Roma.' Letter of Fra Damiano Rubeo to the inquisitor of Bologna, 25 April 1576, Rome, as quoted in Antonio Rotondò 'Nuovi documenti per la storia dell'Indice dei libri proibiti (1572-1638)' *Rinascimento* serie 2, vol 3 (1963) 157. Of course the papacy would not permit anyone else to correct the *Apophthegmata* when it was about to promulgate an authorized expurgation. But the rest of the instruction documents papal hostility toward the entire corpus.

31 'Circa la licenza, che è domandata a Vostro Reverendo da molti di tenere le cose d'Erasmo d'humanità, e del Machiavello, deletis erroribus, si dice, che non dia questa licenza a nessuno.' 2 May 1579. Biblioteca Apostolica Vaticana, ms Vaticanus Latinus 10945, 'Anima del Sant'Offitio spirata dal Supremo Tribunale della Sacra Congregazione raccolta dal Padre Predicatore F. Giacomo Angarano da Vicenza l'anno del Signore MDCXLIV,' f113v. This ms contains summaries of instructions from the Congregation of the Holy Office to the inquisitors of Venice and other cities in the Venetian state.

32 *Cento ragionamenti sopra la Passione di N.S. Giesù Christo ...* (In Venetia: Apresso Giacomo Vincenti 1606) 479. Panigarola delivered these sermons in Milan in the presence of St Charles Borromeo (d 1584) and first published them in 1585.

33 We have changed some of Botero's tenses for the sake of consistency. *Relationi universali di Giovanni Botero ...* (In Venetia, Per li Bertani, MDCLXXI) 361. This is from part three of the *Relationi*, first published in Rome in 1593.

34 See Francesco Panigarola's elaboration of these themes in *Prediche quadragesimali del Reverendiss. Monsig. Panigarola ... predicate da lui in San Pietro di Roma, l'anno 1577 ...* (In Venetia, Appresso Pietro Miloco, MDCXVII) 510-11, 513-14.

35 Panigarola *Cento ragionamenti* 288-9

36 The prevailing hostility toward Erasmus largely explains papal refusal to expurgate the bulk of his works. Yet, the general papal reluctance to expurgate, or to permit others to expurgate, needs further investigation. Although the Tridentine Index rules never authorised individuals to expurgate the copies in their own libraries, they empowered bishops and inquisitors to direct theologians to expurgate. Then, presumably, local printers could publish corrected versions. But very little of this possible expurgation was realized, for publishers issued very few expurgated books before 1590 and not a great number after that date. And most of these were literary titles that had never been banned by the Tridentine Index. The vast bulk of humanistic, legal, medical, and scientific works that seemed to qualify for expurgation under rules II, V, and VII of the Tridentine Index (see Reusch *Indices* 247-9) never appeared in expurgated Italian printings.

We can offer only a limited explanation for this state of affairs. Doubtless the militant Counter-Reformation mentality, the tendency to distrust any kind of intellectual deviation, partially explains it. A few pieces of evidence also suggest that the Congregation of the Index made a start on the mountainous task of expurgation before giving up. While the Index Congregation's surviving papers are locked up in the Palazzo del Santo Uffizio, we have noted what appear to be directions for the expurgation of a number of titles and authors, including Erasmus, in mss Vaticanus Latinus 6149 and 6207 of the Biblioteca Apostolica Vaticana. Perhaps these are remnants of the abortive efforts. John Tedeschi has found limited evidence to

support his surmise that the refusal of Italian scholars to co-operate in a mass expurgation effort forced Rome to abandon the enterprise. See his article 'Florentine Documents for a History of the Index of Prohibited Books,' in *Renaissance Studies in Honor of Hans Baron* Anthony Molho and John A. Tedeschi eds (Florence 1971) 581-6, 594-5. Whatever the reasons, the Tridentine Index's attempt to substitute expurgation for outright prohibition produced meagre results.

37 We wish to caution that the Venetian Holy Office treated Erasmus as a heretic of the first class in a majority of trials, but not always. It paid little attention to Erasmus titles in some trials, and failed to make its attitude clear in others.

38 See the documents printed in Salvatore Bongi *Annali di Gabriel Giolito de'Ferrari da Trino di Monferrato, stampatore in Venezia* vol I (Rome 1890; rpt Rome nd) lxxxv-xcii.

39 Ugo Tucci 'The psychology of the Venetian merchant in the sixteenth century' in J.R. Hale ed *Renaissance Venice* (London 1973) 363; Ester Pastorello *Tipografi, editori, librai a Venezia nel secolo XVI* (Florence 1924) 92; Corrado Marciani 'Editori, tipografi, librai veneti nel Regno di Napoli nel Cinquecento' *Studi Veneziani* 10 (1968) 508

40 ASV, SU, Bu 14, Vincenzo Valgrisi et al 'Contro Vincentium Vadrisium' ff[37r-41v] for the inventory of 18 August 1570

41 For a description of this work, see Bongi *Annali di Giolito* I, 278-9.

42 ASV, SU, Bu 159, Registro Processi 1569, 1570, 1571, ff128v-30r, sentence of 18 December 1570

43 ASV, SU, Bu 30, Francesco Ziletti e Gilio Bonfadio, ff2v-7v, the latter's testimony and inventory, 6 February through 2 April 1571

44 Gino Marchi *La Riforma Tridentina in diocesi di Adria nel secolo XVI descritta col sussidio di fonti inedite* (Rovigo 1946) 166-8. Unfortunately, Marchi lists only the *Colloquia* and *Apophthegmata*, both apparently in Italian translations, among the Erasmus titles found in Groto's library.

45 Paul F. Grendler *Critics of the Italian World 1530-1560: Anton Francesco Doni, Nicolò Franco & Ortensio Lando* (Madison, Milwaukee, and London 1969) 112-13

46 ASV, SU, Bu 49, Francesco Ziletti e Felice Valgrisi, ff[5r-9r], testimony of 4, 11 December 1582

47 It is not clear how many, if any, of Eras-

mus' titles the tribunal confiscated. ASV, SU, Bu 37, Marcantonio Valgolio, testimony of 24 April, 4, 8 May 1574.

48 ASV, SU, Bu 38, Fra Leonardo, testimony of 3-28 September 1574

49 See paragraph V under *De correctione librorum* in Reusch *Indices* 533.

50 Reusch *Der Index* I, 549-59. Sixty years later, the Spanish church published a substantial *Index Expurgatorius* containing, among much else, directions for the expurgation of thirty-one Erasmus titles. *Index librorum prohibitorum et expurgandorum novissimus: Pro Catholicis hispaniarum regnis Philipp IV* ... (Madriti: Ex Typographaeo Didaci Diaz, MDCLXVII) 256-315. Copy in University of Toronto Rare Book Room.

51 'Le dico per ordine de signori cardinali ch'ella può concedere licenze de libri sospesi, Donec corrigantur, a persone idonee et intelligenti, con la clausula, Deletis delendis: et anco de' libri d'humanità ne' quali sono postille d'Autori Heretici con far cassare i loro nomi e dette postille, che fussero cattive. Et in ciò ella si governi conforme alle Regole dell'Indice.' 12 July 1608. Vaticanus Latinus 10945, f113r.

52 '... che sarebbe di poter vedere quattro parole sole scritte di mano d'Erasmo in qualsivoglia materia. Non si desiderando per altro che per conoscere il proprio caratere di quel valent'-huomo.' Letter of Pinelli of 9 February 1601, Padua, in Basel, Universitätsbibliothek, Ms Frey-Grynaeus I, 12, f266r; copy in ms G. II. 39, f153r. Marcella is preparing a study of Pinelli.

PART TWO
The Erasmus Holdings of Florentine and Venetian Libraries

This survey lists the Erasmus holdings from the sixteenth and seventeenth centuries of the Venetian Marciana and five Florentine libraries. Some of the volumes have been examined, but the survey is based on library catalogues, because this enabled us to determine the over-all state of Erasmus holdings relatively quickly. Since the fullness and reliability of Italian library catalogues varies, the reader can expect substantial but not complete accuracy. For example, when two or more Erasmus works were issued together, the catalogues sometimes list only the initial title. Moreover, the survey of works edited or translated by Erasmus, the second part of the inventory, obviously lacks completeness because old catalogues frequently list such titles only under the author (eg, Terence) and provide little or no information on the editor(s). The survey can, however, claim a higher degree of completeness for works written by Erasmus.

The inventory lists two hundred and seventy-seven Erasmus editions. Forty-nine of these are Italian printings, less than half of those included in Erasmus bibliographies.[53] These figures eloquently testify to the effectiveness of the index and inquisition destruction of Erasmus' works.

On the other hand, the inventory contains forty-two editions, fifteen per cent of the total, not found in the bibliographies consulted. Of these forty-two, eighteen are Italian printings. This points to the need for a thorough bibliography of sixteenth-century Italian printings of Erasmus.[54] Despite the difficulties in compiling it, such a publication history would be the fundamental first step toward further study of Erasmus' Italian *fortuna*.

While the Index and Inquisition provide the fundamental reason for the number of Erasmus editions, the histories of the libraries help to explain why individual collections contain fewer or more Erasmus copies.

Although Petrarch left his manuscripts to the Venetian Republic in 1362, Cardinal Bessarion's donation of over a thousand codices in 1468 marked the true beginning of the Biblioteca Marciana. With a magnificent gesture, the Republic commissioned Jacopo Sansovino to build a suitable edifice to house the manuscripts. At first the patriciate seemed proud of the Library of St Mark. Through the sixteenth century, the Procurators of St Mark (a high post in the Venetian constitution, held by only a few long-lived and honored patricians) watched over the library with care.[55] It was the recipient of several important bequests, notably a gift of 1,000 scudi and all the printed books of Melchiore Guilandini (d 1589), a professor of medicine and an herbalist. His library of some 2,000 titles covered all fields, especially medicine, and included several prohibited works. But Erasmus was conspicuous through his absence – although the inventory listed several anonymous *Adagia*.[56]

At the same time, the Republic did little to care for or increase the collection in an official way. It ordered local publishers to deposit a bound copy of each printed work in the 'libraria publica' in 1593, but neither this nor subsequent deposit decrees appear to have been enforced.[57] And the patriciate lost interest in their famed library in the following century. By the last third of the seventeenth century, visitors from northern Europe confirmed the extraordinary beauty of its architecture, but commented that the holdings were 'neglected, disordered, rarely used. No one, it seemed, really cared.'[58]

The library's fortunes did not improve until the appointment of Procurator Lorenzo Tiepolo (1673-1742) as librarian in 1736. His report tactfully confirmed the sad state of the collection. Under him and Anton Maria d'Alessandro Zanetti (1706-1778, custodian of the library from 1737

on), the Marciana began to receive the care it deserved.[59] The collection only grew substantially in the eighteenth century as a result of private donations, and especially through the suppression of many religious institutions between 1784 and 1810.

These events help to explain the relatively small number of Erasmus editions to be found in the Marciana. The librarians who culled the monastic libraries brought into the Marciana significant numbers of sixteenth-century printed works, but probably not many copies of Erasmus. Since the libraries of ecclesiastical institutions could hardly avoid obeying the index, they had few copies of Erasmus to give to the Marciana. Individual collections, especially those of laymen, were more likely to preserve Erasmus' works, but were also subject to the ravages of time. Their preservation depended on the concern of several generations of owners, but they were vulnerable to the neglect or rashness of a single one.

Of the libraries surveyed, the Biblioteca Nazionale Centrale in Florence houses in its Guicciardini, Magliabechi, and Palatina collections the largest number of Erasmus printings. The first of these is of particular interest, for Count Piero Guicciardini (1809-1886), an evangelical Protestant, amassed the best collection of printed sources on sixteenth-century Italian Protestantism to be found anywhere. Although not so numerous as the Erasmus volumes in the Magliabechi group, the Erasmus copies in the Guicciardini collection include a number of titles and printings not to be found elsewhere as, for example, the only copy of the *Bellum* and several printings of the paraphrases of parts of the New Testament. Ironically, Guicciardini only succeeded in presenting his library of eight thousand volumes, many of them extremely rare, to the Biblioteca Nazionale after years of opposition.[60]

The Magliabechi collection is the fundamental and largest repository of early printed works in the Biblioteca Nazionale. Antonio Magliabechi (1633-1714), librarian for the Medici grand dukes, polymath, and passionate book collector, gave his name to it when he bequeathed his own library of possibly 25,000 volumes to the city of Florence to establish a public library for scholars too poor to purchase books. Additional donations, most notably in 1771 and continuing until the mid-nineteenth-century, have added substantially to the collection. Unfortunately, because Magliabechi's successors failed to keep records, and even neglected the collection, it cannot now be determined which volumes came from the original donation.[61]

Ferdinand III (Lorraine), grand duke of Tuscany from 1791 through 1824 and bibliophile, gathered the Palatina collection, given to the library in 1871. He may have acquired many of the seventeenth-century northern European printings of Erasmus listed in the Palatina collection during his fifteen-year exile in Würzburg forced on him by the French conquest of Tuscany in 1799.[62]

The Laurenziana and Riccardiana libraries, famous for their manuscripts but housing only small printed collections, hold additional Erasmus volumes. Finally, the Biblioteca Marucelliana, a public library founded by Francesco Marucelli (1625-1703), a Florentine patrician who collected books during his long career at the papal court, contains some Erasmus titles.

NOTES

53 van der Haeghen, for example, lists an additional sixty-seven Italian printings. On the other hand, annals of individual presses sometimes list Erasmus titles not noted by more comprehensive bibliographies. For example, the vernacular translation of the *Institutio principis christiani* (Venice: Per Francesco Marcolini 1539), not noted in van der Haeghen, is listed in Scipione Casali *Gli annali della tipografia veneziana di Francesco Marcolini* (Forlì 1861; rpt Bologna 1953) 105-8.

54 A new short-title catalogue of all early Erasmus editions is being prepared by Drs E. van Gulik, formerly City Librarian of Rotterdam. It will be a welcome addition to Erasmus bibliography.

55 ASV, Procuratori di San Marco, De Supra, Bu 68, provides much information on the state's concern for the library. Two historical surveys are: Giuseppe Valentinelli *La R. Biblioteca Marciana di Venezia* (Venice 1872), and Maria Luxoro *La Biblioteca di San Marco nella sua storia* (Florence 1954).

56 ASV, Procuratori di San Marco, De Supra, Bu 68, fascicule 4, 'Inventario delli libri lassati dal Sig.r Marchioro Guilandini semplicista publico alla Ser.mo Signoria,' 2 January 1590

57 ASV, Consiglio dei Dieci, Comune, Registro 43, ff38r-v, 12 May 1593

58 Marilyn Perry 'The Statuario Publico of the Venetian Republic' in *Saggi e Memorie di Storia dell'Arte* 8 (Florence 1972) 87

59 Ibid, 87-9

60 This collection has a printed catalogue: *Catalogo e suo supplemento del dicembre 1875 della collezione de' libri relativi alla riforma religiosa del secolo XVI donata dal conte Piero Guicciardini alla Città di Firenze* (Florence 1877-87). Also see Domenico Fava *La Biblioteca Nazionale Centrale di Firenze e le sue insigni raccolte* (Milan 1939) 136-41.

61 Fava, 12-33. The 1771 addition was the Medici family library from Palazzo Pitti, called the Palatina-Medicea-Lotaringia collection. Ibid, 43-6.

62 Fava, 101-20

Abbreviations

Libraries
Florence
Biblioteca Nazionale
  BNF: General Catalogue
  Gui: Guicciardini Collection
  Mag: Magliabechi Collection
  Pal: Palatina Collection
FL: Facoltà di Lettere, Università degli
  Studi di Firenze
Lau: Biblioteca Laurenziana
Mar: Biblioteca Marucelliana
Ricc st: Biblioteca Riccardiana, stampato

Venice
VM: Biblioteca Marciana

Others
Am: Amsterdam
An: Antwerp
B: Basel
L: Lyons
P: Paris
V: Venice
sl: senza luogo (no place)
st: senza tipografo (no publisher)
snt: senza notizie tipografiche (no imprint,
  no date)

Edition marked with an asterisk is not in-
cluded in the following bibliographies:
F. van der Haeghen *Bibliotheca Erasmiana*
  (Ghent 1893; rpt Nieuwkoop 1961)
Bibliotheca belgica new ed Marie-Thérèse
  Lenger (Brussels 1964) II
H.D. Rix 'The Editions of Erasmus' *De
  Copia' Studies in Philology* 43 (1946)
  595-618; J.K. Sowards, Ibid, 55 (1958)
  122-35
Short-title Catalogue of Books printed in

*France and of French Books printed in
other countries from 1470 to 1600 in
the British Museum* (Oxford 1924; rpt
1966)
*Short-title Catalogue of Books printed in
the German-speaking Countries and
German Books printed in other countries
from 1455 to 1600 now in the British
Museum* (London 1962)
*Short-title Catalogue of Books printed in
Italy and of Italian Books printed in
other countries from 1465 to 1600 now
in the British Museum* (London 1958)
Edition marked with a double asterisk is
not included in above bibliographies and
was destroyed in Florentine flood in 1966.

WORKS BY ERASMUS

Adagia
Adagiorum chiliades tres. V, Aldus, mense
  sept. 1508. fo. Lau Delciana 1037
Proverbiorum chiliades. Ferrare, Joan.
  Machiochus Bondenus, ad idus martii
  1514. fo. Ricc st 14183, VM 37.C.28
Proverbiorum chiliades. B, Io. Frobenius,
  mense nov. 1517. VM 389.D.34
Adagiorum chiliades. V, Aldus, 1520. fo.
  Lau Delciana 4, VM Aldine 122
*Proverbiorum seu adagiorum chiliades.
  V, Sessa, 1522. fo. Mag 11.1.246, VM
  61.C.3
Adagiorum opus. B, Hier. Frobenius et Nic.
  Episcopius, mense martio 1533. fo.
  BNF 22.B.2.12
Proverbiorum chiliades. V, Victor de
  Rabanis et c^{ie}, mense sept. 1537. fo.
  Mag. 16.1.13
*Adagiorum. B, Frobenius, 1538. fo. Pal
  23.6.3.6
Adagiorum chiliades quatuor. B, H. Fro-
  benius, 1539. fo. Mag 11.1.298

Adagiorum opus. L, Seb. Gryphius, 1541.
fo. FL XXV.6.8.2 ·

Adagiorum opus. L, Seb. Gryphius, 1550.
fo. VM 18.C.32

Proverbi, tradotti da Lelio Carani. V,
Giolito, 1550. 8vo. VM 9.C.201

Adagiorum epitome. L, Seb. Gryphius,
1553. 8vo. Mar 5.F.XI.12

Adagia. V, Rabanus, 1554. 4to. Mag 1.6.131

Adagiorum epitome. An, Chr. Plantinus,
1564-66. 8vo, 2 vols. Rice st 14701

Adagia cum animadversionibus Henricie
Stephani. P, M. Sonnius, 1571. 8vo.
Mar 1.00.I.33

Adagia, P. Manutio studio ... ab omnibus
mendis vindicata. Florentiae, Juntas,
1575. fo. BNF B.17.2.51

Adagiorum chiliades. [Francofurti], sumptibus Andreae Wecheli, Claudij Marnij, &
Io. Aubrij, 1599. fo. VM 37.C.5

Adagiorum chiliades. Coloniae Allobrogum,
Petr. Aubertus, sumptibus Caldorianae
societatis, 1612. fo. Mar 5.G.II.1,

Adagiorum chiliades. Hannoviae, typis
Wechelianis, apud haered. Io. Aubrij,
1617. fo. VM 54.T.1

Adagia. Francofurti, sumptibus Joh.
Pressii viduae, 1646. fo. Rice st 11339

Adagiorum epitome. Am, Lud. Elzevirius,
1650. 12mo. Mag 3.8.550, Pal 12.1.1.33,
Mar 1.NN.VIII.50

Adagiorum epitome. Am, ex. off. Elzeviriana, 1663. 12mo. Pal 12.1.34, Mar 1.00.
VIII.56

Adagiorum Collectanea
Veterum max. ins. paroemiarum. i.
adagiorum collectanea. [P], in aed.
Ascensianis, xi kal. julias 1516. 4to.
Gui 5.9.46

Antibarbari
Antibarbarorum liber unus. Argentinae,
Io. Knoblouchium, 1520. 8vo. VM

66.C.211

Apologia contra Lopidem Stunicam
*Apologia ad Stunicae conclusiones, in:
Exmologesis s. modus confitendi [sl, st],
1524. In fine: Mense Ianuario, 1525. 8vo.
Printed with: Exmologesis. VM 78.D.112

Apophthegmata
Apophthegmatum, sive scite dictorum libri
sex. B, in off. Frob. per Hier. Frobennium,
Io. Hervagium et Nic. Episcopium, mense
martio 1531. 4to. Ricc st 2958

Apophthegmatum libri octo. B, in off. Fro-
beniana, 1535. 8vo. VM 21.T.283

Apophthegmatum libri octo. L, Seb.
Gryphius, 1539. 4to. Mag 3.3.352

Apoftemmi cioè motti sententiose in bre-
vità di parole per proposta ... trad. in
rime da S. Fausto da Longiano. V, V.
Vaugris [Valgrisi], 1546. 8vo. Mag
21.7.272, Pal. 12.B.B.5.1.29, Gui 12.10.26,
Mar 1.M.XII.44, VM 67.C.182

Apophthegmatum opus. L, Seb. Gryphius,
1547. 8vo. Mag 3.8.551

Apophthegmatum opus. P, Rob. Stephanus,
1547, cal. Iulii. 8vo. VM 66.D.166

Apophthegmata. L, S. Gryphius, 1548.
16mo. Mar 1.00.VIII.131

Auris Batava (Ex adag. chiliad. IV.
cent. VI)
De Batavis sive Hollandis, in adagio Auris
Batava, in: P. Scriverius, Batavia illustrata.
Lugd. B., Lud. Elz., 1609. 4to. Pal 7.4.3.46

Bellum (Ex adag. chiliad. IV. cent. I)
Bellum. Lovanii, Theod. Martinum, 1517.
4to. Gui 5.9.46[v]

Carmen bucolicum
Bucolicon, cum sch. Alardi Aemstelr.
Coloniae, Hero Alopecius, 1539. 8vo.
VM Misc 2180,5

Civilitate (de) morum puerilium libellus
De civilitate morum puerilium libellus.
Coloniae, Iohannes Gymnicus, 1532.
8vo. Pal 29.2.1.39^V
**De civilitate morum puerilium libellus.
Argentorati, Mylius, 1556. Mag 10.7.41
*De civilitate morum puerilium libellus, et
alia alior. opuscula. Francofurti, 1572.
Mag 3.6.121
De civilitate morum puerilium libellus.
Lugduni Bat., Abr. Comelinus, 1626.
8vo. VM Misc. D 205
*De civilitate morum puerilium libellus.
Coburg, Forkelicij(?), Mag 10.7.40
Liber aureus de civilitate morum pueri-
lium. Hamburgi, Joh. Naumannus,
1659. 8vo. Mag 11.9.118

Colloquia (et *famil. colloquiorum formulae*)
*Colloquiorum formulae. Lovanii, Martinus,
1522. 16mo. Mag 15.9.357
Familiarium colloquiorum opus. Argen-
torati, Christ. Egenolph, 1527. 8vo.
Mag 5.7.16
*Familiarium colloquiorum opus. L, Gry-
phius, 1529. 8vo. Mag 3.3.339
Familiarium colloquiorum opus. L, Gry-
phius, 1538. 8vo. Mag 11.8.168
*I colloqui tradotti in italiano. V, Valgrisi,
1544. Mag 3.3.342 (This vol, which is under-
going restoration, may be the same ed as the
next entry.)
Colloquii famigliari. Tradotti per M. Pietro
Lauro Modonese. V, Vincenzo Vaugris
[Valgrisi], 1545. 8vo. Gui 2.4.44
I ragionamenti overo colloqui famigliari ...
in italiano per Pietro Lauro. V, V. Val-
grisi, 1549. 8vo. Gui 2.4.45, VM 75.C.217
Familiarium colloquiorum opus. B, Nico-
laum Brylinger, 1556. FL Comparetti
XXV.20.1.9
Familiarium colloquiorum opus. Argen-
torati, P. Ledertz, 1619. 8 vo. VM 211.
C.182

Colloquia familiaria. Am, Io. Janssonius,
1628. 24mo. Mag 11.9.52
Colloquia familiaria. Am, Guil. Jz.
Caesius [Blaen], 1629. 24mo.
Ricc st 2549
Colloquia. Lugduni Batavorum, ex off.
Elzeviriana, 1636. 12mo. Pal 12.1.1.36,
Ricc st 2409
Colloquia. Lugduni Batavorum, ex off.
Elzeviriana, 1643. 12mo. Pal 12.1.1.26
Colloquia. Am., Lud. Elzevirius, 1650.
16mo. Mag 3.8.508, Pal 12.1.1.27,
FL II.1.6.32
Les colloques d'Erasme, trad. [par
Chappuzeau]. Leyde, Adr. Vingart,
1653. 12mo. Pal 18.5.1.46
Colloquia. Am, ex off. Elzeviriana, 1655.
12mo. Pal 12.1.1.28
Colloquia familiaria, cum annot. A.
Montani. Am, Jo. Janssonius, 1658. 12 mo.
Mag 11.9.141
Colloquia familiaria, cum notis variorum.
Lugduni Batavorum, Ianson, 1661. 16mo.
Mar 7.00.IX.134
Colloquia. Am, ex. off. Elzeviriana, 1662.
12mo. Mag 21.6.162, Pal 12.1.1.29, Mar 6.D.
XIII.144
Colloquia familiaria. Trajecti ad Rhenum,
Gisb. à Zyll, 1662. 12mo. Mag 11.9.55
Colloquia familiaria, cum notis selectis
variorum, accurante C. Schrevelio. Lugd.
Bat. et Roterod., ex off. Hackiana, 1664.
8vo. Mag 3.3.333, Pal 12.1.3.34, VM 75.C.135
Les entretiens familiers, trad. [par Chappu-
zeau]. Genève, I. Herman Widerhold,
1669. 12mo. Mag 3.8.540, Mar 1.00.IX.56
Colloquia. Am, Dan. Elzevirius, 1677.
16mo. Pal 12.1.1.30
Colloquia. Am, ex off. Elzeviriana, 1679.
12mo. Pal 12.1.1.32
Colloquia familiaria, quibus accedunt Dav.
Constantii notae. Genevae, Sam. de
Tournes, 1681. 8vo. Mag 11.9.56, FL
Bardi B.96, VM 184.C.154

Colloquia familiaria, oder gemeinsame
  Gespräche ... übersetzt durch Fried.
  Romberg. Heidelberg, Rüdiges, 1683.
  8vo, 2 vols. Mag 15.9.354
Colloquia, cum annot. A. Montani. Lip-
  siae, Laur. Sig. Cörnerus, 1684. 12mo.
  Mag 11.9.57
Colloquia cum notis selectis variorum,
  accurante C. Schrevelio. Am, ex typogr.
  Blaviana, 1693. 8vo (677 pp). Mag
  21.5.107
Idem, 784 pp. Pal 12.1.3.35
Colloquia familiaria. Petrus Rabus recen-
  suit. Roterodami, Regn. Leers, 1693.
  8vo. Mag 15.8.379
Colloquia, cum annot. A. Montani. Lip-
  siae, Joh. Christiani Cörneri, Bibliop.,
  Typis Andreae Zeidleri, 1699. 12mo.
  Mag 11.9.59

Concio de puero Jesu
Concio de puero Jesu. Argentorati, Io.
  Hervagius, m. aprili 1524. 8vo. Pal
  29.2.1.39[I]

Conficiendarum epistolarum formula
Brevissima maximeque compendiaria
  conficiendarum epistolarum formula.
  Coloniae, ex off. Conradi Caesaris,
  1521. 4to. VM Misc. 778,13

*De conscribendis epistolis libellus,
sive opus*
Opus de conscribendis epistolis. Coloniae,
  Hero Alopecius, 1522. 8vo. Mag 15.9.357
**Opus de conscribendis epistolis. V, Zop-
  pino, 1526. 8vo. Mag 3.5.79
*Opus de conscribendis epistolis. V, [st],
  1528. 8vo. Mag 3.6.362bis
*Opus de conscribendis epistolis. V, per
  N. Zoppinum, 1529. 8vo. VM 57.D.193
Opus de conscribendis epistolis. Mogun-
  tiae, Georg. Wagnerus, 1556. 8vo.
  Mag 11.9.49

*Opus de conscribendis epistolis. B,
  Oporinus, 1558. Mag 15.9.360

*De constructione octo partium orationis
libellus*
*De octo partium orationis constructione
  libellus. V, per I. Antonium et fratres
  de Sabio, 1521. 8vo: VM Misc. D. 2230
De octo partium orationis constructione
  libellus. V, Greg. de Gregoriis, 1522.
  8vo. VM Misc. 2242,3
*De octo partium orationis constructione
  libellus ... cum Iunii Rabirii commentariis. L, Gryphius, 1540. VM 12.C.172
*De octo partium orationis constructione
  libellus, cum Iunii Rabirii commentariis.
  L, Gryphius, 1543. 16mo. FL Bardi 5.A.39
De octo orationis partium constructione
  libellus, cum commentariis I Rabirii.
  L, Tornaeius, 1557. 8vo. Mag 3.5.7

Consultatio de bello turcico
Consultatio de bello turcis inferendo.
  Lugduni Batavorum, Jo. Maire, 1643.
  12mo. Mag 4.7.149, Gui 5.9.36,[IV] FL Bardi
  IX.2.6.55

De contemptu mundi epistola
De contemptu mundi. Lugduni Batavorum,
  Io. Maire, 1641. 12mo. Mag 4.8.390, Gui
  5.9.36[III], VM 97.C.274

*De duplici copia verborum ac rerum
commentarii*
De duplici copia verborum ac rerum
  commentarii duo. Argentorati, M.
  Schurerius, 1516, mense oct. 4to.
  Mag 11.8.257
De duplici copia verborum. V, Rusconibus,
  1520. Mag 3.3.343
**De duplici copia verborum. V, Zoppino,
  1526. Mag 3.5.79
*De duplici copia verborum. V, [Cominum]
  de Tridino, 1545. Mag 3.3.341
*De duplici copia verborum ... L, Gryphium,

1546. FL B.F.A.VII.608
De duplici copia verborum. Add. comm.
Veltkirchij. B, Brylinger, 1560. 8vo.
Mag 15.9.361a
De duplici copia verborum. Brugis Flandr.,
Hub. Goltzius, 1565, xii kal. aug. 8vo.
Mar 1.NN.XI.107
De duplici copia verborum. Add. comm.
Veltkirchij, Col. Agr., 1577. Mag 11.9.143
De duplici copia verborum. Am, Io. Iansso-
nius, 1632. 8vo. Ricc st 2537
De duplici copia verborum. Am, Io. Iansso-
nius, 1645. 16mo. Mar B.XII.28
De duplici copia verborum. Am, Io. Iansso-
nius, 1655. 12mo. Mag 21.8.26
De duplici copia verborum. Francofurti,
Georg. Müllerus, 1658. 12mo. VM 37.T.241
*De duplici copia verborum. P, 1671. Ricc st
2548

De immensa Dei misericordia concio
De immensa Dei misericordia concio. An,
Mich. (Hillen.) Hoochstra, 1524. 8vo.
Gui 5.9.39
Sermone della grandissima misericordia di
Dio, tradotto per Giov. Ant. Alati
d'Ascoli. Fiorentia, L. Torrentino, 1554.
8vo. Mar 4.A.VI.120
De immensa Dei misericordia. Lugduni
Batavorum, Io. Maire, 1641. 12mo.
Gui 5.9.36^{II}

*Dialogus ciceronianus, s. de optimo
dicendi genere*
*Dialogus cui titulus ciceronianus s. de
optimo genere dicendi. Printed with:
De recta latini graecique sermonis pro-
nuntiatione dialogus. V, Melchiorem
Sessam, 1531. 8vo. Mar 6.D.XII.15,
VM 14.C.198
Dialogus cui titulus ciceronianus ... In
J.C. Scaliger, adversus D. Erasmum
orationes duae. Tolosae Tectosagum,
R. Colomerius, 1621. 4to. Pal 29.3.5.9

Dialogus ciceronianus, sive de optimo
genere dicendi. Lugduni Batavorum, Jo.
Maire, 1643. 12mo. Mag 3.8.541, FL Bardi
IX.4.8.2, Ricc st 2546

*Dialogus de recta latini graecique
sermonis pronuntiatione*
De recta latini graecique sermonis pronuntiatione dialogus. L, Gryphius, 1531.
8vo. Mag 5.8.64
*De recta latini graecique sermonis pronun-
tiatione dialogus. V, Melchiorem Sessam,
1531. 8vo. Mar 6.D.XII.15, VM 14.C.198
De recta latini graecique sermonis pronuntiatione dialogus. B, Frobenius, 1558.
8vo. Mag 11.9.142
De recta latini graecique sermonis pronuntiatione dialogus. Lugduni Batavorum, Io.
Maire, 1643. 12mo. Mag 21.8.27, Ricc st
2540

Ecclesiastes
Ecclesiastae sive de ratione concionandi
libri IV. B, Frobenius, 1535. fo.
Mag 15.1.225
Ecclesiastae sive de ratione concionandi
libri IV. B, 1544. Colophon: B, H. Fro-
benius & N. Episcopius, 1545. 8vo.
Mag 5.8.30

Enchiridion militis christiani
*Enchiridion militis christiani. V, de Gre-
goriis, 1523. Mag 15.9.318, Gui 5.9.42^{II}
Enchiridion, Dalla lingua latina nella vol-
gare tradotto per M. Emilio di Emilij
bresciano, con una sua canzone di peni-
tenza in fine. V, Al insegna de S. Hie-
ronymo [Giacomo de Borgofranco],
1539. Gui 5.9.34, Ricc st 2539
Enchiridion militis christiani. Lugduni
Batavorum, I. Maire, 1641. 12mo.
Mag 11.9.116, Ricc st 2542
Instructio militis christiani. Hamburgi,
Naumann, 1662. 12mo. Mag 11.9.119

Enchiridion militis christiani. Cantabrigiae,
Joh. Hayes. Impensis G. Graves, 1685.
12mo. Mag 15.8.380, Ricc st 9197, VM
95.C.325

Encomium matrimonii
Encomium matrimonii. B, Io. Frobenius,
1518. 4to. Printed with: Encomium
artis medicae. VM Misc. 777,1
Encomium matrimonii et artis medicae.
Moguntiae, Io. Schoeffer, m. aprili 1522.
8vo. VM Misc. 2171,2
Encomium matrimonii. V, Gregorius de
Gregoriis, mense augusto 1526. 8vo.
Printed with: Encomium artis medicae.
VM 166.C.80
Suasoria de ineundo matrimonio. Am, Lud.
Elzevirius, 1638. 12mo. Printed with:
Dom. Baudius, amores. Pal 12.1.2.17

Encomium medicinae
Encomium artis medicae. B, Io. Frobenius,
1518. 4to. Printed with: Encomium
matrimonii. VM Misc. 777,1
Encomium artis medicae. Norimbergae, I.
Petreius, 1525. 8vo. Printed with: Paulus
Aegineta, Praecepta salutaria. VM Misc.
1222,2
*Encomium artis medicae. V, Gregorius de
Gregoriis, mense augusto 1526. 8vo.
Printed with: Encomium matrimonii.
VM 166.C.80
Encomium medicinae. Roterodami, A.
Leers, 1644. 8vo. Printed with: Joh.
Beverovicius, Epistolicae quaestiones.
BNF Targioni-Tozzetti Misc. 109.7

Epigrammata
Epigrammata. B, Io. Frobenius, mense
dec. 1518. 4to. VM Misc. 801,1

Epistola ad Franciscum I
Gravissima epistola ad christ. Galliarum

regem Franciscum I. Irenopoli, 1674.
8vo. Mag 3.8.542

*Epistola ad archiepisc. ac cardinalem
Moguntinum*
*Presbyteri theologi ad R. cardinalem
Moguntinum Epistola, in qua de Luthero
qui ipse sentiat, declarat: seguitur Epistola Erasmi ad Lutherum. Lovanii, 1519.
4to. Gui 2.3.60$^{2/I}$

Epistola ad P. Mosellanum
*Epistola quaedam ad P. Mosellanum.
[Lipsiae, 1519]. 4to. Gui 5.9.48

Epistola quid de oscuris sentiat
Epistola quid de oscuris sentiat. Coloniae,
Quentell, 1518. 4to. Printed with:
Lamentationes obscurorum virorum.
Ricc st 9197

Epistolae
Autoriarum selectarum aliquot episto-
larum Erasmi Roterodami. Argentorati,
Schurerius, 1519. 4to. Pal 12.1.2.41
Farrago nova epistolarum. B, Io. Frobenius,
mense oct. 1519. fo. Lau 20328/2
Auctarium selectarum epistolarum. B, Io.
Frobenius, mense martio, 1519. 4to.
Pal F.5.1.32
Epistolae ... ad diversos & aliquot aliorum
ad illum. B, Io. Frobenius, 1521, pridie
cal. sept. fo. Mag 1.5.84
Auctarium select. epistolarum. V, De
Gregoriis, 1524. 8vo. Mag 15.9.358^a,
VM Misc. 2242,2
Epistolae familiares. B, B. Westhemerus,
1541. 8vo. Mag 15.9.369
Epistolae familiares. B, B. Westhemerus,
1546. 8vo. Mag 15.9.359^a
Epistolae. Lugduni Batavorum, Io. Maire,
1642. 12mo. Printed with: Erasmi Vita.
Ricc st 2547

26

Epistolarum libri XXXI. London, M.
Flesher & R. Young, 1642. fo, 2 vols.
Mag 5.1.62, Pal 12.1.6.10, VM 167.C.16-17

Evangelio (de novo)
De novo evangelio, novisque evangelistis
iudicium. Ingolstadii, A. Sartorius, 1611.
4to. Ricc st 9594

Exmologesis sive modus confitendi
*Exmologesis sive modus confitendi.
[sl, st] , 1524. In fine: 1525. 8vo.
Mag 15.9.358^c, VM 78.D.112

*Explanatio symboli apostolorum,
s. catechismus*
Explicatio in symbolum apostol. & deca-
logum. Lugduni Batavorum, I. Maire,
1641. 12mo. Mag 4.8.385

Expostulatio Jesu cum homine
Expostulatio Iesu cum homine suapte
culpa pereunte. Argentorati, Io. Hero-
vagius, 1524. 8vo. Printed with:
Deratione studii. Pal 29.2.1.39^I

Flores ex scriptis Erasmi collectae
Flores una cum septem centuriis sapient.
dictor. collecti opera D. Sim. Partlicii de
Spitsberg. Am, Io. Ianssonius, 1640.
16mo. Pal 29.1.1.39

Hyperaspistes
Hyperaspistes diatribae adversus servum
arbitrium Martini Lutheri. B, Io. Frobenius, 1526. 8vo. Gui 5.9.40
*Hyperaspistes diatribae adversus servum
arbitrium Martini Lutheri. [sl, st] , 1526.
8vo. VM Misc. 2180,2

Institutio christiani matrimonii
Christiani matrimonii institutio. [Coloniae,
Eucharis. Cervicornus, 1525]. 24mo.
VM Ar. VIII. b. 29 (Biblioteca Erasmiana

E 1246?)
Ordinatione del matrimonio de christiani
tradotta [Pietro Rocca]. V, per Francesco Rocca & Fratelli. 1550. 8vo.
Gui 23.3.11, VM 218.C.149

Institutio principis christiani
Institutio principis christiani, et alia
opuscula. Lovanii, Martinus, 1516. 4to.
Mag 2.6.131
Institutio principis christiani saluberrimus
referta praeceptis. V, Aldus, sept. 1518.
8vo. Printed with: Querela pacis. VM
Aldine 579, Lau Delciana 365
Institutio principis christiani. Coloniae,
Euch. Cervicornus, 1525, mense
januario. 8vo. VM Ar.VIII.b.29^{3a}
*Institutione del Principe Christiano ...
tradotta a la lingua volgare. V, Marcolini,
1539. 8vo. VM 218.C.148; 60.D.206;
77.C.199
Institutio principis christiani. Lugduni
Batavorum, A. Cloucquius, 1628. 32mo.
Pal 29.1.0.27
Institutio principis christiani. Lugduni
Batavorum, Io. Maire, 1641. 12mo.
Gui 5.9.36^I, Ricc st 2543, Gui 5.9.37^{II}.

Institutum hominis christiani
Institutum hominis christiani carmine pro
pueris. V, Greg. de Gregoriis, 1522. 8vo.
BNF 3.L.3.343

Lingua
*Lingua opus novum, et hisce temporibus
aptissimum. An, Hillenius, 1525. 8vo.
Gui 5.9.39^I
Lingua. [sl, st] , 1526. Mag 3.3.338
Lingua. Lugduni Batavorum, Andr.
Cloucquius, 1624. Typis Petri Mulleri.
24mo. Mar 1.AA.X.20

Modus orandi Deum
Modus orandi Deum. Lugduni Batavorum,
  Io. Maire, 1641. 12mo. Mag 4.8.390

Moriae encomium, s. stultitiae laus
Opusculum, cui titulus est Moria, id est,
  sultitia. V, Aldus, mense Augusto, 1515.
  8vo. Lau Delciana 916
Moriae encomium declamatio. B, Io. Fro-
  benius, 1519. 4to. Printed with: L.A.
  Seneca, Ludus de morte Claudii Caesaris,
  c. notis B. Rhen. VM Rari 670-674
Opusculum, cui titulus est Moria, id est
  Stultitia ... V, in aedibus Georgij de
  Rusconibus ... et Nicolai Zoppini atque
  Vincentii sociorum impensis, 1520. die
  xxiii Martii. Gui 5.9.42^{III}, Mar 6.D.XII.78,
  VM 221.C.115
La moria d'Erasmo in volgare tradotta
  [da A. Pellegrini]. V, 1539. 8vo.
  VM 90.C.197
Moriae encomium cum comm. G. Listrii.
  B, Frobenius, 1540. 8vo. Mag 15.8.378
Moriae encomium. B, Hier. Frobenius et
  Nic. Episcopius, 1551. 8vo. Mag 11.8.187.1,
  VM 21.T.291
Encomium moriae. Lugduni Batavorum,
  Jac. Marcus, 1617. 12mo. Mag 11.9.115,
  VM 222.C.127
Encomium moriae. Lugduni Batavorum, A.
  Cloucquius. Typis P. Mulleri, 1624. 32mo.
  VM 41.D.218
*Encomium moriae. Editio quinta. Lugduni
  Batavorum, Marcus, 1627. VM 396.D.411
Moriae encomium. Lugduni Batavorum,
  Io. Maire, 1648. 12mo. Mag 3.8.539
Μωριας ἐγχωμιον. Stultitiae laus cum
  comment. G. Listrii. B, typis Genathianis,
  1676. 8vo. Mag 3.3.99, Pal D.8.6.4. Gui 5.9.45,
  Mar 6.J.IX.77, VM 61.C.187
Μωριας ἔγχωμιον. Stultitiae laus. Am,
  Henr. Wetstenius, 1685. 12mo. Mar
  7.C.VII.22

Encomium moriae, aus dem Latein in
  Teutsch von S.F.V.W. [Franck van
  Wörd]. s.l., 1696. 12mo. Mag 9.7.155

De morte declamatio
De morte declamatio. V, Aldus, mense
  sept. 1518. 8vo. Printed with: Querela
  pacis. VM Aldine 579, Lau Delciana 365

Opera omnia
Opera omnia ... in decem tomos distincta.
  Lugduni Batavorum, P. vander Aa,
  1703-1706. fo. 10 vols in 11. Mag 21.-23,
  Pal 1.4.6.3, FL Filos. XV.9, Mar 1.N.II.3,
  Ricc st 11146, VM 16.C.1-10, and 55.D.9-18

Opuscula aliquot
Opuscula. Lugduni Batavorum, 1641.
  12mo. Mar 6.A.XIII.138

Oratio de virtute amplectenda
Oratio de virtute amplectenda. Lugduni
  Batavorum, Io. Maire, 1641. 18mo.
  Mag 3.8.846, 24mo. Mag 11.9.54

Panegyricus ad Philippum Austriae ducem
Panegyricus gratulatoris de felici ex His-
  pania reditu, ad ill. principem Philippum
  Maximiliani filium. Printed with: Que-
  rela pacis. V, Aldus, sept. 1518. 8vo.
  VM Aldine 579, Lau Delciana 365
*Panegyricus ad Philippum. In Rerum
  Germanicarum editi ex Bibliotheca
  Freheri. Francofurti, 1624. Ricc st 10625

Parabolae sive similia
Parabolae sive similia. Argentorati, Matt.
  Schurerius, mense iulio, 1518. 4to.
  BNF 22.B.6.35
Parabolae sive similia. V, G. de Gregoriis,
  1522, 8vo. VM Misc. D.2232

Paraphrasis in acta apostolorum
Paraphrasis in acta apostolorum. B, Io.

Frobenius, 1524. fo. Mag 11.1.214
Paraphrasis in acta apostolorum. L,
  Gryphius, 1544. 8vo. Gui 19.2.6

Paraphrasis in epistolas Pauli
Paraphrases in omnes epistolas Pauli.
  Lutetiae, st, 1523. 12mo. Mag 4.8.546

*Paraphrasis in universas epistolas
apostolorum (s. canonicas)*
In epistolas apostolicas paraphrasis. L,
  Gryphius, 1544. 8vo. Gui 19.2.6

*Paraphrasis in evangelium secundum
Joannem*
In evangelium secundum Joannem.
  B, Frobenius, 1523. fo. Mag 11.1.214
Paraphrasis in evangelium Joannis. L,
  Gryphius, 1544. 8vo. Gui 19.2.6

Paraphrasis in evangelium Lucae
in evangelium Lucae paraphrasis. L,
  Gryphius, 1544. 8vo. Gui 19.2.6

Paraphrasis in evangelium Marci
In evangelium Marci paraphrasis.
  B, Frobenius, 1523. fo. Mag 11.1.214
In evangelium Marci paraphrasis. L,
  Gryphius, 1544. 8vo. Gui 19.2.6

Paraphrasis in evangelium Matthaei
In evangelium Matthaei paraphrasis.
  L, Gryphius, 1544. 8vo. Gui 19.2.6
*Espositione letterale del testo di Matteo
  evangelista, di M. Bernardin Tomitano.
  V, Gio. dal Griffio, 1547. 8vo. Gui 11.7.56

Paraphrasis in quatuor Evangelia
Paraphrasis sive enarratio in epistolas et
  evangelia. Coloniae, haer. Arn. Birck-
  manni, 1555. 8vo. VM 150.C.221

Paraphrasis in elegantias Laur. Vallae
Paraphrasis luculenta iuxta ac brevis in

elegantiarum libros Laur. Vallae. P, Rob.
  Stephanus, 1531, vii. cal. julii. 8vo.
  Mag 5.6.13
Paraphrasis luculenta iuxta ac brevis in
  elegantiarum libros Laur. Vallae. L,
  Gryphius, 1543. 8vo. FL Bardi 5.A.39
Paraphrasis in elegantiarum libros
  Laurentii Vallae. L, Th. Paganus, 1551.
  8vo. Mag 21.7.140

Peregrinatio apostolorum Petri et Pauli
Peregrinatio apostolorum Petri et Pauli,
  cum ratione temporum. L, Gryphium,
  1542. 8vo. Gui 19.2.6

Preparatione (de) ad mortem liber
De preparatione ad mortem liber. P, Chr.
  Wechelus, 1534. 8vo. Mar Misc. 447.1
't Handt-boeckjen van der voorbereydingh
  tot de doodt. Am, Dav. van Wesel. Gedr.
  by Baldus de Wild', 1649. 12mo.
  Mag 9.7.440

Precatio dominica
Precatio dominica in septem portiones
  distributa. B, Frobenius, 1523. 8vo.
  BNF 22.B.8
Precatio dominica. Lugduni Batavorum,
  Io. Maire, 1641. 12mo. Mag 15.8.88

*Psalmi (Enarrationes s. comment.
in psalmos)*
*Paraphrasis in tertium psalmum: Domine
  quid multiplicati. [sl, st], 1524. In fine:
  1525. 8vo. Printed with: Exmologesis.
  VM 78.D.112
Enarratio in psalmum I. Beatus vir.
  Lugduni Batavorum, Io. Maire, 1644.
  12mo. Mar 6.G.XIII.59[1]
Enarratio triplex in psalm. XXII. Lugduni
  Batavorum, Io. Maire, 1645. 12mo.
  Mag 4.7.553, Mar 6.G.XIII.59[2]
Enarratio ... in psalmum XXXIV. Lugduni
  Batavorum, Io. Maire, 1652. 12mo.

Mag 6.G.XIII.59[3]
Concionalis interpretatio ... in psalm.
 LXXXVI. Lugduni Batavorum. I. Maire,
 1652. 12mo. Mag 6.G.XIII.59[4]

Pueris (de) liberaliter instituendis libellus
Libellus novus et elegans de pueris statim
 ac liberaliter instituendis. Argentorati,
 Chr. Egenolphus, 1529. 8vo. Pal 29.2.1.
 39[III]
Della institutione de fanciulli ... tradotto
 per M. Stephano Penello ad istantia di ...
 Madonna Perinetta Grimaldi. V, Giolito,
 1545. 8vo. VM 192.D.419
Della institutione de fanciulii ... tradotto
 per M. Stephano Penello ad istantia di ...
 Madonna Perinetta Grimaldi. V, Giolito,
 1547. 8vo. Gui 2.4.43
De pueris statim ac liberaliter instituendis
 libellus. L, Ant. Vincentius, 1551. 8vo.
 Gui 5.9.41

Querela pacis
Querela pacis undique gentium ejectae
 profligataeque. V, Aldus, Sept. 1518.
 8vo. VM Aldine 579, Lau Delciana 365
Querela pacis. L, Gryphius, 1529. 8vo.
 Mag 5.8.64

Ratio verae theologiae
Ratio seu methodus compendio perve-
 niendi ad veram theologiam. Argumen-
 tum in omnes epistolas apostolorum
 perendum copiosus explicata Theodo-
 ricus. [sl] , Martinus Alustensis, 1518.
 4to. Gui 5.9.46[I].
Ratio seu methodus compendio perve-
 niendi ad veram theologiam. V, de
 Gregoriis, 1522. 8vo. Mag 15.9.386,
 Gui 5.9.42[I]

De ratione studii libellus
De ratione studii ac legendi interpretan-
 dique auctores libellus. Argentorati, Io.

Hervagius, 1524. 8vo. Printed with:
 Concio de puero Iesu. Pal 29.2.1.39[I]

*Responsio (de fratres Germaniae
inferioris) ad epistolam apologeticam
incerto autore proditam*
Responsio ad epistolam apologeticam
 incerto autore proditam, nisi quod
 titulus, forte fictus, habebat per minis-
 tros verbi, ecclesiae Argentoratensis.
 Freiburg im Breisgau, Fab. Emmeus,
 1530. 8vo. FL Comparetti VI 1.1.26

*Responsio ad epistolam paraeneticam
Alberti Pii*
Responsio ad epistolam paraeneticam
 Alb. Pii Carporum principis. B, Frobe-
 nius, 1529, mense martio. 4to.
 VM 154.C.98.2

*Responsio adversus febricitantis
cujusdam libellum*
Adversus febricitantis cuiusdam libellum
 responsio. B, Io. Frobenius, mense
 martio 1529. 8vo. Pal 29.2.1.42[IV]

Scarabeus (Ex. adag. chil. III, cent. VII)
Scarabeus. Lovanii, Th. Martinus Alost.,
 mense sept 1517. 4to. Gui 5.9.46[III]

*Sileni Alcibiadis (Ex adag. chiliad. III,
cent. III)*
Sileni Alcibiadis, cum scholiis Io. Frobenii.
 Lovanii, Th. Martinus, mense oct. 1517.
 4to. Gui 5.9.46[IV]

*Spongia adversus aspergines Hutteni, s.
Purgatio ad expostulationem Ulr. Hutteni*
Spongia adversus aspergines Hutteni. B,
 Frobenius, 1523, mense sept. 8vo.
 VM Misc. 2180,3
Spongia adversus aspergines Hutteni. B,
 Frobenius, 1524. 4to. Mag 15.9.358d

30

Virginis et martyris comparatio
Virginis et martyris comparatio. An, Mich.
  Hellenius, 1524. 8vo. Gui 5.9.39
Il paragone della virgine e del martire ...
  tradotto per Ludovico Domenichi.
  Fiorenza, Lorenzo Torrentino, 1554.
  8vo. Mag 15.9.343ᵃ, VM Misc. 2149,2

Vita Erasmi ex ipsius manu repraesentata
Vita Des. Erasmi Rot. ex ipsius manu
  fideliter repraesentata ... edidit. G.F.P.N.
  Merula, Lugduni Batavorum, Th. Basson,
  1607. 4to. Pal 3.2.29
Magni Des. Erasmi Rot. vita; partim ab
  ipsomet Erasmo, partim ab amicis ...
  descripta. Lugduni Batavorum, Maire,
  1642. 12mo. FL Comparetti VI.8.2.21,
  Ricc st 2547
Magni Des. Erasmi Rot. vita; partim ab
  ipsomet Erasmo, partim ab amicis ...
  descripta. Lugduni Batavorum, Maire,
  1649. 12mo. Mag 15.9.381

AUTHORS PUBLISHED,
TRANSLATED, OR ANNOTATED
BY ERASMUS

Dᵘˢ *Ambrosius, episcopus Mediolanensis*
Opera omnia, edid. Erasmus. B, Frobenius,
  1555. Fo, 5 vols. Pal 23.6.3.16
Opera omnia, primum per Erasmum
  castigata. B, Eus. Episcopius, et haer.
  Nic. Episcopii, 1567. fo, 5 vols.
  Ricc st 4354

Dion. Cato
Disticha moralia, cum scholiis Erasmi. V,
  Greg. de Gregoriis, die 28 martii 1522.
  8vo. VM Misc. D.2231
Disticha moralia. Am, Io. Janssonius,
  1646. 8vo. Pal E.99.36, Ricc st 12595

M.T. Cicero
*Officis, De Amicitia, De Senectute, Para-
  doxa et De Somnio Scipionis cum
  Erasmi annotationibus. V, Apud
  Cominum de Tridino Montisferrati,
  1545. VM 291.C.41
Officiorum libri III ... Acc. Erasmi
  scholia. V, Aldus, 1548. fo. VM 28.D.265

Q. Curtius Rufus
Quintus Curtius de rebus gestis Alexandri
  Magni regis Macedonum, cum annot.
  Erasmi. Argentorati, Schurerius, mense
  junio 1518. fo. BNF 22.B.3.15
Quintus Curtius de rebus gestis Alexandri
  Magni regis Macedonum, cum annot.
  Erasmi. B, Henricpetri, 1556. 8vo.
  VM 77.D.103

Euripides
Euripidis Hecuba et Iphigenia: latinae
  factae Erasmo Rot. interprete. V, Aldus,
  mense dec. 1507. 8vo. BNF Nencini Ald.
  1.1.25, VM 394.D.271
Euripidis Hecuba et Iphigenia: latinae
  factae Erasmo Rot. interprete. B,
  Frobenius, mense febr. 1524. 8vo.
  VM 113.D.143

Claudius Galenus
De optimo docendi genere liber, Erasmo
  interpr. In: Sextus Empiricus, Pyrrho-
  niarum hypotyposeon lib. III, interpr.
  H. Stephano. [P], H. Stephanus, 1562.
  8vo. Ricc st 12653

Dᵘˢ *Hieronymus Stridonensis*
Omnes lucubrationes, per Eras. digestae.
  B, ex off. Frobenius 1565. fo.
  Pal 23.4.6.2ᵛⁱⁱ

Historiae Augustae scriptores
Historiae Augustae scriptores ex recognitione D. Erasmi. C. Suetonius Tranq.,

Dio Cassius, Aelius Spartianus, etc. B,
Hier. Frob. et N. Episc., m. julio 1533.
fo. Ricc st 10546
Vitae Caesarum cum adnotationibus Des.
Erasmi, et Baptistae Egnatii, accesserunt
Velleii Paterculi Libri II. B, 1546. fo.
Ricc 10529

D^us Irenaeus, episcopus Lugduenesis
Divi Irenaei opus in quinque libros digestum
in quibus retegit veterum haereseon opiniones ex codicum collat. emend. opera
D. Erasmi. B, H. Frobenius [et Ioh.
Hervagius], 1528. fo. Ricc st 4106
Divi Irenaei opus in quinque libros
digestum in quibus retegit veterum
haereseon opiniones ex codicum collat.
emend. opera D. Erasmi. B, Frobenius,
1548. fo. Ricc st 4107

D^us Joannes Chrysostomus
Missa graecolatina, Erasmo interprete.
P., Wechel, 1537. 8vo. Mag 22.6.110[1]
*Commentarium in Acta Apostolorum ...
Eras. Roterodamo interprete. P, J.
Roigny, 1545. 8vo. Lau 10.T.7.23

Flavius Josephus
Opera (latine) interpr. Ruffino presb. De
insigni Machabaeorum martyrio liber,
castig. ab Erasmo. Coloniae, Euch.
Cervicornus impendio Godefridi Hit-
torpii, 1524, cal. febr. fo. Ricc st 5736
Opera quae extant, nempe ... de Machabeis
... lib. cum paraphrasi Erasmi. Aureliae
Allobr., P. de la Roviere, 1611. fo.
Ricc st 4658

Libanius sophista
Declamationes tres, Erasmo interpr. B,
[A. Cratander], 1529. 8vo. Printed
with: Dictys Cretensis, de bello Tro-
jano libri VI. VM 116.D.211

Lucianus Samosatensis
Luciani opuscula. Erasmo (et Moro) interpr.
V, Aldus, mense maio 1516. 8vo.
VM Aldine 530
Opuscula, Erasmo interprete. Florentiae,
her. Ph. Juntae, m. jul. 1519. 8vo.
VM 224.D.226

P. Ovidius Naso
Commentarius Erasmi Rot. in Nucem
Ovidij. B, Io. Frobenius, 1524. 8vo.
Mag 3.4.238

M. Accius Plautus
*Elegantiarum e Plauto et Terentio libri
II. P. Syri mimorum et sententiarum ex
poetis similium lib. I, cum expositionibus
D. Erasmi et G. Fabricii. Lipsiae, [st],
1563. 16mo. Mag. 11.9.50

Aurelius Prudentius Clemens
Aurelii Prudentii Clementis ... Psycho-
machia ... Item Commentarius Erasmi
Roterodami in duos hymnos. B, per
Henricum Petrum, mense augusto anno
1540. VM 166.D.207

Luc. Ann. Seneca
Opera per D. Erasmum emendata. B, Hier.
Frobenius et Io. Hervagius, m. martio
1529. fo. VM 218.C.33
Ad Lucilium epistolarum liber ... Erasmi
annotationibus illustr. Excudebat Iac.
Foillet, 1607. 8vo. FL S.R.3.28 (vol 1)
Opera (cum notis Eras.). P, Chevalier,
1613. fo. Ricc st 9999
Flores s. sententiae insigniores excerptae
per D. Erasmum. Am, Lud. Elzevirius,
1642. 12mo. Pal E.B.2.C.17, transferred to
Elz. 152; FL Bardi B 226, Ricc st 2416

32

C. Suetonius Tranq.

XII Caesares ... Annotationes Erasmi in
Suetonium, Eutropium, & Paulum Dia-
conum per literarum ordinem. V, Aldus,
mense maio 1521. 8vo. Pal E.12.5.1

*Duodecim Caesares ex Erasmi recognitione.
L, 1541. 8vo. VM 112.D.187

Duodecim Caesares ex Erasmi recognitione.
B, Henricpetri, mense martio 1542. 8vo.
VM 116.D.237

*Duodecim Caesares ex Erasmi recognitione.
L, 1562. VM 200.C.198-200

*Opera ... cum adnotationibus ... Des.
Erasmi. L, 1593. Ricc st 16598

C. Suetonii Tranq. XII Caesares cum ...
Erasmi ... annotat. P, S. Cramoisy, 1610.
fo. VM 132.D.6, Ricc st 10528

P. Terentius Afer

Terentii comoediae, c. scholiis ex Donati,
Asperi, et Cornuti commentarijs decerp-
tis ... Indicata sunt carminum genera ...
studio et opera D. Erasmi. B., Hier. Frobenius et Nic. Episcop., mense martio
1532. fo. VM 43.D.265

*Terentii comoediae, cum argumentis Donati
et versuum generibus per Erasmum. V,
1536. fo. VM 388.D.60

Novum Testamentum. Editiones Erasmicae

**Novum testamentum ab Erasmo recogni-
tum. Gr. & Lat. [sl, st], 1522. Mag 3.--.296

In Novum Testamentum annotationes ab
ipso autore iam quintum recognitae. B,
in off. Froben., 1535. fo. (784 pp).
VM 131.C.2

In novum testamentum Annotationes. B,
H. Frobenius et Episcopius, 1542. fo.
Mag 2.1.182

Novum Testamentum ab Erasmo recog-
nitum (Gr. & Lat). B, N. Bryling., 1553.
8vo. Gui 4.10.22

Novum Testamentum ab Erasmo recog-

nitum (Lat.). B, H. Frobenius et N.
Episcopius, 1555. fo. Mag 11.--.143

Novum Testamentum ab Erasmo recog-
nitum (Gr. & Lat.). B, 1570. fo, 2 vols.
Mag 11.--.4

Novum Testamentum ex versione Erasmi
(Lat.) Biblia. An, I. Keerbergius, 1616.
fo. Gui 4.4.14

Xenophon

Xenophontis Hieron sive Tyrannus, D.
Erasmo interprete. In: Xenophon,
opera. B, Cratander, 1534. fo.
VM 387.D.35

*Xenophontis Hieron sive Tyrannus,
D. Erasmo interprete. In: Xenophon,
opera. L, [st], 1551. VM 222.C.123

Xenophontis Hieron sive Tyrannus, D.
Erasmo interprete. In: Xenophon,
opera. [P], H. Stephanus, 1561. fo.
Mag 1.4.191, Pal E.3.10.9

Xenophontis Hieron sive Tyrannus, D.
Erasmo interprete. In: Xenophon,
opera. H. Stephanus, 1581. fo.
VM 131.D.18

ERASMI ROTHERODAMI PROVERBIORVM CHILIADES
TRES, ET TOTIDEM CENTVRIAE, ADDITIS QVI,
BVSDAM REBVS OPTIMIS NOVITER EXCVS,
SAE PLVRIMISQVE IN LOCIS DILIGEN,
TISSIME CASTIGATAE.

Lectori Sal.

Habes studiose Lector adagiorū tria milia fere supra trecēta, Habes Annotatio,
nes uarias, acutas, eruditas, Nam et plurima auctorū loca ignorata hactenus,
et multas explicationes Ciceronis ad Atticū inuenies. Ex Homero autem,
Aristophane, Euripide, aliis'q poetis grxcorū prope uersuū decēmilia
in latinitatem uersa. Ex Platone, Luciano, Demosthene, cxteris'q id
genus Oratoribus magnā interp̄tationum Syluam. Physicas
etiam et Mathematicas quxstiones aliquot ingeniose et
prudenter excussas. Tū cōmoda admodū diuerticula,
Ė quibus incertū est plus'ne utilitatis, an uolu,
ptatis mutueris. Si cum re ipsa cōgrediare,
dices multa pollicitum, plura prx,
stisse, Quando hic unus Liber
tibi pro iusta Biblio,
theca esse po
test.

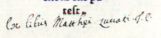

Figure 1
Proverbiorum chiliades (Ferrara: Bondenus 1514)
see page 20 column 2

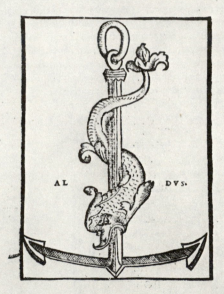

ERASMI ROTERO
DAMI ADAGIORVM CHILIADES QVA
TVOR, CENTVRIAEQVE TOTI
DEM: QVIBVS ETIAM QVIN
TA ADDITVR IM.
PERFECTA.

AL DVS.

Figure 2
Adagiorum chiliades (Venice: Aldus 1520)
see page 20 column 2

Figure 5
Encomium matrimonii
(Venice: Gregorius 1526)
see page 25 column 1

Figure 3
De octo partium orationis
(Venice: Antonium 1521)
see page 23 column 2

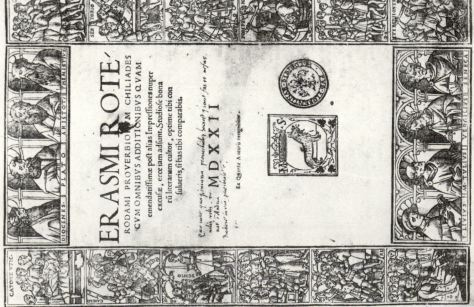

Figure 4
Proverbiorum seu adagiorum chiliades (Venice: Sessa 1522)
see page 20 column 2

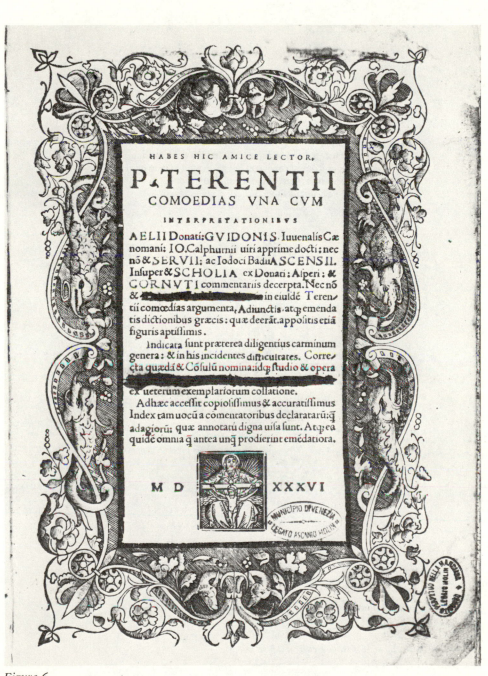

Figure 6
Terentii comoediae, cum argumentis Donati et versuum generibus per Erasmum
(Venice 1536) Expurgated title page. See page 32 column 1

Figure 7
Adagiorum chiliades (Basel: Froben 1538)
see page 20 column 2

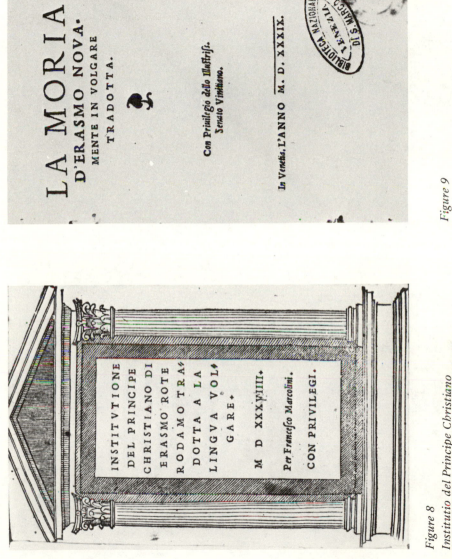

Figure 9
La moria d'Erasmo (Venice 1539)
see page 27 column 1

Figure 8
Institutio del Principe Christiano
(Venice: Marcolini 1539)
see page 26 column 2

DELLA INSTI-
TVTIONE DE FAN-
CIVLLI COME DI BVONA
hora si debbono ammaestrare alla
virtu & alle lettere.
LIBRO DI ERASMO ROTERODAMO,
Tradotto in lingua volgare,
PER M. STEPHANO PENELLO.
AD INSTANZA DELLA MOLTO
MAGNIFICA MADONNA PE-
RINETTA GRIMALDI.
Con Gratia & Priuilegio.

In Vinegia Appresso Gabriel
Giolito de Ferrari.
M D X L V.

Figure 10
Della institutione de fanciulli
(Venice: Giolito 1545)
see page 29 column 1

I RAGIONAMENTI, OVERO
COLLOQVI
FAMIGLIARI
DI DESIDERIO ERASMO
ROTERODAMO:
Di Latino in uolgare già tradotti, ma hora in
tanti luoghi racconci, non solo intorno la
lingua, ma etiandio intorno i sensi, che
piu tosto ritradotti, che racconci
si possono dire.
IN VINEGIA,
NELLA BOTTEGA D'ERASMO
DI VINCENZO VALGRISI:
M. D. XLIX.

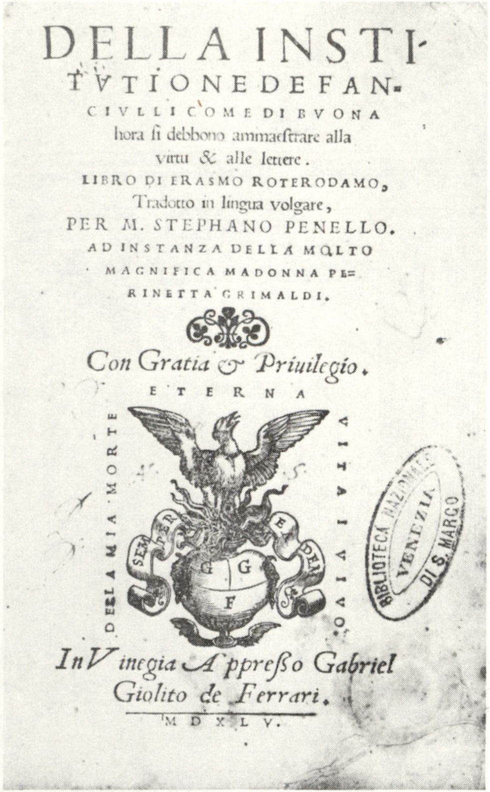

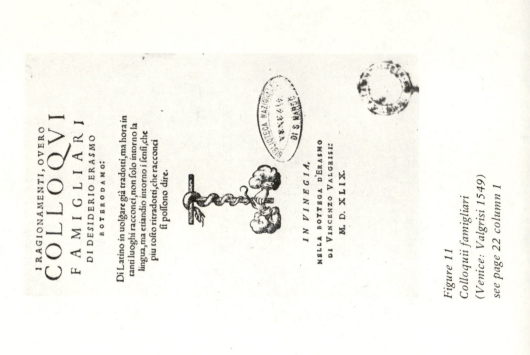

Figure 11
Colloquii famigliari
(Venice: Valgrisi 1549)
see page 22 column 1

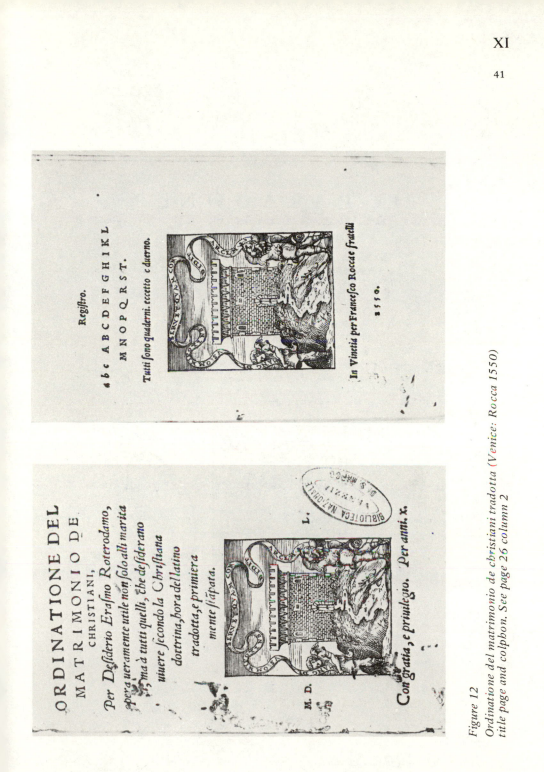

Figure 12
Ordinatione del matrimonio de christiani tradotta (Venice: Rocca 1550)
title page and colphon. See page 26 column 2

Figure 13
Il paragone della virgine e del martire
(Florence: Torrentino 1554)
title page. See page 30 column 1

XII

THE DESTRUCTION OF
HEBREW BOOKS IN VENICE, 1568

The Hebrew press of Venice enormously enriched Jewish learning
and religious life in the sixteenth century. The Hebrew printers did
not achieve their goals easily, however, for the Venetian government twice destroyed large quantities of Hebrew books. Scholars
are aware of the burning of the Talmud in 1553, but perhaps do
not know that the Venetian government again confiscated and
burned thousands of Hebrew books in 1568. This article will
describe the events of 1568, and how the Hebrew publishers then
thwarted Venetian restrictions through smuggling in the early
1570s.[1]

The Venetian Hebrew press probably led Europe both in the
quantity and the significance of its publications. Daniel Bomberg
(c. 1483–1553), a Christian from Antwerp with great sympathy
for Jewish learning, was the key figure.[2] From its establishment
in 1516, his press issued as many as two hundred printings, including the complete Talmud between 1519 and 1523, a landmark
of Hebrew publishing. When Bomberg slowed his pace and ceased
to publish in 1549, others partially took his place. Two presses
carrying patrician names dominated Hebrew printing at mid-

[1] This article identifies the Hebrew titles involved and offers an expanded
account of an incident described briefly in Paul F. Grendler, *The Roman
Inquisition and the Venetian Press, 1540–1605* (Princeton, N.J.: Princeton Uni-
versity Press, 1977), pp. 141–45. I am especially grateful to Professor Frank
Talmage of the Department of Near Eastern Studies of the University of
Toronto; without his help in identifying Hebrew titles, this article would
not have been possible. Fellowships from the American Council of Learned
Societies and the Canada Council assisted the research.

[2] Alfredo Cioni, "Daniel Bomberg," *Dizionario biografico degli italiani*, Vol.
11 (Rome, 1969), pp. 382–87.

104

century: that of Marc'Antonio Giustiniani, who published about eighty-five titles between 1545 and 1553, and Alvise Bragadino who printed about fifteen titles between 1550 and 1553. Giovanni de' Farri e fratelli, Francesco Brucioli, and Me'ir Parenzo, who printed at least ten titles between 1545 and 1552, joined them.[3]

The Venetian Republic demonstrated no more sympathy for the Jews than other Italian states. It distinguished between Levantine Jews, who had for some time lived and enjoyed trading privileges in the maritime empire, and German or local Jews, many of whom had come from other Italian cities. The fugitives from Iberian persecution (called Ponentine or Western Jews) comprised a third group; these most often suffered from Venetian hostility toward Jews. In 1516, the Venetian government enclosed Jews living in the city into a ghetto, and forced them to pay large sums of money for the permission (*condotta*) to remain in Venice for a specified term of years.[4] Hostility toward the Jews mounted in the 1540s. The government did little to punish the perpetrators of anti-Jewish riots on the mainland; it came close to expelling Marranos in 1550, and tightened the fiscal pressure on the local community.[5]

The Venetian patricians viewed the Hebrew press in the same way that they did the Jews as a whole: with suspicion tempered by grudging toleration in exchange for financial compensation. When in October 1525 Bomberg offered 100 ducats for an extension of his permission to print Hebrew books, the Senate refused

---

[3] David W. Amram, *The Makers of Hebrew Books in Italy. Being Chapters in the History of the Hebrew Printing Press* (Philadelphia, 1909; rpt. London, 1963), pp. 146–224; Joshua Bloch, "Venetian Printers of Hebrew Books," *Bulletin of the New York Public Library*, 36 (1932), pp. 71–92; Cecil Roth, *History of the Jews in Venice* (Philadelphia, 1930), pp. 245–55; and *The History of the Jews in Italy* (Philadelphia, 1946), pp. 225–26; Horatio F. Brown, *The Venetian Printing Press 1469–1800. An historical study based upon documents for the most part hitherto unpublished* (London, 1891; rpt. Amsterdam, 1969), pp. 105–06.

[4] Frederic C. Lane, *Venice: A Maritime Republic* (Baltimore and London, 1973), pp. 300–04; Roth, *Jews in Venice*, pp. 1–71, 105–211.

[5] Brian Pullan, *Rich and Poor in Renaissance Venice. The Social Institutions of a Catholic State, to 1620* (Cambridge, Mass., 1971), pp. 510–37.

him on the ground that his publications attacked the Catholic faith. A few months later it accepted his offer of 500 ducats.[6] Similarly, on December 19, 1548, the Republic forbade the Jews to print or publish; but a number of Jews worked as typesetters, proofreaders, and possibly in other capacities.[7] It is likely that the government overlooked violations because it realized that the Hebrew press could not function without Jewish participation.

The papacy became worried about the danger to the faith of Hebrew books, and in November 1548 directed Nuncio Giovanni Della Casa to obtain the expurgation of Venetian Hebrew publications. He readily obtained the consent of Marc'Antonio Giustiniani, but Bomberg objected and argued that no changes could be made in ancient manuscripts. Lacking the advice of Christian experts in Hebrew, Della Casa took no action.[8] The pressure mounted: in December 1550, Cardinal Girolamo Verallo complained vigorously to the Venetian ambassador in Rome that a press run of over 800 copies of the Talmud was more than half finished, and that many other Hebrew books "of the greatest perniciousness" to Christianity were being printed in Venice.[9] Nevertheless, the Giustiniani press completed its publication of the multi-volumed Babylonian Talmud in 1551.

The complaints document growing papal hostility to Hebrew books, but they did not yet produce action. The Venetian har-

[6] Cioni, "Bomberg," p. 385.

[7] Pullan, *Rich and Poor*, p. 521; Amram, *Makers of Hebrew Books*, p. 253. Benjamin Ravid's forthcoming article on the Venetian Hebrew press also lists several Jews. I am indebted to him for allowing me to consult his work.

[8] Correspondence between Della Casa and Rome from November 24, 1548, through February 23, 1549, as quoted in Lorenzo Campana, "Monsignor Giovanni della Casa e i suoi tempi," *Studi storici*, vol. 17 (1908), pp. 269–71.

[9] Letter of Ambassador Matteo Dandolo, December 26, 1550, Rome, in Archivio di Stato, Venice (hereafter ASV), Capi del Consiglio dei Dieci, Lettere di Ambasciatori a Roma, Busta 23, no. 159. Pio Paschini, *Venezia e l'inquisizione romana da Giulio III a Pio IV* (Padua, 1959), pp. 65–66, quotes the letter but misdates it as December 16. Verallo (d. 1555), a veteran papal diplomat, Vatican official, and member of the Congregation of the Holy Office in 1553, appears to have been a zealot.

bored the same fears. In February 1551, the *Collegio* (the doge in concert with his cabinet) ordered the *Esecutori contro la bestemmia* (the civil tribunal charged with punishing blasphemy, moral offenses, and violations of the civil press laws) to examine the Talmud. Having heard that the Talmud is filled with blasphemy and slander against our Lord, the decree read, the Collegio instructed the Esecutori to arrange for Christian experts to note those passages, and to report back to the Collegio.[10]

The attack came as the immediate result of a bitter dispute between the Giustiniani and Bragadino presses over rival editions of a title. Translated to Rome, the denunciations and charges transformed religious fears into destructive action.[11] A papal order of August 12, 1553, condemned the Talmud and similar books to be burned. Executed in Rome, the Congregation of the Holy Office ordered the same throughout Italy on September 12. The Venetians willingly followed suit. On October 18, having heard from the report of the Esecutori contro la bestemmia that the Talmud was filled with blasphemies against God, Jesus, and Mary, the Council of Ten (the supreme disciplinary organ to which the Esecutori were accountable) acted. It ordered the Esecutori to burn all copies of the Talmud collected to date, and authorized them to search in the ghetto and elsewhere, in the houses of Jews, Christians, and bookmen, for others. Originally scheduled for Thursday, October 19, the fire was postponed until the Sabbath, Saturday, October 21. On that morning, "a good fire" (in the nuncio's words) burned in Piazza San Marco. In the next few months the Talmud and other works were burned as far away as Crete in the Venetian Dominion, while across Italy possibly hundreds of thousands of books were burned.[12] The Venetian government burned the Tal-

---

[10] ASV, Collegio, Notatorio, Registro 27, f. 138*v* (February 23, 1550, Venetian style, actually 1551). The vote was 20 yes, 1 no.

[11] Amram, *Makers of Hebrew Books,* pp. 252–76; Kenneth R. Stow, "The Burning of the Talmud in 1553, in the Light of Sixteenth Century Catholic Attitudes toward the Talmud," *Bibliothèque d'Humanisme et Renaissance,* 34 (1972), pp. 435–59.

[12] ASV, Consiglio dei Dieci, Registro 21, ff. 58*v*–59*r*. The votes on three

mud before all other parts of the papal state complied with Rome's order.[13]

The Venetians needed little papal exhortation to join in burning the Talmud. According to the nuncio, no one spoke against the decree. Jewish spiritual and financial distress failed to sway the government; it also rejected the pleas of the two patrician Hebrew publishers. Giustiniani worked behind the scenes to halt the destruction of Hebrew books, and then to prevent the confiscation of his recently printed Talmud. When it was apparent that the Republic would proceed, he appealed to the papacy for financial compensation. He received nothing. The government seized the Giustiniani imprints and, presumably, the Bragadino works as well. Giustiniani's son reported many years later that his father lost 24,000 ducats' worth of books in 1553.[14]

decrees ordering confiscation and destruction were 19 yes, 0 no; 26 yes, 0 no, 2 abstentions; and 26 yes, 0 no. The general decree of October 21 is published in Giovanni Sforza, "Riflessi della Controriforma nella Repubblica di Venezia," *Archivio storico italiano*, 93 (1935), part 2, pp. 44–45; and C. Castellani, "Documenti circa la persecuzione dei libri ebraici a Venezia," *La Bibliofilia*, 7 (1905–06), pp. 304–07, with documents relating to Crete as well. See the letters of Nuncio Ludovico Beccadelli of August 19, 26, September 23, October 14, 21, 1553, Venice, in *Nunziature di Venezia*, Vol. 6, ed. Franco Gaeta. Istituto Storico per l'età moderna e contemporanea. *Fonti per la Storia d'Italia*, no. 86 (Rome, 1967), pp. 255, 258, 267, 274–75, 277 (quote). Some of this correspondence is in Paschini, *L'inquisizione*, pp. 108–111. Also see Ludwig von Pastor, *The History of the Popes*, trans. Ralph Francis Kerr, Vol. 13 (London and St. Louis, 1924), pp. 214–15; Roth, *Jews in Venice*, pp. 255–59; Roth, *Jews in Italy*, pp. 290–93; William Popper, *The Censorship of Hebrew Books* (New York, 1899), pp. 29–37; Salo Wittmayer Baron, *A Social and Religious History of the Jews*. 2nd ed. rev. Vol. 14: *Catholic Restoration and Wars of Religion* (New York, London, and Philadelphia, 1969), pp. 29–31, 127–28, 141–42, 317, 353–54, 357–58.

[13] See the letter of Girolamo Muzio to Fra Michele Ghislieri (the future Pius V) of December 16, 1553, Pesaro, in which he reported that the Talmud had been burned on December 9 in the Dukedom of Urbino, while in nearby Ancona no action had yet been taken. Girolamo Muzio, *Lettere catholiche del Mutio Iustinopolitano* (Venice: Gio. Andrea Valvassori, 1571), pp. 185–86.

[14] Letters of Nuncio Beccadelli of August 26, September 23, October 14, 21, 1553, Venice, in *Nunziature di Venezia*, vol. 6, pp. 258, 267, 274–75, 277;

108

Pope Julius III, in response to Jewish pleas, issued modifying decrees on May 29 and December 18, 1554, permitting Hebrew books to be held after having been censored.[15] But Hebrew publishing did not resume in Venice. It moved to Cremona, Ferrara, Mantua, Sabbioneta, and Riva di Trento, sometimes flourishing in these north Italian cities through the dark days of the pontificate of Paul IV (1555–1559). Cristoforo Madruzzo (1512–1578), the prince and cardinal of Trent, founded and supported a Hebrew press at Riva di Trento, about fifty kilometers southwest of Trent, that lasted from 1558 through 1562.[16]

The Republic did not forbid the publication of Hebrew books; it only insisted on expurgation. In July 1559, the Esecutori followed the papal lead and ruled that Hebrew books, with the exception of the Talmud and its commentaries, might be published after expurgation.[17] The Esecutori appointed two experts in Hebrew, Father Tommaso da Urbino, a Dominican of strict observance, and Felice da Tolentino, a converted Jew, to expurgate titles according to the papal booklet of corrections prepared by Father Jacopo Giraldino (or Geraldino).[18] Hebrew titles still held

ASV, Santo Uffizio, Busta 37, Antonio Giustiniani, no pag., his testimony of November 4, 1574. Antonio may have exaggerated, for his father in 1553 estimated that before the fire the cost of paper and printing of the confiscated books was 3,000 ducats. (*Nunziature di Venezia*, vol. 6, p. 275, letter of October 14, 1553.) On the other hand, calculating the loss from the retail price would raise the figure to at least 6,000 ducats. Additional books may have been confiscated after October 1553.

[15] Pastor, *History of the Popes*, vol. 13, p. 215; Roth, *Jews in Venice*, pp. 259–60.

[16] Amram, *Makers of Hebrew Books*, pp. 277–337. Madruzzo was a patron of arts and letters, generous host to the Council of Trent, and a statesman who successfully balanced his allegiances to emperor and pope; see the brief remarks of Hubert Jedin, *A History of the Council of Trent*, trans. Ernest Graf, Vol. 1 (London, 1957), pp. 566–74. One would like to know why he established a Hebrew press.

[17] The Esecutori specifically referred to edicts of Julius III of May 29, 1554, and of Paul IV of March 26, 1555.

[18] Giraldino, with the title of Apostolic Commissioner, was in charge of Hebrew book censorship in the papal state. Obviously his influence extended beyond it as well. Popper, *Censorship of Hebrew Books*, pp. 40–41, 135–36.

by the Esecutori, as a result of the confiscations of October 1553, were to be returned to their owners after correction. But the Esecutori threatened the punishments decreed by the Council of Ten in 1553 — fines, imprisonment, and the galleys — for those who printed or held unexpurgated Hebrew books.[19]

In the early 1560s the Esecutori continued to exercise keen vigilance over Hebrew books. In 1561 the court discovered several bales of books lacking the proper corrections at the Bomberg press (now led by Giovanni di Gara, sometimes called the "heir of Bomberg") and in the hands of various booksellers. These volumes had to be imports or older Venetian imprints. The Esecutori ordered the titles expurgated but levied no penalties.[20]

The Venetian Jews and their publishers probably felt that this vigilance manifested a continuing hostility toward Hebrew books that made the resumption of printing very risky. Needing a clear signal of a change of attitude, they watched anxiously to see if the Church would give it at the Council of Trent. The council's commission drafting the Index of Prohibited Books discussed the Talmud in 1562 and 1563 without reaching a decision. This heartened the Jews, because they expected kinder treatment from Pius IV than from anyone else. They were not disappointed, for his Index of 1564 (usually called the Tridentine Index) softened the previous condemnation in order to permit the Talmud with its commentaries and glosses so long as they were expurgated and printed without the explicit title "Talmud."[21] Perhaps this was

[19] ASV, Esecutori contro la bestemmia, Busta 56, Notatorio Terminazioni, Registro 1542–1560, ff. 161v–164r, July 24, 1559.

[20] ASV, Esecutori contro la bestemmia, Busta 56, Notatorio Terminazioni, Registro 1561–1582, ff. 4v–5r, September 25, 1561. A number of surviving copies of Venetian Hebrew works printed beween 1564 and 1568 have been expurgated by means of blank spaces and passages inked out. This censorship may have been the result of the action of 1568. See below. Popper, *Censorship of Hebrew Books*, p. 54; Amram, *Makers of Hebrew Books*, p. 257; Meir Benayahu, *Haskamah u-reshut bi-defuse Venetsiah* (*Copyright, Authorization and Imprimatur for Hebrew Books Printed in Venice*) (Jerusalem, 1971), pp. 198–207. I thank Joseph Shatzmiller for reading this book for me.

[21] Salo Wittmayer Baron, "The Council of Trent and Rabbinic Literature,"

110

the assurance that the Venetian Jews sought. In 1564 and 1565, Alvise Bragadino, Me'ir ben Jacob Parenzo, and four newcomers — Zorzi de' Cavalli, Giovanni di Gara, Giovanni Griffio, and Cristoforo Zanetti — began to publish Hebrew books; each of the six published up to fourteen imprints through 1568.[22]

But the times did not favor the Jews in Venice or elsewhere in Italy, for Pius V (1566–1572) gave an example of persecution for the entire peninsula. The Venetians had additional reasons, which focused on Don Joseph Nasi (João Miquez). A wealthy merchant from Portugal, Nasi in 1550 asked the Republic to sell him an island that he might turn into a haven for Jewish refugees. Not only did the Venetians rebuff him, but the Council of Ten in 1553 instigated kidnapping charges against Nasi and his associates for what apparently was the rescue of his aunt from a Venetian prison.[23] Sentenced *in absentia* to hanging, Nasi made his way to the Turkish court in 1554 where he soon became the leading financier and tax farmer for the sultan. Now very anti-Venetian, Nasi organized a commercial network for East-West trade in direct competition with the Republic. In the late 1560s, the Venetians believed that he wished to become King of Cyprus and, when the Turkish invasion came in 1571, held him responsible.[24]

A series of incidents in the last years of the 1560s convinced

in his *Ancient and Medieval Jewish History*. Edited with a Forword by Leon A. Feldman (New Brunswick, N. J., 1972), pp. 353–71, 555–64; Baron, *A Social and Religious History of the Jews*, vol. 14, pp. 19–23, 310–313.

[22] *Short-title Catalogue of Books printed in Italy and of Italian Books printed in other countries from 1465 to 1600 now in the British Museum* [hereafter *STC Italian*] (London, 1958), pp. 796, 806, 830–32, 856, 906–07, 985. Of course, the surviving copies in the British Museum should be viewed as an extensive sampling rather than a complete list of the titles published.

[23] Constance H. Rose, "New Information on the Life of Joseph Nasi, Duke of Naxos: The Venetian Phase," *Jewish Quarterly Review*, 60 (1969–70), pp. 330–44. The lady rescued was his cousin, not his aunt, according to P. Grunebaum-Ballin, *Joseph Naci, duc de Naxos* (Paris, 1968), p. 52, a work unavailable to me. I thank Benjamin Ravid for this information.

[24] Lane, *Venice*, pp. 301–02; Samuele Romanin, *Storia documentata di Venezia*. 3rd ed. Vol. 6 (Venice, 1974), pp. 189–92.

many Venetians that local Jews were Turkish agents attempting
to sabotage the Republic from within. In 1567 the government
intercepted coded Hebrew letters (which may have been counterfeit) giving the details of a joint plot by Jews in Constantinople
and Venice to bribe a Venetian ambassador extraordinary.[25] When
in April 1568 a fire in Constantinople endangered the life of
the *bailo* (the Republic's resident ambassador and governor of
the Venetian colony there), the Venetians again held the Jews
responsible.[26]

At the peak of public hostility toward the Jews, the Esecutori
fell upon the Hebrew press anew. In a series of decisions of September 22 and 24, 1568, it ordered the destruction or correction
of thousands of copies of recent publications and fined those held
responsible.[27] The tribunal began by noting that various Jews
of the city, both "foreigners" and "Levantines," had published
Hebrew books "almost all incorrect and unexpurgated." They had
done this without a governmental imprimatur (permission to print,
granted by the Heads of the Council of Ten) and in contravention
of the decree of the Esecutori of July 24, 1559. These books had
violated the instructions for expurgation drafted by Jacopo Giraldino and Don Agusto Felice.[28] The tribunal further noted that
two local priests, experts in Hebrew, Fra Marco[29] and Fra Paulo

[25] See the letters of Nuncio Giovanni Antonio Facchinetti of July 19,
August 16, October 18, 1567, May 22, 1568, Venice, in *Nunziature di Venezia*,
Vol. 8, ed. Aldo Stella. Istituto Storico per l'età moderna e contemporanea,
Fonti per la Storia d'Italia, no. 65 (Rome, 1963), pp. 251, 260–61, 290, 388.

[26] Letter of Facchinetti of April 10, 1568, Venice, in *Nunziature di Venezia*,
vol. 8, p. 372.

[27] ASV, Esecutori contro la bestemmia, Busta 56, Notatorio Terminazioni,
Registro 1561–1582, ff. 41bisr–47v, September 22, 24, 27, October 29, 1568.
Unfortunately, only the *terminazioni* (sentences), and not the transcripts of
the trials or reports of investigations, survive.

[28] Unidentified.

[29] More than likely this is Fra Marco Marini da Brescia, Hebraist and
biblical scholar. Both he and Fra Paulo appear on lists (c. 1571) of clerical
experts who assisted the Venetian Holy Office in enforcing the Index of Prohibited Books. One of these lists includes two experts "per la lingua hebraica";
they are "Don Marco da Brescia" and "Don Paulo da Venetia," both from

of the Augustinian monastery of San Salvatore, had confirmed that the Hebrew titles had not been expurgated. "Recognizing that the perfidy of many Jews is such that they seek with diverse means to subvert our true and holy Christian faith, and in order to castigate those who have committed these errors and to frighten others," the tribunal had decided to punish the guilty.

The Esecutori found fault with a substantial number of the titles printed since the revival of Hebrew publishing in 1564. The court levied heavy fines on the Venetian Jews who had sponsored publication of the offending works, imposed lesser fines on the publishers and printers, and decreed various dispositions for the books.

The Esecutori began by fining one "Rabi Juda overo Leone" 500 ducats for sponsoring the printing by Zorzi de' Cavalli of 800 copies each of three titles:[30]

> "Rabot" — probably *Midrash Rabba*, commentary on the Pentateuch and M^eghilloth. (Venice: Zorzi de' Cavalli, 1566), folio.[31]

the monastery of San Salvatore. I have been unable to identify further the latter. ASV, Santo Uffizio, Busta 30, Andrea Arrivabene, loose documents, one of them dated December 1, 1571, appended to the trial of Arrivabene. I am grateful to Joanna Weinberg who first suggested that Fra Marco might be Marini.

[30] The documents provide only a one- or two-word title, but they do include the name of the publisher. This is usually enough information to identify title and printing. I do not read Hebrew, not an insurmountable handicap because the secretary recording the decisions did not either. As the Esecutor rendered judgment on various titles, he wrote down in Italian, often with Venetian orthography, a phonetic equivalent of the Hebrew word. (He probably consulted one of the Christian Hebrew experts when in doubt.) For the identifications below I matched the titles as given in the documents with the Hebrew phonetic equivalents found in the *STC Italian*. I identified about three-quarters of this group of titles in this way, and Professor Frank Talmage, who combines expertise in medieval Hebrew literature with a knowledge of Italian, helped me with the rest. Throughout this article I follow *STC Italian* form for Hebrew transliteration of the titles in the booklists.

[31] For the identification, see *STC Italian*, p. 437, item 11 on the page.

"Bacagiai" also described as "Menandes" — probably Bahye (or Bachye) ben Asher (or Moses ben Nahman, pseud.), *Be'ur 'al ha-Torah* (Venice: Zorzi de' Cavalli, 1566), folio.[32]

"Zarozamoth" — probably Abraham Saba, *Ṣeror Ha-Mor* (Venice: Zorzi de' Cavalli, 1567), folio.[33]

The Esecutori ordered these 2,400 volumes burned in Piazza San Marco.

The tribunal next fined Moise Salati of Venice 500 ducats for sponsoring the printing by Giovanni di Gara of 1,000 copies of "bibie... in foglio real con comenti hebrei et caldei in quatro volumi"; the Esecutori especially noted that the third and fourth volumes contained "molte pravità." This was probably Gara's 1568 printing of the rabbinical Bible first published by Bomberg in 1517:

Old Testament (Hebrew) with Aramaic (Chaldean) versions and the commentaries of Rashi, Abraham Ibn Ezra, David Kimhi et al. 4 vols. (Venice: Giovanni di Gara, 1568), folio.[34]

The Esecutori ordered Salati to ship the 4,000 volumes to the Levant within three months, presumably after expurgation. Salati returned on October 29 to plead that he could neither pay the fine nor ship the books to the Levant. Relenting, the Esecutori permitted him to sell the books outside the Venetian state, i.e., elsewhere in Italy or in northern Europe.[35]

The Esecutori fined Benetto Bora da Padua 200 ducats for sponsoring the publication of 1,000 copies each of two titles:

"Opere del forni in latino" published by (Giovanni) "Griffio." Possibly this was the Latin translation of *Or 'Ammim* (*Light*

---

[32] *STC Italian*, p. 67, item 22.

[33] *STC Italian*, p. 594, last item.

[34] *STC Italian*, p. 94, item 19.

[35] ASV, Esecutori contro la bestemmia, Busta 56, Notatorio Terminazioni, Registro 1561–1582, ff. 47*v*–48*r*. Salati probably lacked a Venetian license for Levantine commerce.

114

of Nations, an anti-Aristotelian work) of Obadiah ben Jacob
Sforno (1475–1550). Apparently Sforno made the translation and dispatched it to Henry II of France (reigned
1547–1559), but little is known about the edition.[36]

"Ciscioni" or "Cisconi" published by Giovanni di Gara. Possibly R' Menahem ben R' Meir, *Ṣiyoni*, a Cabbalistic commentary on the Pentateuch, but a Gara printing has not
been located.[37]

The Esecutori ordered Bora to ship the "Ciscioni" to the Levant,
but when he pleaded that he was barred from the Levantine trade
because he was a Jew, they permitted him to sell the books in
Poland and Germany. The documents provide no information on
the disposition of the thousand copies of Sforno's work.

The tribunal found fault with six titles published by Giovanni
Griffio:

"orazechel" — probably *Or ha-Sekhel*, Midrash Rabbah on
Genesis, with commentary attributed to Rashi, and issued
with *Maʿadamei Melekh* by Abraham ben Gedaliah Ben
Asher. (Venice: Giovanni Griffio, 1567), folio.[38] The Esecutori ordered the 1,000 copies seized to be burned.

The other four titles were parts of a joint work:

"Orachini" — probably *Orah hayyim*, which was part I of
Jacob ben Asher, *Arbaʿah Turim*. 4 vols. (Venice: Giovanni
Griffio, 1566), folio.[40]

"Ioredea del Caro" — probably *Yoreh Deʿah*, part II of
Arbaʿah Turim, which included the commentary *Beth Yoseph*
of Joseph ben Ephraim Caro. Gedelia da Genoa Ceroicho,

[36] Salo Wittmayer Baron, *A Social and Religious History of the Jews*, 2nd
ed. rev. Vol. 13: *Inquisition, Renaissance, and Reformation* (New York, London,
and Philadelphia, 1969), pp. 193, 410.

[37] See *STC Italian*, p. 433, item 15, for a printing in Cremona, 1560.

[38] *STC Italian*, p. 437, item 12.

[39] *STC Italian*, p. 431, item 15.

[40] *STC Italian*, p. 344, item 12.

who had sponsored the publication of this title, was fined 200 ducats.

"Ehem" also described as "Laenaser" — probably *Eben Ha-ezer*, part III of *Arba'ah Turim*.

"Copemispat" — probably *Hoshen Mishpat*, part IV of *Arba'ah Turim*.

The Esecutori seized 800 copies each of parts I, II, and IV, ordering them to be corrected. Part III was to be burned, but the quantity is unknown.

The Esecutori ordered three liturgical titles published by Zorzi de' Cavalli burned:

"abudaram" — possibly David ben Joseph Abudirham, *Abudirham* (Venice: Zorzi de' Cavalli, 1566), 4°.[41] One bale — an unknown quantity — was ordered burned.

"Colho" — probably *Kol-bo* (Venice: Zorzi de' Cavalli, 1567), folio.[42] One bale was to be burned.

"Machazorci" — probably *Mahazor*, festival prayers (Venice: Zorzi de' Cavalli, 1567), folio.[43] Six bales were ordered burned.

The Esecutori seized another liturgical title published by Giovanni di Gara:

"Sedurini spagnolo" — probably *Mahazor S^ephardim mi-Yamim Nora'im*, Spanish rite festival prayers for the New Year and the Day of Atonement (Venice: Giovanni di Gara, 1567), 16°.[44]

The Esecutori retained custody of 3,000 copies; their final disposition is unknown.

The Esecutori fined the publisher Cristoforo Zanetti for printing

---

41 *STC Italian*, p. 3, item 29.
42 *STC Italian*, p. 365, item 23.
43 *STC Italian*, p. 354, item 13.
44 *STC Italian*, p. 355, item 22.

116

600 copies of "Rashi," i.e., Solomon ben Isaac of Troyes (1040–1105), called Rashi. There is a likely possibility:

> *Perush Rashi ʿal Ha-Torah*, commentary on the Pentateuch and Five Megilloth (Venice: Cristoforo Zanetti, 1566), 4°.[45] The fate of the books is unknown.

Finally, the Esecutori dealt with two editions of the *Hummash*: "Comas" or "Comas cum targotti" — *Hummash* (Pentateuch) with *Targum Onkelos* (Venice: Giovanni di Gara, 1567), folio.[46] The court seized 1,500 copies whose disposition is unknown.

——. The Esecutori ordered 4,000 copies of an edition published by Cristoforo Zanetti (not identified) exported to the Levant.

In addition to the heavy penalties imposed on Rabbi Juda, Moise Salati, Benetto Bora, and Gedelia Ceroicho, the Esecutori levied fines of 5 to 100 ducats on other Jews for lesser involvement in the publication and export of Hebrew books.[47] Holding the printers guilty to a lesser degree, the Esecutori fined Cavalli, Gara, and Griffio 100 ducats each, Cristoforo Zanetti and Nicolò Bevilacqua (who had printed 3,500 copies of the *Mahazor Sephardim* probably for Gara, and 3,000 copies of the *Hummash* for either Gara or Zanetti) 50 ducats each.[48] In all, the court fined the

---

[45] *STC Italian*, p. 633, item 9.

[46] *STC Italian*, p. 95, items 8 and 20.

[47] The Esecutori fined Cecuo di Solomon da Mestre 100 ducats, and Isach Sacu levantino, Abraham Galico levantino, Rabbi Admai levantino, and Josef Angulaci and Indo Levi (jointly) 50 ducats each. The Esecutori fined Gedelia another 50 ducats for bringing in books from Cremona, Jacob di Rizzo 50 ducats for shipping books to Mantua, and Josef Crespin levantino 5 ducats for attempting to send a title to Salonika.

[48] Nicolò Bevilacqua from the Trentino (1510/20–1573) was one of Paolo Manuzio's most important associates. He operated his own press in Venice from 1554 to 1572, and moved to Turin when Duke Emanuele Filiberto of Savoy offered him substantial financial concessions. This is the first notice that he also printed Hebrew texts. Alfredo Cioni, "Nicolò Bevilacqua," *Dizionario biografico degli italiani*. Vol. 9 (Rome, 1967), pp. 798–801.

Jews 1,805 ducats and the printers 400. With this the action ended.

The destruction of thousands of titles and the heavy fines levied were grievous financial blows. The Esecutori ordered 4,400 folio volumes of the *Midhrash Rabba, Be'ur 'al hat-Torah, Ṣeror Ha-Mor, Or Ha-Sekhel,* and *Maroth Elohim* burned, as well as an indefinite number of four other titles (*Eben Ha-Ezer, Abudirham, Kol-bo,* and *Mahazor*) also burned. If nearly complete press runs (800 to 1,000) of the last four titles were destroyed, the total number consigned to the flames was between 7,600 and 8,400 volumes. The monetary loss was very high. The retail price of a folio volume began at about a ducat and could climb rapidly; perhaps an average price for a folio volume was 1.5 to 2 ducats.[49] Hence, the retail value of the destroyed volumes may have been between 11,400 ducats (7,600 volumes × 1.5) and 16,800 ducats (8,400 volumes × 2). This loss must be added to the fines of 2,205 ducats.

The Esecutori also ordered a large number of volumes exported. Presumably these books were then sold abroad, meaning that the publishers and their sponsors realized some return on their investment. But it is possible, even probable, that the return was lower than it would have been had they been able to sell the volumes normally. Hence, an additional heavy loss may have been sustained.

The financial loss can be calculated; the affliction of spirit is more difficult to measure but must have been severe.[50] For the

[49] This is my calculation, based on contemporary price lists of the retail prices of Latin and Italian folio volumes. See Grendler, *The Roman Inquisition and the Venetian Press*, pp. 12–14. I do not have any information on the retail prices of Hebrew books. But since paper and the cost of printing made up the largest part of production costs, I estimate that Hebrew books sold for about the same as Latin and Italian volumes of the same size.

[50] That is, if the bookburning of 1568 was completely carried out. Because so many of the titles ordered destroyed survive in the British Museum, and in light of what followed (see below), one wonders if the destruction orders were fully implemented. Obviously the Jews and their printers would do all in their power to save the books. Moreover, Venetian policy toward the Jews was full of twists and turns in those years; it is possible that the decree of the

118

second time in fifteen years Venetian Jews saw many volumes
essential to the religious life of the community destroyed.

The exact, proximate reason for the Venetian action is not easy
to determine. Ultimately it can be traced to the prevailing hostility
toward the Jews throughout Italy. But the leaders of the Republic
seldom acted without some immediate and concrete reason spur-
ring them into action, and this is difficult to discover. The papacy
issued no new decrees against Hebrew books at this time, nor
has any directive from the highest organs of the Venetian state
(Collegio, Council of Ten, Senate) come to light. No provocative
act attributable to the Jews has been unearthed.

The Esecutori repeatedly charged that the Jews and their printers
had published these titles without expurgating anti-Christian sentiments, in effect systematically violating the censorship. This could
be true, but it seems unlikely that publishers and Jews would
engage in deliberate and massive deception at this perilous time.
The risks were too great. At the other extreme, it also seems
unlikely that the Venetian government cynically raised money for
the approaching war against the Turks by punishing the Jews for
censorship infractions previously ignored. The Venetian leadership
normally honored its pacts with the Jews until expiration — and
then raised the price.

The most likely explanation is that a combination of hostility
and a desire for vengeance motivated the Venetian government.
The Venetians had granted the Jews a haven from the worst
forms of persecution, but believed that they had been repaid with
treachery. Patricians and commoners alike increasingly feared and
hated the Jews as Turkish agents. In this period of mounting
hostility, the government became increasingly suspicious of the
Hebrew press, viewing the press — as it viewed the Jews — as
an internal threat to the security of the state. The Venetians could
not read what the Hebrew press produced and may have suspected
the worst. Perhaps in this charged atmosphere the leaders reacted

Esecutori was quietly countermanded. When this happened, one seldom finds
official notice in governmental documents.

strongly when Christian Hebrew experts reported that the books were full of anti-Christian sentiments. The experts may now have found intolerable passages which earlier would have occasioned only irritation. Determining the orthodoxy of a book depends very much on the intellectual context and political milieu, then as today. The history of sixteenth-century religious censorship offers many examples of changing standards; Erasmus and Machiavelli, for example, were originally accepted but later condemned. Perhaps in this climate of fear and hostility the government, acting through the Esecutori, engaged in retroactive censorship, and justified the heavy penalties imposed as fair retribution against a people who had supposedly repaid toleration with treachery.

The Hebrew press did not quickly recover from this blow. Cavalli, Griffio, and Zanetti gave up publishing Hebrew titles.[51] Giovanni di Gara continued, but his output dropped substantially in the next few years.[52]

After 1568 the situation of the Venetian Jews became perilous. Public opinion held Nasi's Jewish agents in Venice responsible for the devastating Arsenal fire of September 13, 1569. Crowds celebrated the victory of Lepanto (October 7, 1571) by harassing Levantine Jews.[53] But the fall of Cyprus followed the great naval victory, and anger against the Jews increased. At this ominous moment the *condotta* expired, and the Senate met to decide their fate. Many senators felt that this was the time to rid the city of

---

[51] There is one possible exception to this statement, a Zorzi de' Cavalli printing of *Eben Ha-Ezer* of 1585 is listed in *STC Italian*, p. 344, item 22. But this is so much later as to suggest that the publisher was another person, perhaps a younger relative. Or the entry could be erroneous. Indeed, excluding this work of 1585, the Cavalli firm stopped publishing altogether in 1570, while Giovanni Griffio and Cristoforo Zanetti did very little after 1568. Griffio apparently died at the time of the Great Plague of 1575–1577. See *STC Italian*, pp. 805–06, 855–56, 985.

[52] *STC Italian*, p. 831, lists only three Gara Hebrew titles of 1569 through 1573. Amram, *Makers of Hebrew Books*, p. 360, doesn't list any.

[53] Biblioteca Marciana, Venice, Mss. Italiani, Classe VII, 134 (8035), "Cronaca veneta di Girolamo Savina sino al MDCXV," f. 358r.

120

their presence.[54] One senator depicted the Jews as "the scum of the earth, spies for the Turks, and internal enemies," holding them responsible for the grain shortage and the Arsenal fire. He went on to charge that their moneylending led youths to vice and reduced noble families to penury. The older arguments for toleration carried little weight on this occasion. Another senator asked rhetorically, who will deny that the Jews are perfidious, usurious, miserly, and politically unreliable? Nevertheless, they contribute significantly to the ducal treasury, and make it possible for Christians to avoid staining themselves with the sin of usury. He urged the Republic's traditional policy of tolerance on the grounds of economic utility and in the hope that, someday, they would become Christians. But the Senate, expressing thanks to God for Lepanto and vowing vengeance for Jewish treachery, voted to expel them on December 18, 1571.[55]

Within a few days the Venetians reconsidered, as they calculated the anticipated effects of the loss of the *condotta* payment and the disruption of the monetary exchange. The Senate cancelled the expulsion order, but did not renew the *condotta*, leaving the Jews suspended between toleration and exile, while secret peace negotiations with the Turk began. Turkish acceptance of peace probably depended upon a reprieve for the Jews. Hence, in the summer of 1573 the Senate renewed the *condotta* in exchange for Jewish operation of loanbanks for the poor.[56]

In these very difficult times the Jews and their publishers resorted to clandestine means to print and distribute Hebrew titles. This was the burden of a denunciation that a priest brought to the Venetian Holy Office in April 1570. The target of his allegations

---

54 The speeches are summarized by Agostino Valier, *Dell'utilità che si può ritrarre dalle cose operate dai veneziani libri xiv, del Cardinale Agostino Valerio Vescovo di Verona*. Trans. Niccolò Antonio Giustiniani (Padua, 1787), pp. 358–60. Valier (1531–1606), Venetian noble and cardinal, wrote his history c. 1581.

55 Pullan, *Rich and Poor*, p. 537, quotes the preamble of the expulsion act.

56 Pullan, *Rich and Poor*, pp. 537–40.

was Marc'Antonio Giustiniani, the patrician publisher of Hebrew books since 1545 until the burning of the Talmud in 1553.

Marc'Antonio Giustiniani was born on December 15, 1516, the third or fourth of seven sons of Niccolò.[57] The Giustiniani were one of the "old" noble families called the "longhi" because they were believed to descend from the tribunes who governed in the Venetian lagoon before the election of the first doge (697).[58] One Giustiniani reached the very high office of Procurator (a lifetime post limited to seven men, from whom the doge was almost always chosen) in 903. Marc'Antonio's branch descended from Ferrigo (called Belletto) Giustiniani (d. 1293), a naval hero in the struggle against Genoa in the Greek archipelago. Members of this branch continued to play a prominent role in the eastern Venetian Empire. Bernardo (d. c. 1498), grandfather of Marc'Antonio, had served as governor at Candia (the capital of Crete) and had at his own expense armed three war galleys against the Turk. Niccolò (d. 1550), Marc'Antonio's father, had been *bailo* at Constantinople.

Neither Marc'Antonio nor his brothers enjoyed the political or military prominence of their ancestors. Marc'Antonio was elected to one significant political office, the *Avvogadori di Comun*, on a single occasion, December 13, 1562, for a term of one year.[59] The Avvogadori were State Attorneys charged with bringing suit against officials or magistracies who abused their trust. Although not minor, the office had lost much of its former prestige and influence by the middle of the sixteenth century.[60] It did not begin to compare with such powerful offices as the *Savii del Consiglio*, Ducal Counsellors, or members of the Council of Ten. Marc'Antonio also managed to obtain the appointment of *rettore* (governor) of

[57] For genealogical and other information on Marc'Antonio and his ancestors, see ASV, Marco Barbaro, "Arbori dei Patritii veneti," vol. 7, pp. 449, 464.

[58] Lane, *Venice*, p. 196.

[59] ASV, Segretario alle voci, Serie Misto, Registro 13, f. 63*v*.

[60] Lane, *Venice*, p. 100. For a discussion of its declining influence, see Gaetano Cozzi, "Authority and the Law in Renaissance Venice," in J. R. Hale, ed., *Renaissance Venice* (London, 1973), pp. 293–345.

Cephalonia, an island stronghold in the Ionian Sea, at some point in the mid-1560s. The priest's denunciation to the Holy Office of April 8 (Saturday), 1570, focused on Marc'Antonio's activities at Cephalonia.

The priest charged that Giustiniani had transformed Cephalonia into a center for printing and distribution of Hebrew books during the past five years.[61] Giustiniani had brought in two bookbinders and an engraver-printer skilled in Arabic; he had then established a press in the governor's palace to produce Arabic and Hebrew books. Since this went on without supervision by the Inquisition or any other authority, Giustiniani was printing and selling unexpurgated, even prohibited, Hebrew volumes, in the opinion of the denouncer. The priest concluded with the startling news that Giustiniani had a chest of illicit volumes in his ship now docked in Venice; he urged the Holy Office to seize the chest immediately.

Instead, the cautious Inquisition gathered more evidence. At its next regular sitting (Tuesday, April 11, 1570),[62] it questioned three soldiers who had been with Giustiniani in Cephalonia. They confirmed that Giustiniani trafficked in Hebrew books, but they had been unable to penetrate the veil of secrecy around the press in the governor's palace — or else they were unwilling to reveal all they knew. At the end of this hearing, the Holy Office ordered the chest of books on Giustiniani's ship seized. When opened before the eyes of the denouncer (April 22), it contained only pelts and sponges.[63] A few days later Giustiniani sent a counter-denunciation of the priest as a scandalmonger.

61 ASV, Santo Uffizio, Busta 28, Marco Antonio Giustiniani, no pag., consisting of the denunciation of Don Angelo Fasoli (the priest), his testimony and list of Hebrew titles of April 8, 1570, and the testimony of other witnesses and additional material, from April 11 through May 25, 1570.

62 Year after year, the Venetian Holy Office met on Tuesdays, Thursdays, and Saturdays, days chosen to avoid conflicts with other Venetian magistracies whose meetings the lay deputies (nobles appointed by the government to assist and oversee the Holy Office) might be obliged to attend.

63 It is not clear whether the order was executed on the 11th or later. It makes little difference, for once the Inquisition failed to act immediately (on

The priest did provide with his initial denunciation a list of the titles that Giustiniani allegedly had shipped from Venice to Cephalonia:[64]

"Commasin con Targon" — *Hummash* with *Targum Onkelos*. Several Venetian printings are known, including one published by Giustiniani in 1546 and the most recent one attributed to Giovanni di Gara in 1567.[65]

"Commasin senza Targon" — *Hummash* without *Targum Onkelos*. Again several Venetian printings are known, including two attributed to the Giustiniani press, in 1547 and 1551.[66]

"Sidorin Spagnoli grandi" — probably Spanish Rite daily prayer books in folio size.

"Chitarin" — *Ketuvim*, i.e., Hagiographa, the third of the three Jewish divisions of the Old Testament, usually comprising Psalms, Proverbs, Job, Song of Solomon, Ruth, Lamentations, Ecclesiastes, Esther, Daniel, Ezra, Nehemiah, and Chronicles.

"Bibia in xvi" — probably a Hebrew Old Testament in 16°. Giustiniani published a Hebrew Old Testament in 24° in 1551–1552.[67]

"Sidorin Spagnoli del mise" — probably Spanish Rite festival prayers.

"Maimonin" — unknown title of Moses Ben Maimun (Maimonides).

"Bibia in 4°" — Giustiniani published a Hebrew Old Testament in 4° in 1551–1552.[68]

the 8th) ample time existed for someone (e.g., one of the soldiers) to warn Giustiniani.

[64] The titles as given by Don Fasoli are reproduced in quotation marks and in the original sequence. For the identifications I followed the same procedure described in note 30 but, needed considerable assistance from Professor Talmage.

[65] *STC Italian*, p. 95, items 15 and 20.

[66] *STC Italian*, p. 95, items 2 and 3.

[67] *STC Italian*, p. 94, item 12.

[68] *STC Italian*, p. 94, item 11.

124

"Chomas in 4°" — Giustiniani published a quarto Pentateuch with a glossary of difficult words in 1547.[69]

"Perùs Rassi" — Solomon ben Isaac (called Rashi), *Perush Rashi ʿal Ha-Torah* (commentary on the Pentateuch). Several Venetian printings, including one attributed to Marc'Antonio Giustiniani of 1548, exist.[70]

"Cholbò" — *Kol-bo* (a ritual). A Venetian printing by Giustiniani of 1547 and another by Zorzi de' Cavalli of 1567 are known.[71]

"Chomas con perus amilot con li suoi Apharot" — the Pentateuch with an explanation of words and the Haphtarah, i.e., a portion of the Prophets chanted in the synagogue on the Sabbath and holidays. Several Venetian printings, including those of 1547 and 1551 by Giustiniani, are extant.[72]

"Elacot Gadolot" — Simeon Kayyara, *Halakhoth Gᵉdoloth* (an epitome of the Babylonian Talmud). Ed. Judah ben Isaac [Venice: Marc'Antonio Giustiniani, 1548].[73]

"Cirorà Maor" — Abraham Saba, *Ṣeror Ha-Mor* [Venice: Marc'Antonio Giustiniani, 1545] or [Venice: Zorzi de' Cavalli, 1567].[74]

"Perus Araman sopra il Chomas" — *Perush ha-Ramban*, a commentary on the Pentateuch by Moses ben Naḥman (Nahmanides). The precise edition is difficult to determine; however, the Bomberg press published in 1548 an edition of the Pentateuch with commentaries by Moses ben Naḥman and others.[75]

"Raboth sopra il Chomas" — Midrash Rabbah on the Pentateuch.

"Raboth sopra il chomas megilot" — Midrash Rabbah on the

---

69 *STC Italian*, p. 94, item 10.
70 *STC Italian*, p. 633, item 7.
71 *STC Italian*, p. 365, items 23 and 24.
72 *STC Italian*, p. 95, items 1 through 10.
73 *STC Italian*, p. 628, last item.
74 *STC Italian*, p. 594, last two items.
75 *STC Italian*, p. 95, item 16.

Pentateuch and M^{e}ghilloth (Five Scrolls). Several Venetian printings had appeared in the previous twenty-five years, including one published by Marc'Antonio Giustiniani in 1545, and two by Zorzi de' Cavalli in 1568.[76]

"Chadachim" — Bahya ben Asher, *Kad Ha-Qemaḥ* (an ethical work) [Venice: Marc'Antonio Giustiniani, 1545].[77]

"Barchiaror del Barbarello (or Barbavello)" — unidentified title of Isaac ben Judah Abravanel. Giustiniani published his *Ro'sh Amanah* in 1545.[78]

"En Jacob; et bet Jacob" — Jacob Ibn Habib, *En Ya'akobh* (the aggadhic passages of the Babylonian and Palestinian Talmuds) [Venice: Marc'Antonio Giustiniani, 1546–1547], or [Venice: Zorzi de' Cavalli, 1566].[79]

"Abadarom" — David ben Joseph Abudirham, *Abudirham* (a ritual) [Venice: Marc'Antonio Giustiniani, 1546] or [Venice: Zorzi de' Cavalli, 1566].[80]

"Arasba" — probably Solomon ben Abraham Ibn Adret, *Sh^e'eloth u-T^{e}shubhoth l^e-ha-Rashba* [Venice: Marc'Antonio Giustiniani, 1545–1546].[81]

"Agur" — Jacob Baruch ben Judah Landau, *Agur* [Venice: Marc'Antonio Giustiniani, 1546].[82]

"Thoilin con Kimchi" — Psalms with commentary by David ben Joseph Kimhi. [Venice: Giovanni di Gara, 1566].[83]

"Perush Sachia" — perhaps *Perush Shehitah*, i.e., commentary on the laws of slaughtering or a collection of such laws. Possible identifications are Mordecai ben Hillel, *Hil^{e}khoth Sh^{e}ḥitah* (a compendium in verse on such laws) [Venice: Daniel Adelkind, 1550?][84] or Jacob Weil, *Sh^{e}ḥitoth u-*

---

[76] *STC Italian*, p. 437, items 10, 11, 12, 15.

[77] *STC Italian*, p. 67, item 24.

[78] *STC Italian*, p. 3, item 4.

[79] *STC Italian*, p. 655, items 24 and 25.

[80] *STC Italian*, p. 3, items 27 and 28.

[81] *STC Italian*, p. 632, item 27.

[82] *STC Italian*, p. 367, second last item on the page.

[83] *STC Italian*, p. 97, item 13.

[84] *STC Italian*, p. 448, item 28.

B^e*diqoth*, ed. Me'ir ben Ephraim, ha-Sopher of Padua. [Mantua: Jacob ben Naphtali, ha-Kohen, for Venturino Ruffinelli, 1556].[85]

"Sepher Atermà" — probably Baruch ben Isaac, *Sepher ha-T^erumah*. A printing of 1523 attributed to Bomberg is extant.[86]

"Commassin con Latin con la decchiaration del dicduc per imparar Latin et hebreo" — a Hebrew-Latin Pentateuch with a Hebrew-Latin grammar. A publication answering this description has not been located, although the Giustiniani press issued a Hebrew-Latin Pentateuch with commentary by Sebastian Münster in 1551.[87]

"Rabi Jacob balaturim" — Jacob ben Asher, *Arba'ah Turim*. Giovanni Griffio published in 1566 the most complete recent Venetian printing, with commentary by Joseph ben Ephraim Caro.[88]

"Heliocotolam" — Y^eshu'ah ben Joseph, *Halikoth 'Olam* (a methodology of the Babylonian Talmud) [Venice: Cornelius Adelkind & Judah ben Isaac, ha-Levi, & Jehiel ben Jekuthiel, ha-Kohen, for Giovanni de' Farri and his brother, 1544].[89]

"Sidorsolam" — possibly *Seder 'Olam* (Order of the World, a chronicle). [Venice: Marc'Antonio Giustiniani, 1545].[90]

"Igarot" — Igg^{e}roth (letters). Possibly Moses Ben Maimun (Maimonides), *Igg^{e}roth* [Venice: Marc'Antonio Giustiniani, 1545].[91]

'Biurim sopra il perus Rassi" — supercommentary on Rashi, i.e., a commentary on Rashi's commentary on the Penta-

[85] *STC Italian*, p. 736, item 23.

[86] *STC Italian*, p. 75, item 18.

[87] *STC Italian*, p. 95, item 17. Münster (1489–1552) was a German Hebraist and historian.

[88] *STC Italian*, p. 344, item 12.

[89] *STC Italian*, p. 739, item 4.

[90] *STC Italian*, p. 620, item 11.

[91] *STC Italian*, p. 452, item 15.

teuch. Possibilities include the supercommentary of Israel
ben Petahiah Isserlein, published in Venice by Cristoforo
Zanetti in 1566, or the *Diqduqe Rashi* (anonymous gram-
matical notes on Rashi) published in Riva di Trento, 1560.[92]
"Pelmoet" — possibly Solomon ben Abraham Ibn Adred,
Ohel Mo'ed (a dictionary of synonyms). [Venice: Marc'
Antonio Giustiniani, 1548].[93]

The list of readily identifiable titles argues strongly that the
priest based his denunciation on concrete information, probably
the books themselves. Perhaps he saw them at the loading dock
in Cephalonia or in Giustiniani's ship. Or someone else in Cephalonia read the titles and passed on the information to the priest.
Obviously the denouncer or his informant read Hebrew.

Even though Giustiniani's chest contained sponges rather than
books, the Inquisition continued its investigation. Other witnesses
testified that Giustiniani was trafficking in Hebrew books and that
he operated a printing press in the governor's palace. But they
could not confirm that he printed Hebrew books. Giustiniani had
brought to Cephalonia a German, one Cristoforo Nicostella da
Magonza (Mainz) for the purpose of engraving Arabic maps and
printing Turkish prayers ("orationi Turchesca"). The Holy Office
questioned Nicostella, who acknowledged that he had been engaged in the Arabic and Turkish printing projects, but had with-
drawn over a wage dispute with Giustiniani. He said nothing
about printing Hebrew books but did relay some secondhand information: Zuan Jacopo Bollani of Venice, the first bookbinder
at Cephalonia, had told Nicostella that Giustiniani had trans-
ported twelve boxes of Hebrew books "both good and prohibited"
("fra buoni et prohibitij") from Venice and had had them bound
in the governor's palace in Cephalonia. These books looked like
the Talmud that was burned in Venice, according to Zuan Jacopo.

Cristoforo had also heard that four boxes of these books were
shipped to Zante (the next Venetian island outpost in the Ionian

---

[92] *STC Italian*, p. 633, items 9 and 11.
[93] *STC Italian*, p. 632, item 21.

Sea, directly south of Cephalonia) from whence they were sent to Syria as well. The Holy Office did not question Bollani,[94] but did question the other bookbinder who had succeeded Bollani at Cephalonia. The second bookbinder confirmed that he had bound Hebrew books there, but did not know if they were prohibited titles. He knew nothing about Hebrew printing in Cephalonia.

The list of titles and the corroborative testimony easily establish that Giustiniani dealt in Hebrew books. One can speculate on the chronology and geography of the trade. Perhaps when the Esecutori in 1568 ordered Hebrew volumes exported out of the Venetian state, the Jews and their publishers only sent them to Cephalonia. Giustiniani then quietly returned the books to Venice at the first opportunity.

The additional and more fascinating possibility is that Giustiniani printed Hebrew books in Cephalonia. It is conceivable that the Jews and their publishers smuggled type to Cephalonia and there replaced the titles destroyed in Venice. According to Nicostella, Bollani had told him that the books that he was binding were like the Talmud burned in Venice. He may have been binding, for example, copies of Simeon Kayyara's *Halakhoth G^e doloth*, an epitome of the Talmud published by Giustiniani in 1548, and perhaps reprinted in Cephalonia. Indeed, the list of titles presented by the priest strongly suggests that Giustiniani was both reprinting titles that he had originally published between 1545 and 1553 as well as reprinting titles published by Cavalli, Gara, Griffio, and Zanetti, between 1563 and 1568.[95] In this way the Venetian Hebrew press may have continued to fulfil its traditional role of supplier of liturgical and rabbinical works to Jewish communities all the length of the Mediterranean Sea.

Yet, the evidence for a Hebrew printing press in Cephalonia is circumstantial rather than conclusive. The priest did not claim that

[94] It appears from the documents that Bollani was no longer in Cephalonia nor readily available in Venice.

[95] Of course, Giustiniani would not list Cephalonia as the place of publication of any books printed there. This would only draw attention to his illegal activities.

he had seen it, and the printer and bookbinder said nothing about it. Of course, the latter two may have been lying.[96] It is also possible that Giustiniani only imported unbound Hebrew books from somewhere else in the Mediterranean, bound them in Cephalonia, and sold them in Venice and other lands. The Holy Office could not convict without concrete evidence, so the investigation petered out. But the members of the Inquisition probably strongly suspected that Giustiniani operated a Hebrew press in Cephalonia, and that same suspicion seems justifiable four centuries later.

Certainly the clandestine traffic in Hebrew books continued. When Marc'Antonio Giustiniani died in Cephalonia (July 25, 1571), his eldest son followed in his footsteps. Antonio Giustiniani (1553–1580)[97] brought fourteen chests of Hebrew books from Cephalonia to Venice sometime in the first half of 1574. The Holy Office examined them at the customs dock, released twelve, and sealed two chests pending expurgation. The Holy Office held the key but permitted Antonio to take the sealed chests to his home. The chests then disappeared. Giustiniani blandly explained to the Holy Office that he had needed more room in his house to lodge some French dignitaries in the train of Henry III whom the Venetian government had lavishly hosted in July 1574. So he had sold the books to a Ferrara Jew. The angry Inquisition tried to trace the books, but encountered a series of dead ends. For example, Giustiniani told the tribunal that the sale had been ar-

---

[96] Members of the Venetian booktrade very seldom cooperated with the Inquisition. They often violated the Index of Prohibited Books, especially by smuggling prohibited volumes from northern Europe into Venice, and they endured frequent questioning by the Inquisition without revealing much. They grudgingly admitted their guilt when the Holy Office had overwhelming evidence, such as possession of the illicit volumes. But even under intense questioning, they almost never revealed additional information about any aspect of the booktrade.

[97] ASV, Marco Barbaro, "Arbori dei Patritii veneti," vol. 7, p. 449, with the notation that Antonio was killed. This branch of the Giustiniani family died out with Antonio and his three brothers. Only two of them married, and none produced legitimate heirs. (It is not known if there were any illegitimate offspring, because the Barbaro genealogies do not list them.)

130

ranged by a certain Rialto broker — who had died in the meantime. In the end the Inquisition gave up trying to recover the books, but fined Antonio 100 ducats.[98] Whatever the true story of the disappearance of the books, the significant point is that distribution of unexpurgated Hebrew books persisted despite the controls of church and state.

After the narrow escape of 1571, the lot of Venetian Jewry steadily improved, as its indispensable role in the Republic's commercial and social life grew and was acknowledged by the government.[99] The easing of hostility toward the Jews led to the revival of Hebrew publishing. In 1574 Alvise Bragadino and Me'ir Parenzo began again to publish Hebrew titles. The Great Plague of 1575–1577 brought printing and most other economic activity to a halt. Subsequently, Giovanni di Gara, and the respective Bragadino and Parenzo heirs published Hebrew titles in greater quantity. Eventually a handful of other publishers joined them, especially in the 1590s. Clandestine measures were no longer needed.

The Jewish community and their publishers suffered heavily in 1568, but managed to continue printing and distributing Hebrew books. The titles listed by the priest in 1570 were almost exclusively religious, either liturgical works or learned commentaries necessary for rabbinic scholarship. They were essential for the maintainance of religious life of a community enduring persecution. Although much remains unknown, the fundamental point is clear: the Jews, with the aid of the Giustiniani family, obtained the books they needed.

University of Toronto

[98] ASV, Santo Uffizio, Busta 37, Antonio Giustiniani, no pag., the questioning of Giustiniani and others from October 22, 1574, through April 19, 1575.

[99] Pullan, *Rich and Poor*, pp. 541–78.

[100] Amram, *Makers of Hebrew Books*, pp. 342–44, 360–63.

XIII

BOOKS FOR SARPI: THE SMUGGLING OF PROHIBITED BOOKS INTO VENICE DURING THE INTERDICT OF 1606-1607

Books were important weapons during the interdict conflict. When the Republic refused to hand over to ecclesiastical courts two clergymen accused of crimes, and also declined to revoke laws asserting secular jurisdiction over criminous clerics and ecclesiastical property, Paul V laid Venice under interdict in April 1606. The Venetians sprang to defend themselves, not only with diplomacy, but with pamphlets and treatises designed to win the approval of European public opinion. The Senate appointed Sarpi its theologian, and from this platform he argued the Venetian case. Additional Venetian clergy and laymen also contributed works, while cardinals Cesare Baronio and Robert Bellarmine, and other papal defenders, answered.

The Venetian apologists enjoyed the indispensable aid of the Venetian bookmen.[1] The Republic had an enormous advantage over Rome in the propaganda warfare because it could enlist the support of the largest Italian printing industry, one that ranked among the four or five largest in Europe. The Venetian bookmen brought to the fray a wealth of professional skills developed through years of both legal trade and clandestine operations designed to circumvent the Index of Prohibited Books and the Holy Office. No bookman contributed more than Roberto Meietti, who published several important antipapal tracts, including Sarpi's *Considerationi sopra le censure della Santità di Papa Paulo V*.[2] Equally important were his smuggling skills, for he arranged the publication of antipapal tracts in northern Europe and the importation into Venice of prohibited titles that Sarpi and other authors might find useful. This latter, less noted service to the Venetian cause will be discussed here.[3]

Roberto Meietti was born into the printing trade. His father Paolo published in Venice and Padua concurrently from 1569 through 1596. Roberto began publishing in Venice with a single title in

Padua, 1572, and then continuously in Venice from 1588 through 1617, producing mostly literary and medical titles before the interdict.[4] All were acceptable to the Index, with one exception. When the Roman Congregation of the Index in 1594 ordered the destruction of Francesco Patrizi's *Nova de universis philosophia* (Ferrara, 1591), the Ferrara printer saved some copies and sent them to Meietti, who put a new title page on the work and sold it.[5]

Meietti probably began to deal in prohibited books early in his career. In 1588 the Venetian Holy Office questioned him to learn why he had shipped books from Venice to stock a newly purchased Paduan bookstore without procuring an Inquisition export license. Normally the Holy Office did not investigate such a petty offense, but the tribunal appeared to be generally suspicious of Meietti, since he could not provide an inventory of the existing books in the Paduan store. The tribunal was sceptical that he would spend two hundred ducats without knowing what he was buying, and suspected that the bookstore contained prohibited titles. But without firm evidence, the Inquisition could only warn Meietti.[6]

With the support of the Republic, the Venetian Holy Office attempted to prevent the importation of Protestant books from northern Europe through an inspection at the customs house. The Council of Ten had decreed in 1569 that all books entering the city were to be opened at the customs house in the presence of the inquisitor. In addition, one of the priors of the printers' guild had to prepare inventories of imported titles in the presence of the inquisitorial inspector. Only then might the books be removed from the customs dock.[7]

Nevertheless, the bookmen found ways to avoid the customs check. In 1594 the papacy discovered that Meietti was distributing prohibited German titles in Rome itself. He had brought the banned books into Venice, removed their title pages, substituted innocent new ones, and then shipped the disguised works on to Rome. The Congregation of the Index demanded that the Venetian Holy Office proceed against Meietti and his unnamed accómplices. The Council of Ten promised that the Riformatori dello Studio di Padova, a civil body charged with overseeing the book trade, would investigate. Quite likely, the Riformatori did little or nothing.[8] The Venetian Holy Office did apprehend Meietti and three other publishers importing from Germany works which included a volume of the

Magdeburg Centuries and a banned astronomical title in 1599. The Inquisition confiscated the books, threatened the bookmen with penalties of one hundred ducats, and released them.[9]

During the interdict, the customs inspection collapsed because the Republic withdrew its support. The papacy could only intercept northern contraband if it passed through friendly states. Fortunately for the papacy, the major Venetian trade route from Germany to Venice was through the Brenner Pass, Bolzano, and the Archbishopric of Trent.[10] Having learned through its intelligence network that Meietti's factor had taken some manuscripts north to be printed in Frankfurt, the papacy requested the archbishop of Trent to arrest him upon his return. On October 23, 1606, Cardinal Carlo Madruzzo reported that the disguised factor had slipped through, but that his cargo of books had been seized.[11]

The first three titles were pro-Venetian tracts which Meietti had arranged to have printed in the north. The factor was returning with a thousand copies of each, i.e., a normal press run, probably intended for distribution in Venice and elsewhere in Italy.

Due discorsi sopra la libertà ecclesiastica. Di Giovanni Simone Sardi Venetiano, anno MDCVI. 4°. The tract argues that the Roman curia, with the aid of the Jesuits, sought to undermine all temporal powers and to make itself master of the world. "Sardi" was the pseudonym of Giovanni Battista Leoni, historian, man of letters, and *oratore* in Venice for the Duke of Urbino at the time of the interdict. Since Urbino was a papal dependency, Leoni undoubtedly thought it wise to write under a pseudonym and to arrange for publication abroad. However, reprints identified the author.

Risposta di maestro Pasquino cittadino romano, a quanto gli scrive il Gobbo di Rialto, sopra la scommunica publicata contra la Serenissima Republica di Venetia da Papa Paolo V, et le scritture delli cardinali Baronio e Bellarmino. 1606. 4°. Of unknown authorship, this is an antipapal satire put into the mouth of the famous Roman statue Pasquino. Perhaps the Venetians hoped that this tract would persuade readers to believe that opposition to the pope's stand existed in Rome itself. Some printings of 1606 identify Meietti as the publisher, while others do not.

Duo vota hoc est ex animo voto prelatae sententiae unum illustrissimi, ac reverendissimi D. Caesaris BARONII Sorani S. R. E. cardinalis bibliothecarii contra serenissimam Rempublicam Venetam.

*Alterum excellentissimi D. Ioannis MARSILII Neapolitani theologi,
pro eadem serenissima Republica.* MDCVI. 4°. This composite work
contains a short anti-Venetian tract of Baronius (pp. 4-6) and the
longer reply (pp. 7-22) of Giovanni Marsilio (c. 1562-1612), a
Neapolitan priest, one of the Republic's theologians, and a prolific
controversialist. The papacy excommunicated him on November 1,
1606.[12] Even though the Tridentine authorities undoubtedly destroyed
these press runs, each of the above three titles had two or more
printings. Thus, many copies survive.

Next were two northern tracts supporting the Venetian stand.
Probably the factor was bringing them to Venice for perusal.

*De Venetorum excommunicatione, adversus Caesarem Baronium
S. R. E. Cardinalem dissertatio, in qua vera excommunicationis ratio,
tum ex Sacra Scriptura, tum ex antiquis Ecclesiae christiane monu-
mentis breviter et dilucide demonstratur, autore Nicolao Vignierio.*
Salmuri [Saumer], prostant exemplaria apud T. Portau. MDCVI. 8°.
Six copies. Nicolas Vignier the Younger (c. 1575-c. 1645) was the
Huguenot pastor of Blois and a theologian. The French ambassador
to Venice, who was sympathetic to the Venetian cause, judged that
Vignier's intemperate tract would not aid the Republic. Nevertheless,
it was quickly reprinted and translated into French and English.[13]

Rütger Rulant, *Thesaurus juris executivi ecclesiastici criminalis
et civilis ad Principum et Senatum venetum.* Frankfurt, 1606. One
copy. The Congregation of the Index in 1609 condemned this collection of four tracts dealing with the interdict authored by Rulant (or
Rulandt), 1568-1630, a German jurist.[14]

"Ad Paulum V. Pont. Max. quattuor epistolae." 8°. Twenty-nine
copies. This title remains unidentified. Several pro-Venetian letters
addressed to the pope, including the Republic's official response, two
from anonymous jurisconsults, and others are known. This appears
to be a collection of four of them.

Meietti's factor also carried one or two copies each of several
prohibited northern works, mostly defenses of civil jurisdiction, from
which Venetian defenders might cull useful arguments. One of these
works was destined for Sarpi, another for one of his associates, and
the rest possibly imported to fill specific requests.

Caroli Molinaei, *Consilium super actis Concilii Tridentini.* 8°.
Two copies. The Protestant jurist Charles Du Moulin (1500-66)
authored this treatise, first published in French at Lyons, 1564, and

in Latin at Poitiers in 1565, which opposes the acceptance of the Tridentine decrees. A bull of August 21, 1602, banned all of Du Moulin's works.[15]

"Triumphus Papalis. In folio. Basileae." Two copies. Unidentified.

"De Jurisdictione Auctoritate, et praeminentia Imperiali ac potestate ecclesiastica. Vol. 1." Unidentified.

Marsilius of Padua, *De defensor pacis*. The Tridentine Index banned this title.

Thomas Erastus, *Explicatio gravissimae quaestionis utrum excommunicatio*. Pesclarii, apud Boacium Sultaceterum [i.e., John Wolfe, London], 1589. 4°. Two copies. This is the first edition of the celebrated treatise on excommunication, which argues for the submission of church to state, by Thomas Erastus (1524-83), Swiss medical scholar, theologian, and follower of Zwingli. The Clementine Index of 1596 banned it. One copy carried the notation: "Per il Reverendo Prete Maestro Paolo [Sarpi] de Servi Theologo del Senato. Venetia." A second copy was addressed: "Per il Clarissimo Signore Nobile Giacopo Barrozzi. Venetia." Giacomo di Lorenzo Barozzi was an associate of Sarpi.[16] Either these had been purchased on order, or else northern admirers made presents of them to Sarpi and Barozzi.

(bound with) Wilhelm Holder, *Cuculus Calvinisticus sive de gratitudine Calviniana adversus blasphemam I. I. Grynaei Apologiam commonefactio*. Tubingae, 1585. 4°. Holder (1542-1609) was a Lutheran theologian whose opera omnia were banned by the Clementine Index.

Finally, the factor carried a Quattrocento Italian vernacular literary work which had been banned, Masuccio Salernitano's *Novelle*.

One week later, the Roman Congregation of the Holy Office excommunicated Meietti. The edict condemned him for publishing "pernicious books containing heresies, impieties, and errors of diverse kinds." But it made no mention of his smuggling, suggesting that the decision to excommunicate had been made before news of the smuggling reached Rome. The edict forbade all to purchase or sell Meietti's imprints, past and future, although this was soon modified to permit the buying and selling of those printed prior to the interdict.[17]

By the terms of the interdict, clergy were forbidden to exercise almost all religious functions, such as celebrating mass and administering sacraments. The Republic ordered Venetian ecclesiastics to disobey the papacy. The majority did without murmur, while others were coerced, and the Jesuits, Capuchins, and Theatines expelled. Both Republic and papacy made ostentatious preparations for a war which would only enhance the French and Spanish presences in the peninsula. Within a few months, the belligerents reached an impasse and began to extend peace feelers. Paul V softened his position, and the unanimity of the Senate started to crack. In February 1607 the Venetians accepted mediation by a French cardinal, and on April 21 the pope lifted the interdict. The Venetians handed over to the French king the accused clerics sought by Rome, but retained the laws claiming secular jurisdiction over clergymen and church lands. As usual in Venetian-papal conflicts, much was left unsettled to ignite future disputes. Despite their claims, neither side profited from the interdict. Paul V suffered a distinct defeat, because he levied an interdict and then withdrew it without attaining much of his goal. The Venetians could more legitimately claim a victory but, at the same time, the struggle had underlined the dangers to a small state of isolation in an indifferent world. Perhaps the major outcome of the conflict was to teach doge and pope that they had to settle their differences in the old way of interminable negotiation lest they become the pawns of the great powers.

Despite the reconciliation, the Republic did not restore the inquisitorial check on imported books for several years.[18] If a bookman could elude the Tridentine authorities and reach Venetian territory with his contraband, he need no longer worry. For example, when the Verona inquisitor wished to inspect a shipment of books from the north destined for Venice, the Republic rebuffed him.[19] Unable to halt the traffic into Venice, Rome could only try to stop it elsewhere. The papacy admonished inquisitors in other Italian cities to scrutinize closely books arriving from Venice, and in 1614 the papacy deputized an official in Frankfurt to draft a list of permissible books from which the bookmen might select their purchases.[20] But it is unlikely that the papacy had the local political support to enforce this.

As a result of the smuggling, Venetian readers had access to a broad range of old and new prohibited titles. In August 1608, Fra Fulgenzio Manfredi (c. 1550-1610), one of the Republic's theologians during the interdict, suddenly defected to Rome. He provided the papacy with a brief list of some prohibited books which circulated.

The nobility and the learned had Calvin's *Institutes* in Latin, and such English anti-Catholic titles as *Problema de Romanae fidei ementito catholicismo* (Cambridge, 1604) of the Puritan theologian William Perkins, and the *Disputationum de Antechristo libri* (London, 1605) of the Anglican controversialist Gabriel Powel. He also reported that the majority of the nobles had Machiavelli. Titles circulating among commoners and in nonlearned circles included Calvin's *Catechism* in Italian, the Psalms in Italian printed in Geneva, 1585, a Protestant vernacular version of the New Testament, and the anti-papal *Due dialoghi. L'uno di Mercurio et Caronte, l'altro di Lattantio et di uno archidiacono* (first published in Venice in the 1540s) of Alfonso Valdés.[21]

Once prohibited titles entered Venice, they could turn up anywhere. For example, the father-general of the Franciscan Conventuals visited a Venetian monastery in May 1609. During the mealtime scriptural reading, the father-general suddenly heard passages which deviated from the Catholic Vulgate. Examining the Bible, he discovered that it was a Protestant version lacking title page and colophon.[22] More than likely, the bookseller had torn off the pages which would identify it as an imported Protestant version, and had sold it to the unsuspecting friars.

The nuncio confirmed that "a great quantity" of prohibited books circulated, and that "he who wants them has them." But, he warned Rome, nothing could be done, for there would be great trouble with the Venetians if he were to instruct priests to preach on the subject.[23] At the same time, he counselled Rome to keep the situation in perspective. While "many heretics and others of little piety" certainly had Protestant Bibles, the city was not inundated with heretical literature.[24] The nuncio was undoubtedly correct; if Protestant literature had threatened the city's traditional loyalty to Catholicism, the government would have strongly supported the Holy Office, as it had in the 1560s and 1570s. The leaders of the state opposed the jurisdictional claims of the papacy, but they were not sympathetic to indigenous heresy.

In the lingering hostility, the papacy refused to lift Meietti's excommunication despite repeated intercession by the Venetian ambassador.[25] Rome's caution was justified, for Meietti had not changed his ways. In 1610 he was secretly vending an Italian translation of the *Anticoton* (first published in 1610), the famous French tract attacking Pierre Coton, Jesuit advisor to Henry IV. Although the Italian translation carried the name of a Lyons publisher, the nuncio suspected that Meietti had printed it, either in Venice or abroad. The Holy Office failed to act because the lay members refused to permit the tribunal to confiscate the title or punish Meietti.[26] During his excommunication Meietti carried on his business as before, and even held office in the printers' guild in 1611.[27] Eventually, in 1614, he made his submission and was absolved. Nevertheless, Rome still advised the inquisitors of other cities to observe the prohibitions against Meietti lest "under the pretense of a change of heart he might introduce bad and pernicious books" into their jurisdictions.[28] Again papal suspicions were justified, for in 1621 Meietti was selling anti-Catholic pamphlets printed in Germany in his Venetian store.[29] Thirty-three years after his first brush with the Holy Office, Meietti still trafficked in prohibited books. Disobedience to the Index of Prohibited Books remained an unchanging feature of Venetian life in the late Cinquecento and early Seicento.

[1] Rather than attempting to distinguish among publisher, printer, and bookseller (an artificial distinction in any case, because one man or firm frequently did all three), the general term "bookman" is preferred. *Stampatore*, *libraio*, and *bibliopola* were used interchangeably and indiscriminately in the Cinquecento and early Seicento.

[2] For known Meietti imprints of interdict tracts, see *Lettres et ambassade de messire Philippe Canaye, seigneur de Fresne* (Paris, 1645), vol. III, "Avant-propos," no pag., items XIX, XXIV, XXV, XXVIII, XXIX, XXXIX, XLVI, XLVII, XLVIII, LXXVI, LXXXIX, XCII, XCIII, CIX.

[3] This article describes a few incidents in a large topic, the struggle to enforce the Index in Venice. For a comprehensive picture, see my forthcoming monograph, "The Roman Inquisition and the Venetian Press, 1540-1605," Princeton Univ. Press.

[4] Dennis E. Rhodes, "Roberto Meietti e alcuni documenti della controversia fra Papa Paolo V e Venezia," *Studi secenteschi*, 1 (1960), 165-74; and "Further travels of certain Italian printers," *La Bibliofilia*, 73 (1971), 181-82; *Short-title Catalogue of Books printed in Italy and of Italian Books printed in other countries from 1465 to 1600 now in the British Museum* (London, 1958), 890; Ester Pastorello, *Tipografi, editori, librai a Venezia nel secolo XVI* (Florence, 1924), 54-55.

[5] Luigi Firpo, "Filosofia italiana e Controriforma," *Rivista di filosofia*, 41 (1950), 171-72.

[6] Archivio di Stato, Venezia (hereafter ASV), Santo Uffizio (hereafter SU), Busta 62, Roberto Meietti, no pag., testimony of October 22 and November 8, 1588.

[7] ASV, Consiglio dei Dieci, Parti Comuni, Registro 29, ff. 30r-31r, June 28, 1569. In practice, priests drawn from the local regular clergy acted for the inquisitor, while the priors probably appointed representatives.

[8] Letter of Ambassador Paolo Paruta of November 19, 1594, Rome, in *La legazione di Roma di Paolo Paruta (1592-1595)*, ed. Giuseppe de Leva. Vol. II (Rome, 1887), 488-90; ASV, Consiglio dei Dieci, Deliberazioni Roma, R. 3, f. 59v, November 29,

1594. Because the Riformatori *fondo* is very incomplete for the Cinquecento, I cannot confirm that they did not act. But I have not come upon any notice that they ever punished bookmen for violating the press laws.

[9] ASV, SU, Bu. 49, Libri prohibiti, no pag., documents of August 3 and September 4, 1599. This folder contains miscellaneous charred fragments, difficult to read, of several trials concerning prohibited books. The astronomical title was *Ephemerides novae annorum xxxvi incipientes ab anno mdxcv* (Frankfurt, 1599) of David Origanus (1558-1628), a Copernican. It was banned in 1603. Franz Heinrich Reusch, *Der Index der Verbotenen Bücher. Ein Beitrag zur Kirchen- und Literaturgeschichte.* Vol. II, pt. 1 (Bonn, 1885; rpt. Darmstadt, 1967), 182.

[10] Frederic C. Lane, *Venice: A Maritime Republic* (Baltimore, 1973), map on p. 227.

[11] Archivio Segreto Vaticano, Fondo Borghese, IV, vol. 12, ff. 157r-58v. The following identifications are based on the titles, some full, others brief, listed by Cardinal Madruzzo. Bibliographies of interdict writings are found in *Lettres de Canaye*, III, "Avant-propos;" and Francesco Scaduto, *Stato e chiesa secondo Fra Paolo Sarpi e la coscienza pubblica durante l'interdetto di Venezia del 1606-1607. Con bibliografia* (Florence, 1885). The first four tracts listed are in the Biblioteca Marciana, Venice.

[12] Gino Benzoni, "I 'teologi' minori dell'interdetto," *Archivio veneto*, Serie V, vol. 91 (1970), 78-88.

[13] *Lettres de Canaye*, III, "Avant-propos," item CIII: *British Museum General Catalogue of Printed Books.* Vol. 248 (London, 1964), cols. 793-94; *Catalogue général des livres imprimés de la Bibliothèque Nationale. Auteurs.* Vol. 209 (Paris, 1970), cols. 285-86.

[14] Reusch, *Der Index*, vol. II, pt. 1, pp. 321-22.

[15] Reusch, *Der Index*, vol. I, pp. 441-44.

[16] Paolo Sarpi, *Lettere ai Protestanti*, ed. Manlio Duilio Busnelli. Vol. I (Bari, 1931), 63.

[17] The edict of excommunication of October 30, 1606, is found in Archivio Segreto Vaticano, Miscellaneorum Armarium IV, vol. 31, f. 226r. For the modification, see a letter from Rome to the inquisitor of Bologna of November 25, 1606, in Antonio Rotondò, "Nuovi documenti per la storia dell'Indice dei libri proibiti (1572-1638)," *Rinascimento*, Serie 2, vol. 3 (1963), 184, document 28.

[18] The papacy complained in 1610 and 1611 that the bookmen were unpacking German imports at the customs house without an inquisitorial presence. Biblioteca Apostolica Vaticana, Vaticanus Latinus 10945, "Anima del Sant'Offitio spirata dal Sopremo Tribunale della Sacra Congregatione raccolta dal Padre Predicatore F. Giacomo Angarano da Vicenza l'anno del Signore MDCXLIV," f. 118v.

[19] Letter of Nuncio Berlinghiero Gessi of May 24, 1608, as quoted in Pietro Savio, "Il nunzio dopo l'interdetto," *Archivio veneto*, Serie V, anno 56-57 (1955), 77 n. 1.

[20] Letters from the Congregation of the Holy Office to the inquisitor of Modena of 1613 and 1614 in Rotondò, "Nuovi documenti," 193-97, documents 37, 38, 40, and 42.

[21] Pietro Savio, "Per l'epistolario di Paolo Sarpi," *Aevum*, 10 (1936), 26-27. I have completed some of the identifications. The unfortunate Manfredi was executed as a *relapsus*. Benzoni, "I 'teologi' minori," 67-78.

[22] Letter of the father-general of May 8, 1609, as quoted in Savio, "Epistolario di Sarpi," *Aevum*, 10 (1936), 26 n. 1.

[23] Letter of Nuncio Gessi of February 14, 1609, in Savio, "Il nunzio dopo l'interdetto," 83-84.

[24] Letter of Nuncio Gessi of June 27, 1609, in Savio, "Epistolario di Sarpi," *Aevum*, 16 (1942), 11.

114

[25] Letter of Cardinal Scipione (Caffarelli) Borghese of November 26, 1607, quoted in Savio, "Epistolario di Sarpi," *Aevum*, 16 (1940), 9.

[26] The Venetian Holy Office consisted of the inquisitor, the patriarch, the nuncio, and three nobles appointed by the Venetian government. The tribunal could not arrest a suspect without the approval of the laymen. See the letters of Nuncio Gessi of December 4, 11, 18, 25, 1610, as quoted in Savio, "Epistolario di Sarpi," *Aevum*, 14 (1940), 67-68. The *Anticoton* was formally banned by the Congregation of the Index in 1617, but an Italian translation has not been located.

[27] ASV, Arte dei libreri, stampatori e ligadori, Bu. 163, Registro Atti II (1597 mv-1617), ff. 71v-72r, 74r, 75v, 77r-v.

[28] Biblioteca Apostolica Vaticana, Barberino Latino 5195, "Raccolta di alcuni negotij, e cause spettanti alla Santa Inquisitione nella Città e Dominio Veneto. Dal principio di Clemente VIII sino al presente mese di luglio MDCXXV," ff. 52r-v, July 11, 1614; Rotondò, "Nuovi documenti," 184 n. 2.

[29] ASV, SU, Bu. 77, Roberto Meietti.

INDEX

Abraham ben Gedaliah Ben
  Asher: XII 114
Abraham Ibn Ezra: XII 113
Abravanel,Isaac ben Judah:
  XII 125
Abudirham,David ben Joseph:
  XII 115,125
Aconcio,Jacopo: I 150
Admai,Rabbi: XII 116
Aesop: VI 456;XI 14
Agostini,Ludovico: IV 482,
  487,490,493
Agrippa: II 243
Alamanni,Luigi: II 236
Alberti,Leandro: I 167
Alberti,L.B.: II 231-234,
  237,240;IV 479,487,490
Aleander,Girolamo: XI 1-2
Alexander the Great: IV 481
Alunno,Francesco: VI 459
Amaseo,Romolo: VI 454,455,
  457,458,462
Ammirato,Scipione: I 150
Angelieri,printer: I 156
Angulaci,Josef: XII 116
Appian: I 161
Apuleius: II 235
Aquinas: VII 48
Aretino,Pietro: I 142,179;
  II 230,234,243,248;III 25,
  28,38;IV 483;V 318,319;
  IX 54,57,61;XI 4,9,10
Ariosto,Ludovico: I 141;II
  235,240;IV 485;VI 459;
  IX 54
Aristotle: I 144,149,179;
  II 234,236,241,242;IV 482;
  V 322;VI 455
Atanagi,Dionigi: I 149
Augustine,St: III 32
Avicenna: VI 456

Bacon,Francis: I 179;VIII
  212
Badia,Tommaso: XI 2
Badoer,Andrea di Piero: X
  316,322
Bahye ben Asher(Moses ben
  Nahman): XII 113,125
Baius: VII 38
Barbarigo,Agostino di
  Lorenzo: X 327

Barbarigo,Agostino di
  Zuanne: X 316
Barbarigo,Andrea di
  Gregorio: X 307-309,312,316
Barbarigo,Doge Marco: X 307
Barbarigo,Pietro di Lorenzo:
  X 327
Barbarigo,Sebastiano di
  Francesco: X 330
Barbaro,Marc'Antonio di
  Francesco: X 293
Baron,Hans: II 231;VI 447
Baronius,Caesar: I 155;X
  105,108
Barozzi,Giacomo di Lorenzo:
  XIII 109
Baruch ben Isaac: XII 126
Barzizza,Cristoforo: VI
  459
Beccadelli,Ludovico: X
  302,306
Belegno,Alvise di Bernar-
  dino: X 291,335
Bellarmine,Robert: VIII 214;
  XIII 105
Bembo,Giovanni di Agostino:
  X 291,335,337
Bembo,Pietro: I 140;II 230,
  234,236,240,241;III 27;
  IV 485;VI 455,459
Beni,Paolo: I 150
Benivieni,Girolamo: VI 459
Bernardo,Andrea di Francesco:
  X 325,326,329
Bernardo,Francesco di Marc'
  Antonio: X 315,322,325
Bernardo,Francesco di
  Zaccaria: X 291,338
Bernardo,Giovanni Battista
  di GB: X 335
Bessarion,Cardinal: XI 17
Bevilacqua,Nicolò: I 155
Bevilacqua press: XII 116
Biondo,Flavio: I 147,168;
  VI 459
Boccaccio: II 234,240,241;
  IX 54;XI 4,7
Boccalini,Traiano: I 151
Bodin,Jean: I 149,150,168;
  VIII 212,214-216
Bollani,Zuan Jacopo: XII
  127,128

Bolognetti,Alberto: X 322
Bomberg,Daniel: XII 103-105,
109,113,124,126
Bon,Alessandro di Alvise:
X 291,313
Bonamico,Lazzaro: V 324;VI
449,454-455,457-458,462
Bondumier,Bertucci di
Zuanne: X 335
Bonelli,Michele: X 315
Bonifacio,Giovanni Bernar-
dino: X 307,309
Bora,Benetto: XII 113,114,116
Borromeo,Carlo: X 317
Botero,Giovanni: VIII 218;
XI 7,8
Bracciolini,Poggio: VI 461
Bragadino,Alvise: XII 104,
106,110,130
Bragadino,Antonio di Andrea:
X 294,318
Bragadino,Giovanni Alvise
di Marco: X 322-324
Bragadino,Marcantonio di
Marco: X 322
Brucioli,Antonio: IX 61
Brucioli,Francesco: XII 104
Bruni,Leonardo: I 148,163,168;
II 231,V 323;VI 459,461
Bruno,Giordano: III 38;X 329
Brus,Anton: XI 6
Bruto,Giovan Michele: I 151
Brylinger,Nikolaus: XI 11
Buccella,Nicolò: X 312
Bucer,Martin: III 29,30;XI 2
Buffalo,Nonce: VII 49

Caesar: I 144,146,161;II 233
Calcagnino,Celio: VI 459
Calmo,Andrea: I 142
Calvin,John: III 27;IX 56,61;
XI 8;XIII 111
Camillo,Guilio: VI 459
Campana,Augusto: V 317,321-
323,325;VI 447-449,461
Campanella,Tommaso: I 179;
III 38;IV 490,493,494
Canale,Antonio di Giovanni:
X 334
Cantimori,Delio: III 27
Capella,Galeazzo: I 171
Capello,Vincenzo di
Domenico: X 330,331,335,
337,338
Capponi,Gino di Neri: I 163
Carafa,Gian Pietro: see
Paul IV
Caro,Annibale: VI 459

Caro,Joseph ben Ephraim: XII
114,126
Carnesecchi,Pietro: III 27
Cartari,Vincenzo: I 170
Castiglione,Baldesar: I 141,
171;II 232;III 34;XI 7
Cavalcanti,Bartolomeo: VI 459
Cavalli,Marin de': X 320
Cavalli,Zorzi de': XII 112,
115,116,119,124,125,128
Cecuo di Solomon: XII 116
Centorio degli Hortensii,
Ascanio: I 159,160
Ceroicho,Gedelia: XII 114,
116
Chappuys,Gabriel: II 248
Charles V,emp: I 145,153,171,
177;II 237;IV 480;IX 50;
X 302,303,305,312
Charron,J.D: VII 46-49
Charron,Pierre: VII 46-50;
VIII 212-224
Cherel,Albert: VII 49
Cicero: I 143,149,164;II 230,
232,233,239,240,242,246;
III 34;V 322,324;VI 449-
451,456;XI 4,11,14
Cicogna,Pasquale di Gabriel:
X 287,288,294,324,325
Cieco,Ventura: I 149
Clement VII,pope: I 145;
X 302; XI 1
Clement VIII,pope: X 331,333,
334,337
Coducci,Mauro: XI 9
Collenuccio,Pandolfo: VI 459
Colonna,Vittoria: III 27
Contarini,Alvise di Galeazzo:
X 303,304
Contarini,Domenico di
Francesco: X 319
Contarini,Federico di
Francesco: X 292,294,329-
332,335
Contarini,Francesco di
Zaccaria: X 283,302
Contarini,Gasparo,card: I
162;III 27,28,31;X 291,
294,302,323;XI 2
Contarini,Giovanni Paolo di
Sebastiano: X 332,334, 337
Contarini,Giulio di Zorzi:
X 291,294,296,305,306,
308-310,313,314,317,318
Contarini,Nicolò di Zan
Gabriel: X 331,336-338
Contarini,Nicolò di Zorzi:
X 291